PRINCESS

Jean P. Sasson

BANTAM BOOKS
LONDON · NEW YORK · TORONTO · SYDNEY · AUCKLAND

PRINCESS

A BANTAM BOOK : 0 553 40570 5

Originally published in Great Britain by Doubleday,
a division of Transworld Publishers

PRINTING HISTORY
Doubleday edition published 1992
Bantam Books edition published 1993

17 19 20 18

This book is set in 11/13pt Bembo by
Chippendale Type Ltd, Otley, West Yorkshire.

Bantam Books are published by Transworld Publishers,
61–63 Uxbridge Road, London W5 5SA,
a division of The Random House Group Ltd,
in Australia by Random House Australia (Pty) Ltd,
20 Alfred Street, Milsons Point, Sydney, NSW 2061, Australia,
in New Zealand by Random House New Zealand Ltd,
18 Poland Road, Glenfield, Auckland 10, New Zealand
and in South Africa by Random House (Pty) Ltd,
Endulini, 5a Jubilee Road, Parktown 2193, South Africa.

Printed and bound in Great Britain by
Cox & Wyman Ltd, Reading, Berkshire.

International Acclaim For

PRINCESS

'The startling truth behind the veiled lives of Saudi Arabia's women . . . frank and vivid revelations'

Sunday Express

'*Princess* is a mind-boggling look at the everyday life of a contemporary woman in the 21,000-member-strong royal family . . . absolutely riveting'

People Magazine

'Gripping . . . a fast-paced, enthralling drama rich in detail . . . '

Publishers Weekly

'Anyone with the slightest interest in human rights will find this book heart-wrenching. It is a well-written, personal story . . . It had to come from a native woman to be believable'

Betty Mahmoody, bestselling author of *Not Without My Daughter*

Also by Jean Sasson
and published by Bantam Books

DAUGHTERS OF ARABIA
DESERT ROYAL

This book is dedicated to

JACK W. CREECH

From the first moment, he believed in the importance of telling Sultana's story. He alone knows the anguish I endured in reliving my long friendship with Sultana in the writing of this book; and he, more than any other person, generously gave his friendship and emotional support during difficult times as this book slowly became a reality.

Contents

Acknowledgements

Once I was convinced that I should write this book, I read and reread Sultana's notes and diaries that she had entrusted to me. As I selected the adventures of her amazing life to portray in this book, I felt the excitement of a detective. Yet I was burdened with a solemn responsibility carefully to discard the events that would surely lead trouble to her door. The words are mine, but the story is hers.

Thank you, Sultana, for bravely sharing your life-story with the world. By taking this bold step, you have helped to humanize the Arabs, a people misunderstood by the West. My hope is that by revealing the intimate details of your life as an Arab woman, in all its pain and glory, your story will help to dispel the many negative stereotypes held of your people throughout the world. Readers of your story cannot help but understand that, as in any country of the world, there is good along with the bad. We of the West have heard only the bad of Saudi Arabia. I know, and you know, that, in spite of the primitive customs that cruelly bind females in your land, there are many Arabs, like you, who deserve our respect and admiration for their struggles against centuries of oppression.

Closer to home, I sincerely thank Liza Dawson, my editor at William Morrow, who fell in love with Sultana's story at her first reading of the manuscript. Her comments and suggestions further enhanced it.

Also, I want to thank Peter Miller, my literary agent. His energetic enthusiasm for this book never lagged and is appreciated.

Very special thanks are reserved for Pat L. Creech, PhD, who from the beginning assisted me with comments and editorial revisions. Her brilliance helped to shape this book.

I would have found writing Sultana's story much more difficult without the love and support of my family. I owe a special debt of gratitude to my parents, Neatwood and Mary Parks. Their ever-present love and support was even more deeply felt during the writing of this very personal book.

The story of Princess Sultana is true. While the words are those of the author, the story is that of the Princess. The shocking human tragedies described here are factual.

Names have been changed and various events slightly altered to protect the wellbeing of recognizable individuals.

In telling this true story it is not the intention of the author nor of the Princess to demean the Islamic faith.

SAUDI ARABIA

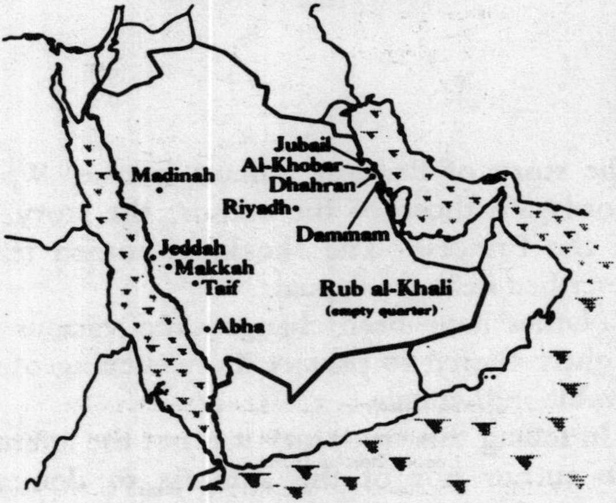

Country Facts

OFFICIAL TITLE:	Kingdom of Saudia Arabia
AREA:	864,866 sq. miles
POPULATION:	Est. 14 million
GOVERNMENT:	An absolute monarchy dominated by the Sa'ud family. The king appoints a Council of Ministers to assist in formulating policy.
RELIGION:	Islam; 95% of the population is Sunni Muslim, with 5% Shiite Muslim, who are concentrated in the Eastern Province.
LANGUAGES:	Arabic. English is widely spoken in business circles.
CLIMATE:	Hot and dry. Temperatures can reach 130°F in the hot summer months. During the winter months, the temperature varies between 50°F and 80°.
CURRENCY:	Saudi Riyals. U.S. $1 = SR3.73
ECONOMY:	Wealth is based on petroleum exports. Saudi Arabia is the largest producer within OPEC. One sixth of the world's total of oil is produced in this country.

SAUDI ARABIA AND NEIGHBOURING COUNTRIES

Facts on Countries Surrounding Saudi Arabia

EGYPT:	Population: 54 m.; Religion: Sunni Muslim (90%), Coptic Christian (10%)
ISRAEL:	Population: 4.7 m.; Religion: Jewish (82%), Sunni Muslim (14%), Christian (2.5%), Other (1.5%)
JORDAN:	Population: 3.2 m.; (East Bank only); Religion: Sunni Muslim (93%), Christian (5%), Other (2%)
IRAQ:	Population: 17.9 m.; Religion: Shiite Muslim (54%), Sunni Muslim (43%), Christian (3%)
KUWAIT:	Population: 2 m.; Religion: Sunni Muslim (63%), Shiite Muslim (28%), Christian (7%), Hindu (2%)
BAHRAIN:	Population: 510,000; Religion: Shiite Muslim (48%), Sunni Muslim (38%), Christian (7%), Other (7%)
QATAR:	Population: 450,000; Religion: Sunni Muslim (93%), Christian (5%), Other (2%)
U.A.E.:	Population: 1.9 m.; Religion: Sunni Muslim (74%), Shiite Muslim (21%), Christian (5%)
IRAN:	Population: 56.7 m.; Religion: Shiite Muslim (92%), Sunni Muslim (7%), Other (1%)
OMAN:	Population: 1.5 m.; Religion: Ibadi Muslim (69%), Sunni Muslim (18%), Hindu (13%)
YEMEN:	Population: 11.8 m.; Religion: Sunni Muslim (53%), Shiite Muslim (47%)
ETHIOPIA:	Population: 54 m.; Religion: Ethiopian Orthodox (53%), Muslim (32%), Traditional (15%)
SUDAN:	Population: 28.6 m.; Religion: Sunni Muslim (74%), Traditional (16%), Christian (8%), Other (2%)

THE HOUSE OF AL SA'UD

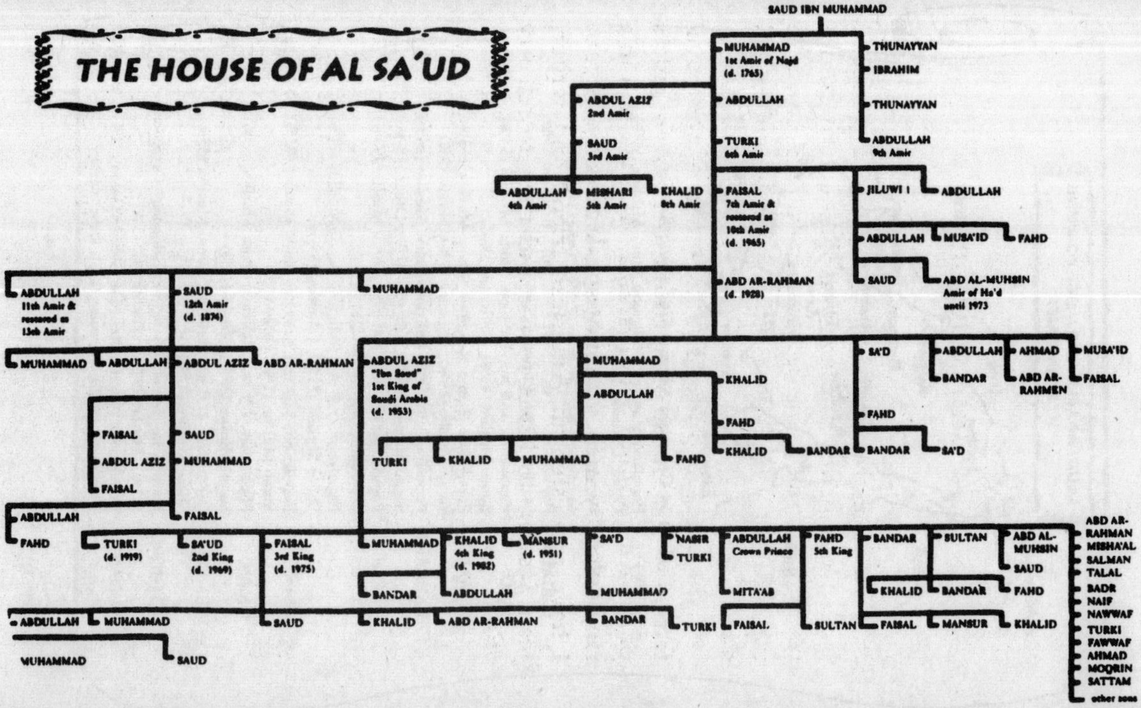

Introduction

In a land where kings still rule, I am a princess. You must know me only as Sultana. I cannot reveal my true name for fear harm will come to me and my family for what I am about to tell you.

I am a Saudi princess, a member of the royal family of the House of Al Sa'ud, the current rulers of the Kingdom of Saudi Arabia. As a woman in a land ruled by men, I cannot speak directly to you. I have requested an American friend and writer, Jean Sasson, to listen to me and then to tell my story.

I was born free, yet today I am in chains. Invisible, they were loosely draped and passed unnoticed until the age of understanding reduced my life to a narrow segment of fear.

No memories are left to me of my first four years. I suppose I laughed and played as all young children do, blissfully unaware that my value, owing to the absence of a male organ, was of no significance in the land of my birth.

To understand my life, you must know those who came before me. We present-day Al Sa'uds date back six generations to the days of the early emirs of the Nadj, the bedouin lands now part of the Kingdom of Saudi Arabia. These first Al Sa'uds were men whose dreams carried them no farther than the conquest of nearby desert lands and the adventures of night raids on neighbouring tribes.

In 1891 disaster struck when the Al Sa'ud clan was defeated in battle and forced to flee the Nadj. Abdul Aziz, who would one day be my grandfather, was a child at this time. He barely survived the hardships of that desert flight. Later he would recall how he burned with shame as his father ordered him to crawl into a large bag which was then slung over the saddle horn of his camel. His sister, Nura, was cramped into another bag hanging from the other side of their father's camel. Bitter that his youth prevented him from fighting to save his home, the angry young man peered from the bag as he swayed with the gait of the camel. It was a turning-point in his young life, he would later recall, as he, humiliated by his family's defeat, watched the haunting beauty of his homeland disappear from view.

After two years of nomadic desert travel, the family of Al Sa'uds found refuge in the country of Kuwait. The life of a refugee was so distasteful to Abdul Aziz that he vowed from an early age to recapture the desert sands he had once called home.

So it was that in September 1901, twenty-five-year-old Abdul Aziz returned to our land. On 16 January 1902, after months of hardship, he and his men soundly defeated his enemies, the Rasheeds. In the years to follow, to ensure the loyalty of the desert tribes, Abdul Aziz married more than 300 women, who in time produced more than fifty sons and eighty daughters. The sons of his favourite wives held the honour of favoured status; these sons, now grown, are at the very centre of power in our land. No wife of Abdul Aziz was more loved than Hassa Sudairi. The sons of Hassa now head the combined forces of Al Sa'uds to rule the kingdom forged by their father. Fahd, one of these sons, is now our king.

Many sons and daughters married cousins of the prominent sections of our family such as the Al Turkis, Jiluwis and Al Kabirs. The present-day princes from these unions are among influential Al Sa'uds. In 1991 our extended family consisted of nearly 21,000 members. Of this number, approximately a thousand are princes or princesses who are direct descendants of the great leader, King Abdul Aziz.

I, Sultana, am one of these direct descendants.

My first vivid memory is one of violence. When I was four years old, I was slapped across the face by my usually gentle mother. Why? I had imitated my father in his prayers. Instead of praying to Makkah, I prayed to my six-year-old brother, Ali. I thought he was a god. How was I to know he was not? Thirty-two years later, I remember the sting of that slap and the beginning of questions in my mind: If my brother were not a god, why was he treated like one?

In a family of ten daughters and one son, fear ruled our home: fear that cruel death would claim the one living male child, fear that no other sons would follow, fear that God had cursed our home with daughters. My mother feared each pregnancy, praying for a son, dreading a daughter. She bore one daughter after another – until there were ten in all.

My mother's worst fear came true when my father took another, younger wife for the purpose of giving him more precious sons. The new wife of promise presented him with three sons, all stillborn, before he divorced her. Finally, though, with the fourth wife, my father became wealthy with sons. But my elder brother would always be the firstborn and, as such, he ruled supreme. Like my sisters, I pretended to revere my brother, but I hated him as only the oppressed can hate.

When my mother was twelve years old, she was married to my father. He was twenty. It was 1946, the year after the great world war that interrupted oil production had ended. Oil, the vital force of Saudi Arabia today, had not yet brought great wealth to my father's family, the Al Sa'uds, but its impact on the family was felt in small ways. The leaders of great nations had begun to pay homage to our king. The British prime minister, Winston Churchill, had presented King Abdul Aziz with a luxurious Rolls-Royce. Bright green, with a throne-like back seat, the car sparkled like a jewel in the sun. Something about the car, as grand as it was, obviously disappointed the king, for upon inspection he gave it to one of his favourite brothers, Abdullah.

Abdullah, who was my father's uncle and close friend, offered him this car for his honeymoon trip to Jeddah. He accepted, much to the delight of my mother, who had never ridden in a car. In 1946 – and dating back untold centuries – the camel was the usual mode of transport in the Middle East. Three decades would pass before the average Saudi rode with comfort in a car rather than astride a camel.

Now, on their honeymoon, for seven days and nights, my parents happily crossed the desert trail to Jeddah. Unfortunately, in my father's haste to depart from Riyadh, he had forgotten his tent; because of this oversight and the presence of several slaves, their marriage remained unconsummated until they arrived in Jeddah.

That dusty exhausting trip was one of my mother's happiest memories. Forever after, she divided her life into 'the time before the trip' and 'the time after the trip'. Once she told me that the trip had been the end of her youth, for she was too young to understand what lay ahead of her at the end of the long journey. Her parents had died in a fever epidemic, leaving her orphaned at the age of eight. She had been married at the age of twelve to an intense man filled with dark cruelties. She was ill-equipped to do little more in life than his bidding.

After a brief stay in Jeddah, my parents returned to Riyadh, for it was there that the patriarchal family of the Al Sa'uds continued their dynasty.

My father was a merciless man; as a predictable result, my mother was a melancholy woman. Their tragic union eventually produced sixteen children of whom eleven survived perilous childhoods. Today, their ten female offspring live their lives controlled by the men to whom they are married. Their only surviving son, a prominent Saudi prince and businessman with four wives and numerous mistresses, leads a life of great promise and pleasure.

From my reading, I know that most civilized successors of early cultures smile at the primitive ignorance of their ancestors. As civilization advances, the fear of freedom for the individual is overcome through enlightenment. Human society eagerly rushes to embrace knowledge and change. Astonishingly, the land of my ancestors is little changed from that of a thousand years ago. Yes, modern buildings spring up, the latest health care is available to all, but consideration for women and for the quality of their lives still receives a shrug of indifference.

It is wrong, however, to blame our Muslim faith for the lowly position of women in our society. Although the Koran does state that women are secondary to men, much in the same way the Bible authorizes men to rule over women, our Prophet Muhammad taught only kindness and fairness towards those of my sex. The men who came behind Prophet Muhammad have chosen to follow the customs and traditions of the Dark Ages rather than to follow Muhammad's words and example. Our Prophet scorned the practice of infanticide, a common custom in his day of ridding the family of unwanted females. Prophet Muhammad's very words ring with his concern at the possibility of abuse and indifference towards females: 'Whoever hath a daughter, and doth not bury her alive, or scold her, or prefer his male children to her, may God bring him into Paradise.'

Yet there is nothing men will not do, there is nothing they have not done, in this land to ensure the birth of male, not female, offspring. The worth of a child born in the Kingdom of Saudi Arabia is still measured by the absence or the presence of a male organ.

The men of my country feel they are what they have had to become. In Saudi Arabia, the pride of a man's honour evolves from his women, so he must enforce his authority and supervision over the sexuality of his women or face public disgrace. Convinced that women have no control over their own sexual desires, it then becomes essential that the dominant male carefully guard the sexuality of the female. This absolute control over the female has nothing to do with love, only with fear of the male's tarnished honour.

The authority of a Saudi male is unlimited; his wife and children survive only if he desires. In our homes, he is the state. This complex situation begins with the rearing of our young boys. From an early age, the male child is taught that women are of little value: they exist only for his comfort and convenience. The child witnesses the disdain shown for his mother and sisters by his father; this open contempt leads to his scorn of all females, and makes it impossible for him to enjoy friendship with anyone of the opposite sex. Taught only the role of master to slave, it is little wonder that by the time he is old enough to take a mate he considers her his chattel, not his partner.

And so it comes to be that women in my land are ignored by their fathers, scorned by their brothers and abused by their husbands. This cycle is difficult to break, for the men who impose this life upon their women ensure their own marital unhappiness. For what man can be truly content surrounded by such misery? It is evident that the men of my land are searching for gratification by taking one wife after the other, followed by mistress after mistress. Little do these men know that their happiness can be found in their own home, with one woman of equality. By treating women as slaves, as property, men have made themselves as unhappy as the women they rule, and have made love and true companionship unattainable to both sexes.

The history of our women is buried behind the black veil of secrecy. Neither our birth nor our death is made official in any public record. Although births of male children are documented in family or tribal records, none is maintained anywhere for females. The common emotion expressed at the birth of a female is either sorrow or shame. Although hospital births and government record-keeping are increasing, the majority of rural births take place at home. No country census is maintained by the government of Saudi Arabia.

I have often asked myself: Does this mean that we women of the desert do not exist, if our coming and our passing go unrecorded? If no-one knows of my existence, does that mean I do not exist?

This fact, more than the injustices of my life, have prompted me to take this very real risk in order to tell my story. The women of my country may be hidden by the veil and firmly controlled by our stern patriarchal society, but change will have to come, for we are a sex that is weary of the restraints of customs. We yearn for our personal freedom.

From my earliest memories, aided by the secret diary I began to keep at the age of eleven, I will try to give you some portrayal of the life of a princess in the House of Al Sa'ud. I will attempt to uncover the buried lives of other Saudi women, the millions of ordinary women not born of the royal family.

My passion for the truth is simple, for I am one of those women who were ignored by their father, scorned by their brother, and abused by their husband. I am not alone in this. There are many more, just like me, who have no opportunity to tell their stories.

It is rare that truth escapes from a Saudi palace, for there is great secrecy in our society, but what I have spoken here and what the author has written here is true.

Chapter One

Childhood

Ali slapped me to the ground, but I declined to hand over the shiny red apple just given to me by the Pakistani cook. Ali's face began to swell with anger as I hovered over the apple and quickly began to take huge bites and swallow them whole. Refusing to give in to his male prerogative of superiority, I had committed a grave act and knew that I would soon suffer the consequences. Ali gave me two swift kicks and went running for our father's driver, Omar, an Egyptian. My sisters feared Omar almost as much as they did Ali or my father. They disappeared into the villa, leaving me alone to face the combined wrath of the men of the house.

Moments later, Omar, followed by Ali, rushed through the side-gate. I knew they would be the victors, for my young life was already rich with precedent. I had learned at an early age that Ali's every wish would be fulfilled. Nevertheless, I swallowed the last bite of the apple and looked in triumph at my brother.

Struggling vainly in the grasp of Omar's huge hands, I was lifted into the air and transported to my father's study. Reluctantly, my father looked up from his black ledger and glanced with irritation at his seemingly ever-present unwanted daughter while holding out his arms in invitation to that treasured jewel, his eldest son.

Ali was allowed to speak, while I was forbidden to respond. Overwhelmed with desire for my father's love and approval, my courage was suddenly reborn. I shouted out the truth of the incident. My father and brother were stunned into silence at my outburst, for females in my world are reconciled to a stern society that frowns upon the voicing of our opinions. All women learn at an early age to manipulate rather than to confront. The fires in the hearts of the once proud and fierce bedouin women have been extinguished; soft women who bear little resemblance to them remain in their stead.

The fear curled in my belly when I heard the shouting of my voice. My legs trembled under my body when my father arose from his chair, and I saw the movement of his arm but never felt the blow to my face.

As punishment, Ali was given all my toys. To teach me that men were my masters, my father decreed that Ali would have the exclusive right to fill my plate at mealtimes. The triumphant Ali gave me the tiniest of portions and the worst cuts of meat. Each night, I went to sleep hungry, for Ali placed a guard at my door and ordered him to forbid me to receive food from my mother or my sisters. My brother taunted me by entering my room at midnight laden with plates steaming with the delicious smells of cooked chicken and hot rice.

Finally Ali wearied of his torture, but from that time on, when he was only nine years old, he was my devoted enemy. Although I was only seven years old, as a result of the apple incident I first became aware that I was a female who was shackled by males unburdened by consciences. I saw the broken spirits of my mother and sisters, but I remained faithful to optimism and never doubted that I would one day triumph and my pain would be compensated by true justice. With this determination, from an early age, I was the family troublemaker.

There were pleasant times in my young life, too. My happiest hours were spent at the home of my mother's aunt. Widowed, too old for further notice and thus complications from men, she was now merry and filled with wonderful stories from her youth of the days of the tribal battles. She had witnessed the birth of our nation and mesmerized us with the tales of the valour of King Abdul Aziz and his followers. Sitting cross-legged on priceless oriental carpets, my sisters and I nibbled on plates of date pastries and almond cakes while immersed in the drama of the great victories of our kinsmen. My aunty inspired me to new pride in my family as she told of the Al Sa'uds' bravery in battle.

In 1891 my mother's family had accompanied the Al Sa'ud clan in their flight from Riyadh when they were defeated by the Rasheed clan. Ten years later, male members of her family returned with

Abdul Aziz to recapture the land; my aunty's brother fought alongside Abdul Aziz. This show of loyalty ensured their entry into the royal family by the marriage of their daughters. The stage was set for my destiny as a princess.

In my youth, my family was privileged, though not yet wealthy. The income from oil production ensured that food was plentiful and medical care available, which at that time in our history seemed the greatest of luxuries.

We lived in a large villa made of concrete blocks painted snowy white. Each year, the sandstorms turned the white to cream, but father's slaves would dutifully repaint the sand-coloured stones white. The thirty-foot block walls surrounding our grounds were maintained in the same fashion. The childhood home I took for granted was a mansion by Western standards; yet, looking back, it was a simple dwelling by today's Saudi royal expectations.

As a child, I felt our family home was too large for warm comfort. The long hallways were dark and forbidding. Rooms of various shapes and sizes branched off, concealing the secrets of our lives. Father and Ali lived in the men's quarters on the second floor. I used to peer into their quarters with the curiosity of the child I was. Dark-red velvet curtains closed out the sunlight. A smell of Turkish tobacco and whisky embraced the heavy atmosphere. One timid look and then with a rush I would return to the women's quarters on the ground floor, where my sisters and I occupied a large wing. The room I shared with Sara faced the women's private garden. Mother had had the room painted a bright yellow; as a result, it had the glow of life that was so glaringly absent in the rest of the villa.

The family servants and slaves lived in tiny airless rooms in a separate dwelling set apart at the back of the garden. While our villa was air-conditioned, the servants' quarters were ill-equipped for enduring the hot desert climate. I remember the foreign maids and drivers speaking of their dread of bedtime. Their only relief from the heat was the breeze generated by small electric fans. Father said that if he provided their quarters with air-conditioning they would sleep the whole day through.

Only Omar slept in a small room in the main house. A long golden cord hung in the main entrance of our villa. This cord was connected to a cowbell in Omar's room. When Omar was needed, he would be summoned by the ringing of this bell; the sound of the bell, day or night, would bring him to his feet and to Father's door. Many times, I must admit, I rang the bell during Omar's naps, or in the middle of the night. Then, lungs bursting, I would rush to my bed and lie quiet, an innocent child sleeping soundly. One night my mother was waiting for me as I raced for the bed. With disappointment etched on her face at the misdeeds of her youngest child, she twisted my ear and threatened to tell Father. But she never did.

Since my grandfather's day, we had owned a family of Sudanese slaves. Our slave population increased each year when Father returned from Haj, the annual pilgrimage to Makkah made by Muslims, with new slave children. Pilgrims from Sudan and Nigeria, attending Haj, would sell their children to wealthy Saudis so that they could afford the return journey to their homeland. Once in my father's care, the slaves were not bought and sold in the manner of the American slaves; they participated in our home life and in my father's businesses as if they were their own. The children were our playmates and felt no compulsion to servitude. In 1962, when our government freed the slaves, our Sudanese family actually cried and begged my father to keep them. They live in my father's home to this day.

My father kept alive the memory of our beloved king, Abdul Aziz. He spoke about the great man as if he saw him each day. I was shocked, at the age of eight, to be told the old king had died in 1953, three years before I was born!

After the death of our first king, our kingdom was in grave danger, for the old king's hand-picked successor, his son Sa'ud, was sadly lacking in qualities of leadership. He extravagantly squandered most of the country's oil wealth on palaces, cars, and trinkets for his wives. As a result, our new country was sliding towards political and economic chaos.

I recall one occasion in 1963 when the men of the ruling family gathered in our home. I was a very curious seven-year-old at the time. Omar, my father's driver, burst into the garden with a manner of great importance and shouted for the women to go upstairs. He waved his hands at us as if he were exorcizing the house of beasts and literally herded us up the stairwell and into a small sitting-room. Sara, my older sister, pleaded with my mother for permission to hide behind the arabesque balcony for a rare glimpse of our rulers at work. While we frequently saw our powerful male uncles and cousins at casual family gatherings, never were we present in the midst of important matters of state. Of course, at the time of each female's menses and subsequent veiling, the cut-off from any males other than father and brothers was sudden and complete.

Our lives were so cloistered and boring that even our mother took pity on us. That day, she actually joined her daughters on the floor of the hallway to peep through the balcony and listen to the men in the large sitting-room below us. I, as the youngest, was held in my mother's lap. As a precaution, she lightly placed her fingers on my lips. If we were caught, my father would be furious.

My sisters and I were captivated by the grand parade of the sons, grandsons and nephews of the deceased king. Large men in flowing robes, they gathered quietly with great dignity and seriousness. The stoic face of Crown Prince Faisal drew our attention. Even to my young eyes, he appeared sad and terribly burdened. By 1963 all Saudis were aware that Prince Faisal competently managed the country while King Sa'ud ruled incompetently. It was whispered that Sa'ud's reign was only a symbol of the family unity so fiercely protected. The feeling was that it was an odd arrangement, unfair to the country and to Prince Faisal, and unlikely to last.

Prince Faisal stood apart from the group. His usual quiet voice rose above the din as he asked that he be allowed to speak on matters that were of grave importance to the family and the country. Prince Faisal feared that the throne which had been so difficult to attain would soon be lost. He said that the common people were tiring of the excesses of the royal family, and that there was talk not only of ousting their brother Sa'ud for his decadence, but also of turning away from the entire Al Sa'ud clan and choosing instead a man of God for leadership.

Prince Faisal looked hard at the younger princes when he stated in a clear, sure voice that their disregard for the traditional lifestyle of bedouin believers would topple the throne. He said his heart was heavy from sadness that so few of the younger royals were willing to work, content to live on their monthly stipend from the oil wealth. A long pause ensued as he waited for comments from his brothers and relatives. As none seemed to be forthcoming, he added that if he, Faisal, were at the controls of the oil wealth, the flow of money to the princes would be cut and honourable work would be sought. He nodded his head at his brother Muhammad and sat down with a sigh. From the balcony, I noticed the nervous squirming of several youthful cousins. Even though the largest monthly stipend was no more than ten thousand dollars, the men of the Al Sa'ud clan grew increasingly wealthy from the land. Saudi Arabia is a huge country, and most of the property belongs to our family. In addition, no building contracts are signed without benefit to one of our own.

Prince Muhammad, the third-eldest living brother, began to speak; and, from what we could gather, King Sa'ud had now insisted on the return of absolute power that had been taken from him in 1958. He was rumoured to be in the countryside, speaking out against his brother Faisal. It was a devastating moment for the family of Al Sa'ud, for its members had always shown a unified front to the citizens of Saudi Arabia.

I remember when my father had told the story of why the eldest living son after Faisal, Muhammad, was passed over as successor to the throne. The old king had declared that if Muhammad's disposition were backed by the power of the Crown many men would die, for Muhammad's violent temper was well known.

My attention returned to the meeting, and I heard Prince Muhammad say that the monarchy itself was endangered; he broached the possibility of physically overthrowing the king and installing Prince Faisal in his stead. Prince Faisal gasped so loudly that the sound stifled Muhammad. Faisal seemed to be weeping as he spoke quietly. He told his kin that he had given his beloved father a deathbed promise that he would never oppose the rule of his brother. In no event would he consider breaking the promise, not even if Sa'ud bankrupted the country. If talk of ousting his brother was going to be the heart of the meeting, then he, Faisal, would have to depart.

There was a hum of voices as the men of our family agreed that Muhammad, the eldest brother next to Faisal, should attempt to reason with our king. We watched as the men toyed with their coffee-cups and made vows of loyalty to their father's wish that all the sons of Abdul Aziz would confront the world as a united force. As the traditional exchange of farewells began, we watched as the men filed as silently from the room as they had entered.

Little did I know that this meeting was the beginning of the end of the rule of my uncle, King Sa'ud. As history unfolded, and our family and countrymen watched in sadness, the sons of Abdul Aziz were forced to evict one of their own from his land. Uncle Sa'ud had become so desperate that in the end he had sent a threatening note to his brother Prince Faisal. This one act sealed his fate, for it was unthinkable for one brother to insult or threaten another. In the unwritten rule of the bedouin, one brother never turns against the other.

A fevered crisis erupted within the family and the country. But we learned later that a revolution, sought by Uncle Sa'ud, had been averted by the soft approach of Crown Prince Faisal. He stepped aside and left it to his brothers and the men of religion to decide the best course of action for our young country. In doing so, he took away the personal drama of the movement so that it became a less volatile matter, with statesmen making appropriate decisions.

Two days later, we learned about the abdication from one of Uncle Sa'ud's wives, for our father had been away at the time with his brothers and cousins. One of our favourite aunties, married to King Sa'ud, burst into our home in great agitation. I was shocked to see her rip her veil from her face in front of our male servants. She had arrived from Uncle Sa'ud's Nasiriyah Palace (an edifice that, to my mind, was both a demonstration of what endless money can buy and a ruinous example of what was wrong with our country).

My sisters and I gathered around our mother, for our aunty was now out of control and screaming accusations about the family. She was particularly incensed at Crown Prince Faisal and blamed him for her husband's dilemma. She told us that the brothers of her husband had conspired to take the throne that had been given by their father to the one of his choice, Sa'ud. She cried out that the religious council, the Ulema, had arrived at the palace that very morning and had informed her husband that he must step aside as king.

I was entranced by the scene before me, for rarely do we view confrontation in our society. It is our nature to speak softly and agree with those before us and then to handle difficulties in a secret manner. When our aunty, who was a very beautiful woman with long black curls, began to tear out her hair and rip her expensive pearls from her neck, I knew this was a serious matter. Finally my mother calmed her enough to lead her to the sitting-room for a cup of soothing tea. My sisters gathered around the closed door and tried to hear their whispering. I kicked around the large clumps of hair with my toe and stooped to gather the large smooth pearls. I found myself with fistfuls of pearls and placed them in an empty vase in the hallway for safe-keeping.

Mother guided our weeping aunty to her waiting black Mercedes. We all watched as the driver sped away with his inconsolable passenger. We never saw our aunty again, for she accompanied Uncle Sa'ud and his entourage into exile. But our mother did advise us against feeling harsh towards our Uncle Faisal. She said that our aunty had uttered such words because she was in love with a kind and generous man, but such a man does not necessarily make the best ruler. She told us that Uncle Faisal was leading our country into a stable and prosperous era, and by doing so he earned the wrath of those less capable. Although by Western standards my mother was uneducated, she was truly wise.

Chapter Two

Family

My mother, encouraged by King Faisal's wife Iffat, managed to educate her daughters, despite my father's resistance. For many years, my father refused even to consider the possibility. My five older sisters received no schooling other than to memorize the Koran from a private tutor who came to our home. For two hours, six afternoons a week, they would repeat words after the Egyptian teacher, Fatima, a stern woman of about forty-five years of age. She once asked my parents' permission to expand my sisters' education to include science, history and maths. Father responded with a firm no; and the recital of the Prophet's words, and his words alone, continued to ring throughout our villa.

As the years passed, Father saw that many of the royal families were allowing their daughters the benefit of an education. With the coming of the great oil wealth, which relieved nearly all Saudi women, other than the bedouin tribespeople and rural villagers, from any type of work, inactivity and boredom became a national problem. Members of the royal family are much wealthier than most Saudis, yet the oil wealth brought servants from the

Far East and other poor regions into every home.

All children need to be stimulated, but my sisters and I had little or nothing to do other than to play in our rooms or lounge in the women's gardens. There was nowhere to go and little to do, for when I was a child there was not even a zoo or a park in the city.

Mother, weary of five energetic daughters, thought that school would relieve her while expanding our minds. Finally Mother, with the assistance of Aunty Iffat, wore Father down to weak acceptance. And so it came to be that the five youngest daughters of our family, including Sara and myself, enjoyed the new age of reluctant acceptance of education for females.

Our first classroom was in the home of a royal relative. Seven families of the Al Sa'ud clan employed a young woman from Abu Dhabi, a neighbouring Arab city in the Emirates. Our small group of pupils, sixteen in all, was known in those days as a *kutab*, a group method then popular for teaching girls. We gathered daily in the home of our royal cousin from nine o'clock in the morning until two o'clock in the afternoon, Saturday to Thursday.

It was there that my favourite sister, Sara, first displayed her brilliance. She was much quicker than girls twice her age. The teacher even asked Sara if she was a primary graduate, and shook her head in wonder when she learned that Sara was not.

Our instructor had been fortunate to have a

modern-thinking father who had sent her to England for an education. Because of her deformity, a club foot, she had found no-one who would marry her, so she chose a path of freedom and independence for herself. She smiled as she told us that her deformed foot was a gift from God to ensure that her mind did not become deformed, too. Even though she lived in the home of our royal cousin (it was and still is unthinkable for a single woman to live alone in Saudi Arabia), she earned a salary and made her decisions about life without outside influence.

I liked her simply because she was kind and patient when I forgot to do my lessons. Unlike Sara, I was not the scholarly type, and I was happy the teacher expressed little disappointment at my shortcomings. I was much more interested in drawing than in maths, and in singing than in performing my prayers. Sara sometimes pinched me when I misbehaved, but after I howled in distress and disrupted the whole class, she left me to my mischievous ways. Certainly the instructor truly lived up to the name given her twenty-seven years before – Sakeena, which means 'tranquillity' in Arabic.

Miss Sakeena told Mother that Sara was the brightest student she had ever taught. After I jumped up and down and yelled, 'What about me?' she thought for a long moment before answering. With a smile, she said: 'And Sultana is certain to be famous.'

That evening at dinner, Mother proudly passed

on the remark about Sara to Father. Father, who was visibly pleased, smiled at Sara. Mother beamed with pleasure, but then Father cruelly asked how any daughter born of her belly could acquire learning. Nor did he credit Mother with any contribution to the brilliance of Ali, who was at the top of his class at a modern secondary school in the city. Presumably the intellectual achievements of her children were inherited solely from their father.

Even today I shudder with dismay while watching my older sisters attempt to add or subtract. I say little prayers of gratitude to Aunty Iffat, for she changed the lives of so many Saudi women.

In the summer of 1932, Uncle Faisal had travelled to Turkey and, while there, he had fallen in love with a unique young woman named Iffat al Thunayan. Hearing that the young Saudi prince was visiting Constantinople, the young Iffat and her mother approached him about disputed property that had belonged to her deceased father. (The Thunayans were originally Saudis but had been taken to Turkey by the Ottomans during their lengthy rule of the area.) Smitten by Iffat's beauty, Faisal invited her and her mother to Saudi Arabia to sort out the misunderstanding of the property matter. Not only did he give her the property; he also married her. Later he was to say it was the wisest decision of his life. My mother said Uncle Faisal had gone from woman to woman, like a man possessed, until he met Iffat.

During the years of Uncle Faisal's reign, Iffat became the driving force behind education for young girls. Without her efforts, the women in Arabia today would not be allowed in a classroom. I was in awe of her forceful character and declared I would grow up to be just like her. She even had the courage to hire an English nanny for her children who, of all the royal brood, turned out to be the most unaffected by great wealth.

Sadly, many of the royal cousins were swept away by the sudden rush of riches. My mother used to say that the bedouin had survived the stark emptiness of the desert but we would never survive the enormous wealth of the oilfields. The quiet achievements of the mind and the pious religious beliefs of their fathers hold no appeal for the vast majority of the younger Al Sa'uds. I believe that the children of this generation have decayed with the ease of their lives, and that their great fortune has deprived them of any ambitions or real satisfactions. Surely the weakness of our monarchy in Saudi Arabia is bound up in our addiction to extravagance. I fear it will be our undoing.

Most of my childhood was spent travelling from one city to another in my land. The nomadic bedouin blood flows in all Saudis, and as soon as we returned from one trip discussions would ensue as to the next journey. We Saudis no longer have sheep to graze, but we cannot stop looking for greener pastures.

Riyadh was the base of the Government, but none of the Al Sa'ud family particularly enjoyed the city; their complaints never ended about the dreariness of life in Riyadh. It was too hot and dry, the men of religion took themselves too seriously, the nights were too cold. Most of the family preferred Jeddah or Taif. Jeddah, with its ancient ports, was more open to change and moderation. There, we all breathed easier in the air of the sea.

We generally spent the months from December to February in Jeddah. We would return to Riyadh for March, April and May. The heat of the summer months would drive us to the mountains of Taif from June to September. Then it was back to Riyadh for October and November. Of course, we spent the month of Ramadan and two weeks of Haj in Makkah, our holy city.

By the time I was twelve years old, in 1968, my father had become extremely wealthy. In spite of his wealth, he was one of the least extravagant Al Sa'uds. But he did build each of his four families four palaces, in Riyadh, Jeddah, Taif and Spain. The palaces were exactly the same in each city, even to the colour of carpets and furniture selected. My father hated change, and he wanted to feel as if he were in the same home even after a flight from city to city. I remember him telling my mother to purchase four each of every item, down to the children's underwear. He did not want the family to bother with packing suitcases. I found it eerie that when I entered my room in Jeddah or Taif it was the same as my room in Riyadh, with the identical clothes hanging in identical wardrobes. My books and toys were purchased in fours, one of each item placed in each palace.

My mother rarely complained, but when my

father purchased four identical red Porsches for my brother, Ali, who was only fourteen at the time, she cried out that it was a shame – such waste – with so many poor in the world. When it came to Ali, though, no expense was spared.

When he was ten years old, Ali received his first gold Rolex watch. I was particularly distressed, for I had asked my father for a thick gold bracelet from the *souq* (market-place) and he had brusquely turned aside my request. During the second week of Ali flaunting his Rolex, I saw that he had laid it on the table beside the pool. Overcome with jealousy, I took a rock and pounded the watch to pieces.

For once, my mischief was not discovered, and it was with great pleasure that I saw my father reprimand Ali for being careless with his belongings. But of course, within a week or so, Ali was given another gold Rolex watch and my childish resentfulness returned with a vengeance.

My mother spoke to me often about my hatred for my brother. A wise woman, she saw the fire in my eye even as I bowed to the inevitable. As the youngest child of the family, I had been the most pampered of the daughters by my mother, sisters and other relatives. Looking back, it is hard to deny that I was spoiled beyond belief. Because I was small for my age, in contrast with the rest of my sisters, who were tall with large frames, I was treated as a baby throughout my childhood years. All of my sisters were quiet and restrained, as befitting Saudi princesses. I was loud and unruly, caring little for my royal image. How I must have tried their patience! But even today each of my sisters would spring to my defence at the first sign of danger.

In sad contrast, to my father I represented the last of many disappointments. As a consequence, I spent my childhood trying to win his affection. Finally, I despaired of attaining his love and clamoured after any attention, even if it were in the form of punishment for misdeeds. I calculated that if my father looked at me enough times he would recognize my special traits and come to love his daughter, even as he loved Ali. As it turned out, my rowdy ways ensured that he would go from indifference to open dislike.

My mother accepted the fact that the land in which we had been born was a place that is destined for misunderstandings between the sexes. Still a child, with the world stretching before me, I had yet to reach that conclusion.

Looking back, I suppose Ali must have had good character traits along with the bad, but it was difficult for me to see past his one great defect: Ali was cruel. I watched him as he taunted the handicapped son of our gardener. The poor child had long arms and strangely shaped legs. Often, when Ali's boyhood friends came over for a visit, he would summon poor Sami and tell him to do his 'monkey walk'. Ali never noticed the pathetic look on Sami's face or the tears that trickled down his cheeks.

When Ali found baby kittens, he would lock

them away from their mother and howl with glee as the mother cat tried in vain to reach them. No-one in the household dared to chastise Ali, for our father saw no harm in Ali's cruel ways.

After a particularly moving talk from my mother, I prayed about my feelings for Ali and decided to attempt the 'Saudi' way of manipulation instead of confrontation with my brother. Besides, my mother used God's wishes as her platform, and using God is always an admirable formula for convincing children to change their actions. Through my mother's eyes, I finally saw that my present course would lead me down a thorny path.

My good intentions were squashed within the week by Ali's dastardly behaviour. My sisters and I found a tiny puppy that had evidently become separated from its mother. The puppy was whimpering from hunger. Overcome with excitement at our find, we rushed about collecting dolls' bottles and warming goat's milk. My sisters and I took turns with feedings. Within days, the puppy was bouncing and fat. We dressed him in rags and even trained him to sit in our pram.

While it is true that Muslims do not favour dogs, it is a rare person who can harm a baby animal of any species. Even our mother, a devout Muslim, smiled at the antics of the puppy.

One afternoon we were pushing Basem, which means 'smiling face' in Arabic, in a pram. Ali happened to walk by with his friends. Sensing his friends' excitement over our puppy, Ali decided that the puppy should be his. My sisters and I screamed and fought when he tried to take Basem from our arms. Our father heard the commotion, and he came from his study. When Ali told him that he wanted the puppy, our father instructed us to hand him over. Nothing we said or did would change our father's mind. Ali wanted the puppy; Ali got the puppy.

Tears streamed down our faces as Ali jauntily walked away with Basem tucked under his arms. The possibility for love of my brother was forever lost, and my hate solidified when I was told that Ali had soon tired of Basem's whimpers and, on the way to visit friends, had tossed the puppy out of the window of the moving car.

Chapter Three

My Sister Sara

I felt wretched, for my favourite sister, Sara, was crying in Mother's arms. She is the ninth living daughter of my parents, three years older than I. Only Ali's birth separates us. It was Sara's sixteenth birthday, and she should have been rejoicing, but Mother had just relayed distressing news from Father.

Sara had been veiling since her menses, two years earlier. The veil stamped her as a non-person, and she soon ceased to speak of her childhood dreams of great accomplishment. She became distant from me, her younger sister who was as yet unconcerned with the institution of veiling. I was left longing for the remembered happiness of our shared childhood. It suddenly became apparent to me that happiness is realized only in the face of unhappiness, for I never knew we were so happy until Sara's unhappiness stared me in the face.

Sara was lovely, much more beautiful than I or my sisters. Her great beauty had become a curse, for many men had heard of Sara's beauty through their mothers and sisters and now wished to marry her. Sara was tall and slim, and her skin creamy and white. Her huge brown eyes sparkled with the knowledge that all who saw her admired her beauty. Her long black hair was the envy of all her sisters.

In spite of her natural beauty, Sara was genuinely sweet and loved by all who knew her. Unfortunately, not only did Sara acquire the curse that comes with great beauty; she was also exceptionally bright. In our land, brilliance in a woman assures her future misery, for there is nowhere to focus her genius.

Sara wanted to study art in Italy and be the first to open an art gallery in Jeddah. She had been working towards that goal since she was twelve years old. Her room was cluttered with books of all the great masters. Sara made my head swim with descriptions of the magnificent art in Europe. Just before the wedding announcement, when I was secretly plundering through her room, I saw a list of the places she planned to visit in Florence, Venice and Milan.

Sadly, I knew that Sara's dreams would not come true. While it is true that most marriages in my land are guided by the hands of the older females of the families, in our family Father was the decision-maker in all matters. Long ago, he had decided that his most beautiful daughter would marry a man of great prominence and wealth.

Now, the particular man he had chosen to marry his most desirable daughter was a member of a leading merchant family in Jeddah that had decided financial influence with our family. The groom was chosen solely because of past and future business deals. He was sixty-two years old; Sara would be his third wife. Although she had never met the old man, he had heard of her great beauty from his female relatives and was eager for the wedding date to be set. Mother had tried to intervene on Sara's behalf; but Father, as was his way, responded without emotion to his daughter's tears.

And now Sara had heard she was to wed. Mother ordered me to leave the room, but her back was turned; I tricked her by making noises with my feet and slamming the door. I slid inside the open wardrobe door and wept silent tears as my sister cursed our father, our land, our culture. She cried so hard that I lost many of her words, but I heard her cry out that she was sure to be sacrificed like a lamb.

My mother wept, too, but she had no words of comfort for Sara, for she knew her husband had the full right to dispose of their daughters in any marriage he liked. Six of their ten daughters were already married to men not of their choosing. Mother understood that the four remaining daughters would follow that darkness; there was no power on earth that could stop it.

Mother heard my squirming in the wardrobe. She narrowed her eyes and shook her head when she saw me, but made no effort to make me move. She told me to bring cold towels, and then she turned her attention back to Sara. When I returned, she placed the towels on Sara's head and soothed her to sleep. She sat and watched her young daughter for many minutes, and finally she rose wearily to her feet. With a long sad sigh, she took me by the hand and led me to the kitchen. Although it was not mealtime, and the cook was napping, Mother prepared for me a plate of cake and a glass of cold milk. I was thirteen, but small for my age; she cuddled me in her lap for a long time.

Unfortunately, Sara's tears served only to harden Father's heart. I overheard her entreaties to him. She became so unbalanced in her grief that she accused our father of hating women. She spat out a verse of Buddha: 'Victory breeds hatred, for the conquered are unhappy.' Father, his back rigid with anger, turned and walked away. Sara wailed at his back that she would have been better off unborn, since her pain so overweighed her happiness. With an ugly voice, Father responded by saying that her wedding date would be moved up to avoid stretching out her pain of anticipation.

Father normally came to our villa once every fourth night. Men of the Muslim faith, with four wives, rotate their evenings so that each wife and family is given an equal amount of time. It is a serious situation when a man refuses to go to his wife and children, a form of punishment. Our villa was in such an uproar with Sara's suffering that Father instructed Mother, who was his first and therefore his head wife, to inform his other three wives that he would rotate among their villas, but not ours. Before he left the villa, Father curtly told Mother to cure her daughter of her feverish resentments and to guide her peacefully to her destiny, which in his words was that of a 'dutiful wife and good mother'.

I barely recall the weddings of my other sisters. I vaguely remember tears, but I was so young and the emotional trauma of marriage to a stranger had not yet penetrated my thoughts. But I can close my eyes today and bring to mind every detail of the events that occurred in the months before Sara's wedding, the wedding itself, and the sad events that unfolded in the weeks afterwards.

I held the family reputation of the difficult child, the daughter who most tried my parents' patience. Wilful and reckless, I created havoc in our household. I was the one who poured sand into the motor of Ali's new Mercedes; I pinched money out of my father's wallet; I buried Ali's gold coin collection in the backyard; I released green snakes and ugly lizards from jars into the family pool as Ali lay sleeping on his float.

Sara was the perfect daughter, with her quiet obedience, and had earned perfect marks for her schoolwork. Even though I loved her madly, I thought Sara weak. But she surprised us all during the weeks prior to her wedding. Apparently she had hidden strength, for she called our father's office daily and left messages for him that she was not going to marry. She even called the office of the man she was scheduled to marry and left a harsh message with his Indian secretary that she thought he was an old disgusting man, and that he should marry women, not girls. The Indian secretary obviously thought better of giving such a message to his employer, for seas did not part and mountains failed to erupt. Determined, Sara called back and asked to speak to the man himself! He was not in his office. Sara was informed that he would be in Paris for a few weeks. Father, wearying of Sara's behaviour, had our telephones disconnected. Sara was confined to her room.

My sister's reality loomed ahead. The day of the wedding arrived. The weeks of fretful mourning had done nothing to diminish Sara's beauty. If anything, she appeared more beautiful, almost translucent, a heavenly creature not made for this world. Because of weight-loss, her dark eyes dominated her face and her features seemed chiselled. There was no end to Sara's eyes, and I could see into her soul through her enormous black pupils. I saw fear there.

Our older sisters, various female cousins and aunties arrived early on the morning of the wedding to prepare the bride for the groom. My unwanted presence escaped the attention of the women, for I sat like a stone in the corner of the large dressing-room that had been converted into a preparation room for the bride.

No less than fifteen women were attending to the various wedding details. The first ceremony, the *halawa*, was performed by our mother and her oldest aunty. All of Sara's body hair had to be removed, except her eyebrows and head hair. A special mixture of sugar, rosewater and lemon juice that would be spread over her body was now boiling over a low fire in the kitchen. When the sweet paste had dried on her body, it would be removed, and Sara's body hair would be ripped off with the sticky mixture. The aroma was sweet-smelling, but Sara's yelps of pain made me shudder in fear.

The henna was prepared for the final rinse through Sara's luxuriant curls; her hair would now shine with beautiful highlights. Her nails were painted bright red – the colour of blood, I reflected gloomily. The pale-pink lacy wedding-gown hung from the doorway. The requisite diamond necklace with matching bracelet and earrings were gathered in a pile on the dressing-table. Although sent over weeks ago as a gift from the groom, the jewels remained unnoticed and untouched by Sara.

When a Saudi bride is happy, the preparation room is filled with the sounds of laughter and eager anticipation. For Sara's wedding, the mood was sombre; her attendants might as well have been preparing her body for the grave. Everyone spoke in whispers. There was no response from Sara. I found her oddly subdued in view of her spirited reactions during the past few weeks. Later, I understood her trance-like state.

Father, concerned that Sara would humiliate the family name by voicing her objections, or even insulting the groom, had instructed one of the Pakistani palace doctors to inject her with powerful tranquillizers throughout the day. Later we discovered that the same doctor had given the groom the tranquillizers in the form of pills for Sara. The groom was told that Sara was highly nervous with excitement over the wedding, and the medicine was prescribed for a queasy stomach.

Since the groom had never met Sara, in the coming days he must have assumed that she was an unusually quiet and docile young woman. But then, again, many old men in my country marry young girls; I am sure they are accustomed to the terror of their young brides.

The beating of drums signalled the arrival of guests. At last the women were finished with Sara. The delicate dress was slipped over her head, the zipper was raised and the pink slippers were placed on her feet. My mother fastened the diamond necklace around her neck. I loudly announced that the necklace might as well be a noose. One of my aunties thumped me on my head, and another twisted my ear, but there was no sound from Sara. We all gazed at her in awed silence. We knew no bride could be more beautiful.

A huge tent had been erected in the backyard for the ceremony. The garden was inundated with flowers sent from Holland. With thousands of overhanging coloured lights, the grounds were spectacular. Taking in the splendour, I forgot for a few moments the grimness of the situation.

The tent was already overflowing with guests. Women from the royal family, literally weighed down by diamonds, rubies and emeralds, were sharing a social event with commoners – a rare occasion. Lower classes of Saudi women are allowed to view our weddings so long as they remain veiled and do not socialize with the royals. One of my friends told me that sometimes men veil and join these women so that they can view our forbidden faces. Supposedly all the male guests were being entertained at a major hotel in the city, enjoying the same socializing as these women guests: talking, dancing and eating.

At weddings in Saudi Arabia, men celebrate at one location and women at another. The only men allowed at the women's celebration are the groom, his father, the father of the bride, and a religious man to perform the short ceremony. In this case, the groom's father was deceased, so only our father would accompany the groom when the time arrived for him to claim his bride.

Suddenly the slaves and servants began to uncover the food. There was a rush towards the feast. The veiled ones were the first to assault the food; these poor women were cramming food under their veils and into their mouths. Other guests began to sample smoked salmon from Norway, Russian caviare, quail eggs and other gourmet delicacies. Four large tables swayed with the weight of the food: appetizers were on the left, main courses in the middle, desserts to the right, and off to the side were the liquid refreshments. No alcohol was visible, of course. But many of the royal women carried small jewelled flasks in their handbags. Now and then, giggling, they would retire to the washrooms for a small sip.

Belly dancers from Egypt moved to the centre of the tent. The crowd of women of all ages quietened and watched the dancers' movements with mixed interest. This was my favourite part of the wedding, but most of the women seemed uncomfortable with the erotic display. We Saudis take ourselves too seriously, and look on fun and laughter with suspicion. But I was startled when one of my older aunties leaped into the crowd and joined in the swaying of the belly dancers. She was amazingly skilled, but I heard the mumble of disapproval from several of my relatives.

Once again the sound of drums filled the air, and I knew it was time for Sara to appear. All the guests looked to the villa entrance in expectation. It was not long before the doors opened wide and Sara, accompanied by our mother on one side and an aunt on the other, was escorted to the dais.

Since I last saw my sister, a cloud-like pink veil had been draped over her face, held in place by a pink pearl tiara. The sheer veil served only to enhance her remarkable beauty. There was a low hum as the guests whispered their approval of her appropriately tortured demeanour. After all, a young virgin bride should look the part: frightened to the core of her being.

Dozens of female relatives followed behind, filling the air with the desert sounds of excitement and celebration: the high-pitched trill which the women produced by flicking their tongues on the roofs of their mouths. Other women joined in with shrill cries. Sara stumbled but was kept upright by our mother.

Soon my father and the groom made their appearance. I knew the groom was older than my father, but I was decidedly revolted by my first sight of him. He looked ancient to my young eyes, and I thought he most resembled a weasel. I cringed at the thought of him physically touching my shy and sensitive sister.

The groom wore a leering smirk as he lifted my sister's veil. She was too drugged to react, and stood motionless, facing her new master. The real marriage ceremony had been performed weeks prior to the wedding; no women had been present. Only men had participated in that ceremony, for it was the signing of dowry agreements and exchange of legal papers. Today the few words would be spoken that would complete the marriage rite.

The religious man looked at Father as he spoke the token words that Sara was now married to the groom in exchange for the agreed-upon dowry. Then he glanced at the groom who, in response, replied that he accepted Sara as his wife and that she, from this time forward, would be under his care and protection. None of the men looked at Sara at any time during the ceremony.

Reading passages from the Koran, the man of religion then blessed my sister's marriage. All at once, the women began to shriek and ululate. Sara was married. The men looked on, pleased and smiling.

As Sara stood motionless, the groom removed a small pouch from the pocket of his *thobe* (a full-length shirt-like garment worn by Saudi men) and tossed gold coins to the guests. I shivered as I watched him smugly accept their congratulations on his marriage to such a beautiful woman. He took my sister by the arm and hurriedly began to lead her away.

Sara's eyes locked on to mine as she passed my way; I knew someone should help her, but I felt certain no-one would. Quite suddenly I remembered Sara's words to Father: 'Victory breeds hatred, for the conquered are unhappy.' In my grieving mind, I found no consolation in the knowledge that the groom would never know happiness in such a bitterly unjust union. There could not be punishment enough for him.

Chapter Four

Divorce

Father forbade us from visiting Sara for the first three months of her marriage. She needed time to adjust to her new life and responsibilities, he said, and the sight of her family would serve only to inflame her desire to return to a useless life of dreams. Our vocal distress over her bondage drew nothing more than passionless nods. Sara, in Father's view, was doing what women are born to do: serve and pleasure the male and produce his children.

Sara had taken nothing from her room. Perhaps she understood that the presence of her books and other objects of delight would only make her present actuality more bleak. To me, it was as if Sara were dead; her absence left a black gaping hole in my life. I mourned her passing by spending long hours in her room with her possessions. I began to take an interest in Sara's hobbies and felt myself assuming parts of her personality. I read her diary, and her dreams felt as if they were my own; I wept with the fury of one who questions the wisdom of a God who allows evil to conquer the innocent.

My mother instructed that Sara's door be locked after she found me in Sara's bed, in her nightdress, reading her art books.

We did not have to suffer through Father's imposed three-month waiting period to see Sara. Five weeks after her wedding, she attempted suicide.

I was in the garden, talking with some of the animals in our newly constructed private zoo, when suddenly Omar tripped completely out of his sandals in his haste to enter the front gate. His skin, which was usually deep bronze, looked pasty white. He brushed off his *thobe* and beat the sand out of his sandals on the side of the wall. He told me to run and find my mother.

Mother had a certain sense about her children, and when she saw Omar she asked him what was wrong with Sara.

No Arab will tell a relative the truth when a family member is sick, dying or dead. We are people who simply cannot handle being the bearer of bad tidings. If a child dies, the unlucky person who receives the task of notifying the family will begin by saying the child is not feeling well. After questioning, the person will acknowledge that a trip to the doctor is necessary and then later admit that the child is in hospital. After intense pleas from the family members for additional information, the messenger will finally say the illness is serious and the family had best prepare for a journey to the bedside of the loved one. Later the person will painfully admit that the loved one's life is in grave danger. It might take a period of several hours to discover the exact degree of seriousness. But no-one will ever admit to the death of a loved one. The furthest an Arab will go in delivering bad news is to prepare the family for worse news from the doctor.

Omar told my mother that Sara had eaten some rotten meat and was now in a private clinic in Jeddah. Father was sending Mother on a private plane within the hour. Mother tightened her lips and turned in a rush to gather her *abaaya* (cloak) and veil.

I screamed and clung to Mother, so that she relented and allowed me to go – with the promise that I would not make a scene in the clinic if Sara were desperately ill. I promised and ran to Sara's room, pounding and kicking at the locked door until one of the servants found the key. I wanted to take Sara's favourite art book to her.

Omar drove us to Father's office since he had forgotten to collect our travel papers. In Saudi Arabia, a man must write a letter granting permission for the females in his family to travel. Without the papers, we might be stopped at the Customs office and prevented from boarding the plane. Father also sent our passports since, as he told Mother, it might be necessary for us to take Sara to London for treatment. Rotten meat? London? I knew what was rotten, and it was Father's story. I thought my sister must surely be dead.

We flew to Jeddah in a small private plane. The ride was smooth, but the atmosphere inside the cabin was clouded with tension. My mother said little and kept her eyes shut for most of the flight. Only a few years before, she had taken her first car ride. Now I saw her lips moving and I knew that double prayers were being spirited to God: Mother was praying first for Sara to be alive and second for the plane to take us safely to Sara.

The pilot and co-pilot were American, and I was immediately attracted to their open friendly manner. They asked me if I wanted to sit in the cockpit. Mother nodded a reluctant permission to my frenzied foot-stamping and arm-flapping. I had never sat in the cockpit before. Ali always sat in the cockpit.

At first I was frightened at the sight of the open sky, and the plane felt like a toy between us and the hard earth. I gave a small cry of alarm and backed away. John, the larger of the two Americans, gave me a reassuring smile, and patiently explained the functions of the various buttons and gadgets. To my surprise, I found myself leaning over his shoulder, completely at ease. For one of the few occasions in my young life, I felt calm and comfortable in the presence of men. Sadly, I was fearful of my father, and I detested Ali and my other half-brothers. It was a strange feeling, yet I felt intoxicated with the knowledge that men, whom I had been brought up to think of as gods, could be so ordinary and non-threatening. This was something new to think about.

When I looked out of the window of the plane, I understood what grips the heart of the eagle as it soars overhead, and I experienced a wonderful sense of freedom. My thoughts drifted to Sara and the shocking realization that birds and beasts were freer than my sister. I made a vow to myself that I would be the master of my life, no matter what actions I would have to take or pain I would have to endure.

I joined my mother for the landing of the plane; she gathered me into her loving arms and held me tenderly as the plane taxied to the terminal. She was veiled, but I knew her every expression, and I heard her breathe a long tortured sigh.

I said goodbye to the kindly Americans. I hoped they would fly us back to Riyadh, for I felt a camaraderie with the two men who had lent such importance to a child's foolish and feverish questions.

Arriving at the clinic, we heard wails and crying as we walked down the long corridor. Mother stepped up her pace and gripped my hand so tightly I wanted to complain.

Sara was alive, but barely. We were distraught to discover that she had tried to take her life by placing her head in the gas oven. She was very quiet, deathly pale. Her husband was not there, but he had sent over his mother. Now, in a loud voice, the old woman began to scold Sara harshly for embarrassing her son and his family. She was a mean old hag. I wanted to scratch her face and see her run, but I remembered my promise to Mother. Instead I stood, barely breathing from anger, patting Sara's smooth still hands.

Mother threw her veil over her head and faced the old woman. She had fretted over many possibilities, but the discovery that her daughter had attempted suicide was unexpected and devastating. When she turned in a cold fury to the husband's mother, I wanted to stamp and cheer. She stopped the woman cold when she asked what her son had done to make a young girl want to take her life. She ordered her to leave Sara's bedside, for this was no place for the ungodly. The old woman left without replacing her veil. We could hear her voice rise in anger as she cried out to God for sympathy.

Mother turned to me and saw my admiring smile. I was awed by her anger, and for a brief shining moment I felt God would not desert us. Sara would be saved. But I knew Mother's life would be one of misery when Father heard of her words. Knowing Father, he would be angry, not sympathetic, towards Sara for her desperate act, and he was sure to be furious with Mother for defending her daughter. In Saudi Arabia, the elderly are truly revered. No matter what they do or say, or how they behave, no-one dares confront someone of age. When she faced the old woman, my mother had been a tigress, protecting her young. My heart felt as though it would burst from pride at her courage.

After three days, without calling once, Sara's husband came to the clinic to claim his property. By the time he arrived, Mother had discovered the source of Sara's agony. She confronted her son-in-law with contempt. Sara's new husband was sadistic. He had subjected my sister to sickening sexual brutality until she felt her only escape was death. Even Father was repelled when he heard of his daughter's sufferings. But Father agreed with his son-in-law that a wife belonged with her husband. Sara's husband promised Father that his relations with her would conform to a life of normalcy.

Mother's hand trembled and her mouth stretched in a howl when Father told her of his decision. Sara began to weep and tried to leave the bed, saying she did not wish to live. She threatened to slit her wrists if forced to return to her husband. Mother stood over her daughter like a mountain and, for the first time in her life, defied her husband. She told him that Sara would never return to the house of a monster, and that she, Mother, would go to the king and the Council of Religious Men with the story, and neither would allow such a matter to continue. Father threatened Mother with divorce. She stood fast and told him to do whatever he had to do, but her daughter would not return to swim in such evil.

Father stood, unblinking. He probably realized that, in all likelihood, Sara would be forced by the men of religion to return to her husband. If the past were any precedent, they would advise the husband to deal with his wife in the manner spelled out by the Koran, and then they would turn their backs on such a disagreeable situation. Father stood, staring, analysing Mother's resolve. Askance at her apparent resoluteness, and wanting to avoid public interference in a family matter, for once in their married life he gave in.

Since we were of the royal family and he did not wish to sever his ties with my father, the husband reluctantly agreed to divorce Sara.

Islam gives the right of divorce to men, without any question of motive. Yet it is very difficult for a woman to divorce her husband. Had Sara been forced to file for the separation, many difficulties would have arisen, for the religious authorities might have ruled, 'You might dislike a thing which Allah has meant for your own good,' and forced Sara to remain with her husband. But Sara's husband relented and uttered the words 'I divorce you' three times in the presence of two male witnesses. The divorce was final in a matter of moments.

Sara was free! She returned to our home.

Every upheaval is a transition. My young world was transformed by Sara's wedding, attempted suicide, and divorce. Fresh thoughts and ideas began to grow in my mind; I was never to think as a child again.

For hours I pondered the primitive traditions surrounding marriage in my land. Numerous factors determine the marriageability of a girl in Saudi Arabia: her family name, her family fortune, her lack of deformities, and her beauty. Social dating is taboo, so a man must depend on his eagle-eyed mother and sisters constantly to seek out proper matches for him. Even after the promise to marry is made and the date is set, rarely does a girl meet her future husband prior to the wedding, though there are times when individual families allow the exchange of pictures.

If a girl is of a good family and without deformity, she will enjoy a number of marriage proposals. If she is a beauty, many men will send their mother or father to beg for marriage, for beauty is a great commodity for women in Saudi Arabia. Of course, no scandal can mar the reputation of the beauty or her desirability will fade; such a girl will find herself married as the third or fourth wife to an old man in a faraway village.

Many Saudi men leave the final decision on the marriage of their daughters to their wives, knowing they will make the best match possible for the family. Still, often the mother, too, will insist upon an unwanted marriage, even as her daughter protests. After all, she herself had married a man she feared, and her life had progressed without the anticipated horror or pain. Love and affection do not last, the mother will caution her daughter; it is best to marry into a family that they know. And then there are men, such as my father, who base their decision concerning their daughters' marriages upon possible personal or economic gain through the union, and there is no higher authority to question the verdict. Sara, for all her beauty, intelligence, and childhood dreams, in the end was no more than a pawn in my father's schemes for wealth.

This intimate view of my beloved sister's predicament filled me with a new resolve: it was my thought that we women should have a voice in the final decision on issues that would alter our lives for ever. From this time, I began to live, breathe and plot for the rights of women in my country so that we could live with the dignity and personal fulfilment that are the birthright of men.

Chapter Five

Ali

A few months after Sara's return, my oldest sister, Nura, convinced Father that Sara and I needed to see the world outside Saudi Arabia. None of us had been able to rouse Sara from her chronic depression, and Nura thought a trip would be just the right medicine. As to the extent of my travels, I had visited Spain twice, but I had been so young my recollections did not count.

Nura, married to one of our first king's grandsons, pleased Father with her marriage and her calm placid outlook on life. She did as she was told, no questions asked. Father actually grew fond of her as the years passed, for few of his daughters had Nura's complaisant qualities. Since Sara's divorce, Father held Nura up as a constant reminder to the rest of his daughters. She had married a stranger, and her marriage had proved to be satisfactory. Of course, the real reason was that her husband was considerate and attentive.

In Father's mind, Sara had obviously provoked her husband into criminal behaviour. It is never the fault of the man in the Middle East. Even if he murders his wife, the man will state 'valid' reasons for his action, which will be accepted by other men without question. In my own country, I have seen newspapers print articles that honour a man for executing his wife or daughter for the crime of 'indecent behaviour'. The mere suspicion of sexual misconduct, such as kissing, can bring death to a young girl. In addition, public congratulations are given from the men of religion for the father's 'notable' act of upholding the commands of the Prophet!

Nura and Ahmed were in the midst of constructing a palace, and Nura wanted to travel to Europe to purchase Italian furnishings. On the way, we were to stop off in Egypt so that Nura's young children could view the pyramids.

Father, with twenty-two daughters from four wives, was often overheard muttering: 'Women are a man's curse.' It did not help his attitude that his younger daughters were in a kind of rebellion against the absolute rule of men. Our talk and actions were unprecedented and unappreciated. Knowing full well we would never reach the heights we desired, our talk alone was a victory of sorts, for no Saudi women had ever approached the topics we discussed with such great abandon.

Nura wanted Mother to go abroad with us, but Mother had been strangely quiet since Sara's return. It was as if her one great rebellion against Father's rule had drained her life's blood. But she encouraged the trip, for she wanted Sara to see Italy. She thought I was too young and should stay at home, but as usual a temper tantrum accomplished the result I wanted. Sara showed little interest, even in the possibility of seeing the artistic wonders of Italy, but I was out of control with happiness.

My joy was shattered by Ali's smug announcement that he was going with us. Father thought I needed a chaperon. In an instant, I lost my mind at the thought of Ali's treacherous presence ruining my vacation, and I was determined to insult him in the worst way. I grabbed his new *ghutra* (headdress) and *igaal* (black cord that rests on the top of the *ghutra*) and raced through the house to my bathroom. I had no notion of what I was going to do with them, but a Saudi man is highly offended if anyone even touches his headdress. I felt an urge to hurt Ali as quickly as possible.

When Ali followed, shouting that he would tell Father, I slammed the bathroom door on him. Since he was wearing sandals, Ali's big toe was broken, and his hand was bruised. From his shouts and moans, the servants thought I was killing him. No-one came to Ali's rescue, though.

I don't know what came over me – perhaps the sound of the big bully groaning and begging for sympathy – but I flushed his headdress down the toilet. The *igaal* would not flush, even as I frantically pushed it with the plunger. The sodden cord became stuck in the toilet! When Ali saw what I had done, he lunged for me. We were struggling on the floor when I got the better of him by pulling and twisting his broken toe. Mother, hearing Ali's screams of agony, intervened and saved him from my years of pent-up wrath.

I knew I was in big trouble. I rationalized that my situation could not be any worse, so when Mother and Omar took Ali to the clinic to get his broken toe bandaged I crept into his room and gathered up his secret hoard of 'treasures' that were forbidden by both our religion and our country.

These 'treasures' were the usual objects that all young boys collect the world over, but their possession is a serious offence under the law of religion in Arabia. Long before, I had located Ali's collection of *Playboy*, *Penthouse* and other similar magazines. Recently I had discovered a new collection of slides. Curious, I had taken them to my bedroom; perplexed, I viewed them on the slide projector. Naked men and women were doing all kinds of strange things; one group of pictures even showed animals with women. Ali had obviously lent them to other boys on occasion, for he had clearly printed his name on every forbidden article.

I was too innocent at the time to know exactly what it all meant, but I knew these 'treasures' were bad because he had always kept his secret cache stacked in the same old tattered box labelled 'School Notes'. I was very familiar with his belongings, having sorted through his stuff for years. I carefully removed every magazine along with the slides. I also found seven miniature bottles of alcohol that Ali had brought home after a weekend trip to Bahrain. I smiled at my plan as I shoved everything in a paper bag.

In Saudi Arabia, mosques are built in every neighbourhood, for the Government has placed top priority on providing a mosque within walking distance of every Muslim male. With prayers to be offered five times a day, it is more convenient to complete all the prayers if a man is a short distance from the mosque. Even though prayers can be given at any location so long as the person faces Makkah, it is thought that access to a mosque is preferable.

Living in one of the wealthiest districts, we were served by a huge mosque made of white opalescent marble. Since it was about two o'clock in the afternoon, I knew the noon prayers were over; it would be safe to carry out my plan without being seen. Even the men of religion nap in the hot climate of Arabia.

I opened the mosque door with dread, and peeped in carefully before entering. Not yet veiled, I thought perhaps my presence would invite little curiosity. I already had my story ready in the event I was caught. If questioned, I would say I was hunting my new kitten that had wandered on to the mosque grounds.

Surprisingly, the mosque was cool and inviting. I had never been inside the huge building, but I had followed my father and Ali to prayer many times. From the age of six, Ali had been encouraged to perform the five daily prayers. I felt my breath sharpen as I recalled the hurt I had felt as I watched my father hold Ali's hand and lead him proudly through the grand entrance of the mosque – always leaving me, a lowly female, at the side of the road to stare after them in sorrow and anger.

Women are forbidden entry into mosques in my country. Even though Prophet Muhammad did not forbid women to pray publicly in the mosques, he did state that it was best for them to pray in the privacy of their homes. As a result, no female in Saudi Arabia has ever been allowed inside a mosque.

No-one was around. I hurriedly walked across the marble floor; the clicking of my sandals sounded loud and strange. I placed the bag containing Ali's forbidden articles in the stairwell leading to the balcony that contains the loudspeakers which broadcast Prophet Muhammad's words throughout our cities five times a day. Just thinking of the intensity of the appeals of the muezzin, the criers who call the faithful to pray, I began to feel guilty about my adventure. Then I remembered Ali's superior smirk as he told me that Father would have me flogged and that he, Ali, would request the pleasure of beating me. I walked back home with a satisfied grin. Let Ali get out of this one.

That night, before Father came home from the office, three *mutawas* (religious men) arrived at our gate. I and three of our Filipino servants peered through one of the upstairs windows as we watched them shout at Omar and gesture wildly at the heavens and then towards some books and magazines which they obviously held in distaste. I wanted to laugh, but kept my face straight and serious.

All foreigners and most Saudis are frightened of the *mutawas* for they have much power, and they watch everyone for signs of weakness. Even members of the royal family try to avoid their attention.

Two weeks earlier, one of our Filipino maids had inflamed some *mutawas* by wearing a knee-length skirt in the *souq*. A group of religious men struck her with a stick and sprayed her uncovered legs with red paint. While the government of Saudi Arabia does not allow tourists to enter our country, there are many women who work as nurses, secretaries or domestic help in our major cities. Many of these women feel the wrath of those who speak God's word yet despise those of our sex. If a woman is so bold as to defy our traditions by exposing uncovered arms or legs, she runs the risk of being struck and sprayed with paint.

This maid had soaked her legs in paint remover, but they were still red and raw-looking. She was convinced that somehow the religious police had traced her to her residence and now they had come to take her to gaol. She ran to hide under my bed. I wanted to tell her the nature of their visit, but my secret had to be guarded – even from the Filipino servants.

Omar was absolutely pallid when he came into the villa screaming for Ali. I saw Ali scuffling down the hallway, gingerly walking with the top of his right foot high in the air while balancing on his heel. I followed and gathered with Mother and Ali in the sitting-room, where Omar was on the phone, calling Father at his office. The *mutawas* had left, entrusting Omar with samples of the incriminating contraband: one magazine, several slides and one miniature bottle of liquor. The rest they kept as evidence of Ali's guilt. I glanced at Ali and saw his face drain of blood when he saw his 'secret treasures' spread out in disarray on Omar's lap.

Catching sight of me, Omar asked me to leave the room, but I clung to my mother's skirts and she patted me on the head. Mother must have hated the way Omar bossed her children and she looked defiantly into his eyes. He decided to ignore me. He told Ali to sit down, that Father was on his way home and the *mutawas* had gone to get the police. Ali was going to be arrested, he announced with booming certainty.

The silence in the room was like the calm before a tempest. For a short moment I was terrified, and then Ali regained his composure and practically spat at Omar, declaring: 'They cannot arrest me; I am a prince. Those religious fanatics are nothing more than pesky mosquitoes at my ankles.' The sudden thought came to me that gaol might do Ali good.

The squealing of Father's brakes signalled his arrival. Rushing into the room barely controlling his anger, he picked up the forbidden articles one by one. When he saw the magazine, he looked hard at Ali. He threw the whisky aside with contempt, for all the princes have liquor in their homes. But when Father held the slide up to the lamp-light, he screamed for Mother and me to leave the room. We could hear him striking Ali with his hands.

All in all, it had been a bad day for Ali.

The *mutawas* must have thought better of calling the police to arrest one of the royal sons, for they returned in a few hours with little besides pious fury leading their way. But even Father had a difficult time with the *mutawas* in excusing the slides of women copulating with animals.

The year was 1968, and King Faisal was not as tolerant with the misdeeds of the young princes as had been his elder brother, Sa'ud. The *mutawas* felt they were in a position of power, for both they and Father knew that his uncle, the king, would be outraged if the contents of the slides became common knowledge. The fears of the *mutawas* were well known regarding the present course of modernization of our land. King Faisal constantly cautioned his brothers and cousins to control their children to avoid the wrath of the religious men upon the heads of the royal men who ruled. The king assured the religious elders that he was leading our country into needed modernization, not degenerate Westernization; the best, not the worst, of the West. The *mutawas* saw proof of the decadent West in the behaviour of the royals. Ali's slide collection did nothing to put their minds at ease about the whispered decadence of the royal family.

We heard the *mutawas* argue long into the night over an appropriate punishment for the son of a prince. Ali was lucky to be a member of the family of Al Sa'ud. The *mutawas* knew that, unless the king gave his approval, no royal prince would be charged in the country's court system. Rarely, if ever, did such an event occur. But if Ali had been a member of a common Saudi family or a member of the foreign community he would have been ordered to serve a long prison sentence.

Our family was all too familiar with the sad story of the brother of one of our Filipino drivers. Four years ago, the brother, who worked for an Italian construction firm in Riyadh, had been arrested for possessing a pornographic film. The poor man was now serving a seven-year prison sentence. Not only was he languishing in prison, but he was also ordered to endure ten lashes every Friday. Our driver, who visited his brother every Saturday, wept as he told Ali that every time he saw his poor brother the man was black from his neck to his toes from the lashings of the previous day. He feared his brother would not live out the coming year.

Unfortunately for Ali, his guilt was established without a doubt – his name was boldly printed on every forbidden item. In the end, a compromise of sorts was made: Father gave a huge sum of money to the mosque, and Ali had to be present for prayers five times each day to appease the men of God, along with God himself. The *mutawas* knew that few of the younger royal princes bothered to go to prayer at all, and that such a punishment would be especially irksome to Ali. He was told he would have to show his face to the head *mutawa* in our mosque at every prayer for the next twelve months. His only excuse would be if he were out of the city. Since Ali generally slept until nine o'clock, he frowned at the mere thought of the sunrise prayer. In addition, he had to write one thousand times on a legal pad: 'God is great, and I have displeased Him by running after the corrupt and immoral ways of the Godless West.' As a final condition, Ali was told he would have to reveal the name of the person who had supplied him with the slides and magazines. As it was, Ali had slipped in the magazines from trips abroad since a prince is ushered through Customs with only a courtesy glance. But a Westerner he had befriended at a party had sold him the slides, and Ali, eager for a foreign villain to take the pressure off him, happily supplied the *mutawas* with the Westerner's name and work address. We would later learn that the man had been arrested, flogged and deported.

I felt terrible. My stupid prank had disgraced my entire family with a stinging humiliation. I did not think the lesson would harm Ali, but I knew my parents had been affected and other innocent people would be injured. Also, I am ashamed to admit, I was petrified that my guilt would be discovered. I prayed to God that, if He would let me escape capture this once, from that day forward I would be a perfect child.

Omar led the *mutawas* out of our grounds. Mother and I waited for Father and Ali to return to the family sitting-room. Father was breathing loudly and gripped Ali by his upper arm, pushing him towards the stairway. Ali looked my way, and our eyes met. A moment, a flash of realization, and I understood that he had concluded I was the guilty party. Sadly, I saw that he looked more hurt than angry.

I began to sob, for I felt the weight of the terrible deed I had committed. Father looked at me in pity. Then he shoved Ali and screamed that he had upset the entire family, including the innocent children. For the first time in my life, my father came and held me in his arms and told me not to worry.

I was now truly miserable. The touch that I had been longing for all my life now felt barren, and the joy I had so often imagined was destroyed in the elusive prize so wrongly taken.

My misdeed had accomplished my target, however. No mention was ever made of Ali's broken toe or the toilet clogged with Ali's headdress. One sin had so outweighed the other that they ended up cancelling each other out.

Chapter Six

The Trip

Despite the recent family turmoil, the trip to Italy and Egypt was still planned, but my heart was no longer joyful. I organized my case and made my lists as I watched Ali warily trudge by my bedroom door. In the past, Ali had given me little thought. I was scorned as a girl, someone to antagonize or push about occasionally – a person of little worth. He looked at me differently now, for he had made the surprising discovery that I, a lowly female and the youngest member of the family, was a dangerous and worthy opponent.

On the day of our departure, six limousines were needed to transport us to the airport. Eleven of us were travelling for four weeks: Nura and Ahmed, with three of their five children; two of their Filipino maids; Sara and myself; and Ali and his friend Hadi.

Two years older than Ali, Hadi was a student at the Religious Institute, a boys' school in Riyadh for those young men who aspired to become *mutawas*. Hadi impressed adults by quoting the Koran and acting very piously in their presence. My father felt confident that Hadi would have a good influence on his children. To those who would listen, Hadi loudly expressed his viewpoint that all women should be confined to the home; he told Ali that women were the cause of all evil on earth.

I could tell it was going to be a pleasant and enjoyable trip with both Ali and Hadi around.

Mother did not accompany us to the airport. For the past few days, she had been listless and sad; I assumed Ali's antics had worried her. She said her farewells in the garden and waved us off from the front gate. She was veiled, but I knew tears were falling on her face. Something was amiss with Mother, I felt, but I had no time to dwell on the possibilities as the prospect of this exciting trip lay ahead of us.

Ahmed had recently purchased a new plane, so our flight was strictly a family affair. I looked to see if the two Americans who had flown Mother and me to Jeddah were piloting; disappointed, I saw they were not. Two British pilots were in the cockpit and they looked friendly enough. The royal family hired a large number of American and British citizens as private pilots. Ahmed conferred with the two men while Nura and the maids settled in with her three little ones.

Sara, her veil now removed, was already bundled in a blanket, clutching her precious books. Hadi looked with distaste at her uncovered face and whispered angrily to Ali, who in turn ordered Sara to replace her veil until we left Saudi Arabia. Sara told Ali she could not see to read through the thick fabric, and if he were smart he would shut his ugly mouth.

Even before we had left the ground there was already a family squabble. I tried to stamp on Ali's sore toe but missed, and Ali took a swipe at my head; I ducked, and he missed. Ahmed, as the oldest male authority figure, shouted at everybody to sit down and be quiet. He and Nura exchanged a look that let me know they were already rethinking the wisdom of their generous invitation.

The three holiest spots in Islam are Makkah, Madinah and Jerusalem. Makkah is the city that captures the hearts of more than a billion Muslims scattered over the globe, for it was there that God revealed His will to His Prophet, Muhammad. The foundations of our religious life are five ritual obligations, called the pillars of religion. One of these obligations requires that every Muslim with the financial ability must attend Haj. No good Muslim feels complete without making the pilgrimage to Makkah at least once in his lifetime.

Our second-holiest city, Madinah, considered 'the city of the Prophet', is the place of Muhammad's burial.

And Jerusalem is our third-holiest city. It was in Jerusalem that Muhammad was taken up by God to heaven on the Dome of the Rock. Muslims weep bitter tears at the mention of Jerusalem, for it is a city now occupied and no longer free and open to our people.

If Makkah, Madinah and Jerusalem are a Muslim's spiritual fountainheads, then Cairo is the crowning glory of a Muslim's self-esteem. Cairo represents fifty centuries of titanic duration, and presents Arabs with the marvel of one of the greatest civilizations to appear on the earth. Egypt is a source of great pride for all Arabs. The might, wealth and accomplishments of the ancient Egyptians make the oil wealth of the modern Gulf Arabs seem puny and inconsequential.

It was in Cairo, that city bursting with life from the beginning of time, that I became a woman. In the Arab culture, with so much importance attached to the change from girlhood to womanhood, every young girl awaits with a combination of dread and deep satisfaction the sight of her first blood. When my Western women friends tell me that they did not know what was happening to them when their first blood appeared, and that they were convinced they were dying, I am struck dumb with surprise. The coming of women's menses is a source of easy conversation in the Muslim world. Suddenly, at that moment, a child is transformed into an adult. There is no going back to that warm cocoon of childhood innocence.

In Saudi Arabia, the appearance of the first menses means that it is time to select the first veil and *abaaya* – with the greatest of care. Even the shopkeepers, Muslim men from India or Pakistan, enquire with ease and respect as to the time the girl-child became a woman. In all seriousness, the shopkeeper will smile indulgently, and proceed to select the *abaaya* and veil that will show the child to her greatest advantage.

Even though the only colour for a veil is black,

there are many possibilities for fabric selection and weight of material. The veil can be of thin material, giving the world a shadowy glimpse of the forbidden face. A medium-weight fabric is more practical, for one can see through the gauzy cloth without the rude glances or sharp remarks from the keepers of the faith. If a woman chooses the traditional thick black fabric, no man can imagine her features under a facial mask that refuses to move with the strongest of breezes. Of course, this selection makes it impossible to examine jewellery in the gold *souq* or to see speeding cars after dusk. In addition to this traditional heavy veil, some of the conservative women choose to wear black gloves and thick black stockings so that no hint of flesh is visible to the world.

For women with a need to express their individuality and fashion sense, there are ways to avoid that endless sea of conformity in dress through creative design. Many purchase scarves with jewelled decorations, and the movement of trinkets turns the heads of most men. Expensive eye-catching decorations are often sewn to the sides and back of the *abaaya*.

Younger women, in particular, strive to set themselves apart by their unique selections. The male shopkeeper will model the latest designer fashions in veils and *abaaya* and show the young girl the stylish way of throwing the scarf over her head to project a look of smart fashion. The method of tying the *abaaya* to show the exact amount of foot that is allowed without being considered risqué is discussed in great detail. Every young girl experiments to find her own method of wearing the *abaaya* with flair.

A child enters the shop, but a woman emerges, veiled and, on that day, of a marriageable age. Her life changes in that split second. Arab men barely glance at the child as she enters the shop but once she dons her veil and *abaaya* discreet glances come her way. Men now attempt to catch a glimpse of a forbidden, suddenly erotic ankle. With the veil, we Arab women become overwhelmingly tantalizing and desirable to Arab men.

But I was now in Cairo, not home in Saudi Arabia, so the full impact of my first blood did little more than irritate me. Sara and Nura showed me all the things a woman should do. They both warned me against telling Ali, as if I would, for they knew he would try to make me veil immediately, even in Cairo. Sara looked at me with great sadness and gave me a long hug. She knew that from that day forward I would be considered a threat and danger to all men until I was safely wed and cloistered behind walls.

In Cairo, Ahmed owned a luxurious apartment that spread over three floors inside the city centre. For privacy, Ahmed and Nura settled on the top floor. The two Filipino maids, Nura's three babies, Sara and I occupied the second floor. Ali, Hadi and the Egyptian caretaker stayed on the first floor. Sara and I hugged each other with delight when we realized Ali and Hadi were separated from us by an entire floor.

On our first evening, plans were made for Ahmed, Nura, Hadi and Ali to go to a night-club to watch belly dancing. Ahmed thought that Sara and I should stay at home with the babies and the Filipino servants. Sara made no protest, but I pleaded our case so eloquently that Ahmed relented.

At fourteen, I came alive in the land of the pharaohs and joyfully anointed Cairo as my favourite city of all time. That attachment to Cairo has never wavered. The excitement of this city inflamed me with a passion I had never known before, and which I cannot fully explain to this day. Men and women of every colour and dress roamed the streets, searching for adventure and opportunity. I recognized that my life before had been dry, without stimulation, for I saw that Cairo was the opposite of our Arabian cities, which were, to my young eyes, sterile and lifeless.

I found the grinding poverty unsettling, yet it was not discouraging, for I saw in it a profound force of life. Poverty can turn a person into a flaming torch for change and revolution, without which mankind would come to a standstill. I thought again of Saudi Arabia and knew that some degree of poverty or need should seep into our lives and force us to renew our spiritual life.

Yes, there are many classes of people in my land, from those various levels of the wealthy royal family down to that of lowly salaried workers. But no-one, including foreign workers, is without the basic necessities of life. Our government ensures the wellbeing of all Saudis. Each male citizen is assured of a home, health care, education, a business where he can earn a living, interest-free loans and even money for food, should the need arise. Our female citizens are provided for by the men of their family, whether it be father, husband, brother or cousin.

As a result of this satisfaction of basic needs, the spark of life generated by material desire is hopelessly lacking in my land. Because of this, I despaired that the pages of history would ever turn on my land. We Saudis are too rich, too settled in our apathy for change. As we drove through the bustling city of Cairo, I mentioned this idea to my family, but I saw that only Sara listened and understood the essence of my thoughts.

The sun was now setting, and the sky turned to gold behind the sharp outline of the pyramids. The generous slow-moving Nile was breathing life throughout the city and into the desert. Watching it, I felt life rush through my veins.

Ali and Hadi were furious that Sara and I – two unmarried females – had been allowed to go into the nightclub. Hadi spoke long and seriously to Ali about the deterioration of our family's values. He declared with smug satisfaction that his sisters had all been married by the age of fourteen, and that they were guarded carefully by the men of his family. He said that, as a man of religion, he had to protest to our father when we returned from the trip. Sara and I, bold in our distance from Riyadh, made faces and told him he had not yet become a religious man. We told him, in slang we had learned from watching American movies, 'to save it'.

Hadi devoured the dancers with his eyes, and made crude remarks about their body parts, yet he swore to Ali that they were nothing but whores, and that if he had his way they would be stoned. Hadi was a pompous ass. Even Ali tired of his holier-than-thou attitude and began to thump his fingers on the table with impatience and to look around the room.

After Hadi's comments and attitude, I was staggered by his actions the following day.

Ahmed hired a chauffeur-driven limousine to take Nura, Sara and me shopping. Ahmed went to meet a businessman. The caretaker, who doubled as a driver, took the two Filipinos and the three children to the pool at the Mena House Hotel. When we left the apartment, Ali and Hadi were lounging about, exhausted from the previous late night.

The sweltering heat of the city soon tired Sara, and I offered to go back to the apartment and keep her company until Nura finished her shopping. Nura agreed, and sent the driver to drop us off. He would return to collect Nura afterwards.

When we entered the apartment, we heard muffled screams. Sara and I followed the noise to Hadi and Ali's room. The door was unlocked, and we suddenly realized what was happening before our eyes. Hadi was raping a young girl, no more than eight years old, and Ali was holding her.

Blood was everywhere. Our brother and Hadi were laughing.

At the sight of this traumatic scene, Sara became hysterical and began to scream and run. Ali's face became a mask of fury as he shoved me from the room, knocking me to the floor. I ran after Sara. We huddled in our room.

When I could no longer endure the sounds of terror that continued to filter up to our floor, I crept back down the stairwell. I was desperately trying to think of a course of action when the doorbell rang. I saw Ali answer the door to an Egyptian woman, about forty years of age. He handed the woman fifteen Egyptian pounds and asked her if she had more daughters. She said that she did and that she would return tomorrow. Hadi ushered out the weeping child. The mother, showing no emotion, took the child, who was limping, tears streaming down her face, by the hand and closed the door behind her.

Ahmed did not seem surprised when Nura, angry, told him the story. He pursed his lips and said he would find out the details. Later he told Nura that the mother herself had sold her child and that there was nothing he could do.

Even though caught in this shameful act, Hadi and Ali acted as though nothing had happened. When I sneered at Hadi and asked him how he could be a religious man, he laughed full in my face. I turned to Ali and told him that I was going to tell Father he was attacking young girls, and he laughed even harder than Hadi. He leaned towards me and said: 'Tell him! I do not mind!' He said that Father had given him the name of a man to contact for the same type of service. He smiled and said young girls were more fun and, besides, Father always did the same sort of thing when he came to Cairo.

I felt as though I had been electrocuted; my brain felt burned, my mouth hung open, and I stared blankly at my brother. I had my first thoughts that all – *all* – men are wicked. I wanted to destroy my memory of that day and lapse once again into the innocence of the mists of my childhood. I walked softly away. I came to dread what I might discover next in the cruel world of men.

I still cherished Cairo as a city of enlightenment, but the decay brought by poverty caused me to rethink my earlier notions. Later in the week, I saw the Egyptian mother knocking on doors in the building with another young girl in tow. I wanted to question her, to discover how a mother could sell her young. She saw my determined look of enquiry and hurried away.

Sara and I talked with Nura for long hours about the phenomenon, and Nura sighed and said that Ahmed told her it was a way of life in much of the world. When I shouted indignantly that I would rather starve than sell my young, Nura agreed, but said it was easy to say such things when the pangs of hunger were not in your stomach.

We left Cairo and its woes behind us. Sara finally had the opportunity to realize her visions of Italy. Was her radiant look worth the travail that had freed her to come here? She dreamily proclaimed that the reality soared above her fantasies.

We toured the cities of Venice, Florence and Rome. The gaiety and the laughter of the Italians still ring in my ears. I think their love of life one of the earth's great blessings, far overshadowing their contributions to art and architecture. Born in a land of gloom, I am consoled by the idea of a nation that does not take itself too seriously.

In Milan, Nura spent more money in a matter of days than most people earn in a lifetime. It was as if she and Ahmed shopped in a frenzy, with a deep desire to fill some lonely void in their lives.

Hadi and Ali spent their time buying women, for the streets of Italy were filled, by day or by night, with beautiful young women available to those who could pay. I saw Ali as I always had, a selfish young man, concerned only with his pleasure. But Hadi, I knew, was far more evil, for he bought the women yet condemned them for their role in the act. He desired them, yet hated them and the system that left them free to do as they would. His hypocrisy was to me the essence of the evil nature of men.

When our plane touched down in Riyadh, I prepared myself for more unpleasantness. At fourteen, I knew that I would now be considered a woman, and that a hard fate awaited me. As precarious as my childhood had been, I had a sudden longing to cling to my youth and not let go. I had no doubt that my life as a woman would be a perpetual struggle against the social order of my land, which sacrifices those of my sex.

My fears regarding my future soon paled with the agony of the moment. I arrived home to discover that my mother was dying.

Chapter Seven

Journey's End

Our one certainty in life is death. As a staunch believer in the words of the Prophet Muhammad, my mother felt no apprehension at the end of her life's journey. She had followed the pure life of a good Muslim and knew her just reward awaited her. Her sorrow was intertwined with her fears for her unmarried daughters. She was our strength, our only support, and she knew that we would be tossed in the wind at her passing.

Mother confessed that she had felt her life ebbing even as we departed on our travels. She had no basis for her knowledge, other than three very extraordinary visions that came to her as dreams.

Mother's parents had died of fever when she was eight years of age. As the only female child, Mother had nursed her parents during their brief illness. They both seemed to be recovering when, in the middle of a swirling fury of a blinding sandstorm, her father had risen on his elbows, smiled at the heavens, uttered four words – 'I see the garden' – and died. Her mother died shortly afterwards without revealing a hint of what she witnessed awaiting her. My mother, left in the care of her four older brothers, was married at an early age to my father.

Mother's father had been a compassionate and kind man. He had loved his daughter as he did his sons. When other men of the tribe sulked at the birth of their daughters, Grandfather laughed and told them to praise God for the blessing of a tender touch in their home. Mother said she would never have been married at such an early age had her father lived. He would have given her some years of the freedom of childhood for herself, she believed.

Sara and I were sitting by her bedside as Mother haltingly confided her disturbing dreams. The first of her visions came four nights before we received word of Sara's attempted suicide.

'I was in a bedouin tent. It was the same as our family tent of my childhood. I was surprised to see my father and mother, young and healthy, sitting beside the coffee fire. I heard my brothers in the distance, bringing in the sheep from a day of grazing. I made a rush for my parents, but they could not see me, nor could they hear me as I cried out their names.

'Two of my brothers, the ones now deceased, came into the tent and sat with my parents. My brothers sipped warm milk from the she-camel, in small cups, while my father pounded the beans for the coffee. The dream ended as Father quoted a verse he had made up about the Paradise awaiting all good Muslims. The verse was simple, yet reassuring to my mind. It went:

Pleasant rivers flow,
Trees shade the yellow of the sun.
Fruit gathers around the feet,
Milk and honey knows no end.
Loved ones are waiting, for those trapped
on earth.'

The dream ended. Mother said she thought little of it, other than that it might be a message of joy from God to assure her that her parents and family were in Paradise.

About a week after Sara came home, Mother experienced a second vision. This time, all the members of her deceased family were sitting in the shade of a palm tree. They were eating wonderful food from silver dishes. But this time they saw her, and Mother's father got to his feet and came to greet her. He took her by the hand and tried to get her to sit and to eat.

Mother said she became frightened in the dream and tried to run away, but her father's hand tightened. Mother remembered that she had young to care for and begged her father to release her, told him that she had no time to sit and eat. She said her mother stood and touched her shoulder and told her: 'Fadeela, God will care for your daughters. The moment is coming for you to leave them in His care.'

Mother awoke from her dream. She said she knew at that instant that her time on earth was passing and that she would soon go to those who went before her.

Two weeks after we left on our trip, Mother began to experience back and neck pains. She felt dizzy and sick. The pain was her message; she knew her time was short. She went to the doctor and told him of her dreams and the new pain. He dismissed the dreams with a wave of his hand, but became serious at the description of the pain. Special tests soon revealed that Mother had an inoperable tumour on her spine.

Mother's most recent dream came the night the doctor confirmed her terminal illness. In the dream, she was sitting with her heavenly family, eating and drinking with great gaiety and abandon. She was in the company of her parents, grandparents, brothers and cousins – relatives who had died many years before. Mother smiled as she saw little ones crawling along the ground and chasing butterflies in a meadow. Her mother smiled at her and said: 'Fadeela, why do you not pay attention to your babies? Do you not recognize those of your very blood?'

Mother suddenly realized that the children were indeed hers – they were the ones lost to her in their infancy. They gathered in her lap, those heavenly five babies, and she began to sway and swing and hold them close.

Mother was going to the ones lost and losing the ones she had known. She was leaving us.

Mercifully, Mother suffered little at her death. I like to think that God saw she had passed the harsh trials of life as a person of godliness and felt no need to wound her further with the pain of passing.

Her daughters surrounded every inch of the deathbed – she lay cloaked with the love of her own flesh and blood. Her eyes lingered on each of us, no words were spoken, but we felt her farewells. When her gaze rested upon my face, I saw her worries gather as a storm, for she knew that I, unbending to the wind, would find life harder than most.

Mother's body was washed and prepared for her return to earth by the older aunties of our family. I saw her as they wrapped the white linen shroud around her thin body, worn down by childbearing and disease. Her face was peaceful, now free of earthly worries. I thought Mother appeared younger in death than in life. It was difficult for me to believe that she had given birth to sixteen children, of whom eleven had survived.

Our immediate family, along with all of Father's wives and their children, gathered in our home; a verse from the Koran was read to offer comfort. Mother's shroud-wrapped body was then placed in the back seat of a black limousine and driven away by Omar.

Our custom forbids females at the burial-site, but my sisters and I showed an unyielding front to our father; he relented on the promise that we would not wail or pull out our hair. And so it was that our entire family followed the car of death, a sad but silent caravan, into the desert.

In Islam, to show grief at a loved one's passing indicates displeasure with the will of God. Besides, our family comes from the Najd region of Saudi Arabia, and our people do not publicly mourn the passing of loved ones.

A freshly dug grave in the endless desert of our land had already been prepared by the Sudanese servants. The body of our mother was tenderly lowered, and the white cloth covering her face was removed by Ali, her only earthly son. My sisters huddled far from Mother's final resting-place, but my eyes could not leave the grave-site. I was the last child born of her body; I would stay with her earthly cloak until the final moment. I flinched as I watched the slaves push the red sands of the Empty Quarter over her face and body.

As I watched the sands cover the body of one I so adored, I suddenly remembered a beautiful verse by the great Lebanese philosopher Kahlil Gibran: 'Mayhap a funeral among men is a wedding feast among the angels.' I imagined my mother at the side of her mother and father, with her own little ones gathered in her arms. Certain at that moment that I would, another day, feel the loving touch of Mother, I ceased weeping and walked towards my sisters, shocking them with my smile of joy and serenity. I quoted the powerful verse God had sent to erase my pain, and my sisters nodded in perfect understanding at the wise Kahlil Gibran's words.

We were leaving Mother behind in the empty vastness of the desert, yet I knew it no longer mattered that there was no stone placed to mark her presence there, or that no religious services were held to speak of the simple woman who had been a flame of love during her time on earth.

Her reward was that she was now with her other loved ones, waiting there for us.

Ali seemed at a loss for once, and I knew his pain was keen also. Father had little to say and avoided our villa from the day of Mother's death. He sent us messages through his second wife, who had now replaced Mother as the head of his wives.

Within the month, we learned through Ali that Father was preparing to wed again, for four wives are common with the very wealthy and the very poor bedouin in my land. The Koran says that each wife must be treated as the others. The affluent of Saudi Arabia have no difficulty in providing equality for their wives. The poorest bedouin have only to erect four tents and provide simple fare. For these reasons, you find many of the richest and the poorest Muslims with four wives. It is only the middle-class Saudi who has to find contentment with one woman, for it is impossible for him to find the funds to provide middle-class standards for four separate families.

Father was planning to marry one of the royal cousins, Randa, a girl with whom I had played childhood games in what seemed like another lifetime. Father's new bride was fifteen, only one year older than I, his youngest child of my mother.

Four months after the burial of my mother, I attended the wedding of my father. I was surly and refused to join in the festivities – I was awash with pent-up emotions of animosity. After the birth of sixteen children and many years of obedient servitude, I knew that the memory of my mother had been effortlessly disregarded by my father.

Not only was I furious at my father; I also felt overwhelming hatred towards my former playmate Randa, who was now going to be the fourth wife, filling the void created by my mother's death.

The wedding was grand, the bride was young and beautiful. My anger towards Randa collapsed as my father led her from the huge ballroom to the marriage bed. My eyes widened as they saw her worried face. Her lips trembled with fear! As a roaring flame is instantaneously extinguished, the sight of Randa's obvious despair quietened and transformed my passion from black hate to tender commiseration. I felt ashamed of my hostility, for I saw that she was as the rest of us, helpless in the face of towering, dominating Saudi manhood.

Father travelled with his virginal bride on an extended honeymoon to Paris and Monte Carlo. In my propitious change of emotion, I waited for Randa's return, and as I lingered I vowed to awaken Father's new wife to a path of purpose: freedom for women in our land. Not only would I provide Randa with new challenges and dreams of power; I also knew I would wound Father in the political and spiritual awakening of his young wife. I could not forgive him for so easily forgetting the wonderful woman who was my mother.

Chapter Eight

Girlfriends

Upon their return from their honeymoon, Father and Randa moved into our villa. Even though Mother was no longer with the living, her younger children continued to reside in Father's villa, and his new wife was expected to assume the duties of a mother. Since I was the youngest child, only one year behind Randa, the custom seemed ludicrous in our situation. However, there is no room for manoeuvring or change to fit the individual conditions in Saudi Arabia, so Randa was installed in our home, a child masquerading as a woman and mistress of our large household.

Randa returned from her honeymoon quiet, almost broken. She rarely talked, never smiled, and moved slowly through the villa, as though she might cause some injury or harm. Father seemed pleased with his new possession, for he spent many hours cloistered in his living-quarters with his youthful bride.

After the third week of Father's undivided attention to Randa, Ali cracked a joke about Father's sexual prowess. I asked my brother what he thought of Randa's feelings in the matter – to be wed to one so much older, one she did not know or love.

Ali's vacant expression told me all too clearly not only that the thought had never entered his head, but also that such a consideration would not find fertile ground in his narrow realm of understanding. He well reminded me that nothing would ever penetrate that dark sea of egotistical matter that constitutes the mind of a Saudi man.

Randa and I held different philosophies. She believed: 'What is written on your forehead, your eyes will see.' I think: 'The picture in your mind will be photographed by your life.' In addition, Randa was painfully shy and timid, whereas I greet life with a certain fierceness.

I noticed Randa's eyes as they followed the hands of the clock; she began to fidget a few hours prior to Father's usual arrival-times for lunch and for the evening meal. She had orders from my father to eat her meals before his arrival and then to shower and prepare herself for him.

At noon each day Randa would order the cook to serve her lunch. She would eat sparingly and then retire to her quarters. My father generally arrived at the villa around one o'clock, had his lunch, and then went to his new wife. He would leave the villa around five o'clock and return to his offices. (In Saudi Arabia, the workdays are divided into two shifts: from 9 a.m. until 1 p.m. and, after a four-hour afternoon break, from 5 p.m. until 8 p.m.)

Observing Randa's pinched look, I thought of asking Father about the teachings of the Koran – the instructions from God that each Muslim was supposed to divide his days and evenings among four wives. Since the day he had wed Randa, his three older wives had been virtually ignored. After consideration, I thought better of my boldness.

And so the evenings were a repeat of the lunch-break. Randa would call for her dinner around eight o'clock, eat, and go to her rooms for her bath and preparation for her husband. I generally would not see her again until after my father left for work the next morning. She had orders to wait in the bedroom until he had left.

The anxiety of watching Randa's bleak life unfold spurred me on to mischief. I had two girlfriends who frightened even me with their boldness; their liveliness might encourage Randa to become more assertive. Little did I know what forces I would unleash by forming a girls' club with Randa, my two indomitable friends and myself as the sole members.

We called our club 'Lively Lips', for we had as our goal to talk ourselves into bravery to battle the silent acceptance of the role of women in our society. We solemnly vowed to uphold the following goals:

(1) At every opportunity, let the spirit of women's rights move our lips and guide our tongues.

(2) Each member should strive to bring in one new member per month.

(3) Our first goal would be to stop marriages of young women to old men.

We young women of Arabia recognized that the men of our land would never pursue social change for our sex, that we would have to force change. As long as Saudi women accepted their authority, men would rule. We surmised that it was the responsibility of each individual woman to foment desire for control of her life and other female lives within her small circle. Our women are so beaten down by centuries of mistreatment that our movement had to begin with an awakening of the spirit.

My two friends, Nadia and Wafa, were not of the royal family, but were children of prominent families in the city of Riyadh.

Nadia's father owned a huge contracting company. Because of his willingness to give large kickbacks to various princes, his company was awarded large government building contracts. He employed thousands of foreign workers from Sri Lanka, the Philippines and Yemen. Nadia's father was almost as wealthy as the royals; he easily supported three wives and fourteen children. Nadia was seventeen, the middle of seven daughters. She had watched with dismay as her three older sisters were married off for the purposes of family connections and convenience. Surprisingly, all three marriages had suited her sisters and they were happy, with good husbands. Nadia said that kind of luck would never continue. She felt with increasing pessimism that she would end up with an old, ugly and cruel husband.

Nadia was indeed more fortunate than most Saudi women; her father had determined that she could continue her education. He had told her she did not have to marry until she was twenty-one. This imposed deadline stirred Nadia into action.

She declared that, since she had only four more years of freedom left, she was going to taste every aspect of life during that time to provide dreams for the remainder of a dull life married to an old man.

Wafa's father was a leading *mutawa*, and his extremism had driven his daughter to extremes of her own. Her father had only one wife, Wafa's mother, but he was a cruel and vicious man. Wafa swore she wanted nothing to do with a religion that appointed such men as her father as a leader. Wafa believed in God and thought Muhammad had been His messenger, but she thought that somehow Muhammad's messages had been conveyed incorrectly by his followers, for no God would wish such grief on women, half of the world's people.

Wafa needed to look no farther than her own home. Her mother was never allowed out of the house; she was a virtual prisoner, enslaved by a man of God. There were six children, five of whom were adult sons. Wafa had been a late surprise to her parents, and her father was so disappointed that he had a girl-child he had virtually ignored her except to give her orders. She was ordered to stay in the home and learn to sew and cook. From the age of seven, Wafa was forced to wear an *abaaya* and to cover her hair. Each morning from the time she was nine, her father would ask her if she had seen her first blood. He was alarmed that his daughter would venture out, face uncovered, after she was classified by God as a woman.

Wafa was allowed few friends. What rare friends she had soon drifted away since Wafa's father made a habit of boldly enquiring in her friends' presence about their first blood.

Wafa's mother, weary and exhausted from the rigid rules of her husband, had made a decision late in life silently to defy his demands. She assisted her daughter in sneaking out of the home and told her husband the child was sleeping or studying the Koran when enquiries concerning Wafa's whereabouts were voiced.

I imagined myself bold and rebellious, but Wafa and Nadia made my stance for women seem puny and powerless. They said that all I did was to provide intelligent stimulation – that my answer to a problem was to talk it to death – but that in reality my efforts to help women were useless. After all, my life had not changed. I realized they were right.

I will never forget one incident that occurred in an underground carpark close to the *souq* area, not far from the spot that foreigners call 'Chop Chop Square' since that is where our criminals lose their heads or their hands on Fridays, our day of religion.

I had hidden the passing of my first blood from my father, since I was in no rush to swathe myself in the black garb of our women. Unfortunately, Nura and Ahmed decided that I had postponed the inevitable long enough. Nura told me that if I did not tell my father immediately, she would. So I gathered my friends around me, including

Randa, and we made the mission to purchase my new 'life's uniform', black scarf on black veil on black *abaaya*.

Omar drove us to the entrance of the *souq* area, and we four young women disembarked, agreeing to meet him in two hours at the same spot. Omar always accompanied us into the *souq* to keep special watch on the women of the family, but that day he had an important errand to run and took the opportunity while we were shopping. Besides, Father's new wife was accompanying his daughter, and Omar was reassured by Randa's acquiescent presence. He had seen no indication that Randa was slowly awaking after the long dull sleep of submission.

We milled about the shops, hands examining the various scarves, veils and *abaayas*. I wanted something special, a way of being an original in the ocean of black-garbed women. I cursed myself for not having an *abaaya* made in Italy, from the finest Italian silk, with an artist's intricate designs, so that, when I breezed past, people would know there was an individual under the black covering, a woman with style and class.

Everyone was veiled except me, and as we made our way to the heart of the *souq* to continue our search I noticed that Wafa and Nadia, heads together, were whispering and giggling. Randa and I stepped up our pace, and I asked them what was so amusing. Nadia looked towards me and spoke through her veil. She said they were remembering a man they had met on their last trip to the *souq*.

A man? I looked back at Randa. We were both confused at their meaning.

It took us only an hour to find a suitable *abaaya*, veil and scarf; the selection seemed rather limited.

Life changed quickly. I had entered the *souq* area as an individual bursting with life, my face expressing my emotions to the world. I left the shopping area covered from head to toe, a faceless creature in black.

I must admit that the first few moments of veiling were exciting. I found the veil a novelty and looked back with interest as Saudi teenage boys stared at me, now a mysterious figure in black. I knew they were wishing for a bit of breeze to blow the veil away from my face so that they might catch a glimpse of my forbidden skin. For a moment, I felt myself a thing of beauty, a work so lovely that I must be covered to protect men from their uncontrollable desires.

The novelty of wearing the veil and *abaaya* was fleeting, though. When we walked out of the cool *souq* area into the blazing hot sun, I gasped for breath and sucked furiously through the sheer black fabric. The air tasted stale and dry as it filtered through the thin gauzy cloth. I had purchased the sheerest veil available, yet I felt I was seeing life through a thick screen. How could women see through veils made of a thicker fabric? The sky was no longer blue, the glow of the sun had dimmed; my heart plunged to my stomach when I realized that, from that moment, outside my own home I would not experience life as it really is in all its colour. The world suddenly seemed a dull place. And dangerous, too! I groped and stumbled along the pitted, cracked pavement, fearful of breaking an ankle or leg.

My friends burst out laughing at the awkwardness of my moves and my futile efforts to adjust my veil. I stumbled over several children of a bedouin woman, and looked in envy at the freedom of her veil. Bedouin women wear veils that fit across their noses, leaving their eyes free to examine their surroundings. Oh, how I wished to be a bedouin! I would cover my face gladly if I could only leave my eyes free to see the infinite changes of life around me.

We arrived early at the meeting-place designated by Omar. Randa glanced at her watch; we had nearly an hour before he was due. She suggested that we go back into the *souq* area since it was too hot in the boiling sun. Nadia and Wafa asked us if we wanted to have some fun. I said sure, without hesitation. Randa balanced from foot to foot, looking for Omar; I could tell she was uncomfortable with the very word *fun*. I, with my marvellous powers of persuasion, convinced Randa to go along with Nadia and Wafa. I was curious, never having broken any of the rules laid down for females. Poor Randa was simply accommodating to a stronger will.

The two girls exchanged smiles and told us to follow them. They made their way to a carpark beneath a new office building not far from the *souq* area. Men who worked in the building and nearby shops parked there.

We four young women inched our way across the busy intersection. Randa squealed and slapped my hand when I raised my veil so that I could see the traffic. Too late, I realized that I had exposed my face to every man on the street! The men appeared stunned by their luck, for they had seen a woman's face in a public place! I instantly realized it was far better for me to be run down by a speeding car than to commit such an act of revelation.

When we reached the carpark lifts, I staggered with shock at my friends' action. Wafa and Nadia approached a foreign man, a strikingly handsome Syrian. They asked him if he wanted to have some fun. For a moment, he seemed ready to bolt and run; he looked to his left and right and punched the lift button. Finally, he thought better of departing, considering the rare opportunity to meet available and possibly beautiful women in Saudi Arabia. He asked what kind of fun. Wafa asked the Syrian if he had a car and a private apartment. He said yes, he had an apartment and a room-mate, a Lebanese. Nadia asked if his friend was looking for a girlfriend, and the Syrian grinned and said, yes, indeed, both of them were.

Randa and I had recovered enough to move our feet. We gathered up our *abaayas* and ran out of the carpark in fear for our lives. In the process I lost my scarf; when I turned to pick it up, Randa ran straight into me. She fell backwards and lay sprawled in the sand, her forbidden legs exposed.

When Wafa and Nadia found us, we were breathing hard and leaning against a shop window. They were hanging on to each other, laughing. They had watched us earlier as I struggled to help Randa to her feet.

We whispered our angry words. How could they do such a stupid thing? Pick up foreign men! What kind of fun were they planning anyway? Didn't they know that Randa would be stoned and the three of us imprisoned, or worse? Fun was fun, but what they were doing was suicide!

Wafa and Nadia simply laughed and shrugged their shoulders at our outburst. They knew that if they were caught they would be punished, but they didn't care. To them, their impending future was so bleak it was worth a risk. Besides, they might meet a nice foreign man and marry him. Any man was better than a Saudi man!

I thought Randa was going to swoon. She ran into the street, looking up and down for Omar. She knew there would be no mercy from Father if she were caught in such a situation. She was terrified.

Omar, wary and perceptive, asked us what had happened. Randa fidgeted and started to speak, but I interrupted and told Omar a story about seeing a youth steal a necklace from the gold *souq*. He had been beaten by the shopkeeper and roughly hauled off to gaol by a policeman. My voice had a tremor as I told Omar we were upset because he was so young and we knew he would lose his hand for his act. I was relieved that Omar believed my story.

Randa inched her hand under my black cloak and gave me a squeeze of gratitude.

Later I found out from Nadia and Wafa what they called 'fun'. They met foreign men, usually from neighbouring Arab countries, occasionally a Brit or an American, in carpark lifts. They selected handsome men; men they felt they could love. Sometimes the men became frightened and jumped into the lift, zooming to another floor. At other times they would be interested. If the man they approached was intrigued, Wafa and Nadia would agree to a meeting-time, at the same lift. They would ask him to try to find a van, instead of a car, to pick them up. Later, at the agreed time, the girls would pretend to go shopping. Their driver would drop them at the *souq*; they would purchase a few items, and then go to the meeting-place. Sometimes the men would become wary and not show up; at other times they would be nervously waiting. If the men had obtained a van, the girls would make sure no-one was around and then jump quickly into the back. The men would cautiously drive to their apartment, and the same degree of caution would be used to smuggle the girls inside. If they were caught, the sentence would be severe, quite possibly death for everyone involved.

The explanation for the van was clear. In Saudi Arabia, men and women are not allowed in the same car unless they are close relatives. If the *mutawas* become suspicious, they will stop the vehicle and check identifications. Also, single men are not allowed to entertain women in their apartments or homes. At the slightest suspicion of impropriety, it is not uncommon for *mutawas* to surround the home of a foreigner and take everyone there, both male and female, to the gaol.

I was fearful for my friends. I warned them again and again of the consequences. They were young and reckless and bored with their lives. They laughingly told me of other activities they did for diversion. They dialled random phone numbers until a foreign man answered. Any man would do, so long as he was not Saudi or Yemeni. They would ask him if he was alone and longing for female companionship. Generally, the reply was yes since there are so few women allowed in Saudi Arabia and most foreign men work there on single-status visas. Once a man's eligibility was established, the girls would ask him to describe his body. Flattered, usually the man would graphically describe his body and then ask them to do the same. Then Wafa and Nadia would portray themselves from head to toe, in lewd detail. It was great amusement, they said, and they sometimes met the man later, in the same fashion as the carpark lovers.

I wondered how intimate my friends became with these pick-up lovers. I was astonished to hear that they did everything except penetration. They could not risk losing their virginity, for they realized the consequences they would face on their wedding night. Their husbands would return them to their homes, and their fathers would turn them away as well. The *mutawas* would investigate. They might lose their lives; if not, they would still have nowhere to live.

Wafa said that in their encounters with these men she and Nadia never removed their veils. They would take off all their clothes but keep their veils intact. The men would tease and beg and even try to force them to remove their veils, but the girls said they felt safe so long as no man saw their faces. They said if any of the men had become serious they might have considered exposing their faces. But, of course, none of them did. They, too, were only having fun. My friends were desperately trying to find an 'out' from their future, which loomed before them like a dark and endless night.

Randa and I wept when we discussed our friends' behaviour. I felt a hatred for the customs of my land creep into my throat like a foul taste. The absolute lack of control, of freedom for our sex, drove young girls like Wafa and Nadia to desperate acts. These were deeds that were sure to cost them their lives if they were discovered.

Before the year was out, Nadia and Wafa were arrested. Unfortunately for them, members of a self-proclaimed Public Morality Committee who roamed the streets of Riyadh in an effort to apprehend people in acts prohibited by the Koran had learned of their forbidden activities. Just as Nadia and Wafa entered the back of a van, a carload of young Saudi zealots wheeled in and blocked the vehicle. They had been watching the area for weeks after one of the committee members, while at work, overheard a Palestinian tell of two veiled women who propositioned him at the lift.

The lives of Wafa and Nadia were spared by the fact that their hymens were intact. Neither the Morals Committee nor the Religious Council, and especially not their fathers, believed their unlikely fabrication that they had simply asked the men for a ride when their driver was late. I suppose it was the best story they could concoct, considering the circumstances.

The Religious Council questioned every man who worked in the area and found a total of fourteen who said they had been approached by two veiled women. None of the men confessed that they had participated in any activities with them.

After three months of bleak imprisonment, owing to the lack of hard evidence of sexual activity the committee released Wafa and Nadia to their respective fathers for punishment.

Surprisingly, Wafa's father, the unbending man of religion, sat with his daughter and questioned her as to the reasons for her misdeeds. When she cried and told him her feelings of rejection and hopelessness, he expressed sorrow at her unhappiness. In spite of his regret and sympathy, he informed Wafa that it was his decision that she should be removed from all further temptations. She was advised to study the Koran and to accept a simple life preordained for women, far removed from the city. He arranged a hasty marriage with a bedouin *mutawa* from a small village. The man was fifty-three; and Wafa, seventeen, would be his third wife.

Ironically, it was Nadia's father who was gripped with a fearsome rage. He refused to speak with his daughter and ordered her confined to her room until a decision was made as to her punishment.

A few days later, my father came home early from the office and called Randa and me into his sitting-room. We sat disbelieving when he told us that Nadia was going to be drowned in her family's swimming-pool, by her father, on the following morning, Friday, at ten o'clock. Father said that Nadia's entire family would witness her execution.

My heart fluttered with fear when Father asked Randa if she or I had ever accompanied Wafa or Nadia on their shameful undertakings. I moved forward and started to voice my denials when Father shouted and shoved me back into the sofa. Randa burst into tears and told him the story of that day so long ago when we had purchased my first *abaaya* and veil. Father sat unmoving, eyes unblinking, until Randa had finished. He then asked us about our women's club, the one with the name of Lively Lips. He said that we might as well tell the truth, that Nadia had confessed all our activities days ago. When Randa's tongue froze, Father removed our club papers from his briefcase. He had searched my room and found our records and membership lists. For once in my life, my mouth was dry, my lips locked as with a chain.

Father calmly put the papers back into a pile on the briefcase. He looked clearly into Randa's eyes and said: 'On this day I have divorced you. Your father will send a driver within the hour to take you to your family. You are forbidden to contact my children.'

To my horror, Father turned slowly to me. 'You are my child. Your mother was a good woman. Even so, had you participated in these activities with Wafa and Nadia, I would uphold the teachings of the Koran and see you lowered into your grave. You will avoid my attention and concentrate on your schooling while I will work towards a suitable marriage.' He paused for a moment, coming close and looking hard into my eyes. 'Sultana, accept your future as one who obeys, for you have no alternative.'

Father stooped for the papers and his case and, without looking at Randa or me again, left the room.

Humiliated, I followed Randa to her room and numbly watched as she gathered her jewels, her clothes and her books into an unruly pile on the large bed. Her face was wiped clean of emotion. I could not form the words that were loose in my head. The doorbell rang too quickly, and I found myself helping the servants carry her things to the car. Without a word of farewell, Randa left my home, but not my heart.

At ten o'clock the next morning, I sat alone, staring yet unseeing out of my bedroom balcony. I thought of Nadia and imagined her bound in heavy chains, dark hood gathered around her head, hands lifting her from the ground and lowering her into the blue-green waters of her family swimming-pool. I closed my eyes and felt her body thrashing, her mouth gasping for air, lungs screaming for relief from the rushing water. I remembered her flashing brown eyes and her special way of lifting her chin while filling the room with laughter. I recalled the soft feel of her fair skin, and considered with a grimace the quick work of the cruel earth on such softness. I looked at my watch and saw that it was 10.10, and I felt my chest tighten with the knowledge that Nadia would laugh no more.

It was the most dramatic hour in my young history, yet I knew that my friends' schemes for fun, as bad or sad as they were, should not have caused Nadia's death or Wafa's premature marriage. Such cruel actions were the worst of all commentaries on the wisdom of the men who consume and destroy the lives and dreams of their women with emotionless indifference.

Chapter Nine

Foreign Women

After the sudden departure of Randa, the marriage of Wafa and the death of Nadia, I sank to the lowest possible level of existence. I can recall thinking that my body no longer required the fresh breath of life. I fancied myself in hibernation and wanted to feel the shallow breathing and lowered heartbeat experienced by creatures of the wild that will themselves away for months at a time. I would lie in my bed, hold my nose with my fingers, and pinch my mouth closed with my teeth. Only when my lungs forced the expulsion of air would I regretfully recognize that I had little control over my vital functions.

The house servants felt my pain keenly, for I was known as the sensitive member of our family and had always shown concern for their situation. The meagre amounts of cash doled out each month by Omar seemed a high price to pay for being so far removed from those they loved.

In an effort to rouse my interest in life, my Filipino maid, Marci, began to revive my thoughts by telling me stories of her country. Our long talks served to thaw the impersonal relationship that exists between mistress and servant.

One day she timidly revealed her life's ambition. She wanted to save enough money, working as a housemaid for our family, to return to the Philippines to study nursing. Filipino nurses are in great demand worldwide, and it is considered a lucrative career for women in the Philippines.

Marci said that after she graduated she would return to Saudi Arabia to work in one of our modern hospitals. She smiled as she reported that Filipino nurses made a salary of 3,800 Saudi riyals each month! Approximately $1,000 a month, compared to the $200 a month she earned as our maid. With such a large salary, she said, she could support her entire family in the Philippines.

When Marci was only three, her father was killed in a mining accident. Her mother was seven months pregnant with a second child. Their life was bleak, but Marci's grandmother tended to the two children while her mother worked two shifts as a maid in local hotels. Marci's mother repeated many times that knowledge was the only solution to poverty, and she frugally saved for her children's education.

Two years before Marci was to enrol in nursing school, her younger brother, Tony, was run over by a car and suffered extensive injuries. His legs were so crushed that they had to be amputated. His medical treatment ate away at Marci's school fund until the small tin can was bare.

Upon hearing Marci's life-story, I wept bitter tears. I asked her how she could maintain her happy smile day after day, week after week.

Marci smiled broadly. It was easy for her, she said, since she had a dream and a way to realize her dream.

Her experiences growing up in a wretchedly poor area in the Philippines left Marci feeling extremely fortunate to have a job and to fill her plate three times daily. People from her area did not actually die of hunger, she emphasized, but of malnutrition that left them vulnerable to diseases that would not have flourished in a healthy community.

Marci shared the stories of her people so vividly that I felt myself a part of her history, her land, her rich culture. I knew I had underestimated Marci and other Filipinos, for, until then, I had given them little thought other than to consider them simple folk lacking in ambition. How wrong I was!

Several weeks later Marci felt confident enough to talk about her friend Madeline. By telling me about Madeline, she opened up the question of the moral values of my land. Through Marci, I first learned that women from Third World countries were held as sex slaves in my own country, Saudi Arabia.

Marci and Madeline had been childhood friends. As poor as Marci's family was, Madeline's was poorer. Madeline and her seven siblings used to beg on the highway that connected their province to Manila. Occasionally, a big car transporting foreigners would stop and huge white hands would drop a few coins into their outstretched palms.

While Marci attended school, Madeline foraged for food.

At an early age, Madeline had a dream and a plan to bring that dream to reality. When she was eighteen, she sewed a dress from Marci's old school coat and travelled to Manila. There she located an agency that employed Filipinos to work abroad; Madeline applied for a maid's position. She was so petite and pretty that the Lebanese owner slyly hinted that he could get her a job in a Manila brothel; there she could earn a substantial amount beyond the imagination of a maid! Madeline, although raised in poor circumstances, was a devout Catholic; her negative reaction convinced the Lebanese that she would not sell her body. Sighing with regret, the man told her to fill in the application form and wait.

The Lebanese told her that he had just received a contract to supply more than three thousand Filipino workers to the Persian Gulf area, and that Madeline would be given priority in the maid positions since the rich Arabs always requested pretty maids. He winked and patted her on the buttocks as she left his office.

Madeline was both excited and frightened when she received confirmation of a maid's position in Riyadh, Saudi Arabia. About the same time, Marci's plans of attending nursing school fell through, and she decided to follow Madeline's footsteps and search for a job outside the Philippines. When Madeline left for Saudi Arabia, Marci joked that she would not be far behind. The good friends hugged their farewells and promised to write.

Four months later, when Marci learned that she, too, was to work in Saudi Arabia, she still had not heard from Madeline. Once there, she did not know where to find her friend, other than in the city of Riyadh. Since Marci was going to work for a family in the same city, she was determined to locate her friend.

I recall the night Marci arrived in our home. Mother was responsible for the running of the household and the placement of the servants. I remembered that Marci seemed a frightened little thing, immediately clinging to the eldest of our Filipino maids.

Since we had more than twenty servants in the villa, Marci was given little notice. As an inexperienced servant, only nineteen years old, she was assigned to clean the rooms of the two youngest daughters of the house, Sara and me. I had given her scant attention during the sixteen months she had patiently and quietly followed me through the villa, asking if I required anything.

Marci surprised me by confessing that other Filipino servants thought her blessed in her job since neither Sara nor I ever struck her or raised our voices in disapproval. My eyes flashed, and I asked Marci if people were struck in our home. I breathed a sigh of relief when she told me no, not in our villa. She did say that Ali was known to be difficult, always speaking in a loud and insulting tone. But his only violent action had been to kick Omar in the shin several times. I laughed, feeling little sympathy for Omar.

Marci whispered as she told me the gossip of the servants. She said that Father's second wife, a woman from one of the neighbouring Gulf states, pinched and beat her female servants daily. One poor girl from Pakistan had a brain injury from being knocked down the stairs. Told that she did not work fast enough, she rushed down to the washroom with a basket of dirty sheets and towels. When she accidentally bumped into Father's wife, the woman became so enraged that she punched the maid in the stomach, sending her tumbling down the stairs. As the girl lay moaning, the older woman ran down the stairs to kick and scream at the girl to finish her chores. When the girl did not move, she was accused of pretence. Eventually, the girl had to be taken to a doctor; she was still not normal, constantly holding her head in her hands and giggling.

Under orders from Father's wife, the palace doctor filled in a form stating that the girl had fallen and suffered concussion. As soon as she could travel, she was to be sent back to Pakistan. She was denied her past two months' salary and sent to her parents with only fifty Saudi riyals ($15).

Why did I act so surprised, Marci wanted to know. Most maids were mistreated in my country; our villa was a rare exception. I reminded her that I had been in many of my friends' homes and, while I had to admit that little consideration was given to servants, I had never witnessed an actual beating. I had seen some of my friends verbally abuse their maids, but I had paid it little heed since no-one had ever been physically assaulted.

Marci sighed wearily, and said that physical and sexual abuse were generally hidden. She reminded me that I live only yards from a palace that hid the sufferings of many young girls, and yet I had no knowledge of them. She softly told me to keep my eyes open, to observe how women from other lands were treated in my country. I nodded sadly in agreement.

Through this conversation, Marci became more aware of my empathetic nature. She decided to take me into her confidence and tell me the full story of her friend Madeline. I remember our conversation as well as if it were yesterday. Our exchanges are clear in my mind. I can see her earnest face before me now.

'Ma'am, I want you to know about my closest friend, Madeline. You are a princess. Perhaps the day will come that you can help us poor Filipino women.'

I was alone on that morning and felt boredom creeping into my day, so I nodded, eager for a morning of revealing gossip, even from a Filipino. I settled myself on my bed; Marci dutifully stuffed pillows behind my head, just the way she knew I liked them.

I told her: 'Before you begin your tale, go and get me a bowl of fresh fruit and a glass of *laban*.' (*Laban* is a buttermilk-like drink common in the Middle East.) After she had returned with a tray of fruit and my cold beverage, I stuck my feet out from under the covers and told Marci to rub them while she told me about this Madeline friend of hers.

Looking back, I burn with shame as I recall my selfish, childish manner. I was intrigued by the thought of a tragic story, yet not content to sit still and listen until all my desires were met! Older and wiser, now I can only look back with regret at the habits I picked up from my Saudi culture. No Saudi I know has ever shown the slightest interest in a servant's life: the number of family members; their dreams and aspirations. People from the Third World were there to serve us wealthy Saudis, nothing more. Even my mother, who was kind and loving, rarely expressed an interest in servants' personal problems; though I do attribute that to Mother's overwhelming responsibilities of running a huge household and also satisfying my demanding father. I had no such excuse. I cringe as I now acknowledge that Marci and the other servants were little more than robots to me, there to do my bidding. And to think that Marci and the household servants thought me kind, for I alone questioned them about their lives. It is a hard remembrance for one who considers herself sensitive.

Pensive, her face without expression, Marci began to rub my feet and started her story.

'Ma'am, before I left my country, I begged that Lebanese man for the address of Madeline's employer. He said no, he was not allowed. I told a lie, ma'am. I said that I had items to take to my friend from her mother. After I begged, he finally agreed, and gave me a phone number and the area of Riyadh that Madeline worked.'

'Is her employer a prince?'

'No, ma'am. He lives in the district called Al Malaz, about thirty minutes by car from here.'

Our palace was in the Al Nasiriyah area, a prestigious location inhabited by many royals, the most wealthy residential district of Riyadh. I had been in the area of Al Malaz once a long time ago and recalled many nice palaces of the upper business society of Saudis.

I knew Marci was forbidden to leave the palace grounds, other than on special monthly shopping trips organized by Omar for the female servants. Since our servants, like most domestics in Saudi Arabia, worked a brutal seven-day week, fifty-two weeks a year, I wondered how she could slip away to visit her friend.

I voiced my interest. 'How did you manage a trip to Al Malaz?'

Marci hesitated for a short moment. 'Well, ma'am, you know the Filipino driver Antoine?'

We had four drivers, two Filipinos and two Egyptians. I was generally driven by Omar or the other Egyptian. The Filipinos were used for grocery shopping and the running of errands. 'Antoine? The young one who is always smiling?'

'Yes, ma'am, that one. He and I like to see each other and he agreed to take me to find my friend.'

'Marci! You have a sweetheart!' I burst out

laughing. 'And Omar. How did you avoid getting into trouble with Omar?'

'We waited until Omar went with the family to Taif and we took our opportunity.' Marci smiled at my look of pleasure. She knew nothing gave me more joy than a successful trick pulled over the men of the household. 'First, I called the telephone number given to me in the Philippines. No-one would give me permission to speak with Madeline. I said I had a message from Madeline's mother. After a lot of hard work of convincing, I was told the location and description of the villa. Antoine drove to the area and located the place to deliver a letter to Madeline. A Yemeni took the letter from Antoine. Two weeks later I received a call from my friend. I could barely hear Madeline, for she whispered, afraid she would be discovered using the telephone. She told me she was in a very bad situation, please to come and help her. Over the telephone, we made a plan.'

I put aside my food and gave Marci my full attention. I told her to stop rubbing my feet. I felt the danger of their meeting and my interest in this brave Filipino whom I did not know grew.

'Two months passed. We knew the hot summer months would give us an opportunity to meet. We were afraid Madeline would be taken to Europe with her employer, but she was told to remain in Riyadh. When you and the family, along with Omar, left the city, I hid in the back seat of the black Mercedes and Antoine took me to Madeline.'

Marci, her voice cracking with her first show of emotion, described Madeline's dilemma: 'I sat in the car while Antoine rang the bell of the villa. While I was waiting, I could not help but notice the condition of the villa wall. The paint was peeling, the gate was rusty, the few bits of greenery hanging over the villa wall were dying from lack of water. I could tell it was a bad place. I knew my friend was in a dangerous situation if she worked in such a home.

'I felt depressed even before I was allowed inside. Antoine had to ring the bell four or five times before we heard activity as someone came to answer our call. Everything happened just as Madeline had said. It was creepy! An old Yemeni man dressed in a tartan wrap-around skirt opened the gate. He looked as though he had been sleeping; his ugly face told us he was none too happy at being awakened from a nap.

'Antoine and I both became frightened, and I heard the shaking of Antoine's voice when he asked, please, to speak to Miss Madeline from the Philippines. The Yemeni could hardly speak English, but Antoine has a little knowledge of Arabic. Together they managed to understand each other enough for the Yemeni to refuse us entry. He waved us away with his hand and began to close the door when I leaped from the back seat and began to cry. Through my tears, I told him that Madeline was my sister. I had just arrived in Riyadh and was working at the palace of one of the royal princes. I thought that might frighten him, but his expression remained the same. I waved an envelope at him that had just arrived from the Philippines. Our mother was gravely ill. I had to speak with Madeline for a few moments to deliver a last message from our dying mother.

'I prayed to God not to punish me for such lies! I think God heard me, for the Yemeni seemed to change his mind when he heard the Arab word for *mother*. I saw that he was thinking. He looked first at Antoine and then at me, and finally told us to wait a moment. He closed the gate, and we heard the flip-flop of his sandals as he made his way back towards the villa.

'We knew the Yemeni was going inside to question Madeline and ask her to describe her sister. I looked at Antoine with a weak smile. It seemed our plan might work.'

Marci paused, remembering that day.

'Ma'am, that was a frightening Yemeni. He had a mean look and carried a curved knife at his waist. Antoine and I almost got in the car and drove back to the palace. But the thought of my poor friend gave me a feeling of power.

'Madeline had told me that two Yemenis guarded the villa. They watched the females of the house. None of the female servants was ever allowed to leave her place of work. Madeline had told me over the telephone that the young Yemeni was without a good heart and would not allow anyone in the gate, even a dying mother herself. Madeline thought we might succeed with the old Yemeni.

'Since the entire family was on holiday in Europe,

the young Yemeni had been given a two-week leave and had returned to Yemen to marry. At this time, the only men in the villa grounds were the old Yemeni and a gardener from Pakistan.

'I looked at my watch, and Antoine looked at his watch. Finally, we heard the shuffling of feet as the old man returned. The gate creaked with a slow swing. I shivered, for I had a feeling I was entering the gates of hell. The old Yemeni grunted and made a motion with his hands that Antoine was to stay outside with the car. Only I would be allowed inside.'

I tensed up as I imagined the fear Marci must have felt. 'How did you dare? I would have called the police!'

Marci shook her head. 'The police do not help Filipinos in this country. We would be reported to our employer and then gaoled or deported, according to the wishes of your father. The police in this country are for the strong, not for the weak.'

I knew what she said was true. Filipinos were a notch below us women. Even I, a princess, would never receive aid if it meant the police had to go against the wishes of the men of my family. But I did not want to think of my problems at that moment; I was wrapped up in Marci's adventure.

'Go on, tell me, what did you discover inside?' I imagined the inner workings of a Saudi Frankenstein's monster!

Having the full interest of her mistress, Marci became enlivened and began to make facial expressions and describe her experiences with relish.

'Following his slow steps, I was able to look all around. The concrete blocks had never been painted. A small block building nearby had no door, just an open space with a stringy old rag pulled across the top. Judging from the clutter of dirty mats, open cans and garbage smells, I knew the old Yemeni must live there. We walked by the family pool, but it was empty of water except for a black foul residue at the deepest end. Three tiny skeletons – which looked like the remains of baby kittens – were lying at the short end of the pool.'

'Kittens? Oh, my goodness!' Marci knew how I loved all baby animals. 'What a terrible death!'

'It looked like kittens. I guessed they were born in the empty pool and the mother cat was unable to get them out.'

I shuddered with despair.

Marci continued. 'The villa was large but had the same coarse look as the wall. Paint had been splashed on the blocks at some time in the past, but sandstorms had left it ugly. There was a garden, but the plants had all died from the lack of water. I saw four or five birds in a cage hanging under a large tree. They looked sad and skinny, without a song in their hearts to sing.

'Through the front door, the Yemeni yelled something in Arabic to an unseen person; he nodded his head at me and motioned for me to enter. I hesitated at the doorway as the bad-smelling air rushed over me. With great fear and trembling, I called out Madeline's name. The Yemeni turned and walked back to his interrupted sleep.

'Madeline came down a long dark hallway. The light was very dim, and after the bright sunshine outside I could barely see her walking towards me. She began to run when she saw it was really her old friend Marci. We rushed to embrace, and I was amazed to see that she was clean and smelled good. She was skinnier than when I last saw her, but alive!'

A feeling of relief flooded my body, for I had expected Marci to tell me she had found her friend half-dead, lying on a dirty mat, struggling to give her final instructions to take her body back to Manila.

'What happened then?' I was in a rush to discover the end to Marci's story.

Marci's voice took on the tone of a whisper, as though her memories were too painful to recall. 'After we completed our cries of greeting and our hugs, Madeline pushed me towards the long hallway. She held my hand and guided me to a small room off to the right. Directing me to a sofa, she sat on the floor facing me.

'She immediately burst into tears now that we were alone. As she buried her face in my lap, I stroked her hair and whispered for her to tell me what had happened to her. After she stopped her tears, she told me of her life since she had left Manila one year before.

'Madeline was met at the airport by two Yemeni servants. They were holding a card with her name spelled out in English. She accompanied the two men, for she did not know what else to do. She was alarmed at their wild appearance, and said she feared for her life as they careered through the city. It was late at night when she arrived at the villa; there was no light, so she did not notice the neglected grounds.

'At that time, the family was away at Makkah for the Haj pilgrimage. She was shown to her room by an old Arab woman who could not speak English. She was given biscuits and dates to eat and hot tea to drink. As the old woman left the room she handed Madeline a note that said she would be informed of her duties the following day.'

'The old woman must have been the grandmother,' I said.

'Maybe – Madeline did not say. Anyhow, I do not know. Poor Madeline's heart sank when sunlight revealed her new home. She jumped at the sight of the bed in which she had slept, for the bedsheets were filthy; last night's glass and plate were swarming with cockroaches.

'With a sinking heart, Madeline located a bathroom only to discover the shower was not functioning. She tried to cleanse herself in the sink with a remnant of dirty soap and tepid water. She wished in vain for God to calm her beating heart. Then the old woman knocked on the door.

'Having no choice, she followed the woman into the kitchen where she was handed a list of responsibilities. Madeline read the hastily scribbled note and saw that she was to assist the cook, be the housekeeper and care for the children. The old woman motioned for Madeline to prepare some food for herself. After eating breakfast, she began to scrub filth off the pots and pans.

'Along with Madeline, there were three other female employees: an old cook from India, an attractive maid from Sri Lanka and a plain maid from Bangladesh. The cook was at least sixty years old; the other two were in their mid-twenties.

'The cook refused conversation with anyone; she was returning to India within the next two months, and her dreams were of freedom and home. The plain maid was silent in her unhappiness, for her work contract had over a year until completion. The pretty maid from Sri Lanka did little work and spent most of her time in front of a mirror. She wished out loud for the return of the family. She hinted strongly to Madeline that she was much loved by the master of the house. She was expecting him to buy her a gold necklace upon his return from Makkah.

'Madeline said she was surprised when the pretty maid ordered her to turn around so she could see her figure. The maid then put her hands on her hips and declared with a grin that the master would find Madeline too skinny for his taste, but perhaps one of the sons would find her favourable. Madeline did not understand the implication and went on with her endless cleaning.

'Four days later, the family returned from Makkah. Madeline saw at once that her employers were of a low-class family; they were crude and ill-mannered, and their behaviour soon proved her assessment correct. They were accidentally wealthy without any effort on their part, and their only education was from the Koran, which in their ignorance they twisted to suit their needs.

'To the head of the household, the secondary status of women indicated in the Koran was understood to be slavery. Any woman who was not a Muslim was considered a prostitute. Matters were not helped by the fact that the father and two sons travelled to Thailand four times a year to visit the brothels in Bangkok and buy the sexual services of young beautiful Thai women. Knowing that some of the women of the Orient were for sale convinced the family that all women outside the Muslim faith were for purchase. When a maid was hired, it was assumed she was to be used like an animal, at the whim of the men of the house.

'Through the mother, Madeline immediately learned that she had been employed to serve as a sexual release for the two teenage sons. She informed Madeline that she was to serve Basel and Faris on an every-other-day basis. This information was given without emotion to Madeline's utter despair.

'To the surprise of the sexy maid, the father decided that Madeline was to his taste. He told his sons they could sleep with the new maid as soon as he had had his pleasure.'

I gasped and then held my breath; I knew what Marci was going to tell me. I did not want to hear it.

'Ma'am Sultana, that first night the family returned, the father raped Madeline!' She sobbed.

'That was only the beginning, for he decided that he liked her so much he continued to rape her on a daily basis!'

'Why did she not run away? Get someone to help her?'

'Ma'am, she did try. She begged the other servants to assist her! The old cook and the ugly maid did not wish to become involved and perhaps lose their salaries. The pretty maid hated Madeline, and said she was the reason she did not get her gold necklace. The wife and old woman were not treated well themselves by the master; they ignored her and said she was hired to please the men of the house!'

'I would have jumped out of a window and run away!'

'She tried to run away, many times. She was caught, and everyone in the house was ordered to guard her. Once, while everyone was sleeping, she went to the roof and dropped notes on the pavement begging for help. The notes were given to the Yemenis by some Saudi neighbours, and she was beaten!'

'What happened after you found her?'

Marci's face was sad and resigned as she continued. 'I tried many things. I called our embassy in Jeddah. I was told by the man that answered that they received many such complaints but there was little they could do. Our country relies on the money sent from workers abroad; our government did not want to antagonize the Saudi government by lodging formal complaints. Where would the poor Filipino people be without money from abroad?

'Antoine checked with some of the drivers about going to the police, but he was told the police would believe any story told by the Saudi employer and Madeline might get into a worse situation.'

I cried out: 'Marci! What could be worse?'

'Nothing, ma'am. Nothing. I did not know what to do. Antoine became frightened and said we could do nothing else. I finally wrote to Madeline's mother and told her of the situation, and she went to the employment agency in Manila and was told to go away. She went to our mayor in our town, and he said he was helpless. No-one wanted to get involved.'

'Where is your friend now?'

'I received a letter from her only a month ago. I am thankful she was sent back to the Philippines at the end of her two-year contract. Two new Filipinos, younger than Madeline, had replaced her. Can you believe, ma'am, Madeline was angry at me? She thought I had left her without trying to help.

'Please believe that I did all that I could. I wrote her a letter and explained all that happened. I have not received a reply.'

I could not say a word in defence of my countrymen. I stared into Marci's face, at a loss.

She finally broke the silence. 'And that, ma'am, is what happened to my friend in this country.'

I could tell Marci was heartbroken for her friend. I myself was stricken with sorrow. How does a person respond to such a tale of horror? I could not. In shame at the men of my country, I no longer felt superior to the young girl who only moments before was my servant, my inferior. Engulfed by remorse, I buried my head in my pillow and dismissed Marci with a flick of my hand. For many days, I was quiet and withdrawn; I thought of the myriad accounts of abuse that torture the minds of the people, both Saudis and foreigners, living in this land I call my home.

How many more Madelines are there, reaching out to uncaring souls and discovering the nothingness that is dressed in the official uniform of those paid to care? And the men of the Philippines, Marci's land, were little better than the men of my country, for they fled from personal involvement.

When I awoke from my unsettling sleep of mortification, I began to interrogate my friends and ferret out their passivity regarding the fate of their female servants. Through my tenacity, I was inundated with firsthand accounts of unspeakable and vile acts committed by men of my culture against women from all nations.

I heard of Shakuntale from India, who at the age of thirteen was sold by her family for a sum of 600 Saudi riyals ($170). She was worked by day and abused by night in much the same manner as the unsuspecting Madeline. But Shakuntale had been bought. She was property that would not be returned – Shakuntale could never go home again. She was the property of her tormentors.

I listened in horror as a mother laughingly

dismissed the plight of her Thai maid who was raped at will by the son of the house. She said that her son needed sex, and that the sanctity of Saudi women forced the family to provide him with his own woman. Oriental women do not care whom they go to bed with, she stated with assurance. Boys are kings in the eyes of their mothers.

Suddenly aware of pervasive evil, I asked Ali why he and father travelled to Thailand and the Philippines three times a year. He scowled and told me it was none of my business. But I knew the answer, for many of the brothers and fathers of my friends made the same trek to the beautiful lands that sold their young girls and women to any beast with money.

I discovered that I had known little about men and their sexual appetites. The surface of life is nothing more than a façade; with little effort I uncovered the evil that lurks under the thin crust of civility between the sexes.

I, for the first time in my young life, comprehended the impossible task facing those of our sex. I knew my goal of female equality was hopeless, for I finally recognized that the world of men harbours a morbid condition of overfondness for themselves. We women are vassals, and the walls of our prisons are unscalable for this grotesque disease of pre-eminence lives in the sperm of all men and is passed along, generation to generation – a deadly incurable disease whose host is male and victim is female.

Ownership of my body and soul would soon

pass from my father to a stranger I would call my husband, for Father had informed me I would be wed three months after my sixteenth birthday. I felt the chains of tradition wrap tightly around me; I had only six short months of freedom left to savour. I waited for my destiny to unfold, a child as helpless as an insect trapped in a wicked web not of its making.

Chapter Ten

Huda

It was ten o'clock at night on 12 January 1972, and all nine of my sisters and I were spellbound with the telling of Sara's future by our old Sudanese slave, Huda. Since Sara's traumatic marriage and divorce, she had taken to studying astrology and was convinced that the moon and stars had played a determining role in her life's path. Huda, who had filled our ears from an early age with stories of black magic, was pleased to be the centre of attention and to provide distractions from the sameness of life in dull Riyadh.

We all knew that Huda, in 1899, at the age of eight, after straying from her mother who was busy digging yams for the family supper, had been captured by Arab slave-traders. In our youth she had entertained the children of the house for countless hours with the saga of her capture and confinement.

Much to our merriment, Huda always re-enacted her capture with great flair, no matter how many times she retold the story. She would crouch by the sofa and sing softly, pretending to scratch in the sand. With a wild screech, she would yank a pillow cover from behind her back and pull it over her head, gasping and kicking against her imagined tormentors. She would moan and fling herself to the floor and kick and scream for her mother. Finally, she would leap on to the coffee-table and peer out of the sitting-room windows, describing the blue waters of the Red Sea from the ship that transported her from Sudan to the deserts of Arabia.

Her eyes would grow wild as she fought imaginary thieves for her small portion of food. She would snatch a peach or a pear from the fruit-bowl and hungrily gobble all but the stone. Then she would march solemnly around the room, hands behind her back, chanting to Allah for deliverance as she was led to the slave-market.

Sold for a rifle to a member of the Rasheed clan of Riyadh, she stumbled as she was led from the streets of Jeddah through blinding sandstorms to the Mismaak fortress, the garrison for the Rasheed clan in the capital city.

Now, in her re-enactment, Huda lurched from one piece of furniture to another. We would squeal with laughter as Huda leaped around the room dodging bullets from our kin, the young Abdul Aziz and his sixty men, as they attacked the garrison and defeated the Rasheeds, reclaiming the country for the Al Sa'ud clan. She would throw her fat body over a chair and scramble for cover as the desert warriors slew their enemies. She told of her rescue by my father's father and would end her playacting by wrestling the nearest one to the floor and kissing her repeatedly as she swore she kissed our grandfather upon her rescue. This is how Huda came to be in our family.

As we grew older, she diverted us from our various dramas by frightening us with supernatural claims of sorcery. Mother used to dismiss Huda's proclamations with a smile, but after I woke up screaming about witches and potions she forbade Huda to divulge her beliefs to the younger children. Now that Mother was no longer with us, Huda returned to her former habit with gusto.

We watched with fascination as Huda peered at the lines running across Sara's palm and squinted her beady black eyes as though she saw Sara's life unfolding before her like a vision.

Sara seemed scarcely affected, as though she expected those very words, as Huda solemnly told her she would fail to realize her life's ambitions. I groaned and leaned back on my heels; I so wanted Sara to find the happiness she deserved that I found myself irritated with Huda and loudly dismissed her prophecies as the mumbo-jumbo I wanted them to be. No-one paid me any heed as Huda continued to scrutinize Sara's lifelines. The old woman rubbed her bony chin with her hand and muttered: 'H'm, little Sara. I see here that you will marry soon.'

Sara gasped and jerked her hand from Huda's grasp. The nightmare of another marriage was not what she wanted to hear.

Huda laughed softly and told Sara not to run from her future. She added that Sara would know a marriage of love and would grace the land with six small ones who would give her great joy.

Sara gathered her brow in a worried knot. Then she shrugged her shoulders and dismissed what she could not control. She looked my way and gave a rare smile. She asked Huda to read my palm, saying that if Huda could foretell what actions her unpredictable baby sister would take, then she, Sara, would be a believer in Huda's powers until the end of time. My other sisters rocked with laughter as they agreed with Sara, but I could tell by their looks that they loved me with a fierce tenderness, their little sister who so tried their patience.

I lifted my head with a haughtiness I did not feel as I plopped myself down in front of Huda. I turned my palms up and demanded, in a loud and bossy manner, to know what I would be doing one year from that date.

Huda ignored my youthful rudeness and studied my upturned palm for what seemed like hours before announcing my fate. She surprised us all with her posturings; she shook her head, muttered to herself and groaned aloud as she pondered my future. Finally, she fixed her eyes on my face and uttered her soothsaying with such confidence that I feared her forecast and felt the sinister hot wind of magic in the words she spoke.

In a freakish deep-throated voice, Huda pronounced that Father would soon inform me of my upcoming marriage. I would find misery and happiness in one man. I would rain destruction on those around me. My future actions would bring good along with bad to the family I loved. I would be the beneficiary of great love and dark hate. I was a force of good and evil. I was an enigma to all who loved me.

With a piercing cry, Huda threw her hands in the air and asked Allah to intervene in my life and protect me from myself. She unseated me as she lunged towards me and wrapped her arms around my neck and began to lament in a wild high-pitched howl.

Nura jumped to her feet and rescued me from Huda's smothering grasp. My sisters comforted me as Nura led Huda from the room, mumbling under her breath for Allah to protect the youngest daughter of her beloved Fadeela.

I was shivering from the impact of Huda's prediction. I began to sob and blurted out that Huda had bragged to me once about being a witch, that her mother had been a witch before her and the power had flowed from her mother's milk into the suckling infant that was Huda. Indeed, I moaned, only a witch could recognize such a one as evil as I!

Tahani, one of my older sisters, told me to hush, a silly game had gone awry and there was no need for dramatics. Sara, in an attempt to lighten the mood, brushed my tears away and said my sorrows were based on the worry that I could never live up to Huda's wild predictions. Joining in Sara's efforts, my other sisters began to joke and recalled with great peals of laughter some of the capers I had successfully pulled on Ali over the years. They reminded me of one of their favourites, which in our camaraderie we began to tell again.

The caper began when I asked one of my girlfriends to call Ali and pretend to be smitten with his charms. For hours we had listened in as he babbled nonsense on the telephone and made elaborate plans to be met by the girl's driver behind a nearby villa under construction.

The girl convinced Ali he must be holding a baby goat on a lead so that her driver could identify him. She told him that her parents were out of town; it was safe for Ali to follow the driver to her home for a secret meeting.

The building-site was across the street from my girlfriend's home, and my sisters and I had joined her on her bedroom balcony. We made ourselves sick with laughter as we watched poor Ali stand for hours, holding on to the baby goat and stretching his neck for signs of the driver. Much to our amusement, the girl managed to talk Ali into the same situation not once, not twice, but on three occasions! In Ali's eagerness to meet a girl, he had lost his sanity. I remember thinking that this silly veiling business works both ways!

Encouraged by my sisters' laughter and confidence, I managed to put Huda's rumblings out of my mind. After all, she was over eighty years of age, and was more than likely senile.

My consternation returned with a rush when Father visited us that evening and announced that he had found a suitable husband for me. With a sinking heart I could only think that the first of

Huda's predictions had come true. In my terror, I failed to ask Father the name of my husband-to-be and fled the room with darkness in my eyes and bile in my throat. I lay awake most of the night and thought of Huda's words. For the first time in my young life, I feared my future.

Nura returned to our villa the following morning to advise me that I was to wed Kareem, one of the royal cousins. As a young child, I had played with this cousin's sister, but recalled little she had said about him other than that he was a bossy brother. He was now twenty-eight years of age, and I was to be his first wife. Nura told me that she had seen a photo of him; he was exceptionally handsome. Not only that; he had been educated in London as a lawyer. Even more unusual, he had distinguished himself from most of the royal cousins in that he held a real position in the business world. Recently, he had opened his own large law firm in Riyadh. Nura added that I was a very lucky girl, for Kareem had already told Father that he wanted me to complete my schooling before starting a family. He did not want a woman with whom he could not share mental exchanges.

In no mood to be patronized, I made an ugly face at my sister and pulled the bedcovers over my head. Nura drew a long breath when I shouted out that I was not the lucky one; instead my cousin Kareem was the one with luck!

After Nura left, I called Kareem's sister, whom I knew slightly, and told her to advise her brother that he had best reconsider marrying me. I threatened that if we married he could not take other wives or I would poison them all at my first opportunity. Besides, I told her, Father had had a difficult time finding a husband for me since I had had an accident in the school lab. When Kareem's sister asked me what had happened, I pretended to be shy but finally admitted that I had stupidly dropped a flask of acid; as a result my face was hideously scarred. I had a good laugh when she hung up the phone in a rush to tell her brother.

Later that evening, Father stamped furiously into the villa with two of Kareem's aunties in tow. I was forced to stand at attention while they looked me over for any signs of facial scars or misshapen limbs. I became so angry at the examination that I opened my mouth and told them to check my teeth, if they dared. I leaned towards them and made loud chomping sounds. Looking back over their shoulders in dismay, they ran out of the room when I neighed like a horse and raised the bottoms of my feet to their faces, which is a terrible insult in the Arab world.

Father stood and looked at me for a long moment. He seemed to be battling his emotions; and then, to my complete astonishment, he shook his head and began to laugh. I had fully expected a slap or a lecture – never in my wildest imagination did I expect him to laugh. I felt a trembling smile form on my face, and then I, too, began to convulse with laughter. Curious, Sara and Ali came into the room and stood, with questioning smiles on their faces.

Father collapsed on the sofa, wiping tears off his face with the hem of his *thobe*. He looked at me and said: 'Sultana, did you see their faces when you tried to bite them? One looked like a horse herself! Child, you are a wonder. I do not know whether to pity or envy your cousin Kareem.' Father blew his nose. 'For sure, life with you will be a tempestuous affair.'

Feeling heady with my father's approval, I sat on the floor and leaned across his lap. I wanted to hold the moment for ever when he squeezed my shoulders and smiled down at his amusing daughter. Taking advantage of the intimate scene, I became brave and asked Father if I could meet Kareem before the wedding.

Father turned and looked at Sara; something in her expression touched his heart. He patted the sofa beside him and asked her to sit. There were no spoken words among the three of us, but we communicated through the bond of generations.

Ali, stunned at the attention given to the females in the family, leaned against the door-frame with his mouth in a perfect circle; he was struck dumb.

Chapter Eleven

Kareem

Much to father's amazement, and to my bitter disappointment, Kareem's family did not break off our engagement. Instead, Kareem and his father arrived at Father's office the following week and politely asked that Kareem be allowed to meet me – under proper supervision, of course. Kareem had heard of my unorthodox behaviour with his relatives and was decidedly curious to discover if I were completely mad or just high-spirited.

Father had not responded to my earlier entreaty to meet Kareem, but a request from the man's family was a different matter. After discussing the issue at length with several of the family aunties and my sister Nura, Father gave a favourable reply to Kareem's request.

Wild with joy, I danced around the room when Father told me the news. I was going to meet the man I would marry before I married him! My sisters and I were electrified, for it was just not done in our society; we were prisoners who felt the ever-present chains of tradition lighten.

Kareem's parents and my father and Nura decreed that Kareem and his mother would come to our villa in two weeks' time for afternoon tea.

Kareem and I would be chaperoned by Nura, Sara, two of my aunties and his mother.

With this possibility of control of my life on the horizon, hope was born, a fantasy I dared not imagine only yesterday. I found myself excited and wondered if I would find Kareem to my taste. Then I was struck with a new and unpleasant thought: perhaps Kareem would not like me! Oh, how I wanted to be beautiful like Sara, so that men's hearts would throb with desire.

Now I stood for hours gazing in the mirror – cursing my small stature, twisting my short unruly curls. My nose seemed too small for my face, my eyes had no lustre. Perhaps it was best to hide me under a veil until the night of the wedding!

Sara chuckled at my agony and tried to reassure me: men loved petite women, particularly ones with small upturned noses and smiling eyes. Nura, whose opinion everyone respected, said laughingly that I was considered very pretty by all the women in the family. I had just never pursued beauty; perhaps the time had come for me to enhance my assets.

Suddenly consumed with yearnings to be considered a desirable woman, I told Father I had nothing to wear. For, even though we Saudi women veil on the streets, our dark coverings are discarded the moment we enter the home of a female friend. Since we cannot awe those of the opposite sex, other than our husbands, with our carefully selected fashions, we females attempt to dazzle each other. Here, we really do dress for other women!

For instance, women in my country will arrive at an afternoon tea-party carefully dressed in lace and satin, with their garments tastefully accented by a display of priceless diamonds and rubies.

Many of my foreign friends have been stunned by the plunging necklines and skimpy clothing hidden under our dowdy *abaayas*. I have been told that we Saudi women resemble bright exotic birds with our choice of attire under our black veils and *abaayas*. Without a doubt, we women in black take more time and effort with our individual clothing under our cloaks than do Western women, who are free to flaunt their fashionable clothes.

Father, delighted that I was displaying an interest in a marriage he had thought I would disrupt, easily gave in to my pleas. Nura and her husband travelled with me to London for a three-day shopping spree at Harrods. I took great pains to tell the Harrods salesladies that I was going to meet my fiancé the following week. Just because I was a Saudi princess, I did not want them to assume I was without choices in my life. I felt disappointed that no-one expressed awe or surprise at my proud announcement. Those who are free cannot fathom the value of small victories for those who live on a tether.

While in London, Nura arranged for me to have a cosmetic makeover and a wardrobe colour chart prepared. When told that emerald green was my most flattering shade, I bought seventeen outfits in that one colour. My unruly hair was pulled back in a smooth twist and I stared in delicious wonder at the sophisticated stranger in the shop windows as I walked through the shopping districts in London.

Sara and Marci helped me dress on the day of the party. I alternately cried and cursed at the impossibility of duplicating my London hairstyle when Huda suddenly appeared at my bedroom door. 'Beware,' she cried, her eyes narrowing to slits. 'First you will know happiness, but then unhappiness will come with your new husband.' I threw my hairbrush at her and loudly told her not to spoil my day with her gibberish. Sara twisted my ear and told me to be ashamed of myself; Huda was just an old woman. My conscience did not hurt me at all, and I told Sara so. Sara replied that the reason was that I did not have a conscience. We sulked with each other until the gate-bell rang; then she hugged me and said I looked lovely in my emerald-green dress.

I was actually going to see my future husband in the flesh! The sound of my pounding heart filled my ears. Feeling all eyes on me watching for my reaction made me blush, which was ruining the sophisticated entrance I had planned. Oh, to return to the safety of my childhood!

I had no need for such emotions. Not only was Kareem the most handsome man I had ever seen; his sensuous eyes caressed my every move and made me feel quite the loveliest creature on earth. Within minutes of our strained introduction, I knew he would never call off our engagement. I discovered in myself a surprising hidden talent, one that is most helpful to women who must manipulate to achieve their goals. I learned I was a natural flirt. With the greatest of ease I found myself pursing my lips and looking at Kareem through lowered lids. My imagination soared: Kareem was only *one* of my many suitors.

Kareem's mother was watching me closely, in obvious distress at my vampish mannerisms. Sara, Nura and my aunties were exchanging pained looks. But Kareem was hypnotized, and nothing else mattered.

Before Kareem and his mother left, he asked if he could call me one evening later in the week to discuss our wedding plans. I scandalized my aunties by failing to ask their permission first and replied: 'Of course. Any time after nine would be all right.' I gave Kareem a woman's smile of promise when he said goodbye.

I hummed my favourite tune, a Lebanese love-ballad, as Nura, Sara and my aunties told me in great detail every wrong move I had made. They declared that Kareem's mother was sure to insist the wedding be called off, since I had practically seduced her son with my eyes and lips. I told them they were just all jealous because I had the chance to see my husband before the wedding. I stuck my tongue out at my aunties and told them they were too old to understand the beatings of young hearts; I left them standing wide-eyed in shock at my audacity. Then I locked myself in my bathroom and began to sing at the top of my lungs.

Later I thought about my performance. Had I not liked Kareem, I would have ensured that he not like me. I liked him, so I willed him to fall in love. My actions had been well thought out: if I had found him repulsive and wanted our engagement cancelled, I would have eaten without any manners, belched in his mother's face, and spilt hot tea in his lap. If Kareem and his family were still not convinced that I was an unworthy wife for Kareem, I had thought I might break wind. Luckily for Kareem and his mother, they were saved from a shocking afternoon since I had found him attractive and pleasing in character. I was so relieved to know I would not be marrying an old man blunted from life that I thought love would find fertile ground in our union.

With such pleasant thoughts in my mind, I gave Marci six pretty outfits from my wardrobe and told her I was going to ask Father if she could go with me to my new home.

Kareem called me that night. With a great deal of amusement, he told me his mother had advised him against our marriage. She had quivered in fury at my boldness and predicted I would bring heartache to her eldest son and, in turn, disaster to the entire family.

Feeling confident in my newly found female wiles, I tartly replied that he had best consider his mother's advice.

Kareem whispered that I was the girl of his dreams: a royal cousin, bright and of good humour. He declared he could not abide the women his mother wanted him to wed; they sat fixed like stones, and he knew they tried to anticipate his every wish. He liked a woman with spunk; he would be bored with the ordinary. He added, in a sexy murmur, that I made his eyes happy.

Kareem then brought up a puzzling subject; he asked if I had been circumcised. I told him I would have to ask Father. He cautioned me: 'No, do not ask. If you do not know, then that means you were not.' He seemed pleased with my reply.

In my innocence, I blurted out the question of circumcision at the dinner-table. It was Father's turn with his third wife on that particular evening, so Ali was sitting at the head of the table. Aghast at my question, he put his glass down with a thump and looked to Sara for comment. I continued to scoop my bread into the dish of houmous, and for a moment failed to see the anxiety in the eyes of my sisters. When I looked up, I saw that everyone was ill at ease.

Ali, thinking himself the leader of the family, banged his fist on the table and demanded to know where I had heard the word. Realizing something was amiss, I remembered Kareem's warning and said I had overheard some of the servants talking.

Ali dismissed my ignorance with a glare in my direction and curtly told Sara to call Nura in the morning and have her speak to 'this child'.

With our mother now dead, Nura, as the eldest, was responsible for my knowledge of such subjects. She arrived at the villa before ten o'clock the next morning and came directly to my room. She had been summoned by Ali. She made a wry face when she said that Ali had informed her that her performance as eldest daughter was sadly lacking. He, Ali, intended to notify Father of his observations and displeasure.

Nura sat on the edge of the bed and asked me in a kind voice what I knew of the relations between a man and a woman. I replied confidently that I knew all there was to know.

My sister smiled as she spoke. 'I fear that your tongue is your master, little sister. Perhaps you do not know all of life.'

As she discovered, I knew plenty about the *act* of sex.

In Saudi Arabia, as in much of the Arab world, the subject of sex is considered taboo. As a result, women talk of little else. Discussions regarding sex, men and children dominate all female gatherings.

In my country, with so few activities to soothe women's minds, the main occupation for women is to gather in each other's palaces. It is not uncommon to attend a women's party each day of the week, excluding Fridays, which is our religious day. We gather, drink coffee and tea, eat sweets, lounge on overstuffed sofas and gossip. Once a woman begins to veil, she is automatically included in these functions.

Since my veiling, I had listened in fascination as young brides told of their wedding night; no detail was too intimate to reveal. Some of the young women shocked the female gatherings by declaring that they enjoyed sex. Others said they pretended to enjoy their husbands' advances, to keep them from taking another wife. Then there were those women who so despised sex that they kept their eyes closed and endured the assaults of their husbands with dread and repulsion. Significantly, there were a few who remained silent during such discussions and shied away from the topic; those were the women who were dealt with in a cruel manner by the men in their lives, much in the same way that Sara had been brutalized.

Nura, convinced that I understood the implications of marital life, added little to my awareness. She did disclose that it was my duty, as a wife, to be available to Kareem at all times, no matter my feelings at the moment. I proclaimed that I would do as I willed, that Kareem could not force me against my inclinations. Nura shook her head. Neither Kareem nor any other man would accept refusal. The marriage bed was his right. I stated that Kareem would be different. He would never use force. Nura said that no man was understanding about such matters. I should not expect it, or I would be crushed with disappointment.

To change the subject, I asked my sister about circumcision. Her voice thin and low, Nura told me that she had been circumcised when she was about twelve years old. She said the rite had been performed on the three sisters that followed her in age. The youngest six daughters of our family had been spared the barbaric custom owing to the intervention of a Western physician who spoke for many hours against the ritual with our father. Nura added that I was blessed not to have endured such a trauma.

I could see that my sister was close to tears; I asked her what had happened.

For more generations than Nura knew, the women of our family had been circumcised. Our mother, like most Saudi women, was circumcised when she became a woman, a few weeks before she was wed. At the age of fourteen, when Nura became a woman, Mother followed the only tradition she knew and arranged for Nura's circumcision to be performed in a small village some miles from Riyadh.

A celebration was held, a feast prepared. A youthful Nura basked in the attention bestowed upon the one of honour. Moments before the rite, Nura was told by Mother that the elder women were going to perform a small ceremony, and that it was important for Nura to lie very still. One woman beat a drum, other women chanted. The oldest women gathered around the frightened child. Nura, nude from the waist down, was held by four women on a bedsheet that had been spread on the ground. The oldest of the women raised her hand in the air; with horror Nura saw that she had a razor-like instrument in her hand. Nura screamed. She felt a sharp pain in her genital region. Dizzy with shock, she was lifted in the air by the women and congratulated on her coming of age. Thoroughly frightened, she saw blood pouring from her wounds. She was carried into a tent and her lacerations were dressed and bandaged.

Her wounds healed quickly, but she did not understand the implication of the procedure until her wedding night; there was unbearable pain and much blood. As the condition persisted, she grew to dread sex with her new husband. Finally, after becoming pregnant, she saw a Western doctor who was appalled at her scars. He told Nura that her entire external genitalia had been removed and that, for sure, the sex act would always result in tearing, pain and bleeding.

When the physician discovered that three more of Nura's sisters had been circumcised and that the remaining six would more than likely suffer the same consequences, he pleaded with her to arrange for her parents to visit him in his clinic.

My other three sisters visited the physician. He said our sister Baher was in much worse condition than Nura, and he did not know how she endured sexual relations with her husband. Nura had been a witness to our sisters' ceremonies and recalled that Baher had fought the old women and had actually managed to run a few yards from her tormentors. But she was caught and returned to the mat, where her struggles caused much mayhem and a great loss of blood.

To the doctor's surprise, it was my mother who had insisted upon the circumcision of her daughters. She herself had endured the rite; she was certain it was the will of Allah. Finally, the physician convinced our father of the utter nonsense of the procedure, as well as of the health risks. Nura said I had been saved from a custom that was cruel and useless.

I asked Nura why she thought Kareem would

enquire of such a matter. Nura said I was fortunate that he was a man of the opinion that it was good for a woman to be complete. She said that many men still insisted upon circumcision of their brides. It was all a matter of the region you were from or the opinion of the family in which a girl was born. Some families continued the practice while others left it in the barbaric past, where it belonged. Nura said it sounded to her like Kareem wanted a wife who would share pleasure, not just be an object of pleasure.

Nura left me with my thoughts. I knew I was lucky to be one of the younger females in our family. I shuddered when I imagined the trauma Nura and my other sisters had endured.

I was glad Kareem was concerned for my welfare. I was beginning to entertain the notion that some women might be happy in my land, in spite of traditions that do not belong in a civilized society. But still the unfairness of it all lingered in my thoughts. We women of Arabia could find happiness only if the man ruling us was considerate; otherwise, sorrow would surround us. No matter what we do, our future is linked to one prerequisite: the degree of kindness in the man who rules us.

Feeling drowsy, I went back to sleep; I dreamed I was in a beautiful emerald-green wedding-gown waiting for my groom, Kareem. He failed to arrive, and my dream turned into a nightmare and I awoke in a trembling sweat; I was being pursued by ghoulish old women in black, razors in hand, screeching for my blood.

I cried out for Marci to bring me cold water. I was in anguish, for I recognized the meaning of my frightening vision: a major obstacle to change and relief from our antiquated customs was the women of Arabia themselves. The women of my mother's generation were uneducated, and had little knowledge other than what their men told them to be true; as a tragic result, such traditions as circumcision were kept alive by the very people who had themselves suffered under the cruel knife of barbarism. In their confusion of past and present, they were unwittingly strengthening the men in their efforts to keep us in ignorance and seclusion. Even when told of the medical dangers, my mother had clung to the traditional past; she could imagine no other path for her daughters than the one she herself had trod, for fear that any shift from tradition would harm their marriage chances.

Only we modern educated women could change the course of women's lives. It was in our power, within our wombs. I looked to my wedding date with determined anticipation. I would be the first of the Saudi women to reform her inner circle. It would be my sons and daughters who would remodel Arabia into a country worthy of all its citizens, both male and female.

Chapter Twelve

The Wedding

On the occasion of my wedding, the preparation room was filled with gaiety. I was surrounded by women of my family; no one person could be heard, for all were speaking and laughing as a singular and grand celebration.

I was in the palace of Nura and Ahmed, which had been completed only a few weeks before my wedding date. Nura was pleased with the outcome and was anxious for word of her gilded mansion to leak throughout the city of Riyadh and cause all to exclaim at the money spent and the glory accomplished.

I myself hated Nura's new palace; for romantic reasons, I had wanted to be wed in Jeddah, by the sea. But my father had insisted upon a traditional wedding; and I, for once, made no outcry when my demands were not met. I had decided months ago to hold back my passion except for matters of paramount importance and to let little irritations slide easily away. Doubtless I was becoming exhausted with the disabilities of my land.

While Nura beamed happily, our female relatives were heaping compliments upon the beauty of the palace. Sara and I exchanged small smiles, for we had agreed some time ago that the palace was in the worst possible taste.

Nura's marble palace was enormous. Hundreds of Filipino, Thai and Yemeni labourers, supervised by unsmiling German contractors, had worked around the clock for months to create the monstrosity. The painters, the woodworkers, the metalworkers and the architects did not speak with one voice; as a result, the palace conflicted within itself.

The halls were gilded and richly adorned. Sara and I counted 180 paintings hanging in the entry-hall alone. Sara recoiled in dismay and said that the works of art had been picked by one with little or no knowledge of the great masters. Garish carpets with embroidered birds and beasts of every type laid across endless floors. The ornate bedrooms made my soul feel heavy; I wondered how children of the same blood could so differ in judgement of style.

While Nura had failed miserably in decorating her home, her gardens were a masterpiece. Nearly a mile of lakes and lawns decorated with beautifully arranged flowers, shrubs and trees encircled her palace. There were many surprises to delight the eye: sculptures, colourful bird-houses, fountains spouting water, and even a children's merry-go-round.

I was going to be married to Kareem in the garden at nine o'clock in the evening. Nura knew that I loved yellow roses, and thousands of them, flown in from Europe, were now floating on the lake beside the rose-covered pavilion where Kareem would come to claim me. Nura proudly announced that people were already whispering that this was the wedding of the decade.

There are no announcements of engagements and weddings in Saudi Arabia; these matters are considered extremely private. But gossip of money spent and grand occasions staged travels throughout the land, with each section of the royal family striving to outspend the other.

I slapped at my aunties and screamed when the hair on my private parts was so rudely removed. Yelping in pain, I asked where such a savage custom had begun. My oldest aunty slapped my face for such impudence. She looked hard into my eyes and announced that I, Sultana, was a stupid child and that as a daughter of the Muslim faith I should know that the Prophet recommended, for the sake of cleanliness, that all pubic and armpit hair should be removed every forty days. I, wilful as ever, shouted that the practice no longer made sense; after all, modern Muslims are equipped with hot water and soap to wash away our dirt. We no longer had to use the sand of the desert for such purposes!

My aunty, knowing the futility of arguing with me, continued with her duties. I shocked all present when I loudly proclaimed that, if the Prophet could speak in this new age of modern amenities, I knew he would end such a silly tradition. Certainly, I announced loudly, this one issue alone proved that we Saudis were like uninspired mules; we trod the same weary track as the mule before us even if it led us to plunge off a cliff. Only when we evolved as spirited stallions, with a strong will of our own, would we progress and leave the era of those primitives behind us.

My relatives exchanged worried glances, for they lived in dread of my rebellious spirit and felt comfortable only with complacent women. My contentment with the one chosen for my husband was considered nothing less than miraculous, but until the final ceremony was complete none of my relatives would breathe easily.

My dress was made of the brightest red lace I could find. I was a bold bride, and I took great delight in scandalizing my family, who had begged me to wear a soft peach or pale pink instead. As was my way, I refused to relent. I knew I was right. Even my sisters finally admitted that my skin and eyes were flattered by the bright colour.

I was in a happy daze when Sara and Nura lowered the dress over my head and shoulders and fastened the delicate buttons around my waist.

A moment of sadness came as Nura draped Kareem's gift of rubies and diamonds around my neck. I could not escape the image of my mother on the sad day of Sara's wedding when I had sat as a child on the floor and watched her fasten the unwanted jewels around the neck of Sara. It had been only two short years ago, yet it seemed another life, another Sultana. I shed my gloom and smiled when I realized Mother must be watching me from a great distance with a satisfied glow in her eyes. I could barely breathe in the tight bodice as I leaned down to pick up a bouquet of spring flowers made entirely of precious stones, especially designed for the occasion by Sara.

Looking into my sisters' smiling faces, I announced: 'I am ready.'

It was time for my new beginning, another life.

The beating of the drums drowned out the orchestra imported from Egypt. With Nura on one side and Sara on the other, I made my proud appearance to the expectant guests, waiting impatiently in the garden.

As with all Saudi weddings, the official ceremony had been conducted earlier. With Kareem and his family in one part of the palace and I and my family in another, the religious sheikh had gone from room to room, asking us if we accepted the other. Kareem and I had not been allowed to say our words of promise in the other's presence.

For four days and nights our family had been celebrating. The celebration would continue another three days and nights after our appearance before our female guests. Tonight's ceremony was merely a stage created for the lovers to bask in the beauty of observance of youth and hope. Our night of glory.

I had not seen Kareem since the day of our first meeting. Our courtship had continued, none the less, by long hours of playful telephone conversation. Now I watched Kareem, escorted by his father, walk slowly towards the pavilion. He was so handsome, and he was going to be my husband.

For some odd reason, I was fascinated with the beating of his heart. I watched the tremor of movement in his throat and counted the beats. My imagination swept me into his chest, to that powerful spot of romance, and I thought: This heart is mine. I alone have the power to make it beat with happiness or with misery. It was a sobering moment for a young girl.

Finally, he stood tall and straight before me; I was suddenly overcome with emotion. I felt my lips tremble and my eyes water as I fought against the urge to weep. When Kareem removed my face-cover, we both burst out laughing, our emotion and joy were so intense. The audience of women began to applaud loudly and stamp their feet. In Saudi Arabia it is rare that a bride and groom find such obvious pleasure in each other.

I was drowning in Kareem's eyes, and he in mine. I was overcome with the emotion of disbelief. I had been a child of darkness, and my new husband, instead of being the expected object of dread, was sweet freedom from the misery of my youth.

Anxious to be alone, we lingered only a short while after the ceremony to receive the congratulations of our female friends and relatives. Kareem threw gold coins from small velvet bags towards various groups of merry guests while I slipped away to change into travelling clothes.

I wanted to speak with my father, but he had hurried from the garden the moment his role was complete. His mind was relieved; his youngest and most troublesome daughter of his first wife was now safely wed and no longer his responsibility. I ached with the desire for a bond between us that had been in my dreams but never broke into reality.

For our honeymoon, Kareem had promised me we would go anywhere and do anything I desired. My every wish was his command. With the glee of a child, I listed all the places I wanted to see and all the things I wanted to do. Our first stop would be Cairo, and from there on to Paris, New York, Los Angeles and then Hawaii. We would have eight precious weeks of freedom from the scars of Arabia.

Dressed in an emerald-green silk suit, I hugged my sisters goodbye. Sara was weeping so violently that she could not bear to turn me loose. She kept whispering, 'Be brave,' and my heart broke for my sister; I understood too well that the remembrances of her wedding night would never disappear. With the passing of years, perhaps the thoughts of her honeymoon would merely fade away.

I covered my designer suit with the black *abaaya* and veil and snuggled in the back seat of the Mercedes with my new husband. My fourteen bags had already been taken to the airport.

For the sake of privacy, Kareem had purchased all the first-class seats on each flight of our trip. The Lebanese air hostesses wore bright smiles as they watched our silly behaviour. We were as adolescents, for we had never learned the art of courtship.

Finally, we arrived in Cairo, rushed through Customs, and were driven to an opulent villa on the banks of the ancient Nile. The villa, which belonged to Kareem's father, had been built in the eighteenth century by a rich Turkish merchant. Restored by Kareem's father to its original splendour, the villa was laid out in thirty rooms on irregular levels with arched windows leading to the lush garden. The walls were covered with delicate dusty-blue tiles, with intricate carved creatures in the background. I felt seduced by the house itself. I told a proud Kareem that it was a wonderful setting in which to begin a marriage.

The impeccably decorated villa brought the garish decorating defects of Nura's palace to mind. I suddenly realized that money did not automatically bestow artistic discrimination on those of my country, even in my own family.

I was only sixteen, still a child, but my husband understood the implications of my youth, and he eased my introduction into the world of adults with a unique solution. He, as I, disagreed with the manner of marriage in our land. He said that strangers should not be intimate, even if those strangers were husband and wife. In his opinion, men and women should have time to understand the secrets of the other that make desire grow. Kareem told me that he had decided weeks before that he and I would have our courtship after our marriage. And, when I was ready for him, I would be the one to say: 'I want to know all of you.'

We spent our days and nights playing. We

dined, rode horses around the pyramids, browsed through the crowded bazaars of Cairo, read books and talked. The servants were puzzled at such a joyous couple who chastely kissed good night and went into separate bedrooms.

On the fourth night, I pulled my husband into my bed. Afterwards, with my drowsy head on Kareem's shoulder, I whispered that I would be one of the scandalous young wives of Riyadh who cheerfully admitted I enjoyed sex with my husband.

I had never been to America and was anxious to form an opinion of the people who spread their culture worldwide yet seemed to know so little of the world themselves. New Yorkers, with their pushy rude manners, frightened me. I was happy when we arrived in Los Angeles, with its pleasant relaxed ambience which feels more familiar to Arabs.

In California, after weeks of meeting transported Americans from practically every state in the Union, I announced to Kareem that I liked these strange loud people, the Americans. When he asked me why, I had difficulty in voicing what I felt in my heart. I finally said: 'I believe this marvellous mixture of cultures has brought civilization closer to reality than in any other culture in history.' I was certain Kareem did not understand what I meant and I tried to explain. 'So few countries manage complete freedom for all their citizens without chaos; this has been accomplished in this huge land. It appears impossible for large numbers of people to stay on a course of freedom for all when so many options are available. Just imagine what would happen in the Arab world; a country the size of America would have a war a minute, with each man certain he had the only correct answer for the good of all! In our lands, men look no farther than their own noses for a solution. Here, it is different.'

Kareem looked at me in amazement. Not used to a woman interested in the greater scheme of things, he questioned me into the night to learn my thoughts on various matters. It was obvious that my husband was not accustomed to a woman with opinions of her own. He seemed in utter shock that I thought of political issues and the state of the world. Finally, he kissed me on the neck and said that I would continue my education once we returned to Riyadh.

Irritated at his tone of permission, I told him I was not aware that my education was up for discussion.

The planned eight-week honeymoon turned into ten weeks. Only after a call from Kareem's father did we reluctantly drag ourselves back to our families. We planned to live in the palace of Kareem's father and mother until our own palace was built.

I knew that Kareem's mother looked upon me with distaste; now it was in her power to make my life miserable. I thought of my foolish disregard for tradition, which had brought about her scorn, and cursed myself for thinking so little of my future by alienating my mother-in-law at our first meeting. I knew that Kareem, like all Arab men, would never side with his wife against his mother. It would be up to me to arrive with an olive branch extended in peace.

I had an unpleasant shock as the plane prepared to land in Riyadh. Kareem reminded me of my veil. I scrambled to cover myself in black and felt a fierce longing for the sweet scent of freedom that had begun to fade the moment we entered Saudi airspace.

With the tightness of dread in my throat, we entered his mother's palace to begin our married life. At that moment, I was unaware that Kareem's mother so disliked me that she had already begun plotting ways to bring our happy union to an end.

Chapter Thirteen

Married Life

If there could be one word that would describe the Saudi women of my mother's generation, it would be *waiting*. They spent their lives waiting. Females of that era were banned from education and job opportunities, so there was little to do but wait to be married, wait to give birth, wait for grandchildren and wait to grow old.

In Arab lands, age brings great satisfaction for women, for honour is bestowed upon those women who fulfil their productive duties with many sons and therefore ensure the continued lineage of the family name.

My mother-in-law, Noorah, had spent her life waiting for a daughter-in-law to bestow the honour she felt was now her due. Kareem was her eldest child, the most beloved son. Saudi customs of the old days demanded that the wife of the firstborn son do his mother's bidding. Like all young women, I knew of this tradition, but reality tends to fade from my thoughts until the time I must confront the facts.

Certainly, desire for male children is common in much of the world; but no place can compare with Arab lands, where every woman must endure boiling tension throughout her childbearing years, waiting for the birth of a son. Sons are the sole reason for marriage, the key to satisfaction for the husband. Male children are so treasured that a fierce bond develops between mother and son. Nothing, other than the love of another woman, can separate the two. From the moment we were wed, Kareem's mother thought of me as her competitor, not as a welcome member of the family. I was the promise of a wedge between Noorah and her son; my presence only intensified her pervasive mood of general unhappiness. Some years before, her life had taken an abrupt turn that had poisoned her outlook.

The first wife of Kareem's father, Noorah had borne her husband seven living children, three of whom were sons. When Kareem was fourteen, his father had taken a second wife, a Lebanese woman of great beauty and charm. From that moment, there had been no peace within the walls surrounding the palaces of the two wives.

Noorah, a mean-spirited woman, was positively malevolent over her husband's second marriage. In her hate, she was driven to consult a sorcerer from Ethiopia – who served the palace of the king but was for hire to the other royals – and paid him a great sum to put a curse on the Lebanese woman so that she would be barren. Noorah, proud of her own productivity, was convinced that the Lebanese would be divorced if she could not produce sons.

As it turned out, Kareem's father loved the Lebanese woman and told her he did not care whether she gave him children. As the years passed, it became evident to Noorah that the Lebanese was not going to give birth or be divorced. Since the greatest driving force in Noorah's life was to rid her husband of his second wife, she consulted the sorcerer and paid an even larger sum to bring a cloud of death upon the Lebanese.

When Kareem's father heard the idle gossip of Noorah's scheming at the palace, he came to her in a rage. He swore that if the Lebanese woman died before Noorah he would divorce Noorah. She would be sent away in disgrace and forbidden contact with her children.

Noorah, convinced that the barren womb was a result of the sorcerer's power, was now terrified that the woman would die; surely black magic was unalterable. Since that time, Noorah was obliged to protect the Lebanese woman. She now spent an unhappy life trying to save the life of the very woman she had tried to kill by voodoo.

It was a strange household.

In her unhappiness, Noorah lashed out at those around her, excluding her children. Since I was not of her blood and was greatly loved by Kareem, I was her natural target. Her intense jealousy was evident to everyone except Kareem, who, like most sons, saw little wrong in his devoted mother. In her maturity, she had apparently gained wisdom, for she made a great pretence of affection to me – when Kareem was within hearing distance.

Each morning I happily walked Kareem to the gate. Hard at work at his law firm, he would leave by nine, which is early for anyone, particularly a prince, to begin work in Saudi Arabia. Few members of the royal family arise before ten or eleven.

I was certain Noorah watched us from her bedroom window, for the moment the gate closed behind him Noorah would begin to call my name with the greatest urgency. None of the thirty-three servants employed in her household would do; she would cry out for me to serve her hot tea.

Since I had spent my childhood mistreated by the men of my family, I was in no mood to spend the second part of my life abused by women, even Kareem's mother.

For the present, I remained mute. But Kareem's mother was soon to learn that I had faced antagonists much more fierce than an old woman with dark mental recesses. Besides, there is an old Arab proverb that says: 'Patience is the key to solutions.' In an attempt to exchange success for failure, I thought it best to heed the wisdom passed down from generations. I would be patient and await an opportunity to reduce Noorah's power over me.

Fortunately, I had little time to wait. Kareem's younger brother, Muneer, had recently returned from his studies in America. His anger at being back in Saudi Arabia bit deeply into the peace of the household.

Although much has been written about the enforced monotony of women's lives in Saudi Arabia, scant attention has been given to the wasted lives of many of our young men. True, their lives are bliss compared with those of women; still, much is lacking, and the young men of Arabia spend many languid hours longing for stimulation. There are no cinemas, clubs or mixed dining since men and women are not allowed in restaurants together unless they are husband and wife, brother and sister, or father and daughter.

Muneer, only twenty-two years old and accustomed to the freedoms of American society, did not relish his return to Saudi Arabia. He had recently graduated from business school in Washington DC, and had plans to be a liaison for government contracts. While waiting for his opportunity to prove his adeptness in acquiring huge sums of money – a passion with all the royal princes – he began to keep company with a group of princes within the family known for their risky behaviour. They gave and attended mixed parties. Foreign women of questionable morals who worked for the various hospitals and airlines were in attendance.

Drugs were abundant. Many of these princes had become addicted to alcohol, drugs, or both. In their drug- or alcohol-induced haze, their dissatisfaction with their kin who ruled the land festered. Not content with modernization, they longed for Westernization; these young men were ardent for revolution. Not surprisingly, their idleness bred dangerous talk and conduct, and before long their revolutionary intrigues were common knowledge.

King Faisal, once a carefree youth himself who was transformed into a pious king, diligently followed the actions of his young kin and attempted, in his solicitous manner, to guide the young men of the family from the excesses of empty lives. Some of the troublesome princes were placed in the family business while others were sent off to the military.

After King Faisal spoke of his concern about Muneer's unseemly behaviour to his father, I heard loud shouting and angry voices from the study. I, like the other female members of the family, soon found some urgent task in the map room, directly opposite the study. With eyes on the maps and ears tuned to the shouting, we gasped when we heard Muneer accuse the ruling family of corruption and waste. Muneer swore that he and his friends would bring the changes so direly needed in the kingdom. With curses on his lips and a call for rebellion, he stormed out of the villa.

While Muneer claimed the country needed to move into the future, his commitment was vague and his real activities troubling. His was a sad tale of misjudgement; alcohol and easy money had seduced him.

Few foreigners today are aware that alcohol was not banned to non-believers (non-Muslims) in the Kingdom of Saudi Arabia prior to 1952. Two separate and tragic events involving royal princes brought about the ban by our first king, Abdul Aziz.

In the late 1940s, Prince Nasir, the son of our ruler, returned from the United States a different man from the one who had departed the kingdom. He had discovered the enticement of the combination of alcohol and uninhibited Western women.

In his assessment, alcohol was the key to idolization by women.

Since Nasir held the position of governor of Riyadh, he found few barriers to his desire to maintain secret supplies of alcohol. Nasir held forbidden parties, entertaining men as well as women. In the summer of 1947, after a late-night gathering, seven of the partakers died from drinking wood alcohol. Some of the dead were women.

Nasir's father, King Abdul Aziz, became so incensed at this needless tragedy that he personally beat his son and ordered him to gaol.

Later, in 1951, when Mishari, another son of the king, while intoxicated shot and killed the British vice-consul and almost killed the man's wife, the old king's patience expired. From that time forward, alcohol was banned in the Kingdom of Saudi Arabia and black-marketing schemes were born.

The people of Saudi Arabia react to the prohibited much in the same manner as people of other cultures. The forbidden becomes even more enticing. Most Saudi men and women I know drink socially; a large number have acquired serious addiction to the substance. I have never been in a Saudi home that did not have a large assortment of the finest and most expensive alcoholic beverages to offer to guests.

Since 1952, the cost of alcohol had risen to 650 Saudi riyals for a bottle of Scotch ($200). A fortune could be made in importing and selling the illegal drink. Since Muneer and two cousins who were high-ranking princes were of the opinion that alcohol should be legalized, they combined their energies and soon became fabulously wealthy transporting illegal alcohol from Jordan.

When border guards became suspicious of the cargo, they were paid off. The only obstacle to the illegal importing of alcohol is the ever-roving bands of the Committees for the Propagation of Virtue and the Prevention of Vice. These committees were formed by the *mutawas*, religious men who tremble in anger at the effrontery of members of the Saudi royal family who, above all others, are presumed to uphold Islamic law yet prove time and again that they consider themselves above the teachings of the Prophet.

One of these committees soon was Muneer's undoing and unwittingly provided the solution to my obtrusive mother-in-law.

It was a Saturday, our first day of the week (Muslims celebrate their religion on Fridays), a day none of Kareem's family will ever forget.

Kareem sullenly walked through the doorway, weary from a hot trying day at his office, and came upon his mother and wife in a rough shoving match. When she saw her son, Noorah widened the twilight war with her new daughter-in-law by sobbing and loudly proclaiming to Kareem that I, Sultana, was filled with disrespect for his mother, and that for no apparent reason I had started the brawl with her.

As she fled the scene she pinched me on the forearm, and I, in a widening mood of anger, rushed after her and would have taken a swing at her but for Kareem's intervention. Noorah looked hard at me and turned to Kareem. She hinted darkly that I was an unfit wife, and that if he investigated my activities he would be prompted to divorce me.

Any other day Kareem might have laughed at our ridiculous and infantile display, for women with little but time on their hands tend to manoeuvre themselves into numerous squabbles. But on that day he had been informed by his London broker that over the previous week he had lost more than a million dollars on the stock market. In his black mood, he rushed to meet violence with a vengeance. Since no Arab man will ever contradict his mother, Kareem slapped me three times across the face. They were slaps meant to insult, since they accomplished little more than to redden my jaw.

My strong character was formed by the age of five. I have the tendency to be nervous at the sight of trouble looming. As the danger draws near, I become less nervous. When the peril is at hand, I swell with ferocity. As I grapple with my assailant, I am without fear and fight to the finish with little thought of injury.

The battle was on. I swung at Kareem with a rare and priceless vase that just happened to be nearby. He saved his face by a quick move to the left. The vase shattered as it struck a Monet painting worth hundreds of thousands of dollars. The vase and the water-lily painting were destroyed. In a fine fury,

I grabbed an expensive oriental ivory sculpture and threw it at Kareem's head.

The crashing and banging, along with our shouts, alerted the household. Women and servants burst suddenly upon us with loud cries. By this time, Kareem realized I was going to destroy the room, which was filled with his father's beloved treasures. To stop me, he punched me in the jaw. Inky darkness surrounded me.

When I opened my eyes, Marci was standing above me, dripping cold water on my face from a soaking cloth. I heard loud voices in the background and assumed that the excitement over my fight with Kareem was continuing.

Marci said no, the new disturbance concerned Muneer. Kareem's father had been summoned by King Faisal regarding a container of alcohol that had leaked the illegal substance in a trail down the streets of Riyadh. The Egyptian driver had stopped at a shop for a sandwich, and the pervasive smell of alcohol had caused a crowd to gather. Detained by a member of one of the committees to prevent vice, he, in his fear, had volunteered the name of Muneer and one other prince. The head of the Religious Council had been alerted and he had contacted the king. The king was in a rare rage.

Kareem and his father left the villa to return to the king's palace. The drivers were sent in search of Muneer. I nursed my swollen jaw and plotted a new plan of revenge on Noorah. I could hear her cries of grief; I gathered myself and walked down the circular staircase, sniffing the air for her sobs.

I, a woman far removed from sainthood, wanted to see and feel the full pleasure of her distress. I followed her cries to the sitting-room. I would have smiled but for my painful jaw. Noorah was crumpled in a corner of the sitting-room, crying out for Allah to save her beloved Muneer from the wrath of the king and the men of religion.

Noorah saw me and instantly quietened. After long moments of silence, she looked at me with contempt and said: 'Kareem has promised me he will divorce you. He agrees that "Who grows up on a habit will die with it" [Arab proverb], and you have grown up wild. There is no place for such a one as you in this family.'

Noorah, expecting tears and pleas, which are common from those deemed helpless, searched my face closely when I replied that I myself was going to demand a divorce from her son. I declared that Marci was at that very moment packing my bags; I would leave her oppressive home within the hour. As an added insult, I called over my shoulder that I was going to influence my father into calling for Muneer to be made an example for those who so disdain the laws of our faith. Her precious son would more than likely be flogged or gaoled, or both. I left Noorah with her jaw hanging in fear.

The tables had turned. My voice rang with a confidence I did not feel. Noorah had no way of knowing if I possessed the behind-the-scenes power that could accomplish my threats. She would celebrate if her son divorced me; she would be mortified if I were the one to seek a divorce. It is difficult, but not impossible, for a woman in Arabia to divorce her husband. Since my father was a prince closer in blood to our first king than Kareem's father, Noorah had a moment of fear that I could be successful in my claim to call for Muneer's punishment. She had no knowledge that my father would more than likely turn me out of our home for my imprudence, and that I would have nowhere to turn.

Appropriate actions to follow my bold threats were required. When Marci and I appeared at the door loaded with travelling-cases, the household broke open like an explosion.

By coincidence, Muneer, located at the home of a friend and ordered home, had just arrived with one of the drivers. Unaware of the seriousness of his predicament, he swore when I informed him that his mother had brought about the pending divorce of her eldest son.

A wave of perverse optimism swept through my body as Noorah, incited to action by the possibility of my vociferous wrath, insisted I not leave the house. The double crisis had impaired Noorah's resolve; she emerged thoroughly weakened in our bitter feud. After much pleading on her part, I reluctantly remained.

I was sleeping when Kareem returned, exhausted from an evening of mortification. I overheard his appeal to Muneer to consider the name of their father before committing acts that were forbidden. I did not have to strain to hear Muneer's insolent response, accusing Kareem of helping to oil the mammoth machine of hypocrisy that was the Kingdom of Saudi Arabia.

King Faisal was revered by most Saudis for his dedicated and devout style of life. Within the family itself, he was held in deep respect by the elder princes. He had led our country from the dark days of King Sa'ud's rule into a position of regard and even admiration from some quarters. But there was a deep divergence between the elder princes and the younger princes within the family.

Devoured by desire for unearned wealth, these young men of the family hated the king, who cut their allowances, prohibited their entry into illegal businesses, and chided them when they strayed from the path of honour. There was not even a flicker of compromise between the two camps, and trouble continuously brewed.

That night, Kareem slept a great distance from me in our large bed. I heard him through the night as he tossed and turned. I knew he was plunged in dark thoughts. I had a rare touch of guilt as I pondered the severity of his troubles. I decided that if my marriage survived that day's grievous wounds I would temper my attitude.

The next morning, a new Kareem emerged. He failed to speak or acknowledge my presence. My good intentions of the previous night vanished into the pale morning light. I told him in a loud voice that I thought a divorce best. In my heart I longed for him to appeal for peace.

He looked at me and replied in a dry frightening voice: 'Whatever you think, but we will settle our differences when this family crisis is behind us.' Kareem continued to shave, as if I had said nothing out of the ordinary.

This new foe, indifference, quietened me and I sat, humming a tune, as one unconcerned, while Kareem finished his dressing. He opened the bedroom door and left me with this parting thought: 'Sultana, you know, you deceived me with your warrior's spirit, hidden behind the smile of a woman.'

After he had departed, I lay in the bed and sobbed until I was exhausted.

Noorah coaxed me to the table of peace, and we settled our differences with gestures of love. She sent one of her drivers to the jewellery *souq* to purchase a diamond necklace for me. I hurriedly travelled to the gold *souq* and purchased the most expensive gold breastplate necklace I could find. I spent more than 300,000 Saudi riyals ($80,000) and cared little what Kareem would say. Now I saw the possibility of peace with a woman who could cause me endless grief should my marriage be saved.

Weeks passed before Muneer's fate was decided. Once again, the family saw no benefit in publicizing the misadventures of the royal sons. The wrath of the king was somewhat tempered by the efforts of my father and various princes who sought to downplay the incident as one of a foolish young man recently influenced by the evils of the West.

Noorah, thinking that I had somehow influenced my father, was grateful and responded by exclamations of the joy in her heart for having such a one as I as her daughter-in-law. The truth was never revealed: that I spoke not a word to my father. His interest stemmed from the very real fact that I was married into the family and he did not desire association with Kareem's brother should a scandal arise. His concern was for himself and Ali. Even so, I was thoroughly pleased at the outcome and was a heroine, admittedly undeservedly, in my mother-in-law's eyes.

Once again, the *mutawas* were quietened by the king's efforts. King Faisal was held in such high esteem by the Religious Council that his appeals were heard and heeded.

Muneer was brought into his father's business and sent to Jeddah to manage the new offices. To buy off his discontent, he was awarded large government contracts. Within a few months, he told his father he wanted to wed, and a suitable cousin was found and his happiness increased. Within months he began to gain weight and joined the ranks of the royal princes who live for making more and more money until their bank accounts overflow and produce enough income from the interest to rival the budgets of small countries.

Kareem had moved into a separate bedroom the day of our conversation. Nothing his mother or father could say or do persuaded him to reconsider our decision to divorce.

Much to my horror, one week after our estrangement, I discovered I was pregnant. After much soul-searching, I decided I had no option but to abort my pregnancy. I knew that Kareem would never agree to a divorce if he discovered I was with child. But one such as I had no use for a husband under duress.

I was in a dilemma, for abortions are not common in my land – many children are desired by most – and I did not have the slightest clue where to go and whom to see.

My investigation was delicate. Finally, I entrusted my secret to a royal cousin who informed me that her younger sister had become pregnant the year before while on holiday in Nice. She had been unaware of her condition and returned to Riyadh. Her fear of her father finding out was such that she had attempted suicide. The mother had shielded the daughter's secret and had located an Indian physician who, for excessive fees, performed abortions for Saudi women. I carefully planned my escape from the palace to the offices of the abortionist. Marci was my confidante.

I was waiting, despondent, in the physician's office when a red-faced Kareem burst through the door. I was a veiled woman among other veiled women, but he recognized me by my unusual silk *abaaya* and my red Italian-made shoes. He pulled and pushed me through the door, screaming to the receptionist that the office had best be closed immediately for he, Kareem, was going to see the doctor in prison.

I was smiling beneath my veil and in the best of tempers as Kareem alternately professed his love for me and cursed me. He glittered and he glared! He cast away my fears of losing him as he vowed that he had never considered divorce; his stance was merely a combination of pride and anger.

Kareem had discovered my plan when Marci divulged the secret to another maid in the house. This maid had gone to Noorah, and my mother-in-law had frantically located Kareem in the office of a client and hysterically reported that I was going to kill her unborn grandchild.

Our child was saved by mere moments. I would have to reward Marci.

Kareem herded me into the house with curses. In our room he covered me with kisses and we wept and made our peace. It had taken a series of mishaps to lead us to our peak of happiness.

Miraculously, all had ended well.

Chapter Fourteen

Birth

The most complete and powerful expression of life is birth. The acts of conceiving and giving birth are more profound and beautiful than any miracle of art. This I learned as I waited for our first child with such great joy and happiness.

Kareem and I had meticulously planned the birth. No detail was too small to take into account. We made reservations to travel to Europe four months before the expected date of arrival. I would give birth at Guy's Hospital in London.

As with so many carefully laid plans, minor occurrences prevented our departure. Kareem's mother, blinded by a new veil made of thicker fabric than usual, sprained her ankle when she stumbled over an old bedouin woman sitting in the *souq*; a close cousin on the verge of signing an important contract requested that Kareem postpone his departure; and my sister Nura frightened the family with what the doctor thought was an appendicitis attack.

Once we were past these crises, false labour pains began. My physician forbade me to travel. Kareem and I accepted the inevitable and set about making arrangements for our child to be born in Riyadh.

Unfortunately, the King Faisal Specialist Hospital and Research Centre that would offer us royals the latest medical care had yet to open. I would give birth at a smaller institution in the city, best-known for harbouring germs and for its lackadaisical staff.

Since we were of the royal family, we had options not available to other Saudis. Kareem arranged for three rooms in the maternity ward to be converted into a royal suite. He hired local carpenters and painters. Interior decorators from London were flown in, tape measures and fabric samples in hand.

My sisters and I were guided through the unit by the proud hospital administrator. The suite glowed a heavenly blue with silk bedcovers and curtains. An elaborate baby-bed with matching silk coverlets was fastened with heavy bolts to the floor, in case a member of the negligent staff should carelessly tip the bed and toss our precious child to the floor! Nura bent double with laughter when told of the precaution and warned me that Kareem would drive the family insane with his schemes to protect our child.

I sat speechless when Kareem advised me that a staff of six would soon arrive from London to assist me in the birth. A well-known London obstetrician, along with five highly skilled nurses, had been paid an enormous fee to travel to Riyadh three weeks prior to the estimated delivery date.

Since I was a motherless child, Sara moved into the palace towards the end of my pregnancy. She watched me as I watched her. I observed her carefully, absorbing the sad changes in my dear sister. I told Kareem I feared she would never recover from her abhorrent marriage; her quiet moods were now a permanent component of what had once been a thoroughly cheerful and joyous character.

How unfair life could be! I, by my very aggressiveness, could have better dealt with an abusive husband, for bullies tend to be less forceful in the face of someone who will stand up to them. Sara, with her peaceful soul and gentle spirit, had been an easy target for the arrogance of her untamed husband.

But I was thankful for her smooth presence. As my body swelled, I became jittery and unpredictable. Kareem, in his excitement over fatherhood, had lost all his good sense.

Owing to the presence of Kareem's brother Asad and various cousins who came and went at will, Sara had been careful to veil when she left our apartments on the second floor. The single men of the family were housed in another wing, but they roamed the palace at all hours. After Sara's third day in our home, Noorah sent word through Kareem that there was no need for her to veil when she entered the main living-areas of the villa or the gardens. I was pleased for any loosening of the tight restraints on women that so encumbered our lives. Sara was apprehensive in the beginning, but soon shed the excess covering of black with ease.

One evening, late, Sara and I were reclining in wicker loungers, enjoying the cool night air of the common garden. (There are women's gardens and common or family gardens in most Saudi palace grounds.) Unexpectedly, Asad and four acquaintances returned from a late-night appointment.

When she heard the men approaching, Sara turned her face to the wall, for she had no desire to bring disgrace on the family by showing herself to strangers. I felt no inclination to emulate her movement, so I loudly proclaimed our presence by shouting to Asad that there were unveiled women in the garden. The men with Asad hurriedly passed our way without a glance and entered one of the side-doors to the men's sitting-room. As a courtesy, Asad casually walked our way to speak and enquire of Kareem's whereabouts – and his eyes happened to rest on Sara's face.

His physical reaction was so sudden that I feared he had been stricken with a heart attack. His body jerked so grotesquely that I moved as rapidly as my belly allowed and shook his arm to get his attention. I was genuinely concerned. Was he ill? Asad's face was flushed, and he seemed unable to move without direction; I led him to a chair and called out loudly for one of the servants to bring water.

When no-one responded, Sara jumped to her feet and rushed inside to get the water herself. Asad, embarrassed, tried to leave, but I was convinced that he was about to faint. I insisted he stay. He said he felt no pain, yet he could not explain his sudden loss of movement.

Sara returned with a glass and a bottle of cold mineral water. Without looking at him, she poured a drink and raised the glass to his lips. Asad's hand brushed Sara's fingers. Their eyes locked. The glass slipped from her grasp and crashed to the floor. Sara swept past me as she ran into the villa.

I left Asad to his friends, who had become impatient and begun to empty into the garden. They were more flustered by the sight of my face than of my huge protruding belly. I defiantly waddled by them, and made a point of greeting them full in the face. They responded with embarrassed mumbles.

Kareem awoke me at midnight. When he arrived at the palace, he had been intercepted by Asad. Kareem wanted to know from me what had happened in the garden. I sleepily related the evening's occurrence and enquired about Asad's health.

I sat up with a start when Kareem replied that Asad was insisting on marrying Sara. He had announced to Kareem that he would never know happiness if Sara were not his wife. This, from the playboy of all playboys! A man who had, only a few short weeks earlier, saddened his mother when he vehemently swore never to marry.

I was astonished. I told Kareem that it was easy to surmise Asad's attraction to Sara by his behaviour in the garden, but that this insistence on marriage was unbelievable! After a few moments of visual pleasure? I dismissed it as nonsense and turned back on my side.

While Kareem was showering, I rethought the event and left our bed. I knocked on Sara's door. Since there was no answer, I slowly pushed the door open. My sister was sitting on the balcony staring at a star-filled sky.

With great difficulty, I manoeuvred myself into a corner of the balcony and sat, silent, in a stupor at this turn of events.

Without looking in my direction, Sara spoke with certainty. 'He wishes to marry me.'

'Yes,' I agreed in a small voice.

With a burning look in her eyes Sara continued. 'Sultana, I saw my life ahead of me when I looked into his soul. This is the man Huda saw when she said I would know love. She also said that as a result of this love I would bring six little ones into the world.'

I closed my eyes in an attempt to bring to mind the comments made by Huda on that day long ago in our parents' home. I remembered talk of Sara's unrealized ambitions and the mention of marriage, but little else of the conversation remained fresh in my mind. I shivered when I realized that much of what Huda had predicted had come true.

I felt compelled to dismiss the idea of love at first sight. But I suddenly recalled my charged emotions the day I first met Kareem. I bit my tongue and made no sound.

Sara patted my belly. 'Go to bed, Sultana. Your child needs rest. My destiny will come to me.' She turned her gaze back to the stars. 'Tell Kareem that Asad should go and speak with Father of this matter.'

When I returned to the bed, Kareem was awake. I repeated Sara's words, and he shook his head in wonder and muttered that life was indeed strange, then wrapped his arms around my belly. Sleep came easily to us, for our lives were fixed on a carefully charted course, and neither of us expected unknowns.

The following morning I left Kareem to his shaving and moved heavily down the staircase. I heard Noorah before I saw her. She, as was her favourite pastime, was quoting a proverb. I cursed under my breath but listened quietly at the doorway.

' "The man who marries a woman for her beauty will be deceived; he who marries a woman for good sense can truly say he is married." '

I had no feeling left to fight so I thought to cough to announce my presence. When Noorah began to speak again I changed my mind. I held my breath and strained my ears to hear her words.

'Asad, the girl has been married before. She was quickly divorced. Who knows the reason? Reconsider, my son. You can wed whom you wish. You will be wise to start with a woman that is fresh, not one that is wilted from use! Besides, my son, you see the ball of fire that is Sultana. Can her sister be of a different substance?'

I followed my stomach into the room, my heart aflutter. She was cautioning Asad against Sara. Not only that; the leopard had not changed its spots: in secret Noorah still hated me. I was a bitter potion for her to swallow.

Aware of Asad's carefree character, I had not been in favour of his and Sara's love. Now I would be a resolute supporter of their wishes. Relieved, I could easily see by Asad's expression that nothing would alter his plans. He was a man possessed.

The conversation folded when they saw my face, for I have difficulty in clothing anger; I was furious that Noorah assumed that grief would arise from her son's union with my sister. Surely, I could not argue against my own rebellious nature. I had assumed the role at an early age and had no inclination to alter. But for Sara to be labelled with my reputation was maddening!

In my youth, I had heard many old women say: 'If you stand near a blacksmith you will get covered in soot; but if you stand near a perfume-seller you will carry an aroma of scent with you.' I realized that, as far as Noorah was concerned, Sara was carrying the soot of her younger sister. My feeling was now bottomless rage at my mother-in-law.

Sara's beauty had sparked jealousy in many of our sex. I knew that her appearance closed the possibility of any consideration given to her gentle character and blazing intellect. Poor Sara!

Asad stood up and nodded slightly in my direction. He excused himself from our company. Noorah looked like someone suffering from a dagger wound when he turned back to her and said: 'The decision is made. If I am acceptable to her and her family, no-one can delay me.'

Noorah yelled at his back about the insolence of youth and tried to load him with guilt when she exclaimed that she was not long for the world; her heart was weakening by the day. When Asad ignored her obvious ploy, she shook her head in sorrow. Brows knitted, she thoughtfully sipped at a cup of coffee. No doubt she was plotting against Sara as she had against the Lebanese woman.

In a state of high emotion, I rang the bell for the cook and ordered yoghurt and fruit for breakfast. Marci came into the room and relieved the pain of my swollen feet with her skilled fingers. Noorah attempted conversation, but I was too angry to respond. As I began to nibble fresh strawberries – flown in daily from Europe – a labour pain took me to the floor. I was frightened and screamed in agony, for this crushing pain was too soon and far too severe. I knew the pain should begin as a twinge, as the false labour that had nudged me in the past.

Chaos erupted as Noorah called out in one breath for Kareem, for Sara, for the special nurses and for the servants. In moments, Kareem lifted me in his arms and bundled me into the back of an extra-long limousine, which had been especially converted for this event. The seats had been ripped out and a bed built in on one side. Three small seats had been made ready to accommodate Kareem, Sara and a nurse. The physician from London and the other four nurses had been alerted and were following in a separate limousine.

I clutched my back while the nurse tried in vain to monitor my heartbeat. Kareem yelled at the driver to go faster; then he reversed his orders and screamed for him to go slower, declaring in a loud voice that his reckless driving would kill us all. He thumped the poor man on the back of the head when he allowed another driver to cut in front of our car.

Kareem began to curse himself for not arranging a police escort. Sara did her best to calm Kareem, but he was like an unleashed storm. Finally, the British nurse spoke loudly in his face; she advised him that his conduct was harmful to his wife and child. She threatened to remove him from the vehicle if he did not quieten himself.

Kareem, a prominent royal prince who had known no criticism in his life from a woman, entered a state of shock and was speechless. We all breathed a sigh of relief.

The hospital administrator and a large staff that had been alerted by the household were waiting at the side-door. The administrator was delighted that our child would be born in his institution, for in those days many of the young royals travelled abroad for the event of birth.

My labour was long and difficult, for I was young and small in size and my baby was stubborn and large. I recall little of the birth itself; my mind was seduced with drugs, and my memory is hazy. The nervous tension of the staff inflated the mood of the room, and I heard the physician insult his staff time and again. Without doubt, they were, as were my husband and family, praying for the birth of a son. Their reward would be great if a male child appeared; if a female child was born, there would be great disappointment. As far as I was concerned, a female child was my desire.

My land was bound to change, and I felt myself smile with anticipation of the agreeable life my baby daughter would know.

The cheering of the physician and his staff awoke me from a shadowy hollow. A son was born! I was sure I had heard the physician whisper to his head nurse: 'The rag-head in the dress will fill my pockets for this prize!' My mind protested at this insult to my husband, but a deep slumber took me from the room and the remark was not recalled for many weeks. By that time, Kareem had awarded the physician with a new Jaguar and fifty thousand English pounds. His nurses were presented with gold jewellery from the *souq* along with five thousand English pounds each. The jubilant hospital administrator from Egypt received a substantial contribution to be used for the maternity wing. He was overjoyed with a bonus of three months' salary.

All thoughts of a daughter vanished when my yawning son was placed in my arms. A daughter would come later. This male child would be taught different and better ways than the generation before him. I felt the power of my intentions creating his future. He would not be backward in his thinking; his sisters would be given a place of honour and respect; and he would know and love his partner before he wed. The vast possibilities of his accomplishments glowed and glittered as a new star. I told myself that many times in history one man has created change that influenced millions. I swelled with pride as I considered the good to mankind that would flow from the tiny body in my arms. Without doubt, the new beginning of women in Arabia could start with my own blood.

Kareem gave little thought to the future of his son. He was enamoured of fatherhood and quite rash with foolish statements regarding the number of sons we would produce together.

We were mindless with joy!

Chapter Fifteen

Dark Secrets

The completion of our birth is in death. Life begins with only one passageway; however, there are unlimited means of exit. The usual and hoped-for method of departure follows the wondrous fulfilment of life's promise. When death claims one blooming with life and cause for hope, it is the saddest of all events. When blossoming youth ends as the result of another man's hand, it is the worst of life.

At the rapturous occasion of the birth of my son, I was confronted with the mindless death of a young and innocent girl.

Kareem and the medical staff attempted to cloister me from the other Saudi women who were short steps away from my suite. While my son slept beside me with an entourage for protection, other sons and daughters were kept in the nursery. Curiosity about their life-stories lured me from my rooms. As with most of the royals, I had led a life sheltered from ordinary citizens, and now my inquisitive nature led me to conversation with these women.

If my childhood had been bleak, the lives of most Saudi women had been more bleak, I soon learned.

My life was ruled by men, but there was protection of sorts because of my family name. The majority of women gathered around the nursery window had no voice in their destiny.

I was eighteen years old at the time of my first child's birth. I met girls as young as thirteen nursing their young. Other young women no more than my own age were delivering their fourth or fifth infant.

One young girl intrigued me. Her black eyes were dulled with pain as she gazed at the mass of screaming infants. She stood so quietly for such a lengthy time that I knew her eyes did not see what was before her; instead she was immersed in a drama far from the spot on which we were standing.

I learned that she was from a small village, not distant from the city. Normally, women in her tribe gave birth in their homes, but she had been in labour five long days and nights, and her husband had driven her to the city for medical assistance. I befriended her over a period of several mornings and discovered that she had been married at the age of twelve to a man of fifty-three. She was the third wife, but much favoured by her husband.

Muhammad, our beloved Prophet of Islam, taught that men should divide their time equally among their wives. In this case, the husband was so occupied with the charms of his young bride that, to please their husband, wives numbers one and two frequently sanctioned their approval of losing their turns for mating. The young girl said her husband was a man of great power and did 'it' many times a day. Her eyes widened as she moved her arm up and down in the pumping motion for added effect.

Now she was frightened, for she had given birth to a daughter, not a son. Her husband would be angry when he came to claim them for the trip back to the village, for the firstborn of the other two wives had been sons. Now, with foreboding, she sensed that she would be scorned by her husband.

She recalled little of her childhood, which now seemed ages ago. She had been raised poorly, and experienced little but hard work and sacrifice. She described how she had helped her numerous brothers and sisters to herd the goats and camels and tend to a small garden. I was anxious to know her feelings of men and women and life, but since she was sadly lacking in education I did not receive the answers I was seeking.

She was gone before I could say goodbye. I felt cold from the thought of her bleak life and wandered back to my suite in a despondent state.

In a fit of anxiety over the safety of his son, Kareem had posted armed guards at the door of my suite. When I had made my morning walk to the nursery, I was surprised to see guards standing in front of another room. I thought that another princess must be in the ward. I eagerly asked a nurse to tell me the name of the princess. A crease formed on her brow when she told me that I was the only princess in the hospital.

She told me the story, but not before she had advised me that she was absolutely scandalized. Then she proceeded to insult all the people on earth before she described the happenings in room 212. She said that nothing of the sort would ever happen in her country, that the British are quite civilized, thank you, and that they make the rest of the world seem simply barbaric.

My imagination could not take me to such depths of anger, so I implored her to tell me what was happening before Kareem paid his afternoon visit.

The day before, she told me, the hospital staff had been dismayed to see a young girl about to deliver, shackled in leg-irons and handcuffs, escorted to the maternity ward by armed guards. A group of angry *mutawas*, followed by the frightened administrator, had accompanied the guards; they, not the administrator, had appointed a physician to her case.

To the physician's consternation, he had been informed that the girl had been tried in the Shari'a (the law of God) courts and found guilty of fornication. Since this was a crime of Hudud (a crime against God), the penalty was severe. The *mutawas*, clothed in self-righteousness, were there to bear witness to the appropriate punishment.

The physician, a Muslim from India, made no protest to the *mutawas*, but he was incensed at the role he was forced to play. He told the staff that the usual punishment for fornication was flogging, but in this instance the father had insisted upon death for his daughter. The girl was to be guarded until she delivered, at which time she was to be stoned to death.

The nurse's chin quivered in indignation as she reported that the girl was no more than a child. She guessed her age at fourteen or fifteen. She knew few other details and left my bedside to gossip with the other nurses in the hallway.

I begged Kareem to uncover the story. He hesitated, saying that this was not a matter of our concern. After much pleading and the shedding of tears on my part, he promised to enquire into the matter.

Sara lightened my day when she brought me bright news of her evolving romance. Asad had spoken with Father and had received the expected positive answer. Sara and Asad were going to marry within three months. I was thrilled for my sister who had known so little happiness.

Then she divulged other news that made my stomach sink with fear. She and Asad had made plans to meet in Bahrain the following weekend. When I protested, Sara said she was travelling to meet Asad, with or without my assistance. She planned to advise Father that she was still at our palace, helping me in my new role of motherhood. She would tell Noorah that she was back at Father's home. She said no-one would guess otherwise.

I asked how she could travel without Father's permission, for I knew he kept all the family passports locked in his safe at the office. Besides, she would require a letter of permission from Father or she would never gain entry to the plane. I cringed when Sara told me she had borrowed a passport and a permission letter from a girlfriend who had planned a trip to Bahrain to visit relatives but had had to cancel when one of the relatives became ill.

Since Saudi women veil, and the security guards at the airport would never dare ask to see a woman's face, many Saudi women borrow each other's passport for such occasions. The letter of permission was the added difficulty; but they, too, are swapped, along with the passports. Sara would return the good deed at a later date by planning a trip to a nearby country and cancelling at the last minute, then lending her credentials to the same friend. It was a detailed, underground operation that none of our men ever figured out. I had always been amused at the ease with which women tricked the airport officials, but now that it was my sister I was shaken with worry.

In an effort to discourage Sara from any reckless acts, I related the story of the young girl waiting to be stoned to death. Sara, as I, was distraught, but her plans remained solid. With increasing trepidation, I agreed to be her cover. She burst out laughing at the thought of meeting Asad without supervision. He had arranged to borrow a friend's apartment in Manama, the capital of the tiny country of Bahrain.

Sara, in her mood of anticipation, lifted my son from his silken cocoon. With joyful eyes, she absorbed his perfection, and said that she, too, would soon know the joys of motherhood, for she and

Asad longed for the six little ones predicted with such certainty by Huda.

I displayed the happy countenance expected by my sister but fear settled in my belly like frozen fire.

Kareem returned early in the evening with information about the condemned girl. He said she was known to be wanton and had become pregnant after having sex with numerous teenage boys. Kareem was disgusted with her behaviour. He said that in her disdain for the laws of our land she had humiliated the honour of her family name; there was no other course possible for her family to take.

I asked my husband of the punishment for the young males who had participated, but he had no answer. I suggested that they had more than likely received a stern lecture in lieu of a death sentence; in the world of Arabs, blame for unsanctioned sex is placed wholly on the shoulders of the female. Kareem stunned me with his calm acceptance of the planned execution of a child, no matter what the crime. In spite of my appeals for him to make some effort to intervene with the king, who could often attain success with a father bent on violent punishment, Kareem dismissed my cries of alarm with unconcealed irritation and insisted that the subject be dropped.

I was withdrawn and sullen when he bade me farewell. He lavished our son with kisses and promises of a perfect life while I sat dull and unresponsive.

I was preparing to depart from the hospital when the British nurse entered my suite in a white glow of anger. She brought heavy tidings of the condemned girl. She possessed an uncanny memory and recalled every painful detail, in perfect clarity, that she had been told by the physician from India. The condemned girl had given birth to a baby daughter in the early hours of the morning. Three *mutawas* had been told of the indignation from the foreign community, and they stood with the armed guards at the entry of the delivery theatre to ensure that no sympathetic foreigner assisted the girl to escape. After delivery, the girl was wheeled back into her room. The *mutawas* informed the physician that the new mother would be removed on that day and taken away to be stoned for her crime against God. The fate of the newborn had not been determined since the family had refused to raise the child as their own.

With horror in her eyes, the nurse stated that the young girl had tearfully told the physician the events that had led to her tragic situation. Her name was Amal, and she was the daughter of a shopkeeper in Riyadh. She had been only thirteen years old when the event occurred that had shattered her world. She had just begun to veil.

It was a Thursday night (equivalent to Saturday nights in the Western world). Amal's parents had travelled to the Emirates for the weekend and would not return until Saturday noon. Three Filipino house-servants were sleeping, and the driver was in his small gatehouse far removed from the main dwelling. Amal's older married siblings were living in other areas of the city. Of the family only she and her seventeen-year-old brother were left at home. Her brother and the three Filipinos had been instructed to take care of her. Her brother had taken the opportunity to entertain a large group of teenage friends while his parents were out of the country. Amal heard loud music and voices late into the evening; the games room was located directly below her bedroom. She thought that her brother and his friends were more than likely smoking marijuana, a substance with which her brother had lately become enamoured.

Finally, when the walls of Amal's bedroom began to vibrate from the sounds of the bass from the stereo, she decided to go downstairs to ask her brother and his friends to turn down their music. Dressed only in her thin nightgown, she had no intention of entering the room, just of poking her head into the doorway to yell for peace and quiet. The lights were dim, and the room was dark; her brother did not respond to her cries, so the girl went inside to look for him.

Amal's brother was not to be found. The other teenage boys in the room were obviously heated with drugs and talk of women, for Amal was pounced upon by several boys at once and found herself pinned to the floor. She screamed for her brother and tried to make the boys understand that she was the daughter of the house, but her pleas did not register in their drugged minds. Her gown was ripped from her body. She was brutally assaulted by her brother's friends, as they had turned into a frenzied mob. The volume of the music muffled the sounds of the attack, and no-one heard her screams for help. Amal lost consciousness after the third boy raped her.

Her brother had been in the bathroom, but he was so drugged that he had slumped against the wall and slept in a haze through the remainder of the night. Later, when the dawn of light cleared the heads of the attackers and Amal's true identity was revealed, the boys fled the villa.

Amal was taken to a nearby hospital by the driver and the Filipinos. The doctor in the emergency room notified the police. The *mutawas* became involved. Owing to Amal's seclusion as a female, she could not identify her attackers by name, only that they were acquaintances of her brother. Their names were taken from Amal's brother, but by the time they were collected and asked to appear before the police for statements they had taken great pains to prepare their story. According to the boys' version of the evening, no drugs had been present. They acknowledged only that they had been playing loud music and having innocent fun. They said the girl had entered the room in a sheer nightdress and enticed them to have sex. She told the boys she had been upstairs reading a book on sex and had a great deal of curiosity. They swore that they had turned her down at first, but that she had behaved in such a bold manner – sitting on their laps, kissing them and fingering her body – that they could not hold back any longer. The girl had been left without a chaperon and was determined to have a good time with some boys. They declared that she was insatiable and had begged them all to participate.

The parents returned from the Emirates. Amal's mother believed her daughter's story; although demented with grief, she was unable to convince her husband of the girl's innocence. Amal's father, who had always been uncomfortable with daughters, was stricken by the event, but felt that the boys had done only what any male would do under the circumstances. With a heavy heart, he concluded that his daughter must be punished for shaming his name. Amal's brother, fearful of severe punishment for using drugs, did not step forward to clear his sister's name.

The *mutawas* offered the father moral support in his strong stance and showered him with accolades for his religious conviction.

The girl would die today. Consumed by emotions of sorrow and fear, I barely heard the continued exclamations of the British nurse. I felt the miserable decline of my happiness as I imagined the girl's innocence and the futility of her mother's efforts to save her from a cruel death. I myself had never witnessed a stoning, but Omar had done so on three occasions and had taken great delight in describing to us the fate that awaited weak women who did not carefully guard their honour which was so prized by their men. I thought of the vivid description with which Omar had burdened my memory.

When I was twelve years of age, a woman in one of the small villages not far from Riyadh had been found guilty of adultery. She was condemned to die by stoning. Omar and our neighbours' driver decided to go and view the spectacle.

A large crowd had gathered since early morning. They were restless and waiting to see the one so wicked. Omar said that just as the crowd was becoming angry with impatience in the hot sun a young woman of about twenty-five years of age was roughly pulled out of a police car. He said she was very beautiful, just the sort of woman who would defy the laws of God.

The woman's hands were bound. Her head hung low. With an official manner, a man loudly read out her crime for the crowd to hear. A dirty rag was used to gag her mouth and a black hood was fastened around her head. She was forced to kneel. A large man, the executioner, flogged the woman upon her back fifty blows.

A truck appeared, and rocks and stones were emptied in a large pile. The man who had read off the crime informed the crowd that the execution should begin. Omar said the group of people, mostly men, rushed towards the stones and began to hurl the rocks at the woman. The guilty one quickly slumped to the ground and her body jerked in all directions. Omar said the rocks continued to thud against her body for what seemed to be an interminable time. Every so often, the stones would quieten while a doctor would check the woman's pulse. After a period of nearly two hours, the doctor finally pronounced the woman dead and the stoning ceased.

The British nurse interrupted my sad ponderings when she returned to my rooms in great agitation. The police and *mutawas* were taking the girl away for her punishment. She said that if I stood in my doorway I could see her face, for the girl was not veiled. I heard a great commotion in the hallway. Quickly, I fastened my veil around my face. My feet moved my body forward without thought or intention.

The doomed one was fragile and childlike between the tall stoic guards who led her to her fate. Her chin rested on her chest, so it was difficult to see the expression on her face. But I discerned that she was a pretty child, one who would have grown into beauty had she been allowed the opportunity to age. She glanced up with dread and peered into the sea of faces that was watching her with great curiosity. I saw that her fear was great. There were no relatives to travel with her to the grave, only strangers to see her off on the darkest of journeys.

I returned to my suite. I held my baby son with great tenderness and considered the relief I felt that he was not of the weaker sex. I gazed into his tiny face with wonder. Would he, too, uphold and thereby harden the system that was so unfair to his mother and sisters? I considered the possibility that all female babies should be put to death at birth in my land. Perhaps the stern attitude of our men would be tempered by our absence. I shuddered, and the question came into my mind.

How could a mother protect the young of her own sex from the laws of the land?

The eyes of the stalwart British nurse were wet with tears. She sniffled and asked why I, a princess, did not intervene in such madness. I told her that I could not help the one condemned; women are not allowed a voice in my land, not even women of the royal family. With sorrow I told the nurse that not only would the girl die as scheduled, but also her death would be hard and her life and death would go unrecorded. With bitterness, I thought of the truly guilty ones roaming free, without thought or care for the tragic death they had wrought.

Kareem arrived with a joyful face. He had organized our return to the palace as carefully as a plan of campaign. Police escorts eased our journey through the bustling traffic of the growing city of Riyadh. Kareem told me to hush when I related the incident at the hospital. He had no desire to hear such sadness with his new son in his arms, travelling towards his destiny as a prince in a land that soothed and nurtured such a one as he.

My feelings for my husband suffered as I saw that he cared little for the fate of a lowly girl. I gave a deep sigh and felt lonely and afraid of what I and my future daughters might face in the years to come.

Chapter Sixteen

Death of a King

The year 1975 holds bittersweet memories for me; it was a year of both glittering happiness and discouraging sadness for my family and my country.

Surrounded by those who loved him, Abdullah, my adored son, celebrated his second birthday. A small circus from France was brought over on our private planes to entertain. The circus stayed for a week at the palace of Kareem's father.

Sara and Asad had survived their daring courtship and were now happily married and awaiting their first child. Asad, in great expectation of the child to be born, had flown to Paris and purchased all the baby clothes in stock at three large stores. Noorah, his disbelieving mother, told all who would listen that Asad had lost his mind. Enveloped in such love, my long-suffering sister Sara beamed with happiness at last.

Ali was studying in the United States and was no longer intimately involved in his sisters' affairs. He gave Father the fright of his life when he announced that he was in love with an American working-class woman but, much to Father's relief, Ali was fickle and soon informed us that he preferred to have a Saudi wife. We later discovered that the woman had struck Ali over the head with a candlestick when he became belligerent and demanding at her refusal to be obedient.

We young modern-thinking Saudi couples embraced the subtle relaxation of the severe restrictions upon women as the years of efforts by King Faisal and his wife Iffat for women's education and freedom proved successful. Along with our education came a determination to change our country. A few women no longer covered their faces, discarding their veils and bravely staring down the religious men who dared to challenge them. They still covered their hair and wore *abaayas*, but the bravery of these few gave hope to us all. We royals would never be allowed such freedom; it was the middle class that showed their strength. Schools for women were now opening without public demonstrations of disapproval by the *mutawas*. We felt certain that women's education would eventually lead to our equality. Unfortunately, the punishment of death for women among the uneducated fundamentalists still occurred. One small step at a time, we grimly reminded each other.

Suddenly, over a six-month period, Kareem and I became the owners of four new homes. Our new palace in Riyadh was finally completed. Kareem decided his new son would grow more hardy if he inhaled fresh sea breezes, so we purchased a new villa by the seaside in Jeddah. My father owned a spacious apartment-house in London only four streets away from Harrods, and he offered the property, at a grand bargain, to any of his children who might be interested. Since my other sisters and their husbands already owned apartments in London, and Sara and Asad were in the process of purchasing an apartment in Venice, Kareem and I eagerly seized the opportunity to have a home in that colourful city so loved by Arabs. And finally, as a special three-year wedding anniversary gift for presenting him with a precious son, Kareem bought me a lovely villa in Cairo.

Upon the occasion of Abdullah's birth, the family jeweller had flown to Riyadh from Paris to bring a selection of diamonds, rubies and emeralds that he had designed into seven distinctive necklace, bracelet and earring sets. Needless to say, I felt richly rewarded for doing what I had wanted to do.

Kareem and I spent as much time as possible in Jeddah. Happily, our villa was located in a coveted spot frequented by the royal family.

We played backgammon as we watched our son, surrounded by Filipino maids, paddle in the warm blue waters that teemed with exotic fish. Even we females were allowed to swim, though we kept our *abaayas* tight around us until we were up to our necks in water. One of the servants relieved me from the *abaaya* held high with my hand, so that I could swim and splash with abandon. I was as free as it was possible for a woman to be in Saudi Arabia.

It was the end of March, not a hot month of the year, so we did not linger long after the midday sun. I told the servants to gather our laughing baby and rinse him under the specially made portable hot shower. We watched him as he gurgled and kicked his short fat legs. Our smiles were broad with pride; Kareem squeezed my hand and said he felt guilty for feeling such happiness. I accused him later of bringing us, and all Saudis, bad luck by voicing his joy with life.

Most Arabs believe in the evil eye; never do we speak aloud of our joy with life or of the beauty of our children. Quite possibly, some evil spirit will hear and steal the object of our joy or cause us some grief by taking away a loved one. To ward off this evil eye, our babies are protected by blue beads pinned to their clothing. As enlightened as we were, our son was no exception.

Moments later, we recoiled in horror as Asad ran towards us with the words 'King Faisal is dead! Murdered by one of the family!' Struck dumb, we sat quivering as Asad told us the scanty details he had learned from a royal cousin.

At the root of our uncle's death was a dispute about the opening of a television station that had occurred nearly ten years before. King Faisal had always stood firm for the progress of modernization for our backward land. Kareem said he had heard him say once that, whether we Saudis liked it or not, he was going to pull us, kicking and screaming, into the twentieth century.

The problems he faced with the extremely religious citizens were a continuation of vexing situations encountered by our very first ruler and Faisal's father, Abdul Aziz. These men of religion fought furiously against the opening of the first radio station, and our first king overcame the objections by ordering the Koran read over the airwaves. The religious ones could find little fault in such a speedy method of spreading God's word. Years later, when Faisal strove to provide television stations for our people, he, like his father before him, encountered much opposition from the Ulema (the religious sheikhs).

Tragically, members of the royal family joined in such protests, and in September 1965, when I was but a child, one of our cousins was shot and killed by the police as he led a demonstration against a television station a few miles outside Riyadh. The renegade prince, with his followers in tow, had stormed the station. This episode ended in a rifle battle with the police, and he was killed. Nearly ten years had passed, but hate had bubbled in the younger brother of the prince until he had now retaliated by shooting and killing his uncle, the king.

Kareem and Asad flew to Riyadh. Sara and I, along with various female royal cousins, congregated within the confines of a family walled palace. We all wailed and shouted our grief to each other. There were few female cousins who did not love King Faisal, for he was our sole chance for change and ultimate freedom. He alone had the prestige with both the religious men and the royal factions of our land to further the cause of women. He felt our chains as his own, and beseeched our fathers to stand behind him in his quest for social change. Once I myself heard him say that even though there are separate roles for men and women, as directed by God, no sex should rule with unquestioned supremacy over the other. With a quiet voice he said that he would know little happiness until each citizen of his land, both male and female, was the master of his or her own fate. He believed that only through the education of our women would our cause be enforced, for our ignorance has surely kept us in darkness. Certainly, no ruler since Faisal has championed our plight. Looking back, our short but heady climb to freedom began its slippery descent the moment his life exploded with the bullets of deceit from his own family. Sadly, we women knew that our one chance for freedom was buried with King Faisal.

Each of us felt anger and hatred for the family that had bred such a one as our cousin, Faisal ibn Musaid, the slayer of our hopes and dreams. One of my cousins shouted out that the slayer's father himself was not right in his mind. He, who had been born prominent in the scheme of Saudi royalty, a half-brother of King Faisal himself, had shunned all contact with family members and responsibility of the throne. One son had been a fanatic, willing to die to prevent the innocent installation of a television station, and another son had killed our beloved and respected King Faisal.

No pain could be worse than the thought of Saudi Arabia without such wisdom to guide us. Never before or since have I witnessed such national grief. It was as if our entire land and all its people were swathed in agony. The best leadership our family had to offer had been struck down by one of our own.

Three days later, Sara's daughter surprised her mother by entering the world as a breach baby. Little Fadeela, named for our mother, joined a nation in mourning. Our grief was so deep that recovery was sluggish, but little Fadeela revived our minds and we recalled the message of joy through her new life.

Sara, in her fear for her daughter's future, convinced Asad to sign a document that said their daughter would be free to choose her husband without family interference. Sara had suffered a troubling nightmare that she and Asad were killed in a plane crash and her daughter was raised in the rigid manner of our generation. Sara, staring pointedly at Asad, said she would commit murder rather than see her daughter wed to a man of evil schemes. Asad, still wild with love for his wife, comforted her by signing the paper and by establishing a Swiss bank account in the baby's name for a million dollars. Sara's daughter would have the legal and financial means to escape her personal nightmares should necessity arise.

Ali returned from the United States for the summer holiday and, if it were possible, he was even more obnoxious than I recalled. He made a great point of telling us of his escapades with American women and announced that, yes, it was true, just as he had been told, they were all whores!

When Kareem interrupted and stated that he had met many women of high morals when he was in

Washington, Ali laughed and suggested that much had changed. He declared that the women he had met in bars took the initiative and proposed sex before he had had the opportunity even to bring up the subject. Kareem told him that was the issue; if a woman were alone in a bar, she was more than likely looking for a one-night stand or a good time. After all, women were free in America, the same as men. He advised Ali to attend church or cultural events, where he would be surprised at the conduct of the women. Ali was adamant. He said that he had tested the morals of women from all walks of life in America; they were *all* definitely whores, in his experience.

Like most Muslims, Ali would never see or understand the customs and traditions of another religion or land. The only knowledge most Arabs have of American society comes from the content of low-grade American movies and trashy television shows. Most important, Saudi men travel alone. Because of their forced seclusion from female companionship, their only interest lies in foreign women. Sadly, they seek out only women who work in bars as strippers or prostitutes. This slanted view distorts Saudis' opinions of the morality of the West. Since most Saudi women do not travel, they believe the stories told by their husbands and brothers. As a result, the vast majority of Arabs truly believe that most Western women are promiscuous.

Admittedly, my brother was handsome in an exotic way that would attract many of the opposite sex, but I knew without a doubt that every woman in America was not a whore! I told Kareem that I longed for the opportunity to travel with Ali. What fun it would be to stand behind him and hold up a sign that proclaimed: THIS MAN SECRETLY DISDAINS YOU AND HOLDS YOU IN CONTEMPT! IF YOU SAY YES TO THIS MAN, HE WILL BRAND YOU A WHORE TO THE WORLD!

Before Ali left to return to the States, he told Father he was ready to acquire his first wife. Life without sex was a hardship, he said, and he would like a woman to be available to him each time he returned to Riyadh for the holidays. Most important, it was time for him, Ali, to have a son. For without sons a man has no value in Saudi Arabia, and is scorned by all who know him.

His new wife could not live with him in the United States, of course; but, rather, would live in Father's villa, carefully guarded by Omar and the other servants. Ali said he must be free to enjoy the relaxed morals of America. His only requirement for his wife – other than virginity, of course – was that she be young, no more than seventeen years of age, exceptionally beautiful, and obedient. Within two weeks, Ali was engaged to a royal cousin; a wedding date was set for December, when he would have more than a month between school terms.

Observing my brother, I recognized my good fortune in having wed a man like Kareem. Doubtless my husband was far removed from perfection, but Ali was a typical Saudi male; to have such a one as him as your master would make life a grinding affair.

Prior to Ali's return to the States, our family gathered at our villa in Jeddah. One evening, the men had too much to drink and became argumentative. After dinner, the volatile issue of whether women should drive cars came out into the open for debate. Kareem and Asad joined Sara and me in our push for a change in the silly custom that had no basis whatsoever in Islam. We brought up the example of women piloting planes in industrialized nations while we were not allowed to drive a car! Many Saudi families could not afford more than one driver, and where did that leave the family when he was on an errand? What would happen if a medical emergency occurred when the driver was unavailable? Did Saudi men think so little of their women's abilities that they would rather twelve- and thirteen-year-old boys drive (which is common in Saudi Arabia) than adult women?

Ali, Father and Ahmed thought the very topic maddening. Ali declared that women and men would be meeting in the deserts for sexual misadventures! Ahmed worried about the veil's hindrance to visibility. Father brought up the possibility of car accidents, and the vulnerability of the female on the street while awaiting the traffic officer. Father looked around the room for confirmation from his other sons-in-law that a woman behind the wheel of a car would endanger herself and others in the process. My other sisters' husbands busied themselves refreshing their drinks or going to the bathroom.

Finally, with brash confidence, as if he had the one bright idea that would win the argument, Ali said that since women are more easily influenced than men they would imitate the youth of our land, who raced their cars through the streets. Naturally, the women would have no thoughts except to emulate them, and this would, as a result, cause our already soaring accident rate to climb.

My brother still infuriated me! Ali mistakenly believed that I had left my youthful impulses behind, but his smug look gave rise to my temper. To everyone's complete surprise, I leaped at Ali, grabbed a handful of his hair, and began to pull as hard as I could. It took both Kareem and Father to force me to release my grasp. My sisters' loud laughter rang throughout the room while their husbands stared at me with a combination of awe and fear.

Ali tried to make peace with me the following day before he departed for the States. My hate was so reckless that I purposely manoeuvred him into a conversation about marriage and the insistence of our men that their wives be virgins while they themselves tried to sample as many women as possible. Ali took the conversation seriously and proceeded to quote the Koran and enlighten me on the absolute necessity of the virginity of females.

The old Sultana of many sly tricks came back to me with ease. I shook my head sadly and sighed a deep sigh. Ali asked what was in my heart. I told him that for once he had convinced me. I agreed with him that all females should be virgins when they wed. I added, with a hidden malice he did not see, that the nature of our young girls had so changed that rarely was a real virgin to be found among them. At Ali's questioning look, I said that certainly there was little misconduct from Saudi women while in Arabia, for what woman wants to lose her life? But when our females travelled, I asserted, they sought out sexual partners and gave their most precious gift to strangers.

Ali became enraged at the thought of any man other than himself, a Saudi, deflowering a Saudi virgin! He enquired, with great agitation, as to where I had learned such information. With a look of appeal on my face, I begged my brother not to reveal our conversation, for surely Father and Kareem would be scandalized. But I admitted to him that we women discussed such issues, and that it was a known topic: the day of the virgin was leaving our land!

Ali puckered his lips and sank deep in thought. He asked me what these young girls did on their wedding night; for if there was no blood, a girl would be disgraced and returned to her father. In Arabia, bloodied sheets are still proudly handed to the mother-in-law of the bride so that she can show friends and relatives that a woman of honour and purity has joined her family.

I leaned closer and told Ali that most young women had surgery to repair their hymen. I added that most young women gave their virginity over and over again to unsuspecting males. It was simple and easy to fool a man. There were plenty of physicians who skilfully performed the operation in Europe, and a few who were known for the service in Saudi Arabia.

Then, to Ali's total horror, I whispered that if, by some chance, the girl could not have a repair job in time for her marriage it was a simple affair to place the liver of a sheep inside her prior to the sex act. The husband could not tell the difference. It was a sheep liver he was deflowering, and not his wife!

A new fear engrossed my self-centred brother. He immediately placed an urgent call to a physician friend; holding the telephone, his face became pale when the friend admitted that such operations were possible. As for the sheep liver, the physician had not heard of it, but it sounded like a viable scheme immoral women would discover sooner or later.

Obviously disturbed, Ali returned twice to the villa on that day, asking my advice as to how he could best guard against such trickery. I told him there was no way, unless he had kept company with his new bride day and night since the day she was born. He, Ali, would just have to accept the possibility that the one he wed might very well be human and have committed mistakes in her youth.

A worried and despondent Ali returned to the States.

When I told Kareem, Sara and Asad of my joke, Sara could not control her glee. Kareem and Asad exchanged looks of worry and glanced at their wives with new thoughts.

Ali's wedding remained on schedule. His young bride was achingly beautiful. How I pitied her. But Sara and I laughed aloud when we saw that Ali was frantic with worry. Later my husband reprimanded me for my mischief when Ali confessed to him that he, Ali, was now dreading the act of sex. What if he had been tricked? He would never know and would be forced to live in doubt with this wife and all future wives.

The worst possible nightmare for a Saudi male would be to follow another in an act of sex with the woman he had wed. If the woman were a prostitute, there was no shame, but his wife represented his family name, bore his sons. The very thought that he might have been misled was more than my brother could bear.

I readily admitted to my husband that I had wicked moments and acknowledged without hesitation that I would have to face up to many sins on my day of judgement. Yet, on Ali's wedding night, I smiled with a satisfaction I had never known. I had discovered and exploited Ali's greatest fear.

Chapter Seventeen

The Woman's Room

Nura's hand was shaking as she retrieved the Koran, our holy book. She pointed out a section to me. I looked at Nura and then, one by one, at my other sisters. My gaze rested on Tahani's stricken face. All hope was lost for her friend Sameera.

Sara, usually quiet and restrained, now spoke. 'No-one can help her. The Prophet, himself, ordered this method of punishment.'

Anger flamed out of my body as I retorted: 'Sameera was not guilty of lewdness. She merely fell in love with a Westerner! These men of ours have determined it is permissible for them to mate with a foreign woman, a woman of another religion, but no, we women are forbidden! It is insane! This law – and its interpretation – is made by men, for men!'

Nura tried to calm me, but I was prepared to fight to the last desperate inch this unnatural tyranny now focused on one whom we all loved: Sameera.

The day before, Sameera had been sentenced by the men of her family and of her religion to be confined to a room of darkness until she was claimed by death. Sameera was twenty-two. Death would come slowly to one so young and strong of limb.

Her crime? While in school in London, she had met and fallen in love with one not of our faith. From our first age of understanding, we Saudi women are taught that it is a sin for any Muslim woman to bind herself to a non-Muslim: the religion of her children cannot be guaranteed if her husband is Christian or Jewish. Since the last word in the Middle Eastern family rests with the husband, the children might well be brought up as Christian or Jewish; the wife and mother would have no say.

Every Muslim is taught that Islam is the final message from Allah to mankind and, therefore, it is the faith superior to all others. Muslims are not allowed to bring themselves knowingly under the patronage of non-Muslims, nor should they ever allow such a relationship to develop. Yet many Saudi *men* do marry women of other faiths without repercussions. Only Saudi *women* pay the supreme price for their association with a non-believer. Our religious scholars say the union of Muslim men with women of other faiths is permissible, for the children are raised in the superior Muslim faith of their father.

Just thinking about the unfairness of it all made me scream out in rage. My sisters and I understood that from this moment the stepping-stones of Sameera's life, one by one, would lead to a great tragedy. And we, her friends from childhood, were helpless in our desire to rescue her.

Sameera had been Tahani's dearest friend since

the age of eight. She was an only child; her mother had fallen ill with ovarian cancer and, although cured, she was told there would be no other children. Surprisingly, Sameera's father had not divorced his now barren wife, which would have been customary for the majority of Saudi men.

My sisters and I had all known women stricken with serious illnesses, only to be thrust aside by their husbands. The social stigma of divorce is severe, and the financial and emotional trauma overwhelming for women. If the children of a divorced woman are not suckling, they, too, can be taken from her. If divorced women are fortunate, they will have loving parents to welcome them home, or an elder son who will give them shelter. Without a supportive family, they are doomed, for no single or divorced woman can live alone in my land. There are government-sponsored homes built specifically to accommodate such women, but life is bleak and each moment is cruel. Those few divorced women who have an opportunity to remarry are lucky enough either to be a great beauty or to have a great fortune. As with everything else in Saudi society, the failure of the marriage and the blame for divorce rest with the woman.

Sameera's mother had been one of the fortunate. Her husband loved her truly and did not think of casting her aside at her time of greatest need. He did not even take a second wife to provide him with sons. Sameera's father is a man considered strange in our society.

Sameera and Tahani were the best of friends.

And, since Sara and I were closest to Tahani in age, we were playmates of Sameera, too. All three of us were envious of Sameera in many ways, for her father bestowed great passion on his only child. He, unlike most Saudi men of his generation, was of a modern mind and promised his daughter that she would be free of the antiquated customs forced upon the females of our land.

Sameera had felt our pain at the obvious failings in our father. In every crisis she had stood firm with the passion of our cause. My eyes stung as I recalled Sameera's tears at Sara's wedding. She had clung to my neck, moaning that Sara would die in the harness of servitude! And now she, Sameera, was locked in the darkest of prisons where even servants were forbidden to speak as they pushed her meals through a special slot at the base of the only door. She was never to hear another human voice. Her total world would be only the sound of her own breathing.

The thought was unbearable. I turned to Sara and suggested that Kareem and Asad might lend some assistance. Tahani looked up in expectation. Sara shook her head slowly. Asad had already made enquiries; neither the uncle nor Sameera's former husband would lift the harsh sentence of darkness with silence until death. This was a matter between the family and their God.

The year of my wedding, Sameera had already charted her future with great care. Since an early age, she had had the odd idea to become an engineer. No woman in Saudi Arabia had such a degree, for we are directed to careers considered appropriate for females: paediatricians, teachers, or social workers for women and children.

In addition, Saudi female students are forbidden contact with male teachers, so Sameera's father had hired his daughter a tutor from London. After years of concentration and effort studying at home, Sameera had been accepted by a technical school in London. Her father, in great pride of his beautiful and clever child, accompanied his wife and daughter to London.

Sameera's father and mother settled Sameera in a private dwelling. Two Indian female servants and an Egyptian secretary were employed to live with their daughter. They bade their child farewell and returned to Riyadh. Of course, no-one had a thought that they would never see each other again. The months passed and, as we expected, Sameera excelled in school.

During her fourth month in London, Sameera met Larry, an exchange student from California. Opposites attract, as they say, for Larry was tall, muscular and blond, a California free spirit, while Sameera was exotic, slim, and mired in the confusions created by our oppressive men.

She wrote to Tahani that love had made her heart heavy, for she knew she was forbidden to marry a Christian. Larry was a Catholic who would never agree to convert to the Muslim faith, a procedure that would help their situation.

Within the month, Tahani received a second, more desperate letter; Sameera and Larry could not survive apart. She was going to live with him while in London, and later she would escape to the States where they would marry. Then, Sameera said, her parents could purchase a home near their daughter in the States. She was certain that their close family relationship would not suffer. But she would be forced to forfeit her Saudi nationality. We would never see her again in our country, for she understood that she could not return to our land after such a scandalous event as marriage to a non-believer.

Tragically, Sameera's parents never learned of their daughter's dilemma, for both of them and their driver were killed instantly when a water-tanker crashed into the side of their car as it crossed a busy street in Riyadh.

In the Arab world, when the head of the family (always a male) dies, the eldest brother takes control of the affairs of the surviving family members. Upon Sameera's father's death, his eldest brother was now her guardian.

Never have two men of the same family borne so little resemblance to each other. Where Sameera's father was permissive and loving, his brother was stern and unbending. A man of the deepest faith, he had often expressed his profound displeasure at the independence of his brother's daughter.

Scandalized, he had not spoken to Sameera's father since the day Sameera enrolled in the school in London. Scornful of the education of girls, he thought it best that females be married at a tender age to a man of years and wisdom. He had recently wed a thirteen-year-old child. She had begun her menses a few months back and was the daughter of a man such as himself.

Sameera's uncle was the father of four daughters and three sons; his daughters had been safely wed at the first sign of puberty. They received little schooling other than the female arts of cooking and sewing, although they had ample instruction in reading skills so that they could recite the Koran.

The day following her parents' death, Sameera received a second shock. A communication of command arrived from her uncle, who was now the head of her family: 'Return to Riyadh on the earliest flight. Bring all that belongs to you.'

Her fear of the brutal realism of life under the care of her uncle caused Sameera to gather her courage and plunge irrationally into a headlong course of unknowns. In what proved to be a fatal mistake for her, Sameera and Larry fled together to California.

The blatant disobedience of this female child burned into the heart of Sameera's new guardian. At that time, he had no knowledge of Sameera's foreign lover. He had no understanding of the wayward girl, for he had no experience with unyielding females.

By the end of the month, with no information of Sameera's whereabouts, the uncle imagined his niece dead, her body decaying in a heathen land. His hunt for her intensified without results, until finally, at the insistence of his eldest son, he relented and employed the services of a detective agency to trace the path of his brother's only child.

Early one morning, Sameera's tyrannical uncle, roaring with rage, arrived at Tahani's villa, clutching the agency's report. He demanded that my sister, Sameera's confidante, reveal the location of his 'ungodly niece and her infidel lover'.

Eyes wide as she described the scene, Tahani marvelled at his anger. He banged his head against the walls of her home; he cried to Allah for assistance in slaying his niece; with fierce denunciations, he promised revenge upon the heathen lover. He cursed the day his brother's child was born. He prayed aloud for God to heap calamities upon his faithless niece. He declared that she had ruined the honour of the family for generations to come.

Tahani, overwhelmed by his shouting and violence, fled from her home to the offices of her husband, Habbib. When they returned to their palace, Sameera's uncle had since departed, but not without a dire warning to the servants that the one who sheltered his niece would feel his wrath. To soothe Tahani's fears, Habbib sought out the uncle and calmed his angry malice. He assured him that his niece was not in contact with our family.

Isolated as she was in another country, Sameera was unaware that her uncle, in a ceaseless effort to locate his niece, now confiscated all family members' mail. By promising great punishment should any contact with his niece escape his attention, he intimidated the family. The girl would eventually long for contact with those of her blood; when the 'one of great sin', as he deemed Sameera, weakened, she would not slip past his vigilant eye. He needed only to wait.

Meanwhile, in California, Larry grew uncertain of his love, and Sameera thrashed about as one lost. Her lover's new indifference bit deeply into her heart; she called Tahani in great fear and uncertainty as to her future course. What should she do? She had few funds and fewer friends in her new land. Without marriage to Larry, she would not be allowed to remain in America. Habbib, while allowing Tahani the freedom of her friendship with Sameera, refused his wife's request to send money.

With only a few thousand dollars left in her bank account, Sameera, in an act of desperation, called her dearest aunty, the youngest sister of her father. The aunty, in dread of her brother's power, dutifully reported the call of her niece. Notified of his niece's difficulties, the uncle carefully planned for her capture and return to his influence.

Sameera was lured to Cairo with the promise of peaceful re-entry into the family she had fled. Money was sent for her return trip. Sameera telephoned Tahani and tearfully confided that she had little choice. Larry's love had dissolved, and he had no inclination to assist her financially. She had not yet earned her degree and could not earn a salary. She had no money. She had placed telephone calls to the Saudi embassies in Washington and London. The embassy staff were unsympathetic. After she had explained her situation, she was curtly told she would have to return to her family. Escape from reality was impossible; she must return to Saudi Arabia.

Sameera told Tahani she was fearfully hopeful that her aunties were speaking the truth, for they had given their oath that their brother had softened and had agreed for her to continue her educational courses in London. Perhaps, after all, her uncle would treat the only child of his brother with kindness. Tahani, certain that the wrath of the uncle had not diminished, was unable to voice her caution, for she saw clearly the futility of Sameera's position.

Sameera was met at Cairo airport by two aunties and two male cousins. They quietened her apprehensions with talk of her return to London, once she had repaired her isolation from her family. Happily, Sameera concluded that all would be well.

Sameera returned to Riyadh.

When Sameera's expected telephone call did not come, Tahani fell into the deepest depression. She finally called Sameera's relatives, only to be informed that the child had a small fever and did not feel well enough to speak to her friends. Tahani was assured that Sameera would contact her the moment her health improved.

The second week of her return, one of Sameera's aunties answered Tahani's plea with the news that a marriage had been arranged, and that Sameera wished for Tahani to cease her contacts, for her future husband did not look favourably upon his wife's girlhood friends.

Sameera finally managed to contact Tahani. Her hopes had been dashed from the moment she saw her uncle, she said. He had been waiting for their meeting, his fury building, until it had peaked at the sight of his 'Godless' niece.

Since the night of her return, Sameera had been confined to her room, awaiting the verdict of her uncle. No member of her family dared raise a voice of protest at her mistreatment. She whispered to Tahani that she had been informed that a suitable marriage had been arranged; she would be wed within the month. Sameera was terrified at the thought, for her relationship with Larry had been one of deep love; she was no longer a virgin.

We were able to discover few details of the wedding, for no-one outside Sameera's family was invited. We knew for certain that it was not a union of joy. We learned that the groom was in his mid-fifties and that Sameera was the third wife.

Much later, Habbib was enlightened of the family gossip by one of Sameera's male cousins. He said that on her wedding night Sameera had fought the husband with such strength and determination that he had barely survived the taking of what was his. The husband, we were told, was short and fat and not overly muscular. Evidently, blood had been lost, but it was that of the husband; in the fierce battle, he had had little time to verify his wife's virginity.

When Tahani questioned Sameera's aunty who now regretted her role in entrapping her niece, she was told that in the beginning the husband had been fond of the tigress he had wed. Her insults and brave defence had done little to deter his resolve to conquer her with force. But, as time passed, he wearied of Sameera's violent gestures of disdain and grew to regret the one he had taken under his roof.

Sameera had bragged to her aunty that, in her distress, she had grown bold and shouted into her husband's round face that she could not love one such as he. She, Sameera, had known the caresses of a real man, a man of strength. She scorned her husband's expertise as a lover and compared him cruelly to her tall handsome American.

Without ceremony, the husband divorced Sameera and deposited her at her uncle's door. He angrily told the uncle that the family had no honour and had knowingly wed him to one who was no longer pure. In great detail, he spoke of Sameera's 'shame' at coming to the marriage bed with memories of another in her mind.

In a bottomless black rage, the uncle sought guidance through the pages of the Koran; he soon found verses that cemented his decision to shut away the one who had shamed his family name. The former husband, still smarting from the insults on his manhood, furthered the decision by vowing to announce to all who would listen the lack of honour in the home of Sameera's uncle, unless serious punishment were meted out to the girl.

Habbib delivered the sad news to Tahani that Sameera had been sentenced to 'the woman's room', a particularly cruel punishment. A special room on the top floor of her uncle's villa had been prepared for her. A windowless padded cell had been completed for the purpose of imprisoning Sameera. The windows were obstructed with cement blocks. Insulation had been installed so that the cries of the one imprisoned could not be heard. A special door had been hung, with a bottom panel adjusted to serve as an entry for food. A hole in the floor had been built for the disposal of body wastes.

Curious foreign workmen were informed that a member of the family had suffered brain injuries from an accident; it was feared that this person might harm herself or perhaps others of the family.

My sisters and I had gathered to console Tahani, who was suffering tremendous grief at the incarceration of one close to her heart. Each of us was in pain, for Sameera was one of us, a Saudi woman with no recourse against injustice.

While I plotted endless schemes of rescue, my older sisters saw the situation more clearly. They had heard stories about other such women, and knew that there was no hope of extricating Sameera from the isolation of her fading life.

For many nights sleep deserted me; I was consumed by emotions of despair and helplessness. I, too, had heard rumours of other condemned women in my country receiving the punishment of the woman's room, but I had never had a picture in my mind of the reality of the drawn and anguished howl of someone I had known, a woman who had embodied the life and hope of our land, a woman now living in utter blacknesss, without sight or sound to sustain her life.

I awoke one night thinking that I had suffered

a bad dream. I was grasping for easement when I realized that the nightmare was real; there would be no relief to those who knew Sameera and the fact that she now suffered helplessly in total captivity and isolation. The never-ending question ran through my mind: What power on earth could release her? As I stared up at the desert night sky sparkling with stars, I had to conclude there was none.

Chapter Eighteen

Second Wife

Thursday, 28 August 1980 is a day I will never forget. Kareem and I had just returned to Riyadh from Taif, a cool mountain resort. I was lounging on the sofa while one of the Filipino servants rubbed my aching feet. Our three children were at a camp in Dubai, in the Emirates, and I was bored without them.

As I looked through the stack of newspapers that had accumulated during our two months' absence, an item of interest leaped from the page of the latest newspaper. One of my relatives, the governor of Asir, Prince Khaled Al Faisal, had recently taken steps to curb the spiralling cost of marriage in his province by limiting the dowry costs that a groom had to pay to acquire a bride in his area.

The prince had placed a limit of 25,000 Saudi riyals ($7,000) as the maximum the bride's parents would be allowed to request for their daughter. The article pointed out that the directive was well received by eligible bachelors since 100,000 Saudi riyals ($27,000) was the average price of brides in the year 1980. As a result, many young men of Saudi Arabia could not afford to purchase a wife.

I read the item to the Filipino servant, but she took little note, for she had few concerns for the plight of Saudi women who were bought and sold. Mere survival was a heavy burden for most Filipinos. They thought we Saudi women were quite fortunate to have endless time on our hands and vast sums of money to spend on whatever we might fancy.

As the mother of two daughters, I did not care about the actual price of a bride, for when the occasion came for our children to wed the bridal price would be of little concern. Kareem and I were exceedingly wealthy; money failed to play a role in my daily frustrations. But I saw a trend of backward moves by the men of our family. In the confines of our homes, they spoke eloquently of freedom for women, while in legal directives they themselves wrote they kept the pressure high for the status quo and steadily pushed us back to the primitive age.

Only the total elimination of dowries would have satisfied my longing. How many years would it take before we women were no longer bought and sold as property?

I was restless and began to feel edgy, for all of my sisters, other than Sara, were still abroad. My dearest sister was in the last few weeks of her fourth pregnancy and now slept most of the daylight hours.

My life, so well planned in my youth, had not turned out as I had envisaged it. Instead, I had settled into much the same routine as my sisters and the other royal princesses I befriended.

Since the servants fed the children their morning meal and organized their days, I generally slept until noon. After a snack of fresh fruits, I would soak in the tub in a leisurely manner. After dressing, I would join Kareem or, if he were occupied, my sisters for a late lunch. We would lounge and read after our meal, and then Kareem and I would take a short nap. Afterwards, he would return to the office or visit his royal cousins while I spent a few hours with the children.

I attended women's parties in the late afternoon and returned to our palace no later than eight or nine o'clock in the evening. Kareem and I made a point of eating our evening meal with the children to learn about their activities that day. We almost always attended a dinner-party in the evenings, for we were of a most select group that entertained mixed couples. Generally, our associates were of the royal family only, but on occasion high-ranking foreigners, foreign ministers, and wealthy Saudi business families would be included in our inner circle. Since our social freedoms had not come, we of the younger generation had decided to take them by force. We knew that the religious groups seethed with anger at our mixed gatherings, yet they made no move to pressure Khalid, our revered and pious king.

For such social gatherings the women dressed with flamboyance, for we had few occasions to show off our jewels and dresses. Kareem and I were often out until two or three in the morning.

Our routine rarely wavered unless we were out of the country.

An eternal question haunted me: Was this all there was?

I could deny the facts no longer. I, the fiery Sultana, had become an ordinary, dull and listless Saudi woman, with little of real importance to occupy my days. I hated my lazy and luxurious life, but was unsure as to the steps I could take to relieve my boredom.

After the relaxing foot massage, I had an urge to walk through the gardens. In planning our own gardens, I had used Nura's lovely grounds as a reference. Nothing gave me as much peace as a stroll in the cool shade of the small forest so vigorously watered and tended by a crew of twelve men from Sri Lanka. We lived in the middle of one of the world's harshest deserts, yet our homes were surrounded by lush green gardens. Because of endless sums of money paid for plentiful water trucked in from the seaports for the four waterings each day, we wealthy Saudis could escape the stark red sands that were waiting for the slightest chance to encroach upon our cities and erase our memory from the earth. In time, the desert would win, but for now we were the masters of our land.

I stopped to rest in the gazebo specially built for Maha, our eldest daughter, who would soon celebrate her fifth birthday. She was a dreamer and spent hours upon hours hidden in the midst of the vine-covered contraption, playing complicated games with imaginary friends. She reminded me so of myself at a young age. Fortunately, she did not share the heavy revolutionary personality of her mother, for Maha enjoyed her father's love and felt no need to rebel.

I picked at the flowers overhanging Maha's favourite spot. She had left an assortment of toys in an unruly pile. I smiled and wondered how she could be so completely removed from her younger sister's character traits; for Amani, who was now three, was a child of perfection, much in the same manner as her Aunt Sara.

As I thought of my children, my depression came to me, fierce and strong. I remembered to thank God for my healthy son and two daughters, but tears welled in my eyes when I thought again about the fact that I would have no more children.

The year before, during a routine examination at the King Faisal Specialist Hospital and Research Centre here in our city, I had been diagnosed as having breast cancer. Kareem and I were shocked, for we thought of illness as belonging only to the aged. I had remained disease-free all of my life and had borne my last two children with ease. The doctors were certain I was now clean of the killer cells, but I had lost one breast. Further, I was also warned not to become pregnant.

As a precaution against desire for more little ones that would overrule common sense, Kareem and I made a decision for me to undergo sterilization. My fears had been so great that I might not live to see my three children grow that my mind was little troubled at the time by the thought of having such a small family. In Saudi Arabia, rarely does a woman stop producing children; age removes the pangs of giving birth, nothing else.

The sound of Kareem's voice interrupted my deep and troubled thoughts. I watched him as he walked briskly across the thick grass. We had suffered many arguments over the past year, for our lives were stressed by my illness. I made a sudden resolve to become the old Sultana, the girl who used to make her husband laugh with great joy and abandon. I smiled at his long athletic legs bound by the tightness of his *thobe*. The sight of him still gladdened my heart.

When he came closer I recognized that trouble was on his mind. I tossed around the possibilities, for I knew my husband's moods; it would take many moments for him to reveal his burden. I gestured with my hand for him to sit beside me. I wanted to sit as closely as our rigid customs allow, which meant our limbs could touch through our clothing so long as no-one could see.

Kareem disappointed me when he settled at the farthest corner of the gazebo. He did not return my smile of welcome. Some harm had come to the children! I jumped to my feet and asked him what bad news he brought. He seemed surprised that I anticipated unpleasant tidings. Then Kareem uttered words that I never, in my wildest expectations, thought I would hear from my husband.

'Sultana, I made a decision, a very difficult decision, some months ago. I have not discussed this matter with you owing to your illness.'

I nodded, unclear as to what was awaiting me, though I was terrified to hear his words.

'Sultana, you are, and will always be, the most important woman – wife – in my heart.'

I still had no notion of what message my husband wanted me to hear, but without doubt his words were meant to prepare me for news I would not embrace. I felt numbness creep into my face; I knew with certainty that I did not want him to reveal what change I would soon know as actuality.

'Sultana, I am a man that can afford many children. I desire ten, twenty, as many as God sees fit to give me.'

He paused for what seemed a lifetime. I held my breath in fear.

'Sultana, I am going to wed another. As the second wife, she will be there to provide children. I need nothing further from her, only children. My love is always with you.'

No sound could be heard because of the pounding in my head. I was trapped in a dark reality that I did not believe. Never, never, never had such a consideration entered the realm of possibility.

Kareem waited for my reaction. At first, I could not move. My breath finally came back to me in deep ragged gasps. The truth of his announcement slowly sank into my mind and came to life; when my strength returned, I could answer him only with a fit of passion that brought us both to the floor.

The depth of my pain could not be expressed in words. I needed to hear Kareem beg for my mercy as I clawed his face and kicked his groin and tried desperately to kill the man who was my husband.

Kareem struggled to get to his feet, but because of the sudden madness that had consumed me with violence I was possessed with great physical strength. To restrain me, Kareem had to pin me to the ground and sit astride my body.

My screams pierced the air. The names I called my husband caused the gathering servants to freeze. Like a wild creature, I spat into Kareem's face and watched his astonishment grow as he witnessed the fury he had triggered. Finally, the servants, in fear of what they were witnessing, rushed to various areas and hid themselves in buildings and behind bushes.

At last my rage was spent. A deadly calm fell over me. My mind was made up. I told Kareem that I wanted a divorce; I would never submit to the humiliation of his taking another wife. Kareem replied that divorce would be out of the question unless I chose to give up my children for his second wife to raise. He would never allow them to leave his home.

In a flash, I saw my life before me. Kareem, far removed from the dignity and decency of a civilized man, assuming one wife after another. Most men and women sense the limits they can bear; philosophically, I did not have the disposition to abide such debauchery.

Kareem could mouth any deception he chose; but I understood the implications of his taking a second wife. The desire for children was not his real reason. The issue was primitive. We had been wed for eight years; sexual licence was his aim. Obviously, my husband was weary of eating the same dish and sought a new exotic fare for his palate.

To think that Kareem thought me mindless enough to accept his well-thought-out explanation further enraged me. Yes, I would accept what God placed before me, but this dispensation did not extend to my earthly husband. I told Kareem to remove himself from my presence; I would, on this day, refrain from murder.

For the first time, I felt keenly the first emotions of dislike towards my husband. His façade was wisdom and kindness; his very bowels were cunning and selfishness. I had lain beside him eight years; yet he suddenly seemed like a stranger I did not know at all. I asked him to leave my sight. I was disgusted to discover that he was merely a shell of a man with little to commend him after all.

I watched him as he walked away, head low, shoulders slumped. How was it possible to love him less than an hour before? Yet the flow of my love had slowed. I had held the character of Kareem high, regarding him in great favour over other men of our society. Yet, sadly, at the core of his being, he was as all the rest.

Yes, we had lived through a year of difficulties. Yes, marriage proves restrictive and irritating. We had enjoyed seven years of immense pleasures and suffered through only one year of trouble and evolution. For that, thoughts of fresh joys, a new uncomplicated woman perhaps, crept into my partner's dreams.

Worst of all, he was a man who could blackmail the one who had borne his children. Without shame, he had dangled the sinister possibility of his second wife determining the happiness of my precious children. That should connect me with the reality of my male-dominated world.

As a plan began to grow in my mind, I thought of my husband with pity. His memory had dimmed of the fiery one he had wed. Kareem would find it difficult to outwit me in the possession of my children.

Chapter Nineteen

Escape

Unlike most saudi husbands, Kareem kept his family's passports and papers within easy reach of his wife. Already I was a master at duplicating his signature. His personal seal was kept on top of his desk in his home study.

By the time I had gathered my thoughts and returned to the house, Kareem was no longer in evidence. So he was a coward, too. I knew with certainty that he would stay at his father's palace for a night or two.

A sudden thought of Noorah came to mind. I seethed with anger as I imagined my mother-in-law's pleasure at my predicament. More than likely, she had already selected the second wife for her eldest son. Until that moment I had not considered who the new wife would be; perhaps she was a youthful royal cousin, for we royals tend to wed royalty.

I calmly packed a travelling-case and emptied our hidden safe of hundreds of thousands of dollars. Like most of the royals, Kareem had plans for the possibility of revolutionary fervour, which springs to life unexpectedly in lands ruled by monarchies. We had talked of his plan to buy our lives should the populous weak ever overthrow the strong. I uttered a murderous prayer for our Shiite minority in the Eastern Province to overthrow our Sunni leaders; a vision of Kareem's head skewered on a post brought a smile to my grim countenance.

After packing my wealth of jewels in a small travel bag, I prepared my travel papers with utmost ease. Finally I was ready.

I could not trust any of my sisters, for they might be tempted to divulge my plan to their husbands. And men stick together; Kareem would be notified immediately.

I called for my most trusted maid, for I suspected she would be the first questioned by Kareem, and told her I was going to Jeddah for a few days and please to advise my husband of my plans, should he enquire.

I telephoned my favourite of the family's pilots and advised him that we would be flying to Jeddah within the hour; he was to meet me at the airport. I called the servants in Jeddah and informed them that I would be visiting a friend in the city; perhaps I would come by the villa for a visit. Should Kareem call and request to speak to me, they should tell him that I was at the home of a friend and would call him back at my first opportunity.

My deceitful actions were an attempt to keep Kareem from my true travel plans as long as possible.

As I was driven to the airport, I looked in wonder at the mass of Thursday-evening traffic in Riyadh.

Our city was filled with foreign workers, for we Saudis could not bring ourselves to work at menial jobs. One day the underprivileged would weary of our ill-treatment; our carcasses would make food for the packs of wild dogs that roamed our cities.

When the American pilot saw the black shadow that was me walking in his direction, he grinned and waved. He had taken me on many journeys, and was a warm reminder of the open and friendly pilots who had flown my mother and me to Sara's side so many years before. The memory caused my heart to flutter and to ache for the healing embrace of my mother.

When I boarded the plane, I told the pilot that our plans had changed; one of the children had become ill in Dubai, and I had just received a telephone call from Kareem advising me that I should go to our child instead of to Jeddah. He, Kareem, would follow tomorrow if it was a real emergency.

I lied with the greatest of ease when I told the pilot that we, of course, imagined that our youngest was simply homesick and that my presence would soothe her feelings. I laughed when I said that they had been away for three weeks, much too long for the little one.

Without questioning me further, the pilot changed his flight plans. He had flown for our family for many years and knew us as a happy couple. He had no reason to doubt my orders.

Once we arrived in Dubai, I told the pilot to stay at his usual hotel, the Dubai Sheraton. I would call him tomorrow or the day after to advise him of my plans. I told him he should consider himself off duty, for Kareem had said he would not need him or the plane for several days. We owned three Lear jets; one was always on standby for Kareem's use.

The children were ecstatic at the unexpected sight of their mother. The headmaster of the British summer camp shook his head in sympathy when I reported that their grandmother was gravely ill. I would be taking the children, that very night, back with me to Riyadh. He hurried off to his office to locate their passports.

When I shook the man's hand in farewell, I mentioned that I could not locate the servants who had accompanied the children to Dubai. They had not answered the telephone in their room; I imagined they were eating their dinner. Would he call them in the morning and tell them I would have the pilot, Joel, waiting for them at the Dubai Sheraton? They should go immediately and present the pilot with this note. With that, I handed the headmaster an envelope addressed to the American pilot.

In the note I apologized for using him in such a deceptive manner; I added a postscript to Kareem describing how I had duped the pilot. I knew Kareem would have a flash of anger at the pilot, but it would pass when he considered the circumstances. The pilot, Joel, was a favourite of Kareem's. He was sure not to lose his job.

The children and I climbed into the waiting limousine, which sped to the airport; a direct flight to London was departing within the hour. I would use whatever lie I could muster to obtain four seats on the plane.

As it turned out, I did not have to damage my soul with God further. The flight was almost empty; most people were returning to the Gulf at the end of the hot summer, not departing. The children were sleepy and asked few questions; I told them they would be surprised at the end of the journey.

As the children slept, I nervously turned the pages of a magazine. Nothing on the pages penetrated my thoughts; I was considering my next move with great care. The remainder of my life would depend upon the events of the next few weeks. Slowly, the feeling overcame me that someone with a purpose was staring directly at me. Had my flight from Kareem already been discovered?

I looked across the aisle. An Arab woman of thirty or so years of age was staring hard at me. She cradled a sleeping three- or four-year-old girl in her arms. I was relieved to see that my mental intruder was a woman, and a mother, for Saudi men would never have such a one in their employ. Her piercing glower was a puzzle, so I stood, threaded my way around the serving-cart and sat in the empty seat beside her. I asked her what her trouble was. Had I offended her in some manner?

Her granite face came to life, and she practically spat her words at me: 'I was at the airport when you arrived; you and your brood.' She glanced with contempt at my children. 'You practically ran over me and my child as you checked in at the ticket counter!' She looked with black malice into my eyes when she emphasized my nationality in her next insulting sentence: 'You Saudis think you can buy the world!'

My warped day had sapped my strength; I surprised myself even more than I surprised the woman when I burst into tears. Through my sobs, I patted her shoulder and told her I was sorry. I had a great tragedy in my life and catching this flight was of utmost importance. With tears streaming down my face, I returned to my seat.

The woman was of a sympathetic nature, for she was unable to remain far from my side after my show of emotion. She carefully placed her daughter in the seat and knelt in the aisle beside me.

My body stiffened, and I turned away, but she manoeuvred her face close to mine and said: 'Please, I apologize. I, too, have had a great tragedy. If I tell you what happened to my daughter in your country, more than likely at the hands of some of your countrymen, you will understand my great bitterness.'

Having absorbed more horror than most people endure in a lifetime, I felt no desire to carry yet another image of injustice in my mind. Unable to trust my voice, I mouthed the words 'I am sorry'. She seemed to understand that I was on the verge of hysterics so she left my side.

But the woman was unwilling to let the dreadful happening go unheard, and before the flight had ended I knew the cause of her despair. Upon hearing her story, my bitterness further hardened towards the degenerate patriarchal society that endangers all females, even children, who dare to tread on the soil of Saudi Arabia, regardless of their nationality.

Widad, the woman, was from Lebanon. Because of the persistence of the heartbreaking civil war of that once-beautiful little country, Saudi Arabia and the Gulf States were overflowing with Lebanese in search of jobs. Widad's husband was one of the fortunate who had been employed as an executive in one of the many booming businesses in Riyadh. After a favourable beginning, he had felt secure enough to bring his wife and young daughter to live in the desert capital.

Widad had been content with her life in Riyadh. The war in Lebanon had taken away any desire to return to the endless shelling and mindless deaths of the innocent. She happily settled herself in a land far different from the one she had known. A spacious villa was rented, furniture was purchased, lives were reassembled. Widad had been most impressed with the lack of crime in our country. With severe punishments meted out to those guilty, few criminals ply their trade in Saudi Arabia, for a convicted thief will lose his hand, and a murderer or rapist his head. With a mind at peace, she had failed to caution her young daughter of the danger of strangers.

Two months before, Widad had given a small women's party for a group of friends. As with Saudi women, there is little for foreign women to occupy themselves in my land. Widad served light refreshments, and her guests played cards. Two of the women had brought children, so Widad's daughter was fully entertained in the garden.

After the last guest had departed, Widad helped her two Indian servants to clear the house for her husband's return in the evening. The phone rang, and Widad chatted much longer than she had realized. When she glanced through the window, she could see only darkness. She called out for one of the servants to go and bring in her child.

Widad's daughter was not to be found. After a frantic investigation, the last guest remembered that the child had been sitting on the kerb holding her doll. Widad's husband returned, and a search of the neighbourhood was begun. No-one had seen the child.

After weeks of searching, Widad and her husband could only surmise that their sole child had been abducted and more than likely murdered. When all hope for her precious daughter was gone, Widad found she could no longer reside in her villa in Riyadh. She returned to her family in war-torn Lebanon. To earn a living for them, her husband remained in his job, in the same villa.

Ten days after Widad arrived in Beirut, she heard a loud pounding on her apartment door. Frightened by the recent militia battles in her neighbourhood, she pretended that no-one was at home until she heard the voice of her neighbour screaming news from her husband in Riyadh.

The neighbour had just received a telephone call from Widad's husband. The line had been disconnected, but not before he had taken down an unbelievable message for Widad. She was to take the boat to Cyprus and go immediately to the Saudi embassy in that country. Her visa for re-entry to Saudi Arabia was waiting. She should return as quickly as possible to Riyadh. Their daughter was alive! She had come home.

Three long days were needed for the boat trip from Jounieh in Lebanon to Larnaca in Cyprus, so that her visa could be stamped, and then the plane trip to Riyadh. By the time Widad arrived in Riyadh, the startling truth of their child's whereabouts was revealed.

Once Widad's husband had recovered from the shock of driving up to his villa to find his long-lost daughter standing by the gate, he had taken the child to a clinic to ascertain if she had been raped, for that was his biggest fear. After a thorough examination, the discovery was chilling. The physician told the astonished father that his child had not suffered from sexual assault. However, she had recently undergone major surgery. Widad's daughter had been used as a kidney donor, the doctor told him. The child's scars were ragged, and infection had set in from filth.

Speculations were wild among the medical staff that examined the child, for many questions arose as to donor-typing and surgical procedures. It was unlikely that the child had undergone surgery in Saudi Arabia; at that time such an operation was not common in the kingdom.

When the police investigated, they suggested that the child had been taken to India by a rich

Saudi who had a child in need of a kidney transplant. Perhaps this person had abducted more than one child and had selected the one most suitable. No-one could determine the events that led to the surgery, for the child could only recall a long black car and a bad-smelling handkerchief held by a big man. She had awakened to severe pain. Isolated in a room with a nurse who could not speak English, she saw no other persons. The day of her release, she was blindfolded, driven for a long time and unexpectedly dropped at her door.

Without a doubt, whoever had abducted the child was wealthy, for when her father had jumped from the car and seized his daughter in his arms she was clutching a small bag filled with more than twenty thousand dollars in cash, along with many pieces of expensive jewellery.

Understandably, Widad despised my land and the oil riches that had shaped a people who considered their wealth the conqueror of all of life's obstacles. Sacred body parts were taken from innocent children and cash left to neutralize the anger of those injured! When Widad saw my look of utter disbelief at her story, she rushed to bring me her sleeping child and exposed the long red scar that showed clearly the moral depths to which some men will stoop.

I could only shake my head in horror.

Widad gazed at her sleeping daughter with rapt love; her return was nothing short of a miracle. Widad's parting words erased the fragile pride I still had left in my nationality: 'You, as a Saudi woman, have my sympathy. In my short time in your country, I saw the manner of your lives. For sure, money may smooth your paths, but such a people as the Saudis will not endure.' She paused for a moment of reflection before continuing: 'While it is true that financial desperation leads foreigners to Saudi Arabia, you are still hated by all that have known you.'

I last saw Widad at Heathrow, clinging fiercely to her precious child. After scheduled medical appointments for her daughter in London, Widad was willing to risk the bombs of Lebanese enemies over the hypocrisy and inconceivable evil of those of my land, the Saudis.

The children and I stayed overnight in London. We crossed the Channel by ferry and arrived in France the following day. From there we went by train to Zurich. I left the children in a hotel for a few hours while I emptied my son's Swiss bank account. With a draft for more than six million dollars in hand, I felt secure.

I hired a chauffeur-driven car to take us to Geneva; from there we flew back to London and then on to the Channel Islands. There, I deposited the money in an account in my name and kept the cash from the safe in Riyadh for our expenses. We then flew to Rome, where I hired another driver to take us back to Paris.

In Paris, I hired a full-time housekeeper, a driver and a bodyguard. Then, under an assumed name, I rented a villa on the outskirts of Paris. After such a confusing trail, I felt secure that Kareem would never find us.

A month later, I left the children in the care of the housekeeper while I flew to Frankfurt. There, I entered a bank and said that I was from Dubai and wanted to make a large deposit. Escorted into the bank manager's office and given preferential treatment, I removed large sums of money from my bag and laid the cash upon the manager's desk.

While he stared in shock at the money, I said that I needed to make a telephone call to my husband, who was away on business in Saudi Arabia. I was, of course, more than willing to pay for the call and laid five hundred dollars in his hand. The manager quickly got to his feet and practically clicked his heels together as he told me to take as much time as I needed. He closed the door and said he would be three offices down the hallway if I needed him.

I telephoned Sara. I knew her baby had been born by now, and she would more than likely be at home. I breathed a sigh of relief when one of the servants answered and said yes, the mistress was at home.

Sara screamed in relief when she heard my voice. I quickly asked her if her telephone lines were tapped, and she said she was not certain. In a rush of words she added that Kareem was out of his mind with worry. He had traced me from Dubai to London, but had lost all evidence of us from that point. He told the family what had happened and was truly filled with deep regret. He wanted nothing more than for me and the children to come home. Kareem had said we must talk.

I asked Sara to give my husband a brief message. I wanted him to know that I found him despicable; he would never see us again. Furthermore, I had made arrangements for citizenship for the children and me in another country. Once I was fully protected in a new land, I would advise my sisters of my new life, but Kareem must never know where I was. And, as an added worry for Kareem, I told Sara to let him know that Abdullah, his son, no longer wanted contact with his father.

With that, I left the subject of Kareem behind. With delight, I learned that Sara had a new baby son and that the rest of my family was in good health. She said Father and Ali were furious and insisted I return to Riyadh and adhere to Kareem's every wish, as was my duty. I had expected nothing more from those two of my very blood.

Sara tried to soothe me and asked if it would not be better to accept a new wife rather than to live my life as a refugee. I asked her if she would consider such an arrangement with Asad. Her silence was my answer.

After the call was made, I shoved my money back into my bag and slipped out of the bank without further notice from the eager manager. I felt a twinge of regret for my trickery, yet I knew I could not risk a call from a payphone, for an operator might well announce the country calling to hidden tape machines linked to Kareem.

In deep contemplation of Sara's words, I felt a smile spread across my face. My plan was working.

But I thought it best to let Kareem suffer additional agony. He would need some time to recognize that I would never accept the multiple-wife existence, no matter the ultimate price.

Actually, the children knew nothing of the drama in our lives. I had told them a convincing tale of their father's business taking him to the Orient for many months. Instead of remaining in Riyadh to suffer boredom, he had thought we would enjoy a pleasant time in the French countryside. Abdullah was curious as to why he received no calls from his father, but I kept him occupied with his lessons and numerous social activities; young minds adapt more easily than we could ever imagine. Our two daughters were still babies unable to consider dire circumstances. They had spent their lives travelling; the missing link was the absence of their father. I did my best to compensate.

I consoled myself by considering the alternatives. Life for my children in Riyadh with their parents in constant turmoil was unacceptable in my mind. Life without their mother would be unnatural. For if Kareem brought another woman into our lives the murder of my husband was a real possibility. What good would I be to the children without my head, for it would surely be parted from my body after I took the life of their father! For a moment I considered the sharp blade of the executioner's sword and shuddered at the thought that I might one day feel that coldness. I knew I was fortunate to be a royal, for I, like Ali so many years ago, could ease through difficult legal and ethical situations without the interference of the men of religion. Were I not of royal blood, the pounding of stones would end my life for such actions. But we royals keep our scandals inside our walls; no-one outside the family would know of my defection. Only Kareem could call for my death; and, no matter what my actions, I knew with certainty that my husband did not have the stomach to call for my blood.

I called Sara once a month. During this lengthy absence from my family and country, my days and nights were restless. But I knew there was gain to be had; my determination and patience would alter Kareem's plans of cluttering our lives with other wives.

Five months after my departure I agreed to speak with Kareem over the telephone. I flew to London to place the call. Our conversation convinced me that Kareem was desperate with desire to see me and the children. He would now enter the second stage of my carefully laid trap.

We made plans to meet in Venice the following weekend. My husband was stunned to see me accompanied by four hefty German bodyguards. I told Kareem I no longer trusted his word; he might have hired thugs to kidnap me and bundle me off to Riyadh to face the unjust way our legal system dealt with disobedient wives! His face began to redden. He swore he blushed with shame; I thought perhaps he was angered by his inability to control his wife.

Our impasse ended with a compromise. I would return to Riyadh only if Kareem signed a legal document stating that so long as he and I were wed he would not take another wife. If he were to break his word, I was to be given a divorce, custody of our children, and half of his fortune. In addition, I was to retain, under my control, the money I had taken out of our son's account in Switzerland. Kareem would replace Abdullah's funds. In addition, he would deposit a million dollars in each of our daughters' names in a Swiss bank account. I would keep in my possession our passports with updated papers stating we could travel without restrictions.

I told Kareem that after he signed the necessary papers I would remain in Europe with the children for an additional month. He had been warned of my determination; perhaps his desire for me would fade after consideration. I was not interested in replaying the same song twice. Kareem winced at my words, delivered with a hardness he had seldom heard.

I accompanied Kareem to the airport. My husband was not a happy man. I walked away less content than I had anticipated after the biggest gamble of my life had produced such a stunning victory. I had found that there is little joy derived from forcing a man to do what is right.

One month later I called Kareem to hear his decision. He confessed that I was his strength, his life. He wanted his family back, with everything as it was before. I bluntly told him that surely he could not expect to sever our love with the cold knife of indifference and then expect that a seamless union would remain in our grasp. We had been among the most fortunate of couples with love, family and unlimited wealth. He was the destroyer of all that, not I.

I returned to Riyadh. My husband was waiting, with trembling lips and a hesitant smile. Abdullah and my daughters went wild with joy at seeing their father. My pleasure slowly grew from the happiness of my children.

I found I was a stranger in my home, listless and unhappy. Too much had happened for me to go back to the Sultana of a year ago. I needed a real purpose, a challenge. I decided I would return to school; there were now colleges for women in my country. I would discover normal life and leave behind the mindless routines of a royal princess.

As far as Kareem was concerned, I could only wait for time to erase the bad memories of his behaviour. I had undergone a transition in the fight to save my marriage from the alien presence of another woman. Kareem had been the supreme figure in my life until he weakened our union with talk of wedding another. A substantial part of our love was destroyed. Now he was simply the father of my children and little more.

Kareem and I set about rebuilding our nest and providing our children with the tranquillity we so valued for our young. He said he keenly felt the loss to our love. He valiantly tried to redeem himself in my eyes. He said that if I continued to sit in judgement of his past behaviour we and the children might well lose the enjoyment of our future. I said little but knew it was true.

The trauma of our personal war was past, but the taste of peace was far from sweet. I reflected often on the emotional scars I had acquired in such a short lifetime; sadly, all my wounds had been inflicted by men. As a result, I could hold not even one member of the opposite sex in high esteem.

Chapter Twenty

The Great White Hope

Suddenly it was August 1990.

A glittering dinner-party was in progress at our villa in Jeddah when we heard the horrifying news that two of our neighbours were locked in a deadly struggle across the border in the tiny country of Kuwait. Kareem and I were entertaining twenty guests from our exclusive circle when the news was shouted out from the top of the stairwell by our son, Abdullah, who had been listening to the BBC on his shortwave radio. After a long dry silence, a disbelieving roar rose throughout the room.

Few Saudis, even those royals involved in the negotiations between Kuwait and Iraq, had really believed that Saddam Hussein would invade Kuwait. Kareem had been present at the conference that ended in a stalemate on that very day, 1 August 1990, in Jeddah. The crown prince of Kuwait, Sheikh Saud Al Abdullah Al Salem Al Sabah, had just returned to Kuwait with the hope that war could be averted.

When our son cried out that Iraqi troops were advancing on Kuwait City, the seriousness of the attack was evident. I wondered if the huge family of Al Sabah would escape with their lives. As a mother, my thoughts were with the innocent children.

I watched Kareem's face across the crowded room. Underneath his calm façade, he was furious. The Iraqis had gone against their word; as a result, the leaders of our government had played a role in minimizing the danger. His brown eyes had a glow that caused a shiver to run down my spine. I knew that he, along with other Al Sa'uds present, would soon leave for a hastily called family conference.

I had heard Kareem speak often of the barbarity of the Baath regime in Iraq. He had said many times that the Iraqis were by nature aggressive and prone to violence in their private lives. He thought that might explain their national acquiescence in a brutal police state.

I myself knew little of the true politics of the area, for Saudi news is heavily censored and our men reveal little of their political activities to their wives. But Kareem's opinion was justified by a story I had heard from an Iraqi. Several years ago, while dining out in London, Kareem, Asad, Sara and I had listened in complete fascination as a casual Iraqi acquaintance bragged of killing his father over a misunderstanding over money.

The son had sent the father his earnings from an investment in Paris. The widowed father had become enamoured with a village woman and had spent the son's earnings on the purchase of expensive gifts for his mistress. When the son returned to Iraq on a visit, he discovered that his money had been squandered. He knew what he had to do, which was to shoot his father dead.

With a loud shout, Kareem had protested at the unbelievable act. The Iraqi was surprised at my husband's bewilderment and disbelief, and responded: 'But he had spent my money! It was mine!' As far as the man was concerned, he had had a reasonable cause to take the life of his father.

His act was so unthinkable and repulsive to Kareem that, departing from his usual mild manner, he jumped towards the man and told him to leave our table. The Iraqi left in a rush. Kareem muttered that such attitudes were not uncommon in Iraq, but social acceptance of murdering one's father found great doubt in his mind.

Kareem, like all Saudi men, revered his father and showed him much respect. He would not think of raising his voice or even presenting his back to his father. I had seen Kareem leave a room backwards on numerous occasions.

Like most Arabs, I am sorry to acknowledge, I am a heavy smoker, yet I was never allowed to smoke in front of Kareem's father.

Kareem, as a member of an outdated monarchy, was acutely interested in the movements of the Middle East that had ousted royals from their throne. As Arab history unfolded, kings were unceremoniously dumped, and quite a number had ended with their bodies riddled with bullet holes. As a royal, Kareem felt fear at the possibility of unrest visiting our land.

In addition, like most Arabs, Kareem felt great shame at the never-ending spectacle of Muslim fighting Muslim. For the most part, we Saudis laid down our arms when our country was bonded from the land of tribes to a kingdom united. Blood-letting is not the manner our men choose to fight our enemies; purchasing power is considered the civilized method of victory.

But, for now, our lives were erupting with the insanity of the drama of real war. While our men rushed to intrude on the momentous decisions of diplomacy, we women called for Abdullah to bring his radio to the sitting-room. The news was sparse, but appeared to be going from bad to worse for the unfortunate Kuwaitis. Before we retired, we learned that Kuwait was occupied; our country was being invaded by thousands of refugees. We Saudis felt ourselves out of harm's way and gave no thought to our personal safety or to danger for our country.

The following week would shake our confidence in our observations. As Saddam's soldiers drew near to our borders, rumours filled our country that he had in mind to swallow two neighbours in one meal!

Streams of Saudis joined the Kuwaitis in the exodus from the eastern area of our country. We received frantic telephone calls from nervous family members with the news that Riyadh was crowded with thousands of panicked people. Soon, many Saudis felt Riyadh to be unsafe; the planes and roads to Jeddah were jammed. Madness had erupted in our quiet kingdom.

Sara and I were thrilled to hear that Kuwaiti

women, who are allowed to drive and go unveiled, were even driving down our roads and into the streets of our capital. No Western women could ever imagine our mixed emotions. We were crashing into a storm and, while our glee was mixed with wonder, at the same moment we were frothing with jealousy that our Arab sisters were driving cars and exposing their naked faces in our land! Were our essentials of life, the veil and Saudi customs, now considered nothing more than clutter so easily dismissed in the heat of hostility? Life had been easy for these Kuwaiti women, in stark contrast with our heavy endurance of male mastery. The sting of envy bubbled through our veins. While sympathetic to these women who had lost their country, their homes and loved ones, we were undeniably swollen with resentment at the ones who had exposed the ridiculousness of our puritanical situation. How we hungered for the rights they had assumed with such ease!

There was a rumour a minute in those dark days of August. When Kareem told me that the latest rumour was true, that our king had agreed for foreign troops to travel to our land, I knew our lives would never again be the same.

With the arrival of the American troops, Saudi feminists' most ambitious dreams felt the spark of life. No Saudi had ever imagined seeing women in military uniforms, guarding that ultimate bastion of male dominance that is Saudi Arabia. It was unthinkable! Our men of religion were aghast and spoke with heavy tidings of the coming harm to our land.

The disruption to our lives can never be measured. No earthquake could have shaken us more.

While I was happy at the turn of events, and felt the change would be beneficial, many Saudi women raged with contempt. There were those I deemed silly who fretted with the possibility of these foreign women stealing their husbands! I suppose such a worry was real, for most Saudi women endure their husbands' trips abroad with trepidation, few believing their spouses would remain faithful in the midst of Western blonde temptations. Many of my friends reassured themselves with the thought that only a prostitute or a woman with little else to promote herself would consider such degradation as shared living-quarters with strange men. Saudi women whispered that they had read that these American women were allowed in the armies solely to service the men and keep them from sexual deprivation.

Our emotions were in conflict over these superwomen who came and went at will in a country not their own. We had known little of American female soldiers, for our country censors all news of women who control their destiny from the citizens of Saudi Arabia. And during our infrequent travels abroad our paths led us to shopping districts, not military bases. When Asad brought Sara uncensored copies of American and European magazines and newspapers, we were astonished to see that the women soldiers were quite attractive. Many were mothers.

Our understanding could not let us imagine such freedom. Our modest goals involved only the acts of uncovering our faces, driving and working. Our land now harboured those of our sex perfectly prepared to meet men in battle.

We women of Arabia were on an emotional roller-coaster. One moment we hated all the foreign women, both Kuwaiti and American, in our land. At the same moment, the Kuwaiti women warmed our hearts with their show of defiance of our centuries-old tradition of male supremacy. While conservative, they had not completely succumbed to the insane social custom of male dominance. Yet moments of jealousy came and went as we realized that they had somehow lifted the status of all Muslim women by their very attitude, while we Saudi women had done little to elevate our lives other than to complain. Where had we gone wrong? How had they managed to discard the veil – and obtain freedom to drive at the same time?

We felt the agony of envy, yet we were ecstatic, too. Confused at the happenings around us, we women met daily to dissect the shift of attitudes and the sudden universal awakenings to the plight of Saudi women. In the past, few women dared express their desire for reform in Islamic Saudi Arabia, for the hope of success was so dim and the penalties too severe for challenging the status quo. After all, our country is the home of Islam; we Saudis are the 'keepers of the faith'. To cover our shame at our forced repressions, we spoke proudly to our Kuwaiti sisters of our unique heritage: we Saudi women hold high the symbols of Muslim belief the world over. Then, suddenly, middle-class Saudi women threw down their shackles. They faced the fundamentalists head-on and called out for the world to free them in the same instant they freed the besieged Kuwaitis!

Sara caused me to tremble when she rushed into the palace screaming. My only thought was that of chemicals invading the air my children were breathing! Had an enemy plane filled with chemical bombs escaped the detection of the forces guarding our land? I stood still, holding my breath, undecided as to where to go or what to do. Any moment I would more than likely be writhing on the floor, thinking my last thoughts. I cursed myself! I should have followed Kareem's wishes and taken our young ones to London, far from the possibility of a painful slow death for those I had carried in my womb.

Sara's words finally penetrated my fear, and the news she told rung as a celebration in my ears. Asad had just called her; Saudi, yes *Saudi*, women were actually driving cars up and down the streets of Riyadh!

I cried out with joy; Sara and I hugged and danced. My youngest daughter began to sob in fear when she came into the room and saw her mother and aunty rolling and screaming on the floor. I soothed her fears when I grabbed her in my arms and assured her our silly nonsense was a result of great happiness; my prayers had been answered.

The American presence was going to alter our lives in a wonderful, wonderful way!

Kareem burst through the door with a dark look in his eyes. He wanted to know what the trouble was; he could hear our cries in the garden.

Did he not know? Women had broken the first of the unyielding barriers – they were claiming their right to drive! Kareem's response sobered our reaction. I knew his opinion on the matter; there is no mention of such in our religion, he would say. He, like many other Saudi men, had always thought it absurd that Saudi women were not allowed to drive.

With a weary tone, my husband now voiced the unthinkable. 'This is exactly the type of action that we did not want you women to take! We have been battling the fanaticals for every concession! Their biggest fear is that our decisions will result in women moving towards more privileges. What is more important to you, Sultana,' he cried out, 'to have soldiers to protect our lives from the Iraqi menace, or to choose this time to drive?'

I was furious with Kareem. Many times he had protested against the silly custom that chains Saudi women to their homes. And now his fear of the men of religion brought his cowardly soul to the surface. How I yearned to be wed to a warrior, a man with the hot flame of righteousness to guide his life.

In a temper, I hotly replied that we women could not be 'beggars with conditions'. What luxury to be able to pick our time and place! We had to take what small opportunities were presented. Now was our time, too, and Kareem should stand by our side. Surely, the throne would not be toppled over the mere fact that women drove in our streets!

My husband was angry at all women at that moment and told me in a hard voice that this incident would delay women's causes for decades. He told us our joy would turn to sorrow when we witnessed the punishment meted out to those so foolish. The proper time will come for women to drive, he warned, but this was not the moment for such drama. His words hung in the air as he made his retreat. A man had spoken!

Kareem had stolen our small moment of pleasure. I hissed like a cat at his back, and Sara's lips trembled as she held back her smile. She dismissed Kareem's words with contempt. She reminded me that the men in our family talked sympathetically about women's rights, but in reality they were little different from the extremists. All men liked a heavy hand on the heads of their women. Otherwise, we would have seen some lifting of our heavy burdens. Our husbands and father were of the royal family that ruled the land; if they could not help us, who could?

'The Americans!' I said with a smile. 'The Americans.'

Kareem's words proved to be true. The forty-seven brave young women who demonstrated against the informal ban on driving became the scapegoats of every grievance the *mutawas* considered. They were women of the middle class, women who were teachers of other women or students – our thinkers and doers. As a result of their bravery, their lives were devastated by their actions: passports taken, jobs lost and families harassed.

While shopping in a local mall, Sara and I overheard young religious students as they aroused Saudi men against these women by saying they were leaders of vice and made their living as prostitutes; they had been denounced in the mosque as such by men who had reason to know! My sister and I lingered at a shop window to hear the young men loudly proclaim that the temptations transported from the West would cause the honour of all Saudis to disintegrate!

I wanted to meet the women, to share in their glory. When I proposed my idea to Kareem, his reaction violently closed the possibility. He threatened to have me shut in the house should I attempt such an outrage. At that moment I hated my husband, for I knew he was capable of fulfilling his threat; he was suddenly wild with fear for our country as well as of the havoc we women could bring to the royal family.

Within a few days I built up my courage and tried to locate those brave women. I returned to the mall. When I saw throngs of men in a circle, I told my Filipino driver to go to them and say he was a Muslim (there are a number of Muslim Filipinos in Saudi Arabia) and request the paper with the telephone numbers of the 'fallen women'. He was to say that he wanted to call their fathers or their husbands to protest at the behaviour of their daughters or wives.

He returned with the paper; I warned him against telling Kareem. Fortunately, unlike Arab servants, the Filipinos tend to avoid our family conflicts and make no mention of our small freedoms to our husbands.

The paper listed thirty names and telephone numbers. My hand shook as I dialled the first number. Only three calls were answered in weeks of constant dialling. No matter what I said, I was told that I must have the wrong number. The harassment had been so insistent that the families chose either denial or not to answer their phones.

On his way out of the country, Ali came by to visit. He and his family of four wives and nine children were travelling to Paris for a few weeks. My brother claimed he wanted to fight the Iraqis, but his plate was filled with business responsibilities that were indeed more important to our country than another man in uniform. He, Ali, must do his duty and leave Saudi Arabia.

I knew my brother was going to wait out the war in safety. I had no desire on that day to confront his cowardice; I merely smiled and wished him a good trip.

The topic of the women drivers was introduced when Ali hinted slyly that one of the protesters had been put to death by her father for shaming the family. The father had thought that by executing his daughter, the religious fanatics would leave him and the remainder of the family in peace. Ali actually smiled; how I hated this brother of mine. He was well suited to a land that kept women at his feet. He would fight to the end to keep women in a lowly position, for a man such as he would be terrorized by a woman of strength and character.

When I questioned Kareem, he claimed not to know of the incident, but told me to put it out of my mind. This was not our affair. He mentioned that he would not be surprised, since the families of the women had suffered along with the trouble-makers. He smugly said, 'I told you so,' reminding me of his prediction on the day of the protest. I felt that Kareem had tricked me with his past talk of free women; surely he now was little advanced over Ali in his thinking. Was there not one man in my country who desired women's bonds loosened?

The rumour of the death of the young woman held fast in our land, and to this day her fate has not been denied or confirmed; it hangs over us women, a veiled threat of the ultimate sacrifice awaiting those with courage.

The war we so dreaded came and went. Our men fought and died, but I heard from Kareem that many of our soldiers had not fought bravely. In fact the Allies had found it necessary to invent tactics to ensure that we Arabs were not offended when the truth about our warriors was revealed. My husband blushed when he told of Saudis running away from, instead of towards, the enemy. Our only pride in our military was for the prowess of our pilots, who performed with honour.

Asad gave his opinion that we should not feel

shame but relief at this assessment. A strong military would be a risk to our very heads; the throne could not survive a precise military machine. In the Arab world, a capable military overthrows monarchies; for truly people desire a voice in the policies of their land. Our family had seen such happenings and maintained a family-run organization of men unwilling to fight. Certainly, our ruling family is sly and purposely keeps the Saudi soldier slovenly and far from his peak.

In the end, events of the war served to abort our confidence in legendary social change for the women of Saudi Arabia. The fight that brought forth Western eyes from around the world to probe the disorders of our society ended all too quickly. The fading power of our enemy, Saddam, lifted the interest in our plight and transferred the whispered pledges of help to the distressing predicament of the Kurds, who were languishing in the mountain snows.

At the end of the war, our men tended to their prayers with great diligence, for they had been saved from the threat of invading armies – and free women.

Who is to say which threat gave them the most worry?

Epilogue

The haunting sound that lifts the heart of every Muslim with joy filled the air. The faithful were being called to pray. 'God is great, there are no other Gods, but God; and Muhammad was his Prophet. Come to prayer, come to prayer. God is great; there is no God, but God.'

It was dusk; the big yellow circle that was the sun was slowly sinking. For faithful Muslims, the time had come for the fourth prayer of the day.

I stood on the bedroom balcony and watched my husband and son leave our palace grounds and walk, hand in hand, to the mosque. I saw that many men were gathering, greeting each other with the spirit of brotherhood.

The turbulent memories of my childhood came back to me, and I was a young girl again, shut out from the love exclusive to my father and his treasured son, Ali. Nearly thirty years had passed, yet nothing had changed. My life had come full circle.

Father and Ali, Kareem and Abdullah, yesterday, today and tomorrow, immoral practices passed from father to son. Men I loved, men I detested, leaving a legacy of shame in their treatment of women.

My eyes followed the movements of my beloved flesh, my most precious blood; my husband and son entered the mosque hand-in-hand, without me.

I felt quite the loneliest figure ever to have lived.

Afterword

At the end of the Gulf War of 1991, there was a universal desire for peace to come to the turbulent Middle East. Endless proposals from leaders of many nations were presented to those in power in an effort to end the interminable violence in this part of the world.

Along with a desire for peace, many who care about the Middle East and its people yearned for change in ancient traditions that have no religious basis yet serve to bind the women of the Middle East to the whims of the men who sired or wed them. While the reality of lasting peace gains momentum in the diplomatic moves of President George Bush, the elusive dream of freedom for women in Arabia languishes. Western men in power have little interest in holding high the banner of justice for ones without political prestige; that is, women.

The Gulf War to free Kuwait also turned out to be a war of sharply growing conflict between the men and women of Arabia. Where women saw hope for social change, men felt the danger of any change in a society that differed little from what it was two centuries ago. Husbands, fathers and sons were unwilling to challenge radical religious forces for women's rights. The cause of freedom for women in Arabia withered in a backlash from religious extremists, for the arrival of foreign troops had unleashed their power. The promise of bitter strife from the men of religion spread fear throughout the land. Sadly, in 1992, Sultana, along with other Saudi women, has been forced to retreat to the trenches of yesterday.

Surprisingly, the rich and powerful, for the first time, are now targeted by the religious police and are suffering raids and arrests like other Saudis. Ordinary citizens, instead of being concerned over the loss of freedom for all citizens, laugh with abandon at the thought of the royals and rich citizens enduring the same fierce scrutiny from the *mutawas* that they themselves have always known. Freedom to drive, to toss aside the veil, to travel without permission are lost dreams among more life-threatening concerns such as the growing menace of regional religious extremists. Who knows when another opportunity with such potential for social change as a war will come for the women of Arabia?

As modern societies strive to improve the living conditions of all peoples, women throughout the world still face the authentic threat of torture or death under the primitive control of the male sex. The seams of the cloak of female slavery are sewn with the strong thread of male resolve to cling to their historic power over women.

In the spring of 1983 I met a Saudi woman

who has changed my life for ever. You know her as Sultana. Our mutual attraction and desire for friendship flourished, for almost instantly we were in harmony. Sultana's passion for life and her amazing mental capacity altered my Westerner's incorrect perceptions of the 'women in black', whom at that time I viewed as an incomprehensible species of the human race.

As an American who had lived among the Saudis since 1978, I had met and socialized with many Saudi women. But, to my foreign eyes, all presented the same tainted mask of defeat. Life for the rich merchant class, or the royal family of the cities to which they belonged, was too comfortable to shift the delicate balance of their lives. The bedouin women of the villages bore their intolerable life with surprising dignity. Indeed, upon meeting me, they moaned in sympathy for one such as I who was 'forced' to venture out into the cruel world on my own, without the protection or guidance of a man. 'Haram [What a pity],' they would say, while patting my shoulder and expressing their despair for one such as I. Behind the veneer of contentment or sympathy, the truth of their condition was concealed.

Sultana exposed me to the vociferous wrath that borders on despair in the minds of many Saudi women hidden behind the veil. With this new perspective, I became convinced that Saudi women did little to influence Saudi culture; instead Saudi culture had created them.

In the autumn of 1988, Sultana approached me

with the request that I, her friend, write her life-story. Much had transpired in her young life and in the lives of other Saudi women of her acquaintance that deserved redress, she believed. But my common sense prevailed. I expressed my doubt of the ultimate advantage such a risky endeavour would bring for her. Other thoughts of my personal interests came to mind and valid excuses for my pacifism sprang to my lips: I loved the Middle East; my dearest friends were in the area; I knew numerous happy Saudi women.

My doubt and denial had no end, for I had personally wearied of the constant criticism by Western journalists of the land I now called my home. Undeniably, the isolation of the Muslims sprouted from endless negative reports from the world's press. An overabundance of articles and books censorious of the Middle East were already in print; I did not want to join the common pattern of 'Arab-bashing', committed by many who took shelter under the economic umbrella of the oil-rich land.

I told Sultana: 'No, I do not wish to condemn.' My desire was to show the Arabs in the favoured light of understanding, to point out their kindness, hospitality and generosity.

Sultana, the princess feminist, forced my eyes upon the naked truth. While it is true that much good thrives in Saudi Arabia, there could be no celebration of life in this society until its women were free to live without fear. Sultana pointed out the conspicuous: 'Jean, as a woman, your loyalties are misplaced!' Sultana could not face defeat: she continued to expound upon the reality of the corruption of her own sex. She was a better woman than I. She did not flinch from risk of life or limb for the cause she sought.

As is the story of her life, Sultana overcame all obstacles, including my stubborn resistance. After I made the difficult decision to collaborate with her to write her story, I knew in my heart that I could have taken no other course. The Christian West and the Islamic East are knitted together by a bond that can withstand the fear I felt in the conception of this undertaking. This was a book that was meant to be.

Much has been sacrificed by many people in the writing of this book: peace of mind for the safety of Sultana and her family; fear for friends still in Arabia who have no knowledge of the existence of this book; but, most of all, I face the loss of the love, support and companionship of Sultana, the person who has thrilled and inspired me with her fiery spirit. For the sad fact is, the moment this publication becomes common knowledge, our paths can no longer cross. My dearest friend will be locked away from me behind the darkness of silence. This is our loving mutual decision, I should add. To reveal our association would ensure grave punishment for many people; most of all, for Sultana.

At our final meeting, in August 1991, a feeling of perverse futility mired my joy, while I marvelled at Sultana's wave of optimism. She felt joyous hope at the outcome of our endeavour and declared that she would rather perish than live as one conquered. Her words gave me strength for the approaching storm: 'Until these despicable facts are made public, there can be no help; this book is like the first steps of a baby who could never run without that first brave attempt to stand on its own. Jean, you and I will stir the ashes and start a fire. Tell me, how can the world come to our aid if it does not hear our cry? I feel it deep in my soul; this is the beginning of change for our women.'

Many years of my adult life were spent living in the Middle East. For three years, I have been reading and rereading Sultana's notes and diaries. Clandestine meetings have been held with her in many of the major capitals of the world. I have shown her the final manuscript, which she read with great delight – and pain. After Sultana read the final sentence of this book, my friend began to weep. When she composed herself, she said I had perfectly captured her spirit, her life's experiences, as clearly as if I had been by her side, as indeed I had for many years. She then asked that I fill in the blanks of her life not covered in her diaries. Here is what Sultana wants you to know.

Sultana's father still lives. He maintains four wives and four palaces in his six favourite cities throughout the world. He has many young children from his youthful wives. Sadly, his relationship with Sultana has not been tempered by age. He rarely visits any of his daughters, but takes great pride in his sons and grandsons.

Ali has not experienced maturity, and his habits remain much the same as those of a spoiled child. His streaks of cruelty are reserved for his female children, whom he treats as he saw his sisters managed by his father. Today, Ali has four wives and countless mistresses. Recently, he was chastised by the king for excessive corruption, but no action was taken to curb his behaviour.

Sara and Asad have maintained their wedded bliss. As of this date, they are the parents of five lively children. Who knows if Huda's prediction of six will come true? Only Sara, of all Sultana's sisters, knows of the existence of this book.

The remainder of Sultana's sisters and their families are well.

Omar was killed in a car accident on the road to Dammam. His family in Egypt is supported by Sultana's father.

Randa's father purchased a villa in the south of France, where Randa now lives most of the year. She has not remarried after being divorced by Sultana's father. There is a rumour in the family that Randa has a French lover, but there is doubt if this is true.

Sultana never again heard from Wafa; she imagines her in a village surrounded by a large number of children, leading the life so dreaded by educated young women in Saudi Arabia.

Marci returned to the Philippines and realized her life's ambition as Sultana knew she would. She worked as a nurse for a while in Riyadh, but once wrote Sultana a letter outlining her plans to take a job in Kuwait; restrictions in Saudi Arabia were too severe to tolerate, she said. Sultana has not heard from Marci since. She fervently hopes that Marci was not raped or killed during the Iraqi invasion, the fate of many beautiful young women.

Huda died years ago. She was buried in the sands of Arabia, far from her native land of Sudan.

Saddest of all, Sameera remains locked in the woman's room. Tahani heard two years ago that Sameera had gone mad. The servants reported that she had screamed for days on end and finally began to speak in a gibberish that none could understand. They occasionally hear her sobbing, and the food-tray is emptied daily, so she still lives. The family swears that the girl will be released when the old man of the family dies, but he is in fine health even at an old age. In any case, it is thought that freedom will no longer benefit Sameera.

Sultana received her master's degree in philosophy two years ago. She does not work at her profession, but says the knowledge she acquired has given her an inner peace and a feeling of oneness with the world. In her studies, she discovered that many other peoples have survived grave injustices. Human progress is indeed slow, she has found, but brave souls continue to push forward, and she is proud to be one of them.

Kareem and Sultana are settled into a relationship that is bound by custom and the mutual love of their children. She regrets that their love never fully revived after the incident of the second wife.

Six years ago Sultana was stricken with a venereal

disease; after much distress, Kareem admitted that he participated in a weekly adventure of sex with strangers. Several of the high-ranking princes send a weekly plane to Paris to pick up prostitutes for a trip to Saudi Arabia. A madam then selects the most beautiful girls from all around the world who ply their trade in France. Each Tuesday they board a plane to Arabia; the following Monday the weary prostitutes are flown out. Kareem told of special palaces in the major cities of Saudi Arabia that house up to a hundred prostitutes. Most of the high-ranking princes of the royal family are invited to participate and to feel free to select any of the women. For these men, women continue to exist only as objects of pleasure or as a vehicle to provide sons.

After the scare of the disease, Kareem promised he would avoid the weekly tryst, but Sultana says she knows that he is weak in the face of such a feast, and that he continues to indulge himself without shame. Their wonderful love has vanished except in memory; Sultana says she will stand with her husband and continue her struggle for the sake of her daughters.

Sultana says that the saddest aspect of her life continues to be watching the black forms of her two young daughters, now wrapped in the black cloaks and veils that, after all the years of rebellion, still cling to a new generation of young women in Saudi Arabia. As always, primitive customs determine women's roles in Saudi society.

The presence of the American troops during the

Gulf War that gave such hope of freedom for Sultana has only brought the *mutawas* greater strength; they now boast of ruling the king who occupies the throne.

Sultana asked that I tell the reader this. Her defiant spirit still rebels through the pages of this book. But her rebellion must be kept in secret; for, although she has the heart for all of life's trials, she could not face the possibility of losing her precious children. Who knows what punishment might be meted out to the one who speaks out truthfully about the hidden lives of women in the land of the two holiest shrines of Islam?

Sultana's destiny was formed in January 1902 when her grandfather Abdul Aziz fought and regained the lands of Saudi Arabia. A dynasty was born. Princess Sultana Al Sa'ud will remain by the side of her husband, Prince Kareem Al Sa'ud, in the Royal House of Al Sa'ud of the Kingdom of Saudi Arabia.

God [illegible] that [illegible] such [illegible] of freedom for [illegible] tans has only brought the [illegible] greater [illegible] they now [illegible] of calling the king [illegible] as the [illegible]

[illegible] the de- [illegible] spirit [illegible] through the pages of [illegible] book. [illegible] although the [illegible] the [illegible] Who knows [illegible] might [illegible] and [illegible] of [illegible] in the land of the two holiest shrines of Islam.

[illegible] history [illegible] when [illegible] grandfather Abdul Aziz fought and [illegible] gained the lands of [illegible] dynasty [illegible] by the [illegible] the Royal House of Al Saud in the Kingdom of Saudi Arabia.

Appendix A

The Laws of Saudi Arabia

The criminal laws of Saudi Arabia adhere to strict Islamic precepts. The word *Islam* means 'surrender to the will of God'. The most important concept of Islam is the Shari'a, or the 'path', which embraces the total way of life ordained by God. All peoples of the Islamic religion are expected to conduct their lives by the traditional values set by Muhammad, the Prophet of God, who was born in AD 570 and died in AD 632.

It is difficult for most Westerners to understand the complete and total submission of Muslims to the laws of the Koran in every aspect of their daily life. The Koran, along with traditions set by Muhammad, is the law of the land in Saudi Arabia.

While living in Saudi Arabia, I once asked a noted scholar of Islam, who made his living as a lawyer, to describe the application of justice in Saudi Arabia that stems from the teachings of the Prophet. His explanations helped dispel my misunderstandings of Saudi law.

Here is a portion of his written report to me that I thought might appeal to the reader's interest:

(1) There are four main sources of the Shari'a: the Koran, which is compiled from thousands of religious verses revealed by God through his Prophet, Muhammad; the Sunna, which are the traditions the Prophet addressed that are not recorded in the Koran; the Ijma, which are the perceptions of the Ulema, or religious scholars; and the Qiyas, which is a method whereby known jurists agree upon new legal principles.

(2) The king of Saudi Arabia is not exempt from the regulations set forth by the Shari'a.

(3) The court system itself is complicated, but if a judgement is taken to appeal it is reviewed by the court of appeals. This court, usually consisting of three members, increases to five members if the sentence imposes death or mutilation. The king is the final arbitrator who serves as a final court of appeal and as a source of pardon.

(4) Crimes are classified into three divisions: Hudud, Tazir and Qisas. Crimes of Hudud are crimes that are denounced by God; the punishment is made known in the Koran. Crimes of Tazir are given to the appropriate authority to determine punishment. Crimes of Qisas give the victim the right to retaliate.

CRIMES OF HUDUD

Crimes of Hudud include theft, drinking of alcohol, defamation of Islam, fornication and adultery.

Persons found guilty of theft are punished by payment of fines, imprisonment, or amputation of the right hand. (The left hand is amputated if the right has already been amputated.)

Persons found guilty of drinking, selling or buying alcohol, sniffing drugs, taking injections of drugs or stirring drugs into dough are punished by a sentence of eighty lashes.

Persons found guilty of defamation of Islam are sentenced according to the circumstances. The harshness of the sentence varies depending on whether the person is a Muslim or a non-Muslim. Flogging is the general punishment for Muslims.

Persons found guilty of fornication are flogged. Men are flogged while standing and women while sitting. The faces, heads and vital organs of the guilty are protected. The usual number is forty lashes, but this number may vary according to the circumstances.

Adultery is the most serious of crimes. If the guilty party is married, he or she is sentenced to death by stoning, beheading or shooting. Stoning is the usual method of punishment. Proof of this crime must be established by confession or by four witnesses to the act.

CRIMES OF TAZIR

The crimes of Tazir are similar to misdemeanour crimes in America. There is no set punishment, but each person is judged on an individual basis, according to the seriousness of the crime and the sorrow shown by the criminal.

CRIMES OF QISAS

If a person is found guilty of crimes against an individual or his family, the aggrieved family has the right to retaliate. The sentence is decided in private by the family, and the actual punishment is carried out in private.

If murder has been committed, the family has the right to kill the murderer in the same method their loved one was murdered, or in any method they choose.

If a member of the family was accidentally killed (such as in a road accident), the family of the deceased may collect 'blood money'. In the past, camels were used as pay for blood money; today the rate of exchange is in currency. There are set damages according to the various circumstances: the payment can be anywhere from 120,000 to 300,000 Saudi riyals ($45,000–80,000). If a woman is killed, the payment is half that of a man.

If a person cuts off another person's body part, the family or the victim may commit the same act upon the guilty party.

WHO MAY TESTIFY IN CRIMINAL PROCEEDINGS

The witness must be deemed sane, the age of an adult, and a Muslim. Non-Muslims may *not* testify in criminal court. Women may not testify unless it is a personal matter that did not occur in the sight of men. Actually, the testimony of a woman is not regarded as fact but rather as presumption. The court may decide whether the testimony is valid according to the circumstances.

WHY WOMEN ARE FORBIDDEN TO TESTIFY IN CRIMINAL PROCEEDINGS

There are four reasons given why women's testimony is not valid in a Saudi court.

(1) Women are much more emotional than men and will, as a result of their emotions, distort their testimony.

(2) Women do not participate in public life, so they will not be capable of understanding what they observe.

(3) Women are dominated completely by men, who by the grace of God are deemed superior; therefore, women will give testimony according to what the last man told them.

(4) Women are forgetful, and their testimony cannot be considered reliable.

Appendix B

Glossary

abaaya: a long black cloak worn over the clothing of Saudi Arabian women.

Abu Dhabi: a city located in the United Arab Emirates.

Al Sa'ud: the family that rules the kingdom of Saudi Arabia.

Asir: the traditional name for the south-west region of Saudi Arabia.

Baath: a political movement that began in Syria and spread to Iraq. Arab unity is at the centre of its doctrine.

Bahrain: an island nation that is linked to Saudi Arabia by a causeway.

bedouin: the original Arabs, a nomadic desert people.

Dammam: the city in Saudi Arabia where oil was first struck in 1938.

Dar'iyah: the old city of Riyadh.

Dubai: a city located in the United Arab Emirates.

Empty Quarter: the great desert occupying the south-east corner of Saudi Arabia. Its Arabic name is Rub al Khali.

ghutra: the Arabian headdress worn by men.

Haj: the pilgrimage, one of the five pillars of Islam.

The journey to Makkah is the life's ambition of most Muslims. All Muslims are required to make this journey, if they can afford it.

halawa: the ceremony of removing body hair.

Haram: an expression that means 'pity' or 'sympathy'.

Hijaz: the traditional name for the area of western Arabia. Jeddah, located on the Red Sea, is in the Hijaz area.

houmous: an Arabic dish made of chickpeas, usually scooped up with a piece of pitta bread.

Hudud: crimes of a serious nature which are denounced by God in the Koran.

ibn: means 'son of' (Khalid ibn Faisal, son of Faisal).

igaal: the black cord worn on top of the Arabian headdress.

Ijma: perceptions of the Koran by the religious scholars of Islam.

Jeddah: a beautiful city in Saudi Arabia located on the Red Sea. Jeddah is popular with the expatriate population, who swim and dive in the pristine waters.

Jerusalem: the third-holiest city of Islam, now under the control of the Israelis.

Koran: the holy book of the Islamic faith containing the words of God as they were given to the Prophet Muhammad.

Kurds: a transnational ethnic and linguistic group numbering 18 per cent of Iraq's population. Nationalistic, with the aim of forming their own country, this group of people continues to fight for Kurdish autonomy.

kutab: a common group method of teaching girls in Saudi Arabia prior to the days of education for females.

laban: a refreshing buttermilk-like drink common in the Middle East.

Madinah: the second-holiest city of Islam, called 'the city of the Prophet', and burial-place of Prophet Muhammad.

Makkah: the holiest city of Islam, where God revealed His will to Prophet Muhammad. It is the destination of millions of Muslim pilgrims each year.

Malaz: a residential section of Riyadh popular with wealthy Saudis.

Manama: the capital city of Bahrain, an island nation connected to Saudi Arabia by a causeway.

Mena House: a popular hotel in Cairo frequented by tourists.

Mismaak: the fortress in Riyadh used by the Rasheed clan in the battle of 1902 that returned the Al Sa'uds to power.

mutawa: the morals police of Islam.

Najd: the traditional name for central Arabia. Riyadh is located in this region. The inhabitants are generally known for their conservative behaviour. The Al Sa'ud family are Najdis.

Nasiriyah: a residential section of Riyadh inhabited by members of the royal family and exceptionally wealthy Saudis.

Qisas: a crime committed against a person. The victim or the victim's family can retaliate against the one convicted of such a crime.

Qiyas: the method of agreement of new legal principles in Islam.
Ramadan: the Islamic month of fasting when Muslims worldwide celebrate God's gift of the Koran to man.
Riyadh: the capital of Saudi Arabia.
riyal: the Saudi riyal is the currency of Saudi Arabia.
Shari'a: the law of God for those belonging to the Islamic faith.
Shiite: the branch of Islam that split from the Sunni majority over the issue of the Prophet Muhammad's successor.
souq: the native market-place or bazaar.
Sunna: the traditions of the Islamic faith as addressed by Prophet Muhammad.
Sunni: the majority orthodox branch of Islam. Saudi Arabia is 95 per cent Sunni.
Suras: the chapters of the Koran. There are 114 Suras.
Taif: a mountain-resort village in Saudi Arabia located near Makkah.
Tazir: crimes of misdemeanour under Islamic law.
thobe: a long shirt-like garment worn by Saudi men. Traditionally, the *thobe* is made of white cotton, but during the cool winter months men often wear a *thobe* of a heavier fabric and a darker colour. (As soon as a male child can walk, he is dressed in a tiny *thobe* and headdress identical to his father's.)
Ulema: Islamic religious scholars who regulate religious life in Saudi Arabia.

Yemen: a country located in the south-west corner of the Arabian peninsula. In the past, Yemenis provided much of Saudi Arabia's manual labour force. When the government of Yemen remained loyal to Saddam Hussein during the Gulf War, most Yemeni labourers were expelled from the kingdom.

Yemen: a country located in the south-west corner of the Arabian peninsula. In the past, Yemenis provided much of Saudi Arabia's unskilled labour force. When the government of Yemen remained loyal to Saddam Hussein during the Gulf War, many Yemeni labourers were expelled from the kingdom.

Appendix C

Chronology

570 Prophet Muhammad is born in Makkah, Saudi Arabia.

610 Prophet Muhammad sees a vision from God proclaiming him to be the messenger of God. Islam is born.

622 Prophet Muhammad flees an angry mob in Makkah and escapes to Madinah. This flight is forever after known as 'the Hegira', the great crisis of Muhammad's mission on earth. The Muslim calendar begins on that date and is called Hegira in honour of that journey.

632 Prophet Muhammad dies in Madinah.

650 The sayings of Prophet Muhammad are collected and written down. Known as the Koran, this book, which recorded the word of God as told by Muhammad, became the holy book of Muslims.

1446 The first documented Al Sa'ud, ancestor of Sultana, leaves the nomadic life of the desert and settles in Dar'iyah (old Riyadh).

1744 Muhammad Al Sa'ud establishes a

partnership with Muhammad Al Wahhab, a teacher who believes in the strictest interpretation of the Koran. Combined forces of a warrior and a teacher unleash a rigid system of punishment upon the people.

1802–6 Sons of Muhammad Al Sa'ud and Muhammad Al Wahhab, inspired by the teachings of the Koran, attack and capture Makkah and Madinah. They are ruthless, massacring the entire male population of Taif, a settlement above Makkah. With this victory, most of Arabia unites under one authority.

1843–65 The Sa'uds extend authority southwards to Oman.

1876 Sultana's grandfather, Abdul Aziz ibn Sa'ud, founder of the kingdom, is born.

1887 The city of Riyadh is captured by the Rasheeds.

1891 The Al Sa'ud clan flees Riyadh into the Empty Quarter.

1893–4 The Al Sa'ud clan marches across the desert to Kuwait.

1901 *September*. Abdul Aziz, now twenty-five years old, along with his warriors, leaves Kuwait for Riyadh.

1902 *January*. Abdul Aziz and his men capture Riyadh. The new Al Sa'ud dynasty begins.

1915 Abdul Aziz Al Sa'ud enters into an agreement with the British government to receive £5,000 per month to fight the Turks.

1926 Sultana's father is born.

1932 Unification of the dual kingdoms of Hijaz and Najd. Named the Kingdom of Saudi Arabia, it becomes the twelfth-largest country in the world.

1933 Sultana's mother, Fadeela, is born.

May. The United States of America wins concessions (over the British) to search for oil in Saudi Arabia.

1934 Saudi Arabia goes to war against Yemen; peace is established one month later.

15 May. In revenge for the Yemen war, King Abdul Aziz is attacked at the holy mosque in Makkah by three knife-wielding Yemenis. His eldest son, Sa'ud, flings himself in front of his father and is wounded instead.

1938 *20 March*. Oil is discovered in Dammam, Saudi Arabia.

1939 War in Europe halts oil production.

1944 Oil production in the kingdom rises to 8 million barrels a year.

1945 *14 February*. President Roosevelt meets King Abdul Aziz aboard USS *Quincy*.

17 February. Britain's prime minister, Winston Churchill, meets King Abdul Aziz aboard USS *Quincy*.

1946 Oil production soars to 60 million barrels a year.

December. Sultana's parents marry in

Riyadh, Saudi Arabia.

1948 Radio Makkah, the first radio station in the kingdom, is opened despite fierce opposition from the Ulema (religious men).

14 May. The state of Israel is established. The first Arab–Israeli war begins.

1952 King Abdul Aziz bans alcohol imports for non-believers.

1953 *9 November*. King Abdul Aziz, Sultana's grandfather, dies at the age of seventy-seven. His eldest son, fifty-one-year-old Sa'ud, becomes king. His half-brother Faisal becomes crown prince.

1956 Sultana is born into the family of Al Sa'ud, the tenth daughter of her parents.

1958 *March*. With the kingdom in financial turmoil, Crown Prince Faisal takes administrative control of the Government.

1960 *December*. King Sa'ud dismisses his brother from administrative duties and assumes control of the Government.

1962 Slavery is abolished in the Kingdom of Saudi Arabia. Most slaves continue to live with the families that owned them.

1963 The first girls' school opens; religious factions riot.

1964 *3 November*. King Sa'ud abdicates and leaves the kingdom for Beirut. Faisal is declared king, and his half-brother Khalid crown prince.

1965 Despite protests, the first television station is opened in Riyadh.

September. Prince Khalid ibn Musa'id, nephew of King Faisal, is killed as he leads an armed protest against the opening of the television station.

1967 *June*. The Six-Day War begins between Israel and her Arab neighbours. Saudi Arabia sends forces.

1969 *February*. Deposed ex-king Sa'ud ibn Abdul Aziz dies in Athens after spending more than $15 million each year of his exile.

1973 *6 October*. The October 1973 war begins between Israel and her Arab neighbours. Saudi Arabia sends troops.

20 October. Furious at America's military assistance to Israel, King Faisal announces a holy war and oil embargo against America.

1975 *25 March*. King Faisal is assassinated by his nephew Prince Faisal ibn Musa'id, brother of the prince who was shot and killed during a riot in 1965. Crown Prince Khalid is declared king. His half-brother Fahd is named new crown prince.

1977 King Khalid issues a government decree that forbids women from travelling outside their homes unless accompanied by a male family member. A second order follows that forbids women from travelling abroad to study. Both decrees resulted from an international incident involving Princess Misha'il, who was publicly executed after meeting and falling in love with another Saudi student at the American University in Lebanon. Her lover was beheaded.

1979 *November*. The Grand Mosque in Makkah is attacked. Protesters complain of women working outside the home in the kingdom. In the months to follow, women's freedom is curtailed in response to government fear of increased fundamentalist unrest.

1982 *June*. King Khalid dies of a heart attack. Fahd, his half-brother, is declared king; his half-brother Abdullah is named new crown prince.

1990 *5 August*. Kuwait is invaded by Iraq. Western Allied forces gather in Saudi Arabia to join Arab armies in repelling Saddam's army.

1991 *Mutawas* react with fear and hostility to the presence of foreign female soldiers. Pressure increases to force the Saudi government to tighten restrictions on the female population of all nationalities as religious factions return to strict interpretation of the Koran.

DAUGHTERS OF ARABIA
by Jean Sasson

Readers of Princess Sultana's extraordinary story, *Princess*, were gripped by her powerful indictment of women's lives behind the veil within the royal family of Saudi Arabia. Now, the princess turns the spotlight on her two teenage daughters, Maha and Amani.

As second-generation members of the royal family who have benefited from Saudi oil wealth, Maha and Amani have never known the poverty which their parents experienced as children. Surrounded by untold opulence and luxury from the day they were born and which they take for granted, but stifled by the unbearably restrictive lifestyle imposed on them, they have reacted in equally desperate ways.

Their dramatic and shocking stories, together with many more which concern other members of Princess Sultana's huge family, are set against a rich backcloth of Saudi Arabian culture and social mores which she depicts with equal colour and authenticity. We learn, for example, of the fascinating ritual of the world-famous annual pilgrimage to Makkah as we accompany the princess and her family to this holiest of cities. Throughout, however, she never tires of her quest to expose the injustices which her society levels against women. In her courageous campaign to improve the lot of her own daughters of Arabia, Princess Sultana once more strikes a chord amongst all women who are lucky enough to have the freedom to speak out for themselves.

'Women with everything but freedom . . . "Sultana" has described her family life to American writer Jean Sasson – and if it didn't come from within palace walls, no one would believe it . . . gripping revelations'
Daily Mail

A Bantam Paperback (0 553 40805 4)

DESERT ROYAL
by Jean Sasson

In *Desert Royal* Princess Sultana continues her gripping story, at a period of crisis in her own life, and that of her family. The forced marriage of her niece to a cruel and depraved older man, and her discovery of a harem of sex slaves kept by a cousin, make her more determined than ever to fight the oppression of women in Saudi Arabia.

Princess Sultana's cause is given an extra sense of urgency against the background of increased dissent against the Al Sa'uds, and the looming spectre of Islamic fundamentalism. But an extended family 'camping' trip in the desert brings the luxury-loving Sultana and her relatives closer to their nomadic roots, and gives her the strength to carry on the fight for women's rights in all Muslim countries.

A Bantam Paperback (0 553 81218 1)

INTERNATIONAL ACCLAIM FOR
JEAN SASSON

DAUGHTERS OF ARABIA

'Women with everything but freedom . . . "Sultana" has described her family life to American writer Jean Sasson – and if it didn't come from within palace walls, no one would believe it . . . gripping revelations'
Daily Mail

'Brutality hidden behind the veil . . . more horrific stories'
Sunday Express

'The first book [was] instrumental in bringing to the attention of the western world a situation in Saudi Arabia which is a continuing violation of the fundamental principles of human rights . . . The stories of oppression and brutality are horrific'
Australian Bookseller & Publisher

PRINCESS

'Unforgettable in content, fascinating in detail . . . a book to move you to tears'
Fay Weldon

'The startling truth behind the veiled lives of Saudi Arabia's women . . . frank and vivid revelations'
Sunday Express

'Mind-boggling . . . absolutely riveting'
People Magazine

'Anyone with the slightest interest in human rights will find this book heart-wrenching. It is a well-written, personal story about the violation of human rights in Saudi Arabia . . . It had to come from a native woman to be believable'
Betty Mahmoody, bestselling author of
Not Without My Daughter

Also by Jean Sasson

THE RAPE OF KUWAIT

PRINCESS

DESERT ROYAL

DAUGHTERS OF ARABIA

Jean Sasson

BANTAM BOOKS
LONDON · NEW YORK · TORONTO · SYDNEY · AUCKLAND

DAUGHTERS OF ARABIA
A BANTAM BOOK : 0 553 40805 4

Originally published in Great Britain by Doubleday,
a division of Transworld Publishers

PRINTING HISTORY
Doubleday edition published 1994
Bantam Books edition published 1994

10

Set in 10pt Linotype Sabon by
Chippendale Type Ltd, Otley, West Yorkshire.

Bantam Books are published by Transworld Publishers,
61–63 Uxbridge Road, London W5 5SA,
a division of The Random House Group Ltd,
in Australia by Random House Australia (Pty) Ltd,
20 Alfred Street, Milsons Point, Sydney, NSW 2061, Australia,
in New Zealand by Random House New Zealand Ltd,
18 Poland Road, Glenfield, Auckland 10, New Zealand
and in South Africa by Random House (Pty) Ltd,
Endulini, 5a Jubilee Road, Parktown 2193, South Africa.

Printed and bound in Great Britain by
Cox & Wyman Ltd, Reading, Berkshire.

This is a true story. Names have been changed and various events slightly altered to protect the well-being of recognizable individuals.

In telling this true story it is not the intention of the author nor of the Princess to demean the Islamic faith.

This book is dedicated to my parents

NEATWOOD JONES PARKS

and

MARY HARDEN PARKS

Acknowledgements

Special thanks go to Jack W. Creech, my most loyal supporter, along with loving members of my family who have been there for me at every turn: my sister, Barbara, my brother-in-law, George, their daughter, Roxanne, and her husband, David.

Warm thanks go to three special friends, David Abramowitz, Nancy Apple and Richard Billingsly.

And, without Frank and Lydia, it would have been difficult for me to work the long hours that I worked.

I want to thank Marianne Velmans and Sally Gaminara for their support, and all the staff at Transworld for their special attention to the story of one very brave woman.

I am deeply grateful to my 'super agent', Frank Curtis, for his enthusiasm for the book and his expert handling of all matters pertaining to the sale of *Daughters of Arabia*.

There are a few others that I dare not name: trusted Saudi couriers that hand-carried messages between myself and Sultana when communication was impossible, but they know who they are, and I thank them.

I cannot forget two special friends in Australia. One day, I hope that it will be safe to publicly thank them for their enduring love and support.

Thanks to my numerous Saudi and other Arab friends who have not deserted me for writing Sultana's story. They know, as I do, that my writing books that detail one Saudi woman's life does not mean that I condemn all Arabs. They, better than anyone, know of my love for the Arab people.

And, of course, most of all, I thank Sultana.

Acknowledgements

[illegible]

Contents

SAUDI ARABIA

THE REGIONS OF ARABIA

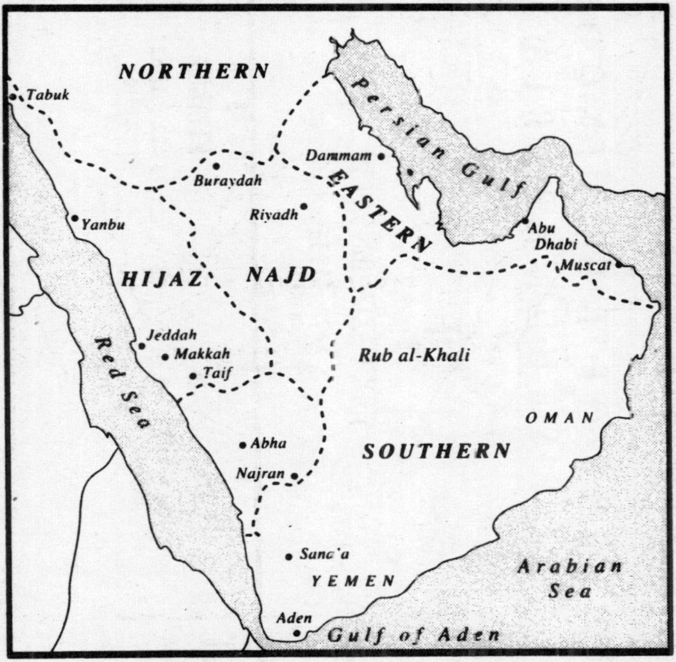

RULERS OF THE KINGDOM OF SAUDI ARABIA

The First Five Kings

ABDUL AZIZ, 'IBN SA'UD'
1876 – 1953
FIRST KING

SA'UD
1902 – 1969
SECOND KING

FAISAL
1904 – 1975
THIRD KING

KHALID
1912 – 1982
FOURTH KING

FAHD
1922 –
PRESENT & FIFTH KING

Foreword

Daughters of Arabia is a true story. It tells of the women who live behind the veil in Saudi Arabia.

An earlier work, *Princess*, published in 1992, set the arena for this work by depicting the life of Princess Sultana from early childhood to the Gulf War of 1991. This book is the continuing story of Princess Sultana and her two daughters.

While it is hoped that readers have the time to read both books, *Daughters of Arabia* is a story in itself and can be read without *Princess*.

While many facts are revealed of a land little understood by the Western world, neither book is meant to be a history of Saudi Arabia, or to reflect the lives of all women who live in that land. The two works are the story of one Saudi princess and her family.

These two books, linked by one woman, come to one conclusion: that subjugation and degradation of women is a worn-out habit in Saudi Arabia. The double standard is alive and well in most countries and it is time for male dominance over women to end.

These adventures of one Saudi princess aim to show that an end to male abuse of females will evolve from knowledge, courage and action.

Prologue

A great rock is not disturbed by the wind; the mind of a wise man is not disturbed by either honour or abuse.
Buddha

Once I read that any good pen can stab any king. As I study the photograph of my uncle, Fahd Ibn Abdul Aziz, the King of Saudi Arabia, I contemplate the fact that I harbour no desire to stab our king, or even to spark the wrath of a man whom I know to be kindly.

I trace my fingers across his face, recalling the Fahd of my childhood days. The photograph portrays the King in maturity and reveals nothing of the youthful man I remember. The King's stern brow and strong jaw belie the charming man whom I wistfully call to mind. My thoughts wander back in time, remembering the King before he was crowned. Standing tall and broad-shouldered, with his large hand outstretched, he had offered a sweet date to a child in awe. That child had been me. Fahd, like his father before him, was a robust man, and to my young eyes had looked more like the son of a bedouin warrior whom he was, than the statesman he would become. Contrary to my usual boldness, I had reacted timidly, accepting the desert fruit from his fingers reluctantly, then running into my mother's arms. I had heard Fahd laughing fondly as I savoured the sweetness of the date.

As is our Saudi custom, I have not been unveiled in the presence of the King since the age of puberty. Since that time, he has grown into a man of age. The King now appears a sombre figure, and I cannot help but conclude that, while the years of statesmanship have strengthened him, the responsibilities of leadership have chastened him. And, though massive and regal, our king cannot be judged handsome. His eyelids droop too heavily over his protruberant eyes, his nose overshadows his upper lip, which tightly frames a delicate mouth. In the picture so familiar to all Saudis and visitors to the kingdom – the official photograph that hangs conspicuously in every business and institution in my country – the King appears to be what I know he is not: forbidding and insensitive.

In spite of his unquestioned power and vast wealth, his position is not to be envied. As absolute sovereign of one of the wealthiest nations on earth, King Fahd's rule over the hot, dreary land of Saudi Arabia is a perpetual struggle between ancient and modern.

While most nations maintain themselves by abandoning or recasting the old ways, growing slowly into newer and better systems that advance civilization, our king has no such options. He, a mere mortal, must unite and keep the peace between four divided and completely distinct groups of citizens: the religious fundamentalists, stern, unyielding men of power who demand a return to the past; the prominent, well-educated middle class that cries out for release from the stifling, old traditions; the bedouin tribes who struggle against enticements to abandon their nomadic way of life and yield to the lure of the cities; and lastly, members of the vast royal family who want nothing more than wealth, wealth, and yet more wealth.

Behind these four factions is the one group of natives who have been forgotten: the women of Saudi Arabia, as diverse in our desires and demands as the individual men who rule our daily lives.

Yet, strangely, I, a woman of great frustrations, have little anger with the King over our plight, for I know that prior to moving against the disciplined men of religion, he must have the loyal backing of ordinary husbands, fathers, and brothers. These clerics claim that they correctly interpret the historic code of laws in allowing men to rule harshly over their women. Too many ordinary men of

Saudi Arabia are content with the *status quo*, discovering that it is easier to ignore the complaints of their women, rather than follow their king in negotiating change.

In spite of the difficulties, the bulk of Saudi citizens support King Fahd. It is only the religious fundamentalists who call for his downfall. To the remainder of Saudi citizens, he is known as a man of generosity and good cheer.

And, I remind myself that the women of our family know that the King is well loved by his wives, and who knows a man better than his wives?

While King Fahd rules with a milder hand than did his father and his three brothers, it does not require the wisdom of a sage to know that *Princess*, the earlier book that tells the story of my life, will be viewed as a slap in the face to the man who rules my country.

That, alone, I regret.

I admonish myself that, under no duress, I made the decision to break the precedent of generations by flinging family secrets to the wind. Now, for the first time, I wonder if I acted with passion rather than wisdom; perhaps my earnestness and enthusiasm led me to overestimate my capacity for intrigue.

In an attempt to assuage my conscience and calm my fears, I vividly recall the intensity of my emotions as I wrote it – my anger that our rulers' world has continued to dominate, oblivious of the fact that we women languish in oppression.

It was my fury at male indifference that led me to revolution.

Chapter One

UNVEILED

Despair weakens our sight and closes our ears. We can see nothing but spectres of doom, and can hear only the beating of our agitated hearts.

Kahlil Gibran

It is October 1992, and I, Sultana Al Sa'ud, the Princess of a revelatory book, follow the days of the calendar with a mixture of feverish excitement and morose depression. The book that exposed the life of women behind the veil was released in the United States in September 1992. Since its publication, I carry with me a sombre presentiment of my doom, feeling as though I am precariously suspended in space, for I am aware that no deed great or small, bad or good, can be without effect.

Taking a deep breath, I hopefully remind myself that I am likely to be safe in the anonymity of the extended Al Sa'ud family. Still, my trusty instincts warn me that I have been discovered.

Just as I conquer my conflicting guilt and fear, my husband, Kareem, enters our home in a rush, shouting out that my brother, Ali, has returned early from his trip to Europe and that my father has called an urgent family meeting at his palace. With black eyes glaring, his pale face blotched fiery red, my husband looks madder than a mad dog.

I am struck by a horrifying thought. Kareem has been told of the book!

Imagining suffocating confinement in a subterranean dungeon, deprived of my beloved children, I surrender to my agitation for a moment, and in a thin high voice that bears no resemblance to my own, ask, 'What has happened?'

Kareem shrugs his shoulders, answering, 'Who can know?' His nostrils flare with irritation when he remembers, 'I informed your father than I have an important appointment in Zürich tomorrow, that you and I could see him when I return, but he was adamant that I cancel my plans and escort you to his home this evening.'

Like a figure blown by the wind, Kareem charges into his office exclaiming, 'Three meetings have to be cancelled!'

Weak-kneed, I collapse on the sofa with relief, thinking I had been premature in my conclusions. Kareem's anger has nothing to do with me! My courage flickers hopefully.

Still, the threat of discovery persists, and I have many long hours before the unexpected family meeting.

Feigning gaiety that I do not feel, I smile and chat as Kareem and I walk through the wide entrance hall and over the thick Persian carpets into an enormous and grand sitting-room in my father's newly constructed palace. Father has not yet arrived, but I see that Kareem and I are the last of the family to make an appearance. The other ten living children of my mother, without their spouses, have been summoned to my father's home. I know that three of my sisters had to fly into Riyadh from Jeddah, while two sisters flew in from Taif. Looking around the room, I verify that Kareem is the only outside member of the family present. Even Father's head wife and her children are nowhere to be seen. I surmise that they have been dismissed from the premises.

The urgency of the meeting leads me back to the book,

and my chest tightens with fear. My sister Sara and I exchange worried glances. As the only member of my family aware of the book's publication, her thoughts reflect mine. Each of my siblings greets me warmly, except for my only brother, Ali, and I catch a glimpse of his sly eyes following me.

Within moments of our arrival, Father enters the room. His ten daughters stand respectfully to their feet, and each of us express our greetings to the man who has given us life without love.

I have not seen my father in some months, and I think to myself that he looks exhausted and prematurely old. When I lean to kiss his cheek, he impatiently turns away, failing to return my greeting. Giving my fears full range, I know at that moment that I have been naïve, thinking that the Al Sa'uds are too busy accumulating wealth to care much for books. My trepidation mounts.

In a stern voice, Father asks us to sit, saying that he has some disturbing news to relay.

Lured by a stare, I see that Ali, with his morbid interest in the suffering of others, is gloating, regarding me with a pitiless stare. There is little doubt in my mind that Ali is privy to the evening's business.

Father reaches into his large, black briefcase and retrieves a book that none of us can read. It is written in a foreign language. My mind in conflict, I think that I have made a mistake with my earlier fears, wondering what this particular book has to do with our family.

In a voice filled with undisguised rage, Father says that Ali recently purchased the book from Germany, and that the book tells about the life of a princess, a stupid and foolish woman who is not aware of the royal obligations that accompany the privileges of royalty. While circling the room he holds the book in his hands. The picture on the cover is plainly that of a Muslim woman, for she is veiled, and is standing against a backdrop of Turkish minarets. I have a wild thought that an aging, exiled princess from Egypt or Turkey has written a revealing book, but quickly realize that such a tale would hold no interest in our land.

When Father steps closer, I read the title: *Ich, Prinzessin aus dem Hause Al Sa'ud.*

It is my story!

As I have not been in touch with the book's author since learning of its sale to a large and respected American publishing house, I am unaware at the time that the book, *Princess*, is a huge success and has been sold to numerous foreign publishers. The book in front of me is quite obviously a German edition of it.

I have a short moment of elation followed by sheer terror. I feel the blood rush to my face. I am numb and can barely hear my father's voice. He explains that Ali had been curious when he saw the book upon his arrival at Frankfurt Airport. Since my brother was spending two months in Europe, he had taken the time and expense to have the book translated when he saw that our family name was written on the cover.

At the time, Ali had an irritated thought that some obscure, disgruntled princess within the Al Sa'ud family had divulged gossipy secrets of her life story. Once Ali read the book and clearly recognized himself from our childhood dramas, the truth of the book was revealed, and he cancelled the remainder of his holiday and hastily returned to Riyadh in a fury.

Father had copies of the translated version made for the meeting.

He nods at Ali, while giving a small signal with his hand. My brother gropes with a bulky pile of papers at his side and proceeds to hand each person a bundle of papers secured with a large rubber band.

Confused, Kareem nudges me, raising his eyebrows and rolling his eyes.

Until the last possible second, I express my denials, returning a face of bewilderment. I shrug my shoulders and stare, unblinking and unseeing, at the papers in my hand.

With mounting voice, Father shouts out my name, 'Sultana!'

I feel my body jump.

Father begins to speak rapidly, spitting out words as I imagine a machine-gun expels bullets, 'Sultana, do you recall the marriage and divorce of your sister, Sara? The wickedness of your childhood friends? The death of your mother? Your trip to Egypt? Your marriage to Kareem? The birth of your son? Sultana?'

I have stopped breathing.

Relentlessly, my father continues to accuse. 'Sultana, if you have difficulty in recalling these momentous events, then I suggest that you read this book!'

Father throws the book at my feet.

Unable to move, I stare mutely at the book on the floor.

My father orders, 'Sultana, pick it up!'

Kareem grabs the book and stares at the cover. He gasps – a deep, ragged breath – and then turns to me. 'What is this, Sultana?'

I am paralysed with fear. My heart stops beating. I sit and listen, longing for the life-giving thump.

Quite out of control, Kareem drops the book to the floor, grabs my shoulders and shakes me like a rag doll.

I again feel the familiar heart beat, though I have a childlike thought – a moment of sorrow that I cannot die on the spot and so burden my husband's conscience with lifelong guilt.

I can hear my neck muscles snapping from the force of Kareem's strength.

My father yells. 'Sultana! Answer your husband!'

Suddenly, the years evaporate. I am a child again, at my father's mercy. How I long for my mother to be alive, for nothing less than maternal fervour can save me from this vicious encounter!

I feel a whimper forming in my throat.

I have told myself many times in the past that there can be no freedom without courage, yet my courage fails me when I need it the most. I had known that if members of my immediate family read the book, that my secret would be discovered, since they are key figures in my life, and in the book. Foolishly, I had felt protected by the fact that, in my family, only Sara reads books. Even if gossip of the book had spread throughout the city, I had assumed that my family would take little note of the event, unless a mention was made of a particular incident that they would recall from our youth.

Now, ironically, my brother, a man who scorns the mention of women's rights, has read the book that focused attention on abuses of women in my land. My demon of a brother, Ali, has foiled my precious anonymity.

Timidly, I look around the room at my father, my sisters and brother. Together, as if they had practised, their looks of surprise and anger are slowly forged into a united, hard stare.

After only one short month, I have been discovered!

Finding my voice, I weakly protest, blaming my deed on the highest authority, saying what all good Muslims say when caught in an act that will bring punishment on their heads. I thump the papers with my hand. 'God willed it. He willed this book!'

Ali is quick to retort, scoffing, 'God? Not so! The devil willed it! He willed it! Not God!' Ali turns to my father and says with perfect seriousness, 'Since the day of her birth, Sultana has had a little devil living inside her. This devil willed the book!'

Quite rapidly, my sisters begin to leaf through the pages in their hands, to see for themselves if our family's secrets had been made public.

Only Sara gives me her support. She quietly stands up and slips behind my back, resting her hands on my shoulders, reassuring me with her soft touch.

After his initial outburst, Kareem is quiet. I see that he is reading the translated copy of the book. I lean sideways and see that he has discovered the chapter that tells of our first meeting and consequent marriage. Sitting perfectly still, my husband speaks aloud the words that he is seeing for the first time.

Father's angry shouting arouses Ali's enthusiastic hatred, and my father and brother quite outdo each other in their verbal assaults on my stupidity. Amid the passionate disorder, I hear Ali shout out the accusation that I have committed treason.

Treason? I love my God, country, and King, in that order; and I shout back that 'No! I am not a traitor! Only a haphazard council of mediocre minds can reach a conclusion of treason!'

As my anger builds, my fear is receding.

I think to myself that the men in my family are proof that men and women can remain at peace only when one sex is strong enough to dominate the other completely. Now that we women in Saudi Arabia are becoming educated, and are beginning to think for ourselves, our lives will be filled with additional discord and mayhem. Still, I welcome renewed battle if it means more rights for women, for a false peace does nothing more than further women's subjugation.

Yet, I know that this is not the most opportune moment for refutations.

The hot controversy continues to rage, and I become lost in the details. My initial fright makes me forget why I requested Jean Sasson to write my story in the first place. I stop listening to the accusations, and force myself to remember my friend Nada's death by drowning and Sameera's crushing imprisonment, wondering if their tragic lives have yet touched readers' hearts. Even before the book was published, I had realized that neither tale seemed credible, unless the book's readers acknowledged the barbarities that men inflict upon women. Yet, something was telling me that those with genuine knowledge of my land – its customs and traditions – had recognized the truth of my words.

The memory of my unfortunate friends and their sad fate gives me fresh strength.

With mounting exasperation I think that those who want freedom must be willing to pay for it with their lives. The worst has happened. I have been discovered. Now what?

It is a pivotal moment. Feeling my strength return, I get to my feet and face my foes. I feel the warrior's blood of my Grandfather Abdul Aziz surge through my body. From the time that I was a child, I am most to be feared when I stand in real danger.

My courage gives me a hardened resolve. Thinking back, I remember the face of a kind man that offered a little girl succulent dates. I have a wild idea. Without hesitating, I shout brave words over the din of confusion, 'Take me to the King!'

The shouting stops. Incredulous, my father repeats my words, 'The King?'

Ali makes an impatient tskking sound with his tongue. 'The King will not see you!'

'Yes. He will! Take me to him. I wish to tell the King the reasons why the book came to be. To tell him of the tragic lives of the women he rules. I will confess, but only to the King.'

My father looks askance at his son, Ali. Their eyes lock in a shocked look. It is as if I can read their minds: 'One must be honourable, but not too much!'

'I insist upon confessing. To the King.' I know this King well. He hates confrontation. Even so, he will punish me for what I have done. I realize I will need someone from outside Saudi Arabia to keep my memory alive. I say, 'But before I go to the King, I must talk to someone on a foreign newspaper to make my identity known. If I am to be punished, I refuse to be forgotten. Let the world know how our country deals with those who unveil the truth.'

I walk toward the telephone that sits on a small table next to the hallway door, thinking that I must notify someone of my plight. I am desperate, trying to recall a telephone number of an international newspaper that I had memorized for such an occasion.

My sisters begin to wail, crying out to our father that he must stop me.

Kareem jumps to his feet, rushing to beat me to the phone. My husband stands tall over me, blocking my path. With a stern face, he holds out his arm and points to my chair as if it were the executioner's block.

Despite the serious moment, something about Kareem's expression amuses me. I laugh aloud. My husband can be a foolish man and still has not learned that to silence me, he must bury me. That, I know, he can never do. My knowledge of Kareem's inability to commit violence has always given me strength.

Neither Kareem nor I move. Keenly feeling the drama of the moment, I shout out, 'When the beast is cornered, the hunter is in danger.' The thought enters my mind to ram his stomach with my head, and I am considering the option just as my oldest sister, Nura, takes centre stage and quietens us all with her calm approach.

'Enough! This is no way to solve a problem.' She pauses, glancing at Father and Ali. 'All this shouting! The servants will hear every word. *Then* we are in a true dilemma.'

Nura is the only female child of my father to gain his love. Father motions for everyone to be quiet.

Kareem leads me by the arm and we return to sit in our chairs.

Father and Ali continue to stand, both quite speechless.

Since the book's publication, I have been weakened by my fear. Now, for the first time in weeks, I feel absolutely fierce, recognizing that the last thing on male minds is to turn me over to the authorities.

The meeting continues much more calmly, with serious talk of how to keep my identity a secret. We understand that there will be much talk and speculation within the kingdom about who the princess in the book is. My family decides that it will be impossible for the common man of Saudi to uncover the truth, for they are outside our family circles. And there is no real danger from male relatives within the extended Al Sa'ud family, for females and their activities are carefully guarded from male view. In Father's mind, there is genuine concern regarding close female relatives, since they sometimes participate in our intimate gatherings.

There is a moment of panic as Tahani remembers that one old auntie who was closely involved in Sara's calamitous marriage and divorce is still living. Nura calms their fears by revealing that our auntie, just a few days ago, has been diagnosed as having a disabling brain disorder that affects the elderly. Nura says that our auntie is rarely, if ever, coherent. If by some remote chance she hears of the book, nothing she says or does would now be taken seriously by her family.

Everyone breathes a sigh of relief.

I, myself, have no fear of the old woman. She is an anomaly in her time. I understand her frisky character better than others. My intimate knowledge has come from past conversations when she whispered in my ear that she supported me in my quest for small female freedoms. This auntie has bragged to me that she was the world's first feminist, long before the European women thought of such matters. She said that on the night of her marriage, she had insisted to her startled husband that she handle the money from the sale of the sheep, since she could figure numbers in her head and he had to use a stick in the sand. Not only that, her husband never even thought of taking another wife, saying often that with my auntie he had women enough.

With a toothless laugh, my auntie had confided in me that the secret to controlling a man was a woman's ability to keep her husband's 'leather stick' rigid and ready. I was a young girl at that time, and had no idea what a 'leather stick' might be. Later, in my adult years, I often smile, thinking of the lusty activities that must have shaken their tent.

After her husband's early death, my auntie confessed that she missed her husband's tender caresses and that it was his memory that kept her from accepting another mate.

Over the years, I have jealously guarded her happy secret, fearing that such a confession would nibble at my auntie's soul.

For several hours, my family pore over the translated pages and satisfy themselves that no-one else alive, or traceable outside our immediate family, is aware of the family dramas and squabbles divulged in the book.

I can see that my family feels a keen sense of relief. In addition, I catch a trace of mild admiration that I had so cleverly altered the pertinent information that would have led the authorities directly to my door.

The evening closes with Father and Ali warning my sisters not to notify their husbands of the night's business. Who knows which husband might feel compelled to confide in a sister or mother? My sisters are instructed to tell their husbands that the meeting involved nothing more than personal female matters that were not worthy of their husband's attention.

Father sternly orders me not to 'come out' in public and announce my 'crime'. The fact that the book is the story of my life must remain a well-kept secret within our family. My father reminds me that not only would I suffer dire consequences, house arrest, or possibly imprisonment, but that the men of the family, including my own son, Abdullah, would be scorned and shut out by Saudi Arabia's patriarchal society that values nothing more highly than a man's ability to control his women.

As a token of submission, I lower my eyes and promise compliance. My heart is smiling, for on this night I have made a brilliant discovery, that the men of my family are locked to me like a chain, that their dominant role imprisons them as surely as it does me.

As I say goodnight to my father and brother, I think to myself that: complete power poisons the hand of the person who holds it. The men of my family cannot punish me without risk to their own well-being within the kingdom.

Cheated of my blood, Ali is displeased and gruff in

our parting. He would like nothing better than to see me placed under house arrest, but he cannot risk the wound to his male pride to be associated by blood with someone like me.

I give him an especially warm farewell, whispering in his ear that: 'Ali, you must remember that not *every-one* in chains can be subdued.'

It is a great triumph!

Kareem is sullen and stubborn as we make our way home. He smokes one cigarette after another, soundly cursing the Filipino driver on three occasions for not driving to suit his master.

I lean my face against the car window, seeing nothing of what we pass on the Riyadh streets. I brace myself for a second battle, for I understand that I cannot escape Kareem's great anger.

Once locked in our bedroom, Kareem grabs the pages of the book. He begins to read aloud the passages that are most insulting to him: 'His façade was wisdom and kindness; his very bowels were cunning and selfish. I was disgusted to discover that he was merely a shell of a man with little to commend him, after all!'

There is a thread of sympathy in my thoughts, for what human would not feel pain and fury at a public statement of their weakest traits. I fight the emotion, forcing myself to recall my husband's activities that led to my own pain and grief so vividly portrayed in the book.

I am in a dilemma, not knowing whether to laugh or cry.

Kareem solves the problem for me with his exaggerated behaviour. My husband waves his arms and stamps his feet. I'm reminded of the Egyptian puppet show that I attended a week ago at my sister Sara's palace, a hilarious event, featuring puppets dressed in full Saudi dress. The closer I look, the more Kareem resembles Goha, a lov-able but eccentric imaginary figure in the Arab world. Goha the puppet had been his usual foolish self in the play, prancing across the stage, disentangling himself from complex situations.

My lips quiver with the urge to laugh. At any moment now, I expect my husband to fall to the floor and throw a childish temper tantrum.

'He swore, he blushed with shame; I thought perhaps he was angered by his inability to control his wife.'

Kareem glares hatefully at me. 'Sultana! Don't you dare smile! I'm truly angry.'

Still battling conflicting emotions, I shrug. 'Do you deny that what you're reading is the truth?'

Ignoring my words, Kareem foolishly continues to seek out the most damning passages concerning his character, reminding his wife of the particular traits of her husband's temperament that had led her to leave him years ago.

Actually shrieking, he reads aloud, 'How I yearned to be wed to a warrior, a man with the hot flame of righteousness to guide his life.'

His rage growing with every word, Kareem holds the book under my nose and points with a finger to the words that he deems most insulting,

> Six years ago, Sultana was stricken with a venereal disease; after much distress, Kareem admitted that he participated in a weekly adventure of sex with strangers . . . After the scare of the disease, Kareem promised he would avoid the weekly tryst, but Sultana says she knows that he is weak in the face of such a feast, and that he continues to indulge himself without shame. Their wonderful love has vanished except in memory; Sultana says she will stand with her husband and continue her struggle for the sake of her daughters.

Kareem is so angry at that particular revelation that I fear he will start to cry. My husband accuses me of 'poisoning paradise', claiming that, 'our lives are perfect'.

Admittedly, over the past year, I have regained some of

my earlier love and trust for Kareem, but it is in moments such as this that my dismay grows over the cowardice of the men in our family. I realize by his behaviour that Kareem gives not a thought to the reasons I risked my safety and our happiness to make known the events of my life, or to the very real and tragic events ending the lives of young and innocent women in his own land. Kareem's only concern is that of his appearance in the book, and the fact that he has fared poorly in many passages.

I tell my husband that he and other men of the Al Sa'ud family alone hold the power to make change in our country. Slowly, quietly, in their subtle manner, they can pursue and encourage change. When he makes no response to my plea, I understand that the men of the Al Sa'ud family cannot risk their power for their women. They are passionately in love with the crown.

Kareem regains his composure, after I remind him that no-one outside our family, other than the author, knows who he is! And those persons know him well, aware of his good and bad traits, even without this published book.

Kareem sits beside me and lifts my chin with his finger. He looks almost appealing as he ponders, 'You told Jean Sasson about the disease I caught?'

I wiggle in shame as Kareem slowly shakes his head from side to side, visibly disappointed in his wife. 'Is nothing sacred to you, Sultana?'

Many battles end in an outpouring of goodwill. The evening ends with unexpected displays of affection. Strangely, Kareem says that he has never loved me more.

I find myself being courted by my husband and the intensity of my feelings increase. My husband reawakens the desire that I had once deemed lost for ever. I wonder at my own ability to both love and hate the same man.

Later as Kareem sleeps, I lie awake by his side and replay in my mind, moment by moment, the events of the day. I realize that despite the evening's end – the guaranteed protection promised by my family (due solely to their own fears of royal banishment and/or punishment) and the renewal of my marriage – that I cannot rest peacefully until genuine social adjustment for the women whose burden I share comes to the land I love. The hard necessities of female lives are pushing me to continue my efforts to gain personal freedom for the women of Arabia.

I question myself: am I not the mother of two daughters? Do I not owe my daughters and their daughters after them every effort to bring transformation?

I smile, once again thinking back to the puppet show that I had watched with Sara's youngest children, and recall the words of the funny but wise puppet Goha. 'Does a faithful saluki[1] stop barking in his master's defence when a single bone is thrown his way?'

I shout, 'No!'

Kareem stirs and I rub the back of his head, whispering sweet words, lulling my husband back to sleep.

I know at that moment that I will not keep a pledge that was made under coercion. I will let the world community decide when I should return to silence. Until people choose to close their ears to the plight of women in despair, I will continue to reveal the true happenings behind the secrecy of the black veil. This is to be my destiny.

I make a decision. Contrary to the promises I had made under threat of detention, when I next travel out of the kingdom, I will contact my friend, Jean Sasson. There is more to be accomplished.

When I close my eyes to sleep, I am a more focused but a much sadder woman than the Sultana who awoke this morning, for I know that, once again, I am entering a risky arena, and even though my punishment – and possibly even my death – will be cruel, failure will be more bitter, for failure is everlasting.

[1] Desert dog.

Chapter Two

MAHA

The more prohibitions you have, the less virtuous people will be.

Tao Te Ching

Those whom Kareem and I love best have proved the worst. Abdullah, our son, troubles us; Maha, our eldest daughter, frightens us; while Amani, our youngest daughter, puzzles us.

I had no foreboding of doom as our only son Abdullah smiled with boyish happiness and told us with relish of his wonderful success on the soccer field. Kareem and I were entranced, as most parents would be, upon hearing the successful exploits of their well-loved child. From a young age, Abdullah was seldom surpassed in physical games, and this fact was a particular source of glee for his athletic father. As we proudly listened, we took no note of his younger sisters, Maha and Amani, who were amusing themselves with a video game.

When Amani, our youngest child, began to scream in alarm, it was with a terrible shock that Kareem and I saw flames licking at Abdullah's clothing.

Our son was on fire!

Acting on instinct, Kareem quickly threw our son to the floor and extinguished the flames by rolling Abdullah in a Persian carpet.

After we assured ourselves that our son was unharmed,

Kareem tried to find the source of the inexplicable fire.

I cried out that the fire was caused by an evil eye, that we were too boastful of our beautiful son!

Fighting back tears, I turned to comfort my daughters. Poor Amani! Her small frame was racked with sobs. While I held my baby, I motioned with my free arm to her older sister, Maha, to come to me. Suddenly, I drew back in horror, for Maha's face was a frightful mask of anger and hate.

After investigating the confusing incident, we learned a terrible truth: Maha had set her brother's *thobe* on fire.

Maha, meaning 'She Gazelle', has not fulfilled the promise of her gentle name. From the age of ten, it was apparent that our eldest daughter was possessed by the demonic energy of her mother. Often I have thought that there must be a battleground of good and evil spirits hovering over Maha, with evil spirits usually overpowering the good. Neither her life amid imperial splendour, nor the unconditional love of a devoted family, has tempered Maha's spirit.

Without justification, she has tormented her brother Abdullah and her younger sister Amani for as long as they both can remember. Few children have brought so many crises to one family as Maha.

In appearance, Maha is a stunningly attractive girl, with a frighteningly seductive personality. She has the look of a Spanish dancer, all eyes and hair. Combined with this great beauty is a gifted mind. Ever since her birth, it seemed to me that too many blessings had been bestowed upon my eldest daughter. With so many abilities, Maha is unable to focus on one goal, and lacking a unifying purpose, she has failed to harness her talents in one direction. Over the years, I have watched as a hundred promising projects have been started, but none completed.

Kareem said once that he feared that our daughter was nothing more than a girl of brilliant fragments, and would fail to accomplish one single idea in her lifetime. My greatest concern is that Maha is a revolutionary seeking a cause.

As I too am such a person, I am aware of the turmoil raised by a mutinous character.

In her earlier years, the problem seemed a simple matter. Maha loved her father to distraction. The intensity of her feelings increased with her years.

Whereas Kareem adored his two daughters as he did his one son, and strove to avoid the resentments that I endured as a child, the make-up of our society drew Abdullah more closely into Kareem's life outside our home. This basic fact of our Muslim heritage was the first shock of Maha's young life.

Maha's intense jealousy of her father's affections brought to mind my own unhappy childhood – a young girl who had chafed under the harsh social system into which she was born. For that reason, I failed to comprehend the seriousness of my child's discontent.

After Maha set fire to Abdullah's *thobe*, we knew that her possessiveness of Kareem went far beyond that of normal daughterly affection. Maha was ten years old and Abdullah was twelve. Amani was only seven, but she had watched her sister slip away from their game, fetch her father's gold lighter, setting fire to the edge of Abdullah's *thobe*. Had Amani not cried out a warning, Abdullah could have been seriously burned.

The second shocking incident occurred when Maha was only eleven. It was the hot month of August. Our family had left the sweltering desert city of Riyadh and gathered at my sister Nura's summer palace in the cool mountain city of Taif. It was the first time in years that Father had attended a family gathering of his first wife's children, and his attentions were devoted to his grandsons. While admiring Abdullah's height and figure, my father ignored Maha, who was tugging on his sleeve to show him an ant farm that the children had built and proudly displayed. I saw Father as he brushed her aside and proceeded to squeeze Abdullah's biceps.

Maha was stung by her grandfather's preference for her brother and his indifference to her. My heart plunged for the pain that I knew was in her heart.

Knowing Maha's ability to create a scene, I walked over to comfort my daughter just as she assumed a masculine stance and began cursing my father with fiery invectives of the coarsest indecency, peppered with vile accusations.

From that moment, the family gathering rapidly deteriorated. Though humiliated, I had a quick thought that Maha had expressed to my father his manifest due.

Father, who had never held a high opinion of the female sex, made no pretence of his feelings. Scornfully, Father ordered, 'Remove this horrible creature from my sight!'

I saw plainly that my daughter had awakened Father's contempt for me. His eyes were penetrating, and his lips were curled in scorn as he looked from his daughter to his granddaughter. I overheard him mutter to no-one in particular, 'A mouse can only give birth to a mouse.'

In the blink of an eye, Kareem snatched Maha from Father's sight and took her squirming and cursing into the villa to wash out her mouth with soap. Her muffled cries could be heard in the garden.

Father left soon after, but not before announcing to the entire family that my daughters were doomed by my blood.

Little Amani, who is too sensitive for such accusations, collapsed into hysterics.

My father has not acknowledged the existence of either daughter since that day.

Maha's belligerence and hostility did not prevent her from occasional bouts of kindness and sensitivity, and her temperament cooled somewhat after the incident in Taif. My daughter's angers ebbed and flowed. In addition, Kareem and I doubled our efforts to assure our daughters that they were as loved and esteemed as our son. While this proved fruitful in our home, Maha could not ignore the fact that she was considered less worthy than her brother in the world outside our walls. It is a distressing habit of all Saudi Arabians, including my own family and Kareem's, that they pour attention and affection on the heads of male children, while ignoring female children.

Maha was a bright girl who was hard to deceive, and the uncompromising facts of Arab life burned into her consciousness. I had strong presumptions that Maha was a volcano that would one day erupt.

Like many a modern parent, I had no clear notion of how to help my most troubled child.

Maha was only fifteen during the Gulf War, a time that no Saudi Arabian is likely to forget. Change was in the air, and no-one was more tempted by the promise of female liberation than my elder daughter. When our veiled plight piqued the curiosity of numerous foreign journalists, many educated women of my land began to plan for the day that they could burn their veils, discard the heavy black *abaayas*, and sit at the steering-wheel of their own cars.

I, myself, was so caught up in the excitement, I failed to notice that my older daughter had become involved with a teenage girl who took her idea of liberation to the extreme.

The first time that I met Aisha I was uncomfortable – not because she was unrelated to the royal family, for I, myself, had cherished friends outside the royal circle. Aisha was from a well-known Saudi Arabian family who had made their fortune importing furniture into the kingdom to sell to the many foreign companies who needed to fit out numerous villas for the swarm of expatriate workers invading Saudi Arabia.

I thought that the girl was too old for her years. Only seventeen, she looked much more mature, and acted in a tough manner that smelled of trouble.

Aisha and Maha were inseparable, with Aisha spending many hours at our home. Aisha had an unusual amount of freedom for a Saudi girl. Later, I discovered that the girl was virtually ignored by her parents, who seemed not to care about their daughter's whereabouts.

Aisha was the oldest of eleven children, and her mother, the only legal wife of her father, was embroiled in a never-ending domestic dispute with Aisha's father over the fact that her husband took advantage of a little-used Arab custom called *mut'a*, which is a 'marriage of pleasure', or a 'temporary marriage'. Such a marriage can last from one hour to ninety-nine years. When the man indicates to the woman that the temporary arrangement is over, the two involved part company without a divorce ceremony. The Sunni sect of Islam that dominates Saudi Arabia considers such a practice immoral, condemning the arrangement as nothing more than legalized prostitution. Still, no legal authority would deny a man such an arrangement.

As an Arab woman belonging to the Sunni Muslim sect, Aisha's mother protested the intrusion of temporary, one-night or one-week brides that her depraved husband brought into their lives. The husband, disregarding his wife's challenge, claimed validation through a verse in the Koran which says, 'you are permitted to seek out wives with your wealth, indecorous conduct, but not in fornication, but give them a reward for what you have enjoyed of them in keeping with your promise'. While this verse is interpreted by the Shiite sect of the Muslim faith as endorsement of the practice, these temporary unions are not common with Sunni Muslims. Aisha's father was the exception rather than the rule in our land, in embracing the freedom to wed young women for the sole pleasure of sex.

Occupied by the plight of helpless girls and women in my country, I questioned Aisha closely on the indecent practice that I had heard discussed by a Shiite woman from Bahrain, whom Sara had met and befriended in London some years before.

It seemed that Aisha's father did not want the responsibility of supporting four wives and their children on a permanent basis, so he sent his trusted assistant on monthly trips into Shiite regions in and out of Saudi Arabia to negotiate with various impoverished families for the right of temporary marriages with their virgin daughters. Such a deal could easily be struck with a man who had four wives, many daughters, and little money.

Aisha sometimes befriended these young girls who were transported into Riyadh for a few nights of horror. After Aisha's father's passion waned, the young brides were sent away, returned to their families wearing gifts of gold and carrying small bags filled with cash. Aisha said that most of the youthful brides were no more than eleven or twelve years old. They were from poor families and were uneducated. She said that they seemed not to know what exactly was happening to them. All the girls knew was that they were very frightened, and that the man Aisha called father, did very painful things to them. Aisha said that all of the girls cried to be returned to their mothers.

The hard-eyed Aisha wept as she related the story of Reema, a young girl of thirteen who had been brought to Saudi Arabia from Yemen, a poverty-stricken country that has a large number of Shiite Muslim families. Aisha said that Reema was as beautiful as the deer after which she was named, and as sweet as any girl that she had ever known.

Reema was from a nomadic tribe who roamed the harsh land of Yemen. Her father had only one wife, but twenty-three children, of which seventeen were girls. Even though Reema's mother was now shrivelled and bent from childbearing and hard work, she had once been a lovely girl and had given birth to seventeen beautiful daughters. Reema proudly said that her family was known as far away as Sana'a, the capital of that country, for the beauty of their women.

The family was very poor, with only three camels and twenty-two sheep. In addition, two of the six sons were handicapped from difficult births. One son's legs were twisted and he could not walk, and the other had strange, jerking spasms and could do no work. For these reasons,

Reema's father strove to sell his sought-after daughters to the highest bidder. During the summer months, the family would travel through high mountain passes, along narrow, tortuous roads into the city, and a deal would be struck for the daughter who had reached a marriageable age according to Islam.

The year before, at the age of twelve, Reema had reached puberty. She was her mother's favourite child, and the girl attended to her handicapped brothers. The family had pleaded with her father to let her remain with them for a few more years, but he sadly confessed that he could not allow it. There were two sons after Reema, and the sister closest in age was only nine years old. Reema's younger sister was small and undernourished, and her father feared that the girl might not reach puberty for another three or four years. Reema's family could not exist without the marriage money.

Reema was taken to Sana'a to be wed. While her father scouted the city for a suitable bridegroom, Reema remained in a small mud house with her sisters and brothers. On the third day, her father returned to the hut with a rich man from Saudi Arabia. Reema said that her father was very excited, for the man represented a wealthy man from Saudi Arabia, a man who would pay much gold for a beautiful girl.

The Saudi agent insisted upon seeing Reema before he paid the money, a request generally met with the blade of a Yemeni sword rather than humble compliance from a Muslim father. The gold in the agent's hands overcame the family's religious convictions. Reema said that she was inspected in the way that her father inspected the camels and sheep at market. Reema confessed that she did not protest the shame, for she had always known she would go to another family, as the purchased property of another man. But she squirmed and pushed when the man insisted upon viewing her teeth.

The agent pronounced Reema satisfactory and paid a portion of the agreed money. The family celebrated by killing a fat sheep, while the agent had Reema's documents prepared to fly to Saudi Arabia. Reema's father happily announced that the family could wait out the four years until Reema's younger sister reached the proper age, for the man from Saudi Arabia had paid a large sum for Reema.

Reema herself forgot her anxieties, even becoming excited, after her father told her that she was the most fortunate of girls. Reema was going to a life of leisure, that she would eat meat every day, have servants at her beck and call, and that her children would be educated and well fed. Reema asked her father if the man might purchase her a doll, one like she had seen in a discarded European magazine that the children had discovered in the rubbish bins in Sana'a.

Her father promised that he would make Reema's request a high priority.

When the man returned a week later, Reema first learned the terrible truth, that the marriage would not be honourable, that it was a marriage of *mut'a*, a temporary union. Her father became angry, for his honour was at stake, his daughter should not be treated in such a lowly manner. He pleaded with the man from Arabia, mentioning that it would be difficult to find another husband for his daughter, who would no longer be considered fresh and clean. He might be forced to provide for Reema for many years while seeking a man who would accept her as a second, less honoured wife.

The man sweetened the deal with a bundle of bills. He said that if Reema's father refused, then he would be forced to insist upon the return of money already paid.

Reluctantly, Reema's father had relented, admitting that he had already spent a portion of that sum. Ashamed, he turned his face to the ground and told Reema that she must go with the man, that it was God's will. Reema's father requested the Saudi man to find Reema a permanent husband in Saudi Arabia, since there were many Yemeni labourers working in that rich country.

The agent had agreed to try; otherwise, he said, Reema could become a servant in his own home.

Reema said goodbye to her family, and left the land of her birth, haunted by the pitiful weeping of her two handicapped brothers.

During the trip, the man had promised a homesick Reema that he would buy her a doll, even though such an item was expressly forbidden by the men of religion.

Like most Arab girls, Reema had full knowledge of a wife's responsibilities. She had slept in the same room with her parents since the day of her birth. Reema understood that a woman must submit to her husband's every wish.

Aisha said it was the girl's calm acceptance of her life of slavery that she found so distressing, recalling that the girl's tears belied her declaration that she was not displeased with her lot. Reema wept for the six days that she was in Aisha's home, all the while defending the right of Aisha's father to do with her as he pleased.

Aisha told me that her father's employee easily located a Yemeni man who worked as a tea boy in one of their offices, a man who had been willing to accept Reema as his second wife. His first wife was in Yemen, and he admitted that he needed a woman to cook his meals and serve him.

The last day that Aisha had seen Reema, the young girl was clutching a small doll, obediently following one man out of their home, to go and wed another man whom she did not know.

Aisha's mother, a pious Sunni Muslim, had become so distraught over Reema's situation that she had gone to her husband's family to complain. Her desperate act had created quite a furore in the family, but nothing the man's parents could say or do convinced their son to cease the godless act. Their advice had been for Aisha's mother to pray to God for her husband's soul.

I often wondered what became of those children, the *mut'a* brides, for it is quite difficult in the Muslim world to arrange a good marriage for a girl who is no longer a virgin. As dispensable girls in fortuneless families, I suppose they were eventually married off as the third or fourth wife to a man without wealth or influence, much in the same manner as Reema, or of my childhood friend, Wafa, who had been wed to such a one against her will.

Aisha's home life was agony for a thinking girl, and the stress and strain of her father's debauchery pushed Aisha into inevitable teenage decline.

My daughter, Maha, who was imprudent by nature, was captivated by Aisha's antics. Recalling my own rebellious youth, I knew the futility of prohibiting Maha from meeting Aisha.

Forbidden fruit is too tempting for all children, regardless of nationality or sex.

During the height of the Gulf War, our King harnessed the most aggressive of the roving bands of 'morals police', forbidding them to harass Western visitors to our land. Quite sensibly, the men of our family knew that it would not do for journalists from the West to view life as it really is in our country. Happily, the women of Saudi Arabia benefited from this royal order. The absence of sharp-eyed religious police patrolling the cities of Saudi Arabia, searching for uncovered women to strike with their sticks, or spray with red paint, was too good to be true. This policy endured no longer than the war itself, but for a few months we Saudi women enjoyed welcome respite from probing eyes. During this heady period, there was a universal call for the women of Saudi Arabia to take their proper place in society, and we foolishly thought that the favourable situation would continue for ever.

For some of our women, too much freedom given quickly proved disastrous. Our men were disappointed that all women did not behave as saints, without understanding the confusion caused by the contradictions of our lives.

Now I know that Aisha and Maha were two Saudi

girls not yet psychologically prepared for unfamiliar and complete freedom.

Due to the unusual times brought about by war, Aisha had managed to have herself appointed a volunteer at one of the local hospitals, and nothing would do but for my daughter to seek the same appointment at that institution. This she did two days a week after her school day ended. It was a marvellous experience for Maha, for although she was forced to wear her *abaaya* and head scarf, she was not required to wear the hated veil once inside the hospital doors.

Once the war ended, Maha refused to go back to the old ways. She held tight to her newfound freedom and begged her father and me to allow her to continue her work at the hospital.

Our approval was reluctantly given.

One afternoon Maha was expected at the hospital, and our driver was waiting in the front drive. I decided to go and hurry her. By some whim of circumstance, I happened to enter Maha's room just as my daughter was strapping a small calibre pistol to a brown leather holster attached to her thigh.

I was struck dumb! A weapon!

Kareem happened to be home for the afternoon siesta, and upon hearing our raised voices, he came to investigate. After an emotional scene, Maha confessed that during the war, she and Aisha had begun to arm themselves, in the event that the Iraqi army broke through to Riyadh! Now that the war was over, she thought she might need protection from the morals police who had begun to threaten women on the street.

The 'morals' or 'religious police', sometimes called the *Mutawwa*, are members of the 'Committee for Enforcing Right and Forbidding Wrong'. During the Gulf War period, these men were instructed by King Fahd to relax their harsh enforcements against improper attire worn by females. Now that the foreign journalists had departed the kingdom, these zealots were more active than we could ever recall, initiating arrests and prosecutions against women in my country.

Maha and Aisha had decided that they would not endure the attentions of the zealots let loose upon innocent women.

I looked at my daughter in alarm and disbelief! Was she planning to fire upon a man of religion?

Kareem learned that the weapon belonged to Aisha's father. He, like many Arab men, had quite a collection of firearms and had not missed two pistols that his daughter and Maha had stolen.

Imagine our horror when we learned that the pistol was loaded, but had no safety-catch. Maha tearfully disclosed that she and Aisha had practised firing the pistols in a vacant lot at the back of Aisha's home!

To Maha's dismay, her enraged father confiscated the illegal weapon and bundled her into his Mercedes. Dismissing his driver, Kareem drove like a madman across the city of Riyadh to Aisha's home in order to return the gun and warn Aisha's parents of our children's dangerous activities.

The result of our bizarre discovery was a hasty conference called between ourselves and Aisha's parents. Both of our daughters were sent to Aisha's room.

Aisha's mother and I, covered still by our black veils, sat in our separate worlds and discussed the children to whom we had given life. Oddly enough, for once in my life I was pleased to be veiled, for I could stare in undisguised contempt at Aisha's father, a man I knew to be a molester of young girls. Surprisingly, he was a youthful man with a dignified appearance.

I thought to myself, beware of those who look like a rose, for even roses have thorns. With the main topic of the evening being our daughters, I had little time to dwell upon the dark secrets of the home we were visiting.

What Kareem and I uncovered that evening about our elder daughter's shocking convictions will haunt our memories until we cease to walk the earth.

While I question the unjust practices and cruel customs inflicted upon the female population of Saudi Arabia by those who so rigidly interpret – and thus often misinterpret – the laws laid down by the Prophet, there is no doubt in my mind of the existence of one God as preached by his messenger, Mohammed. Our three children have been raised to revere the teachings of the Prophet and the Koran which was passed down from God. That a child of mine would curse God and denounce his word brought a chill to my heart and numbed me.

When the decision was announced to Aisha and Maha that their parents had arrived at the reasonable conclusion that the two girls should henceforth avoid each other's company, and seek out other friends and new interests, my daughter Maha yanked the veil from her face, raised her head in fury and displayed such a look of evil that she terrorized her own mother who had carried her in her womb and suckled her at her breast. If I had not heard Maha's words with my own ears, no person could convince me of their validity.

Her full lips tight with determination, our daughter yelled. 'I will *not* do as you say! Aisha and I will leave this land we hate and make our home in another place. We hate it here! *We hate it!* To be a woman in this awful country you must defile your life with the most tremendous injustices.'

Spittle dripped from Maha's lips. Her body moved with uncontrolled rage. Her eyes sought my eyes. 'If a girl lives modestly, she is a fool. If she lives normally, she is a hypocrite. If she believes there is a God, *she is an imbecile*!'

Unable to move, Kareem did manage to find his voice. 'Maha! You blaspheme!'

'Blaspheme? What is there to blaspheme? *There is no God*!'

Kareem jumped to his feet and squeezed Maha's lips together with his fingers.

Aisha's mother screamed and fainted, for such a statement can cost a life in the land of my birth.

Aisha's father shouted out for us to remove our unbelieving daughter from his home.

Kareem and I struggled with Maha, who suddenly had the strength of a giant. My daughter had lost her mind! Only the insane have such unnatural power! After much pulling and pushing, Kareem and I shoved our child into the back seat of the car and raced back to our home. Kareem drove while I tried to quieten my child, who no longer knew her mother. Finally, she lay still, as someone in a swoon.

An Egyptian physician, who was a trusted family doctor, was summoned. In a vain attempt to calm us, he said that there were many such disorders in teenage girls the world over, and proceeded to cite statistics on the strange malady that seems to affect females only.

The physician had his own theory. He claimed that at puberty, a girl often produces large doses of hormones, and such an event drives them crazy for short periods of time. He said that he had treated many such psychological cases within the royal family, without any complications or permanent effects. He grinned and stated that he had not lost a patient yet.

In the doctor's opinion, Maha should be kept sedated for a few days, and she would recover from the case of hysterics on her own.

Leaving us with an ample supply of tranquillizers, the physician said that he would return in the morning to check on his patient.

Kareem thanked the doctor, and walked him to the door. When he returned, we exchanged a long and thoughtful look. There were no words necessary between us.

While Kareem arranged for our private plane to be made ready, I telephoned my sister, Sara, and gained permission for Abdullah and Amani to stay with her until our return. Kareem and I were taking Maha to London. She was in desperate need of the best psychiatric care available. Sara was asked to keep Maha's condition a secret. If enquiries were made, our families were to be told that Maha was in need of dental care that required a number of visits to London.

Many members of the Saudi royal family routinely travel abroad for medical and dental treatment. Such a trip would arouse little curiosity.

While packing Maha's clothing, I came across disturbing books and documents that were hidden under her underwear. There were numerous writings on astrology, black magic, and witchcraft. Maha had underlined many passages detailing revelations and prophecies. Most alarming to my mind were malevolent items that were supposed to wreak dire evils upon people who had offended her, or induce love at a glance, or cause death by a spell.

I caught my breath when I saw a clothing item of Abdullah's wrapped around a black stone with some bits of loose, grey-coloured substance that I could not identify. I stood, hand to forehead, thinking. Could it be true? Had Maha plotted to harm her only brother? If this were the case, then I was a failure as a mother.

In a state of upheaval, I moved about in a turmoil, collecting damning evidence of my child's barbaric interests. Confused, I traced in my mind Maha's activities from the days of her childhood. Where had my daughter learned of such matters, accumulating a treasure-house of dark paraphernalia?

I remembered Huda, my father's long-deceased slave, and her obvious abilities at predicting the future. But Huda had died before my daughter's birth. As far as I knew, there were no other freed slaves or servants from Africa in our homes who possessed Huda's power of sorcery.

I recoiled, as if hit, as I thought of my mother-in-law, Noorah. It had to be Noorah! Disappointed that her son had neither divorced me nor taken a second wife, Noorah had never ceased to hate me, although she was careful to hide her dislike under a thin veneer of false affections.

From Kareem's revelations to his mother, Noorah had detected with her eagle eyes that Maha was my weakest point. From a young age, Maha's mental life had been one of conflict and pain, and Noorah had seized on that pain and found it vulnerable.

It was plain to see that Noorah had always favoured Maha over her other granddaughters, and her attention had been gratefully received by the confused child. Maha had spent long hours alone with her grandmother. Noorah, an avid believer in the occult, had lost no time in teaching my daughter her own ominous beliefs. How could I, Sultana, be so stupid to believe that Noorah had my best interests in mind?

I had been a fool, for my heart had been softened by Noorah's obvious delight in Maha, and I had often expressed my profound appreciation for her generous attentions towards my most troubled child. Noorah, in her dislike of me, had chosen to lead my emotionally fragile daughter deeper into the abyss.

I knew that I must confide my findings to Kareem. My actions would have to be delicate, for Kareem would have great difficulty in believing that his mother was capable of such a shameful deed. The truth could become twisted, and I, Sultana, might bear the brunt of his anger, while Noorah would sit contentedly in her palace gloating at her most hated daughter-in-law's failure as a mother and wife.

Chapter Three

LONDON

Not for ever can one enjoy stillness and peace. But misfortune and obstruction are not final. When the grass has been burnt by the fire of the steppe, it will grow anew in summer.

Wisdom from the Mongolian Steppe

Under the influence of strong medication, Maha lay as one dead, while her father and I attempted to make some sense of the precarious situation in which we found ourselves. On the aeroplane to London, Kareem sat like a stone, pale-faced as he handled the distasteful objects that I had brought in a small bag from Maha's room. He, like myself, was appalled at our daughter's fascination in the supernatural.

After a few silent moments, Kareem posed the question that I had been dreading. 'Sultana, where did Maha come across such madness?' His brow furrowed, and he wondered aloud, 'Do you believe it was that foolish girl, Aisha?'

I squirmed in my seat, not knowing how to answer my husband. Recalling a wise Arab proverb spoken often by my gentle mother, 'A fly will never be able to enter a mouth which knows when to stay shut', I felt that this was not the time to implicate Noorah, my husband's mother. Kareem had endured too many shocks for one day.

Biting my lip and shaking my head, I answered him, 'I don't know. We'll tell the doctor what we found. Perhaps

Maha will confide in him, then we'll know who or what is behind her knowledge of such matters.'

Kareem nodded his head in agreement.

For the remainder of the flight, we took turns sleeping, and watching our child, who appeared in her drug-induced sleep as sweet as an angel. For some unexplained reason, I was reminded of another Al Sa'ud royal, Princess Misha'il, a young woman who hid her deception of illicit love. When her secret was discovered, my royal cousin's life ended in the face of a firing-squad.

While Kareem slept, I watched Maha, and remembered Princess Misha'il.

Misha'il was the granddaughter of Prince Mohammed Ibn Abdul Aziz, the same Prince Mohammed who had been passed over for the crown, because of his father's ruling that the ferocious behaviour of a warrior had no place on a throne.

While I did not have a close friendship with Misha'il, I had met her at various royal functions. She was known in the family as a rather wild girl. I thought perhaps her unhappy temperament had something to do with her marriage to an old man, who failed to placate her. Whatever it was, she was miserable and became romantically involved with Khalid Muhalhal, who happened to be the nephew of the special Saudi Arabian envoy to Lebanon.

Their love affair was hot and filled with the tension caused by the impossible social climate of Saudi Arabia. Many members of the royal family had heard of their illicit relationship, and when the young couple were on the brink of discovery, they made a fatal decision to run off together.

My oldest sister, Nura, was in Jeddah at the time, and heard the story firsthand from a member of Misha'il's immediate family. Misha'il, fearing the wrath of her family, attempted to stage her own death. She told her family that she was going for a swim at their private beach on the Red Sea. Misha'il piled her clothes on the shore, then dressed herself as a Saudi man and tried to flee the country.

Unfortunately, for Misha'il, her grandfather, Prince Mohammed, was one of the shrewdest and most powerful men in the country. He did not believe she had drowned. Officials manning all exits from the country were alerted to search for the granddaughter of Prince Mohammed. Misha'il was caught – intercepted trying to catch a flight from the airport in Jeddah.

Telephones were ringing all over the kingdom, with each royal professing to know more than the next. There was a rumour a minute. I heard that Misha'il had been set free and allowed to leave the kingdom with her lover. Then I was told that a divorce would be granted. Later, a hysterical cousin called and claimed that Misha'il had been beheaded, and that it had taken three blows to separate her head from her body. Not only that, Misha'il's lips had moved and had called out her lover's name, causing the executioner to run from the scene! Can you imagine, my excited cousin asked, words from a bodiless head!

Finally, the very real and ugly truth was made known. Prince Mohammed, in a fit of anger, said that his granddaughter was an adulteress and that an adulteress should submit to Islamic law. Misha'il and her lover were going to be executed.

King Khalid, who was our ruler during this time of tragedy, was known for his indulgent nature. He recommended that Prince Mohammed show mercy, but mercy was not an emotion that was agreeable to that fierce bedouin.

On the day of the execution, I waited with my siblings for news of the event. My sisters and I hoped for a last-minute reprieve. Ali, not surprisingly, expressed the opinion that adulterous women should submit to the laws of Islam and prepare themselves for death.

On that hot day in July of 1977, my cousin Misha'il was blindfolded and forced to kneel before a pile of dirt. She was shot by a firing-squad. Her lover was forced to watch her die. He was then beheaded with a sword.

Once again, unsanctioned love had cost two young people their lives.

The affair was hushed up, and the Al Sa'ud clan hoped that talk of a young woman murdered for the simple act of love would soon disappear. It was not to be. Though buried in the sands of the desert, Misha'il was not forgotten.

Many Westerners will recall the documentary about her death, called, appropriately, *Death of a Princess*. As divided as our family was over her punishment, nothing compared with the arguments and hostility generated by the film.

Having comfortably mastered the role of dictators, the men in our family grew furious over their inability to control the news releases and films shown in the West. Offended to the edge of madness, King Khalid ordered the ambassador from Great Britain to leave our country.

I heard later from Kareem and Assad, Sara's husband, that our rulers had seriously considered forcing all British citizens out of our country!

International tensions ran high over the sexual misconduct and execution of one Saudi Arabian princess.

I despaired of the memory. I held my head in my hands. Now, I was the mother of a child who had gone mad. In her madness, what act might Maha commit that would disrupt our family and introduce the pain of young death into our home? My uncharitable father would surely insist upon the harshest of punishments for the child of my womb who had so spitefully and vigorously pointed out his shortcomings as a grandfather.

Maha stirred.

Kareem awakened, and once again we shared our tortured fears for our daughter.

While we were *en route* for London, as agreed, Sara had made the necessary medical arrangements by telephone. We called my sister from Gatwick Airport. Sara reported that Maha was expected at a leading mental institute in

London and that her bed was waiting. Sara had thoughtfully arranged for an ambulance to transport us to the institute.

Once we had fulfilled the tiresome admission procedures, Kareem and I were informed by the hospital staff that Maha's physician would meet us the following morning after his initial consultation and his examination of our child. One of the younger nurses was especially kind. She held my hand and whispered that my sister had found one of the most respected physicians in the city, that he had years of experience with Arab women and their unique social and mental problems.

At that moment, I envied the British. In my land, shame over a child's madness would close the minds and mouths of my countrymen, and sympathy would never be shown.

Anguished at leaving our precious child in the hands of strangers, albeit capable strangers, Kareem and I walked sluggishly to the waiting car which would take us to our apartment in the city.

Aroused from sleep, our permanent staff at our London home were clearly not expecting us. Kareem was irritated, but I calmed him with the thought that our personal comfort was the last thing on Sara's mind. We could not fault her for not telephoning our servants prior to our arrival.

Due to the Iraqi invasion of Kuwait, and the recent Gulf War, it had been almost a year since we had visited London, one of our favourite spots in the Western world. In our absence, our three servants had grown slovenly and careless. Whether we were in London or Riyadh, they had strict instructions to maintain the apartment as if we were in the city.

We were too depressed over Maha's condition to complain. Kareem and I sat among the dust-sheets in the sitting-room and ordered strong coffee. Servants scurried about the place as best they could, considering they had been awakened at three o'clock in the morning.

I found myself apologizing for intruding on their sleep, and Kareem snapped at me, ordering, 'Sultana! Never apologize to those who are paid by us. You'll ruin their work habits!'

I felt peevish and wanted to retort that we Saudis could benefit from a little humility. Instead, I changed the subject and began to talk once again about our daughter.

I thought to myself that I too must be coming down with some form of insanity. Twice in one day I had chosen to avoid an argument with my husband.

After our bed was prepared, Kareem and I rested without sleeping.

Never had a night seemed so long.

The British psychiatrist was an odd-looking man whose head sat large on his small body. His brow was vast, and his nose slightly skewed to one side. I could only stare in surprise at the tufts of white hair that sprouted strangely from his ears and nose. While his appearance was disconcerting, his manner was encouraging. With his small, blue, penetrating eyes, I could tell that he was a man who took the problems of his patients very seriously. My daughter was in good hands.

Kareem and I quickly discovered that he was a man who spoke what was on his mind. Without caring about our wealth, or Kareem's princely status in the royal family of Riyadh, he spoke with fearless honesty of the system of our land that so hobbled the will of women.

Well-informed of the traditions and customs of Arab lands, he told us, 'As a child I was fascinated by the Arabian explorers: Philby, Thesiger, Burton, Doughty, Thomas, and of course, Lawrence. I devoured their adventures. And, quite determined to view what I had read about, I convinced my parents to send me to Egypt. It wasn't Arabia, but it was a start, anyway. To my misfortune, I arrived just as the Suez Crisis occurred. But, I was hooked.'

His eyes took on a faraway look. 'I went back years later . . . set up a small practice in Cairo . . . learned a bit of Arabic,' he paused, looking at Kareem, 'and found out more than I wanted to know about the way you fellows treat your women.'

Kareem's love of his daughter proved stronger than his love of honour. To my relief, he remained quiet, his face free of all expression.

The doctor looked pleased. He seemed to be thinking that 'here is an Arab who would not spout nonsense about the need to lock females in *purdah*'.

The worry in Kareem's voice told the doctor of his love of Maha. 'Will our daughter recover? Fully recover?' He asked.

I moved to the edge of my seat. I could hear my heart pounding in my ears.

The doctor clasped both hands together, rubbing them as if he were lubricating his palms. Looking from Kareem to me, he heaped drama upon an already dramatic situation. His face remained bland as he answered, 'Will your daughter recover? *Fully* recover? I have talked to her for just an hour. Therefore, it's difficult to summarize her case completely.' Looking upon my stricken face, he added, 'But, her case seems quite typical. I've treated a good number of Arab ladies who suffered from hysterics, women who were visiting our city. Generally speaking, given time and proper care, I would say that your daughter's prognosis is favourable.'

I wept in my husband's arms.

Maha's physician left us alone in his office.

For three months, I remained in London while Maha underwent psychiatric tests and treatment. Once we understood that our daughter required lengthy care, that cure could not be pronounced in a matter of days, Kareem travelled back and forth to Riyadh, making a point of being in London on Tuesdays and Thursdays, the two days of the week that we were allowed to visit our child.

During our visits, we offered Maha peace, but she preferred to fight. It was as if a thousand terrors limited her ability to speak calmly and reasonably. Nothing we could say or do pleased her. Following the physician's instructions, Kareem and I refused to argue with our child. At those moments, Maha argued with herself, even going so far as to speak in two voices! Maha's doctor reassured us that the time would come when Maha's mental state would improve beyond our expectations.

How we prayed for that moment to arrive!

The intense visits wore poorly on Kareem. I could see my husband aging before my eyes. I said to him one evening, 'If nothing else, I have learned that aging has nothing to do with accumulation of years. Aging is the inevitable defeat of parents by their young.'

A small twinkle came into Kareem's eyes, the first sign of joy that I had seen in many days. He claimed, in all seriousness, that it could not be so. 'If that were the case, Sultana, your long-suffering father would appear the oldest living man on the planet.'

Pleased that my husband showed a glimmer of life, I let the reference pass and leaned fondly on his shoulder, relieved that our family tragedy had brought us closer together rather than pushed us further apart. At that moment I reminded myself that no person leads an irreproachable life, and I forgave my husband for the trauma I had endured in his futile quest for a second wife. Full of emotions I had assumed I'd lost for ever, I congratulated myself on the worth of the man I had wed.

In time, Kareem and I witnessed a miracle.

Maha's doctor was, as I had expected, a man of genius and perseverance, a devoted physician whose natural abilities diluted my daughter's frightful demons. In happy obscurity, while locked in the drabbest of offices in the dreariest of hospital wards, he combined his medical knowledge with rich experiences learned in the world of Arab women, and gained my daughter's trust. With this trust, the physician opened her wounds, and torrents of jealousy, hate, and anger spilled from Maha's trembling hands onto the pages of an ordinary note-pad, producing an extraordinary journal.

Weeks later, while reading one of these short but disturbing stories from her notes, given freely from Maha's hands to her parents, Kareem and I discovered the depths into which our child had plunged in a world more sinister than either of us could have ever imagined.

Living in the Mirage of Saudi Arabia
or
The Harem of Dreams
by
Princess Maha Al Sa'ud

During the dark period of Saudi Arabian history, ambitious desert women could only dream of harems stocked with hard muscled men, well endowed with instruments of pleasure. In the enlightened year of 2010, when the matriarchal family ascended into power, with the most intelligent woman crowned Queen, women became the political, economic, and legal authority of society.

The great wealth accumulated during the oil boom of the year 2000, the boom that had crippled the powers of the United States, Europe, and Japan to that of third world powers, assured the land of Arabia plenty for generations to come. With little but time on their hands, women addressed social issues that had plagued the land for more years than they could remember.

A small minority of women voted to abolish polygamy, the practice of taking four husbands, while the majority, remembering the evils the practice had spawned when the kingdom was a patriarchal society, recognized that while the system was not the best that they could devise, it was the only social system that embittered women would receive. The pleasures of love that had been forbidden now wormed their way into the mind of every woman, even that of the waif-like Malaak, the daughter of the Queen of Saudi Arabia.

Malaak danced a hot dance of love, challenging her favourite lover, Shadi, with a gold sovereign between her lips, motioning with her head for the man to pull it out with his teeth.

Malaak was small and brown-skinned with delicate features. Her lover was large and heavy with muscles of steel. Wanting desperately to achieve his goal of being appointed the most influential man in the harem, Shadi moved his tongue over every part of Malaak's body, enticing her senses in an agony of passion.

In a frenzy of movement, Shadi removed the coin with his teeth, and lifted Malaak into his arms, taking her behind the flimsy curtains of his assigned section of the harem. There, the lovers pressed against each other, the warmth of their breath spreading over their faces, and down their necks, to their chests. Shutting out the world, they began to kiss.

Malaak opened her eyes to watch her lover perform his rhythmic movements. Her muscles tensed when she saw that the man Shadi had softened into a woman!

Life having produced a cynical soul, Malaak adjusted herself to the power at hand, and she became enamoured of the loveliness of the woman who shared her bed. Choosing between being feared without love and being loved without fear, Malaak could not sacrifice the love.

With Machiavellian subtlety, Malaak became what she had to be in the circumstances and atmosphere of her time.

With a pale, sickly look, Kareem laid the pages of Maha's journal on the doctor's desk. Bewildered, he asked, 'What does this mean?' He gestured toward the note-pad, his tone accusatory. 'You said that Maha was much improved. This writing is nothing more than the ramblings of a lunatic.'

I know not the source of my instinct, but I knew what the doctor was going to say before he said it. I could not breathe, I could not speak, I saw the room through a haze of blue. The doctor's voice came to me from a distance.

The doctor was gentle with Kareem. 'It's quite simple, really. Your daughter is telling you that she has made the discovery that men are her enemies, and that women are her friends.'

Kareem still did not comprehend what the doctor was saying. He was impatient in his ignorance. 'Yes? So?'

There was nothing else to do but to speak bluntly. The doctor verbalized what I already knew. 'Prince Kareem. Your daughter and her friend, Aisha, are lovers.'

Kareem was quiet for many minutes. When Kareem regained his senses, he had to be restrained, and kept from Maha's side for three days.

Muslims are taught that love and sex between two of the same is wrong, and the Koran forbids experimenting: 'Do not follow what you do not know.' In Saudi Arabia, love and sex are considered distasteful, even between those of the *opposite* sex, and our society pretends as if relationships based on sexual love do not exist. In this atmosphere of shame, Saudi citizens respond to social and religious expectations by *saying* exactly what is expected. What we *do* is another matter altogether.

Arabs are by nature sensuous, yet live in a puritanical society. The topic of sex is of national interest to everyone, including that of our Saudi Government which spends enormous amounts of money employing countless censors. These men sit in government offices, searching out what they deem are odious references to women and sex in every publication allowed into the kingdom. Rarely does a magazine or newspaper make it past Saudi censors without losing a number of pages, or having sentences or paragraphs blacked out by the censor's every-ready pen.

This form of extreme censorship against all conventional social behaviour affects every aspect of our lives, and the lives of those who compete to claim our business.

When one of Assad's companies contracted with a foreign film company to make a simple food commercial for Saudi Arabian television, the list of restrictions that accompanied the contract would have been amusing had it not been authentic. The list of restrictions read:

1. There can be no attractive females in the commercial.
2. If a female is included, she cannot wear revealing clothing such as short skirts, pants, or swimming suits. No flesh can be exposed other than the face, and hands.
3. No two people can eat from the same dish, or drink from the same cup.
4. There can be no fast body movement. (It is suggested in the contract that if a female is used, she has to sit or stand without moving at all.)
5. There can be no winking.
6. Kissing is taboo.
7. There can be no burping.
8. Unless it is absolutely necessary to sell the product, (it is suggested) that there be no laughter.

When the normal is forbidden, people fall into the abnormal.

That, I believe, is what happened to my daughter.

In my country, religious law prohibits single men and women from seeing each other. While inside the country, men socialize with men and women with women. Since we are prevented from engaging in traditional behaviour, the sexual tension between those of the same sex is palpable.

Any foreigner who has lived in Saudi Arabia for a length of time becomes aware that homosexual relations are rampant within the kingdom.

I have attended many all-female concerts and functions where quivering beauties and suggestive behaviour triumphs over heavy veils and black *abaayas*. An orderly gathering of heavily perfumed and love-starved Saudi women festers into spontaneous exuberance, bursting forth in the form of a wild party with the singing of forbidden love accompanied by lusty dancing. I have watched as shy-faced women danced lewdly with other women, flesh to flesh, face to face. I have heard women whisper of love and plan clandestine meetings, while their drivers wait patiently in the parking lots. They will later deliver them to their husbands who are at that same evening captivated by other men.

While the conduct of men is overlooked, the behaviour of women, even with other women, is often carefully guarded. This is apparent by the various rules and regulations governing females.

Some years ago I cut out a small item from one of our Saudi Arabian newspapers to show to my sisters. I was particularly irritated by yet another foolish restriction placed upon women. A ban on cosmetics had been announced in a girls' school. Recently I ran across this clipping while throwing out some papers.

This article reads:

Cosmetics Ban in School

> The Director of Girls Education at Al Ras, Abdullah Muhammad Al Rashid, urged all students and staff of the school under the directorate to refrain from using cosmetics, dyestuffs, ornaments and other make-ups, inside the school compounds.
>
> The Director added that some staff and students were noticed of late to have been using transparent garments and cosmetics as well as high-heel

shoes, hence, such adornments are prohibited. While the students must keep uniformity in dress, the teachers should set good examples to the students. The authorities would not hesitate to take punitive measures against violators of school regulations, Al Rashid added.

I remember well what I had said to my sisters at the time. I waved the clipping angrily under their noses, raging, 'See! See for yourself! The men of this country want to regulate the wearing of our shoes, the ribbons in our hair, the colour of our lips!'

My sisters, while their anger did not equal mine, had sullenly complained that our men were obsessed with controlling every aspect of our lives, even that part of our daily living which was supposedly private.

In my opinion, the control fanatics that govern our traditional lives had driven my daughter into the arms of a woman! While I was greatly distressed and did not condone my daughter's relationship with another woman, in view of the harsh restrictions against those of her sex that she had inherited by the mere fact of being born female, I understood how she had come to seek solace with one of her kind.

Knowing the problem, I now felt more capable of seeking solutions.

Kareem feared that Maha's character was now marred by her experiences. As a mother, I could not agree. I told Kareem that the fact that Maha wanted to share her darkest secret with those who love her best pointed to recovery.

I was right in my assessment of the situation.

After months of professional treatment, Maha was ready for maternal guidance. For the first time in her young life, she drew close to her mother, wanting to communicate, tearfully acknowledging that from her earliest memory, she had hated all men but her father. She had no ready explanation for it.

I felt a twinge of guilt, wondering if my own prejudices against the male sex had seeped into the embryo to which I had given life. It was as if my daughter had been forewarned of the wicked nature of men, while lying cradled in my womb.

Maha confessed that the early trauma she had endured on the occasion of her parents' long separation had further eroded her trust in men. She asked, 'What was so wrong with Father that we had to flee from his presence?'

It had been many years since I had taken my children from their summer camp in Dubai and fled to safety into the countryside of France, not wishing to share my wifely status with another woman. France, with its humane people who shelter those in distress, had seemed the perfect spot to protect my young while I negotiated during those long months with my husband over his scheme to wed another woman. How I had tried to shield my children from the trauma of my own failing marriage, and our separation from Kareem!

What folly! As a parent, I know now that it is preposterous to believe that even minor parental conflict does not impinge upon the emotional well-being of a child. Hearing Maha say that my action in leaving her father had furthered her mental pain, allowing abnormal thoughts to creep into her consciousness, caused me more anguish than any previous agony I have known.

Maha confessed that even after Kareem and I had patched over our differences and we were united with our children again, our continuing strife had pierced the cocoon in which they lived.

When I prodded my daughter on her relationship with Aisha, Maha confided that she had not known that women could love women and men could love men. Such a possibility had never entered her mind, until the day that Aisha had shown her some magazines she had taken from her father's study. The magazines revealed photograph after photograph of beautiful women, in acts of female love. At first the photographs were a novelty, but later Maha came to see them as beautiful, sensing that the love between women was more tender and caring than the aggressive, possessive love of man to woman.

There were other disturbing revelations.

Aisha, a girl who had experimented with many social taboos before knowing my daughter, thought nothing of spying on her father's sexual misdeeds. The girl had made a small peephole in the study adjoining her father's bedroom. There, my daughter and her friend had watched as Aisha's father deflowered one young virgin after another. Maha claimed that the cries of those young girls had closed her mind to wanting a relationship with a man.

She told me an unbelievable tale that I would brush aside as fabrication, had my own daughter not witnessed the event.

Maha said that on one particular Thursday evening, Aisha had telephoned her, urging her to come over quickly. Maha said that Kareem and I were out so she had one of our drivers deliver her to Aisha's home.

Aisha's father had gathered together seven young girls in his home. Maha did not know if he had wed the girls, or if they were concubines.

My daughter watched as those young girls were made to prance naked around the room, each with a large peacock feather stuck up her backside. With these feathers, the girls were forced to fan and tickle the face of Aisha's father. Over the course of a long night, the father had had sex with five of the seven girls.

Afterwards, Maha and Aisha had stolen a feather and had played together on Aisha's bed, giggling and tickling each other's bodies. It was then that Aisha showed Maha the pleasure that women could have with one another.

Ashamed of her love for Aisha, Maha cried in my arms, sobbing that she wanted to be a happy, well-adjusted girl with a productive life. She cried out, 'Why am I different from Amani? We came from the same seed, but we have blossomed into different plants!' She screamed, 'Amani is a beautiful rose! I am a prickly cactus.'

Not knowing the ways of God, I could not answer my child. I held her in my arms and comforted her with the thought that the remainder of her life would be that of a beautiful flower.

Then my troubled daughter asked me the most difficult question of my life. 'Mother, how can I ever love a man, knowing all that I know of their nature?'

I had no ready answer, yet it was with profound happiness that I understood that Kareem and I had another chance with our daughter.

It was time to go home to Riyadh.

We did not leave before Kareem offered Maha's British physician a position in Riyadh as our family's personal doctor.

Much to our amazement, the physician refused. 'Thank you,' he said. 'I am honoured. Fortunately, or unfortunately, whatever is the case, my aesthetic sensibilities are too keen for Saudi Arabia.'

Undaunted, Kareem insisted upon rewarding the man with a large sum of cash. He even went so far as to try to put the money into the man's hand.

Maha's doctor firmly waved aside the offer, uttering words that had they not been spoken softly would have been a keen insult. 'My dear man, please, do not. The shallowness of wealth and power holds no appeal for me.'

While staring in awe at one of the least prepossessing figures I have ever beheld, I suddenly had the answer to Maha's earlier, unanswerable question! Later, I told Maha that she would one day meet a man deserving of her faithful love, for such men existed. She and I had met one in London.

Once back in Riyadh, the source of Maha's knowledge of black magic was revealed. It was as I had thought. Noorah was the culprit.

Maha told her father, in my presence, that it was her grandmother who had introduced her to the dark world of the occult. When we confronted her with Abdullah's clothing wrapped around a charm, Maha denied wanting to cast a spell on her brother.

Hoping that Maha had learned a great lesson, we did not press the issue.

I wanted nothing more than to confront my mother-in-law, spit in her face, and yank out her hair.

Kareem, wisely recognizing the dangers of pent-up anger, refused to let me accompany him when he went to confront her about her misdeeds. Nevertheless, I did coax my unenthusiastic sister, Sara, into paying a visit to our mutual mother-in-law's palace at the time of Kareem's visit.

Sara arrived at Noorah's villa shortly after my husband and waited in the garden until Kareem left. Sara said that she overheard Kareem's shouts and Noorah's pleas of mercy, for Kareem forbade his mother to visit his children unsupervised.

Long after my husband had left his mother, Sara said that Noorah's moans of despair could be heard in the garden. 'Kareem, most beloved, you came from my womb! Come back to your mother, who cannot live without your precious love.'

Sara accused me of being as wicked as Noorah, for I radiated much happiness when she told me of my treacherous mother-in-law's deserved wretchedness.

Chapter Four

MAKKAH

God, Great and Glorious is He, said: 'And proclaim among men the pilgrimage, they will come to you on foot and on every lean camel, coming from every deep ravine.'

Al-Haj, 22:27

There is no means of calculating the number of pious Muslims who have perished while making the gruelling journey across the deserts of Saudi Arabia since the time of Prophet Mohammed and the first pilgrimage, but the total of dead is estimated to be in the thousands. While I am pleased to report that it is no longer necessary for devout Muslims to do battle with raiding bedouin parties, or even to travel through Saudi Arabia on foot or on lean camels, in order to fulfil their fervent desire to perform one of the basic tenets of Islam, still, the annual pilgrimage to the holy city of Makkah remains a chaotic affair. Each year, hundreds of thousands of pilgrims converge on the cities, airports, and highways of Saudi Arabia for the rite of pilgrimage during the time of *Haj*. (*Haj* begins in Dhu al-Qida, the 11th month of the hegira calendar, and ends during Dhu al-Hijah, the 12th month of the hegira calendar.)

I performed the traditional pilgrimage many times in my youth, as a laughing child in my mother's arms, and later as a rebellious girl seeking communication with my

God, whom I prayed would administer peace of mind to an unhappy child.

To my great dissatisfaction, since the moment Kareem and I wed, I had not worshipped in Makkah during the official time of *Haj*.

While Kareem and I, along with our children, have made the *Umrah*, or the lesser pilgrimage, which can be made any time of the year, never had we joined the multitudes in the massive annual celebration of *Haj*, a time that Muslims remind themselves of the lessons of sacrifice, obedience, mercy and faith, models of conduct that are required in the Islamic faith.

Many times over the years, I pointed out to my husband that our children should experience the moving occasion of the pilgrimage during the designated time of *Haj*. Much to my chagrin, Kareem was forever adamant that our family flee the pandemonium of Saudi Arabia during the annual pilgrimage, which brings the largest, and most concentrated gathering of human beings on earth into our country.

Each time I requested of Kareem the justification for his nonperformance of *Haj*, my husband would provide me with a multitude of lame explanations laden with contradiction.

Bewildered at his attitude and determined to get to the heart of the matter, I once purposely entangled Kareem in the discrepancy of his excuses, trapping him on the issue. Kareem was groping for a way out of his dilemma, when I plainly told my husband, a man who believes in the God of Mohammed, that it seemed to me that he abhorred the ritual that brings such joy to all Muslims. There was no other explanation for his bizarre behaviour.

I crossed my arms across my chest and waited for his response to an insulting charge that demanded clarification.

Kareem's face swelled with revulsion at the accusation so vile to a Muslim! Shocked at such a scandalous idea,

Kareem swore to me that he did not abhor the pilgrimage!

In the manner in which all men respond when they are in the wrong, Kareem then yelled out that 'I was ugly to his eyes', and he turned his back to me in an angry effort to leave the room, but I ran around his side and with outstretched arms blocked the door with my body, demanding he be more specific.

I screamed out that I was displeased with what I had heard, and that I would wait for ever for a compelling explanation for his addiction to annual *Haj* flight from the kingdom. Sensing that Kareem was in a position of weakness, I became reckless and added a small lie, saying that, 'Others have noticed your strange distaste for *Haj*, and people are beginning to talk.'

When Kareem saw that I would not remove myself without physical force, he stared down at me and hesitated for a long moment. I could see that Kareem was examining and weighing the wisdom of his reply. Making a decision, he pulled me by the arm and forced me down on the side of the bed by pushing my shoulders with his hands. He paced for a short time to the balcony doors and back, and then his defences fell.

Kareem confessed in a rush that as a young man he had once suffered a realistic and terrifying nightmare that he was crushed to death in a crowd of Hajiis (people of the Muslim faith who attend *Haj*).

I made a sound in my throat. Many baffling episodes regarding my husband's odd behaviour were now clear in my mind. Since the time I had first met him, Kareem had seen crowds where there were none, interpreting the smallest groups of people as a mass of humanity. I shook my head in confoundment, at the perplexing intimacies of my husband's inner life that I had never known. So! Kareem was frightened of the masses of pilgrims!

Being a strong believer in the powerful message of dreams, I turned my attention once more to Kareem's words, my mood grim as I listened to his vivid description of the imaginary yet frightening experience that he had endured while sleeping.

My husband's face became pale as he described the graphic illusion of being asphyxiated under the trampling feet of frenzied worshippers. He told me that since the time of his dream, when he was 23, that he had purposely avoided the congested conditions endured by the faithful in making the annual pilgrimage to Makkah.

Kareem so intensely felt that his nightmare would be fulfilled if he attended *Haj*, that I had little heart to haggle with a man and his visionary forebodings.

Once again, everything was as before, as our family continued to depart the kingdom during the time of *Haj*.

When the very real and ghastly tragedy of the 1990 *Haj* occurred, as over 1,500 pilgrims were crushed to death in a mountain tunnel in Makkah, Kareem took to his bed in Paris and trembled for a whole day, declaring that the cataclysmic disaster was yet another extraordinary omen from God that he should never again worship at the Holy Mosque!

After the fateful accident of 1990, when hundreds of worshippers died, Kareem's extreme reaction to a dream began to annoy me, and I told my husband that his fears were inherently unsound. Nothing I could say or do at the time comforted my husband, even when I pointed out the obvious, that his dream had been realized in the death of others. In my opinion, the exact catastrophe was unlikely to occur again.

I saw that my observation failed to quieten Kareem's fierce apprehension when he replied that, evidently, he would be crushed as a singular tragedy if he failed to heed his dream, or the recent mishap, which to his mind was nothing less than a direct warning from God.

Since it is true that a number of Hajiis are trampled or crushed to death every *Haj* season, I could not reason further with Kareem. I wanted to dismiss Kareem's obsession with his nightmare, to ignore his terrors, but I could not. I struggled successfully to indulge his fears.

Sadly, I pushed the possibility of ever again making the happy journey of *Haj* far into the back of my mind, but not from my heart.

After our triumphant return from London, with a loving Maha in our arms, I felt an irresistible desire to embrace the ritual of glorifying God in unison with other Muslims. The time of *Haj* was upon us, and I gently approached the topic with my husband once again, suggesting that I take our children to Makkah. Since women of our country rarely travel without the protection of a male escort, I wondered aloud about the possibility of accompanying my sister, Sara, and her family to Makkah.

Much to my surprise, Kareem responded favourably to my ardent wish to undertake a journey to the city of Mohammed. My mouth fell open when he said that he would consider taking the journey to *Haj*. Kareem acknowledged that his change in attitude was in spite of his continued fear of personal harm, but that he, too, shared my need to give special thanks to God for the return of our precious Maha.

We were discussing the forthcoming trip with members of Kareem's family when we received a warning from Kareem's brother-in-law, Mohammed, who was married to Kareem's youngest sister, Hanan. Mohammed said that over two million pilgrims were expected to unite in our holiest city of Makkah, and of that total, 150,000 worrisome worshippers were expected from Iran, the Shiite country that makes an annual call to revoke King Fahd's exclusive custodianship over Islam's holiest places.

In 1987, the inflamed Shiites had gone so far as to lead a violent protest during the traditional holy event, and in the process of breaching Saudi laws, had desecrated the Holy Mosque, causing the deaths of 402 pilgrims. Two years later, in 1989, Tehran had instigated two deadly bombings, killing one and wounding sixteen others.

In Mohammed's view, *Haj* was becoming a dangerous religious ceremony for peaceful Muslims. Radical

Muslims were on the move the world over, and they favoured the holiest of Islamic sanctuaries to make known their political grievances.

Mohammed, a prince of high authority in Public Security, a Saudi public service organization that strives to ensure the security of the Saudis and visiting Muslims to our country, was privy to knowledge that most Saudis do not have. Blind to my emotion, and absorbed only in our personal safety, Mohammed suggested that Kareem and I wait until the masses of pilgrims left the kingdom. Then, we could take our children and perform the sacred rites.

Kareem had a pale face and said little, and I knew that my husband was not in the slightest concerned over Iranian danger but was considering the dreaded effects of four million tramping feet.

Stubborn and determined to fulfil my personal desires, as is my way, I challenged Mohammed's warning, saying that, in my opinion, as a result of the Iranians' past capers, those pilgrims travelling from Iran would be so carefully screened and observed by Saudi Security, that they would be of little danger to *Haj* worshippers.

Mohammed, with a stern, and uneasy look on his face, said, 'No. The Iranians can *never* be trusted. Do not let yourself forget, Sultana, that we are dealing with Shiite fanatics who dream of overthrowing our Al Sa'ud-led Sunni Government!'

Seeing that my reasoning was not going to achieve the reassuring response that I was seeking, I used a female tactic, mischievously asking Mohammed and my husband if they failed to remember that, according to Islamic teachings, to die while in Makkah ensures immediate ascension to heaven?

My husband and brother-in-law failed to see any humour in the current situation, and my religious argument made little impact with Kareem, but obviously, he too, felt the wonderful release of anxiety regarding Maha's miraculous revival even more than I had imagined.

Kareem took a deep breath, gave a weak smile, and said, 'Sultana, I will face a thousand dangers if it will give you peace of mind. Together, we will take our children and go on the pilgrimage.'

Mohammed hid a disappointed face with a smile, and I gave my husband an unexpected kiss on the cheek, and began to pull on his earlobes, promising him that he would never regret his decision.

Mohammed looked scandalized at my affectionate display, and made some small excuse to leave the room. Kareem's younger sister, Hanan, who had been married for some years to Mohammed, gave us a knowing smile and said that we should ignore her husband's prudish façade, that Mohammed was the most loving, affectionate, and attentive of men behind closed doors.

I laughed aloud, wondering about their secret life of sweet sex, for Mohammed had always seemed strict and stand-offish, and in the past I had pitied my sister-in-law.

I looked at my husband and saw that his face had reddened at the idea of his sister's marriage bed. I thought to myself that our Saudi men are too uptight, and unbearably puritanical when it comes to married passion, even their own.

Remembering that we were soon going to Makkah, I kissed my husband again! I was elated!

Kareem and I invited Sara, Assad, and their growing brood to accompany our family on our long-awaited religious odyssey. Sara never failed to do *Haj* and was immensely pleased that our family was not going to travel abroad on our usual lengthy European holiday during the religious occasion.

We made excited plans to depart Riyadh for Makkah in two days' time.

Finally, it was the day of our trip to Makkah. There was much to be accomplished! Our plan was to meet Sara and her family at the airport in Riyadh at seven o'clock in the evening. Prior to that time, each member of the family had to enter *Ihram*, which is marked by an all-consuming intention of the heart to fulfil all the rites of pilgrimage.

During the time of *Ihram*, nothing involving normal life is acceptable. Hair cannot be cut, nails cannot be trimmed, beards cannot be shaved, perfumes cannot be worn, garments with seams cannot be worn, animals cannot be killed, sexual relations must be postponed, and direct contact between men and women avoided, until the sacred time of *Ihram* has ended.

Each member of our family started their rituals for the pilgrimage before leaving Riyadh. It was important for each person to enter into a state of purity even before the long awaited journey began.

Startling my Filipino maid, Cora, who was dusting in my bedroom, I entered my private quarters while chanting the famous cry uttered by all pilgrims as they perform the rites while in the holy city of Makkah, 'Here I am, God! Here I am! Here I am to do your bidding.'

After Cora recovered herself, I, in a happy frame of mind, explained the significance of our upcoming religious journey.

Cora, a dedicated Catholic, had little understanding of Muslim traditions, but as a girl of deep religious convictions, she did appreciate my delight at going on a pilgrimage.

I continued to chant my cry to God as a smiling Cora filled my bath.

I counted off on my fingers all the tasks I had to accomplish. My face had to be cleansed of all make-up, and I had to take off my jewellery, even the 10 carat flawless diamond earrings given to me by my husband the year before, pieces of jewellery that I rarely removed from my pierced ears.

After removing my earrings and placing them in the large bedroom safe that holds my collection of precious jewels, I submerged myself for hours in a hot tub, to cleanse myself symbolically of any impurities. While soaking, I prepared myself for the journey by repeating aloud God's command to Muslims to visit Makkah, 'And proclaim among men the pilgrimage, they will come to you on foot and on every lean camel, coming from every deep ravine.'

I put aside any and every thought of my family and myself, and concentrated instead about things of peace and feelings of love for fellow man.

After my long bath, I wrapped myself in a seamless black garment and covered my hair with a lightweight black scarf. Facing the holy city of Makkah, I prostrated myself on the bedroom floor, and performed my prayers, appealing to God to accept the rites of *Haj* from me.

Finally, I was prepared for my journey.

I met my husband and children in the sitting-room downstairs. Kareem and Abdullah were immaculate in white seamless robes and plain sandals. Maha and Amani were dressed in modest, dark coloured garments that covered all flesh except their faces, feet and hands. They, as I, were not veiled. It is not necessary to cover female faces while doing *Haj*. 'The true veil is in the eyes of men,' runs a saying of the Prophet. Thus, women on pilgrimage are forbidden to cover their faces while on *Haj*.

As a child, I often queried my mother on the strange necessity of covering her face before man but not before God. My mother, reared never to question the authority of men, appeared baffled and confused at the sane logic put forth by her enquiring daughter, but having spent a lifetime under the rigid jurisdiction of men, hushed her child and made no answer to what I believe is still a justifiable question.

Now, looking at my daughters' faces in all their innocence, the memory came flowing into my mind.

I hugged each of my daughters, and said in an irritated tone, 'When man comes to share God's wisdom, you can discard the veils that you so hate!' I could not help but to toss a glance of contempt at my husband and son.

Kareem moaned, 'Sultana,' admonishing me for what I had done!

I was struck with the horrible thought that I had broken my *Haj* vow! I had lapsed into a moment of discord, thinking of worldly concerns, when I must rejoice in topics of peace and love.

Embarrassed by my indiscretion, I left the room in a rush, explaining that I must perform my rituals once again.

Kareem was smiling, and my children began to laugh, as they seated themselves on the chairs and sofas, patiently waiting for my return.

I prostrated myself on the bedroom floor, asking God to quieten my tongue and assist me in entering *Ihram* once again.

While I was praying, sad thoughts of my mother once again crept into my mind, and angry images of my father played across my eyes, ending the tranquillity so necessary in entering *Ihram*. With a frowning face, I had to begin my prayers again, from the very beginning.

I was on the verge of tears when I rejoined my family, and my husband gave me a tender look of love which I mistook for a sexual thought. I shouted at Kareem, and then burst into tears, declaring that I could not go to *Haj*, that my family would have to leave without me, for I could not calm my active and spiteful mind in order to enter the state of *Ihram*!

Kareem gave a nod to my daughters, for our flesh was forbidden contact, and Maha and Amani laughingly pushed me from the room into the waiting car. We were going to the airport.

Kareem calmed my protests by saying that I could go through my rituals once again on the aeroplane, or at our home in Jeddah before we made the short drive the following morning to Makkah.

Assad, Sara and their children were waiting for us in the royal waiting lounge at the King Khalid International

Airport, which is a forty-five-minute drive out of the city of Riyadh.

I greeted my sister and her family with strained silence, and after Maha whispered in my sister's ear, Sara gave a knowing smile that told me she understood our delay.

Our family travelled by air in one of Kareem's private Lear jets to Jeddah. It was a quiet journey, with adults thinking of God, and their planned communication with him. The older children played quiet games, while the younger ones slept or looked through some books.

Respectful of my inability to control my tongue, I spoke not a word until moments before we landed, and then I spoke too much.

It was night when we arrived at the King Abdul Aziz International Airport at Jeddah, and I was pleased when Kareem instructed the American pilot to take us through the *Haj*, or Pilgrim's Terminal, which is a surrealistic tent city that covers 370 acres of land. The Pilgrim's Terminal is for incoming pilgrims from other lands, but our royal status made it possible for us to land wherever we might wish.

A few years before, Kareem had taken Abdullah to the grand opening of the terminal, but neither of my daughters had yet been inside the spectacular building.

Forgetting my earlier vow to remain silent until my feet touched the streets of Makkah, I felt an unexplained urge for my daughters to discover a source of pride in their heritage, even if that pride were linked implicitly with economic wealth.

Initially, I spoke in a quiet voice that I knew would not be offensive to God. I explained to my daughters that the terminal had won an international award as a unique design and as an advanced engineering innovation. I felt a surge of pride in the infrastructure that Saudi Arabians had accomplished in one short generation. No longer feeling the shame of my ancestors' wrenching poverty, which had haunted me in my younger days, the old passions left me, and my sense of the past was sharpened. What had once seemed bleak and shameful was now lovely and of great value. I thought to myself: from a forbidding land where scarcely fifty years ago, warring tribes had fought over camels and goats, we Saudis have become an economic force. My own family had guided lawless tribesmen from a stark desert land into one of the wealthiest peoples and nations on earth.

While Western minds have always claimed that only the oil paved our way into prosperity, I paid that analysis little heed, for oil had been discovered in other lands, and the ordinary citizens of those countries had never enjoyed the substantial lifestyle experienced by all Saudis. The secret lay in the wisdom of the men who guided the proceeds from our resources. While I have always found much fault with the men of my family, particularly regarding their stance on women's issues, on this one subject I recognized and commended their clever and insightful leadership.

Thinking the opportunity was ripe to instil ancestral pride into those that I had given life, I became enthusiastic and began to talk loudly, reminding the children of past events and the virtues of the ones who came before us: the courage, endurance, self-reliance, and intelligence of our bedouin ancestors. Recalling the impoverished life lived by my parents, and then the extravagant life enjoyed by their children and grandchildren, a reversal which was nothing short of miraculous, I became animated, telling family tales with dramatic intensity, and convincing realism.

Thinking myself quite the storyteller, remembering happy moments spent at the feet of my own mother and older aunties, I was immersed in the drama of the founding of our country, when suddenly, I realized that I had no audience.

Sara, Assad and Kareem shared pained looks, but as I had quite forgotten the purpose of our journey, their expressions of disbelief at my conduct made no impact on my mind.

I glanced at our young ones, and I was keenly disappointed when I looked into the faces of our disinterested young, so absorbed in present activities. I knew at that moment that poverty not endured does not affect the privileged, and that the younger Al Sa'ud generation had fallen under the enfeebling influence of great wealth.

Plainly, the children were bored at the thought of the bedouin seed from which they had sprung.

Abdullah was playing a game of backgammon with Sara's oldest son, while the smallest children were cavorting with some small cars and trucks that Assad had brought back from his last trip to London.

Recalling the face of my loving mother and her poignant stories of the wonderful grandparents that I had never known, my palms itched with the desire to slap the unresponsive faces of the descendants of those tender souls that had been dead for so very long. I looked around for someone to pounce upon, and just as I reached over to pinch the skin on Abdullah's arm, my eyes met Sara's, and she mouthed the word, *Ihram*.

Once again, I had failed to remember where I was going! Thinking, too late, I will perform my rituals once again when I reach my home in Jeddah, my thoughts strayed back to where they had come, and tears came without warning at the thought of the hardy and brave ancestors that we would see no more. Sara gave me a gentle smile of forgiveness, and I knew that my dearest sister knew my thoughts and forgave me my transgression.

Struck by the memory of an apt proverb, 'Only our own eyes will cry for us,' I was saddened at my family's ability to discard the memory of those who had come before us. I cried out in a forceful voice, 'Those that seem dead to you are alive to me!'

My family looked at me in astonishment, except for Kareem, who failed to control a fit of laughter. I glared at him as he wiped his wet eyes with a tissue and mumbled something to Assad that I tried to hear but could not, regarding the woman that he had wed.

To calm my emotions I turned my attention to my two daughters, and saw that they, at least, had heard something of what I had spoken.

Maha, preferring Europe and America over anything Saudi Arabian, was of little comfort. She had ignored my boastful commentary on our family history, and began to complain bitterly about the terminal, disbelieving that the designers had designed an airport terminal as a tent!

'Why dig up the past?' she muttered with a tinge of dismay in her voice. 'It *is* the twentieth century, you know.'

Amani, though, was entranced by the spotlights which were mounted on the support pylons. They gave an amazing view of the striking engineering wonder, and she gave a squeal of delight.

Showing off his earlier knowledge of the terminal, Abdullah glanced at his youngest sister and casually remarked that, at the present time, the fabric roof of the tent covers the world's largest space, though there were plans in motion to cover a larger space in the city of Madinah.

Amani, my most sensitive child, squeezed my hand and smiled sweetly, saying, 'Mummy, thanks for bringing us here.'

I gave my daughter a happy look. All was not lost!

Who could have known that a journey made with virtuous thought and the desire to praise God for the return of my eldest daughter's lucidity would have significance for my youngest child, Amani, and enduringly disastrous consequences for her mother and father?

Chapter Five

AMANI

Makkah, 'the blessed', known as Umm al Qurrah, 'Mother of Cities', is the spot towards which every believer faces five times a day in prayer. For millions of Muslims, it is the goal of a lifetime to travel to Makkah for Haj. *The city is strictly banned to non-Muslims, but non-believers feel the keen disappointment of what they are missing and want to know what lies within. As a Saudi, I have been personally selected by God to protect the true faith that got its start in the holiest city in the world that is located in my country.*

The explanation given to the author by an elderly Saudi bedouin of why Saudi Arabians are the chosen people of God

On the joyous occasion of Amani's birth, my sister Sara joined me in the pangs of delivery, giving birth to her second child, a daughter that she and her husband, Assad, gave the name Nashwa, meaning ecstasy. While Amani has brought bliss into our lives, Nashwa is a loud and obnoxious girl, and has often introduced havoc into Sara and Assad's happy home.

Many times I have secretly questioned Kareem on the fearful possibility that Amani was the true child of Sara and Assad, while Nashwa was of our blood, for Nashwa's character is remarkably similar to mine. Amani, though, bears a startling resemblance to her Auntie Sara, whom she doubles in lovely countenance and calm spirit.

Could the staff at the hospital have accidentally mistaken our two daughters? Our children were born eleven hours apart, but Sara and I occupied adjoining royal suites. Infant confusion seemed likely to my mind. Many times over the years, Kareem has attempted to push away my fears, quoting meaningless statistics showing that such mix-ups rarely occur, but each time that I gaze on my perfect child, I dread the thought that she belongs to another.

Amani, an absorbed and melancholy spirit, treasured books more than toys, and from an early age was an enthusiastic student of art and language. Unlike her elder sister Maha, Amani for the most part created little turbulence and instead generated tranquillity and affection in our home.

While Amani's sensitive soul had penetrated more deeply into my heart than that of her two older siblings, I nevertheless should have been alerted to the shadowed tenacity in Amani's complex temperament. My daughter's alarming attraction to animals caused open conflict with other members of our family. Her youthful devotion to all living creatures clashed with the Saudi male requisite to hunt and kill to extinction every creature which inhabits our land. While Abdullah and his father gleefully joined other royal cousins in desert hunts, machine-gunning gazelles and rabbits by the light of huge spotlights mounted on specially equipped jeeps and open trucks, Amani crept into her father's hunting room, hiding ammunition, successfully dismantling weapons, and tossing expensive firearms into the garbage. Because of Amani's intense love of animals, she was willing to relinquish her strong desire for family harmony.

This humane but troubling trait showed up at an early age. Owing to Amani's fervour, our home was overrun with stray beasts of many species, sizes and colours.

Most Arabs, unlike many Westerners, feel little devotion for animals, and starving and injured cats and dogs run wild on our city streets. Since the early 1980s there has been an active government policy in Saudi Arabia of collecting strays and abandoning these creatures in the vast empty quarter of the desert to die slow and painful deaths. Yet many animals do outwit their slayers and manage to find a safe haven with those of a tender nature.

While I appreciated and sympathized with Amani's pressing compulsion to protect abused animals, Kareem and others in our home were greatly distressed that our property was becoming a sanctuary for strays. Not content with the mere act of saving their lives, Amani pampered these abandoned creatures as if they were rare and expensive breeds, and when they died, the animals were buried after having solemn funerals in our garden. The surviving strays that she had trained to be lap pets joined our family on our grounds and in our home.

Many times it seemed to me that Amani cared more for animals than she did for members of her own family, but I am a mother that has difficulty in penalizing or restraining her young, and Amani was allowed her one unfortunate idiosyncracy.

Kareem employed two young men from Thailand to clean and disinfect after the animals and to train the dogs in obedience lessons. We even took the extreme action of building our own small zoo on the grounds, equipping the facility with spacious caged areas and purchased numerous breeds of exotic animals in the hope that Amani's personal zoo would satisfy her need to collect and coddle large numbers of animals. Next to the zoo area, Kareem had a sizeable area walled off for Amani's strays. He commanded his daughter to restrict those animals to that special section of the yard. After Amani shed many tears, Kareem reluctantly agreed that our daughter could select her ten favourite cats and dogs that would be allowed inside our home and free access to the general grounds area.

In spite of these efforts, our daughter remained alert to street strays, and these creatures invariably found their way to our door.

Once Kareem came home to a strange sight. Three Filipino men who worked for our neighbours were caught in the act of delivering five cats in a bag to one of the Thai zoo-keepers. Confronting the Filipinos, who were frightened into silence, Kareem was handed a poster that stated our household would reward the bearer 100 *riyals*[1] for each stray cat or puppy. Kareem flew into a fit of wild anger. After threatening the Thai employees with the sack, they confessed to Kareem that Amani had instructed them to attach the reward posters to the walls of neighbouring palaces and villas. In addition, the two men had been told to roam the local streets, abducting cats and dogs, and to bring them to Amani. Our daughter had sworn the two men to secrecy, and since Kareem had employed them to work directly for our daughter, they had kept her confidence.

Kareem forced a head count of strays, and when he discovered that he was feeding over forty cats, and twelve dogs, he slumped to the ground in a daze. After a long period, without a glance directed at his family, my husband got to his feet and not speaking a word, left our home. We heard the wheels of his car spin as he left the neighbourhood. He was away for two days and three nights. I later learned that Kareem had been visiting his parents during this time. I heard from gossipy servants that Kareem had told his startled parents that he must have a few days' respite from the complex women in his life, or he would be forced to commit us all to an institution.

While Kareem was away, I decided that I must find some manner of dulling my daughter's extreme sensitivity to animals. I made many strange discoveries that had gone undetected. The forty cats were dining on fresh fish

[1]About £17.

from the Red Sea, while the twelve dogs were treated to gourmet meats from an expensive Australian-supplied meat shop. Amani had been appropriating money from the weekly funds that are deposited in a small cash box in the kitchen, money that our servants used for our personal shopping. Our household expenses are so enormous that our bookkeeper had failed to notice the sum taken by our daughter to be used for her animals. When I discovered that Amani was using large amounts of money to purchase caged birds, in order to free them, I seriously threatened my child with visits to a psychiatrist, and for a while she became less involved with the animal kingdom.

I distinctly recall one dramatic occasion that involved my brother, Ali. In the past, Ali had made a point of complaining about Amani's pets. He would grumble to me that no self-respecting Muslim could enter my home for fear that the animals roaming at will would create a need for purification. Ali's unmistakable dislike of animals evidently made an impression on the psyche of Amani's greatly loved creatures, since the dogs generally made themselves scarce and hid behind bushes until my brother passed through the garden.

There was one particular incident that stands out in my mind. Ali dropped by our palace for a brief visit and had just entered the garden gate, when he stopped to order one of our servants to wash his car while he was visiting our home. While Ali was speaking, one of Amani's favourite dogs, Napoleon, chose to lift his leg on Ali's freshly laundered *thobe*. Ali, a vain man who is proud of his handsome and impeccable appearance, became speechless with rage. He kicked the poor creature brutally before Amani could rush to Napoleon's rescue. My daughter was so infuriated that she flung herself on her uncle, beating him on his arms and chest with her fists.

Urinated upon by a dog and physically assaulted by his niece, Ali lost no time in leaving our home, shrieking to the smirking servants that not only was his sister completely mad, but that she had given birth to demented children who preferred beasts to humans for companionship!

From that moment, Amani hated her Uncle Ali with the same intensity that I had hated my unfeeling brother as a young girl.

In the Muslim faith, a dog is considered impure, and that fact was a factor in Ali's extreme anger and disgust. In the Islamic faith, if a dog drinks out of any container, it should be washed seven times, the first of which should be water mixed with dust.

Ali is my only brother, and in spite of our continued explosive differences, he chooses to maintain a relationship with my family. Kareem forced Amani to telephone and apologize to her uncle, but the episode with Napoleon kept Ali away from our home for over two months. When he finally recovered from his anger and embarrassment, Ali returned for a visit, calling ahead to insist that our servants shut away Napoleon.

I was apprehensive about Amani's anger, which I knew was thinly veiled, and was pleased with my daughter when she entered the sitting-room on the day of Ali's visit, playing hostess and offering her uncle a glass of freshly squeezed grapefruit juice.

With an expression of relief over the forgotten incident, Ali said that he happened to be quite thirsty.

Noting the similarities between Sara and Amani, I beamed with motherly pride when my beautiful child graciously handed Ali a glass of juice and a plate of almond cookies. Her demeanour was above reproach. I gave her a happy smile, thinking to buy her a special present the next time that I went shopping.

Ali smiled his approval and commented that Amani would, one day, make some lucky man very happy.

It was only after Ali left that I discovered Amani in her bedroom, laughing so loudly that the servants came from all around to learn the cause of her merriment.

Amani told an amazed audience that her uncle had drunk his juice out of a glass that had been licked clean by her entourage of stray pets! My daughter had filled the glass with cool water for her beasts prior to pouring juice for her uncle! Not only that, but she had given the recovered Napoleon a few licks on the cookies before serving them to Ali!

The servants grinned with satisfaction, for Ali is not a popular man with them.

While I tried to appear stern at Amani's unconscionable act, my lips paid no heed, and my face trembled as I struggled to control a laugh. Giving up the charade of parental guidance, I held my daughter in my arms and roared with uncontrollable laughter.

For the first time in her life, Amani exhibited traits that led me to hope that she was a child born of my body instead of my sister, Sara's.

I know now that I should have scolded my child for a deed that would have caused Ali a heart attack had he known the truth, but I could barely control my glee, and when I laughingly confided the story to Kareem, he had such a look of sheer horror at my amusement, that I knew that my husband feared for the sanity of those he loved.

Kareem's patience snapped at my revelation. Seething with Muslim anger at the prank and disturbed by Amani's preoccupation with animals, which he insisted was ruining our lives, Kareem demanded that we sit down with our daughter and have a frank discussion.

Before I could respond, my husband spoke into the house intercom and instructed Amani to come into our living quarters, immediately.

Together, Kareem and I waited for Amani in the sitting area that is attached to our master bedroom.

Amani's black eyes sparkled with interest as she swept with sprightly grace into the room.

Before I could diffuse the situation, Kareem bluntly asked, 'Amani, tell me, what is your object in life?'

Amani, with childlike serenity, replied without hesitation, 'To save all the animals from man.'

'Saving animals is nothing more than a pampered passion of rich Europeans and Americans,' Kareem angrily responded. He looked at me as if I were to blame and said, 'Sultana, I thought that your child would be more intelligent.'

Tears began to well in Amani's eyes, and she asked to leave the room.

Uncomfortable with female tears, my husband thought better of his sarcastic tactics. Kareem tempered his opinion, and spoke with perfect seriousness. 'And, Amani, after you save all the animals, of what consequence will you be to yourself, or to your family?'

Amani squeezed her lips together and looked off into space. Without responding, she gradually came back into our world. Unable to formulate her thoughts, she looked at her father and shrugged her shoulders.

Remaining wisely uncritical of her great love of animals, Kareem clarified the need for greater purpose in human life, to create and inspire those of our own kind. He reminded Amani that she could perform good deeds for four-legged beasts while still influencing civilization. He added, 'Advancing civilization is the responsibility of the minorities in a society, for only out of discontent with imperfection does mankind seek to better the society in which he lives.'

Amani scoffed at his message. She raised her voice and asked her father the obvious question, 'In Saudi Arabia? What can a female do that will make a difference in *this* country?'

My daughter looked at me and waited for my expected agreement.

Just as I was about to argue with Kareem, he interrupted me, and to my astonishment, Kareem pointed me out to our daughter and said that I, as an unheard minority in Saudi Arabia, had not reconciled myself to the life of a royal idler, but that I had become educated and was utilizing my knowledge to further women's causes. He continued by saying that one day women's roles would develop, and our influence would be felt outside the home.

Dumbfounded at Kareem's words, I could add little to

the conversation. Never had my husband acknowledged the righteousness of my vision of freedom for women.

After a discussion of more than an hour, Amani promised her father that she would look beyond her furry friends and find a second, equally challenging purpose in her life.

As affectionate a child that has ever lived, Amani kissed each of us goodnight, and said that she had much thinking to do. As she was closing our bedroom door, she turned back and, giving us a wonderful smile, said, 'I love you Dada, and Mummy, you too,' bringing back to mind the innocent girl that our youngest daughter still was.

Thrilled at what he declared a huge success, Kareem held me in his arms and spoke of his dreams for his daughters, as well as his son, saying that if it were up to him, 'All the ridiculous restrictions placed upon the heads of women would disappear, just like magic.' Kareem snapped his fingers in the air and gave me a tender look.

A thought cynically brushed my mind that there is nothing like a beloved daughter to induce a man to clamour for adjustments in an unfair world.

Longing for unaccustomed peace in a household of three lively children, I welcomed the idea of the peaceful family life that Kareem promised would come, now that Amani would surely get over her affair with the world of animals.

Shortly afterwards, the Gulf War occurred, followed by the culmination of Maha's mental instability. During this stressful period, a stymied and solitary Amani had no-one to help her search for a more fitting, fresh objective to life.

Now, retracing Amani's pattern of obsession with causes that held her interest, I, a woman schooled in philosophy, which is the critical study of fundamental beliefs, should have recognized that my youngest child possessed the traits often connected with those we deem fanatics, frightening people who eagerly embrace extremist convictions.

Perceiving the resolute earnestness of my daughter, I now reproach myself for initiating an impressionable and mentally disoriented child to that most religious occasion, *Haj*, at a time of maximum teenage upheaval.

During our pilgrimage to Makkah, by one of the strangest transformations in our family history, Kareem and I observed our daughter, Amani, arise almost overnight from her dormant religious faith and embrace the Islamic beliefs with unnerving intensity. I was nothing more than a mother tending her child, offering her the outlines of her heritage, but it was as if Amani's mind was caught by a high vision, a secret that was in herself, too intimate to reveal to her mother or father.

The morning after our arrival in Jeddah, we made the short drive in an air-conditioned limousine from that Red Sea city to the Holiest city of Islam, the city of the Prophet Mohammed, Makkah. I was thrilled to find myself at the *Haj*, with my most beloved family members in attendance. I tried to concentrate on my prayers but found myself peering out of the car window, thinking of ancient times when enormous numbers of the faithful had come by camel caravan or trodden with bare feet on rugged and rocky terrain in the eager quest to fulfil one of the five pillars of the Islamic faith.

I wanted desperately to share my thoughts with Kareem and my children, but I saw that each was busy contemplating God and his or her relationship with him. Maha's eyes were closed, while Abdullah was fingering his prayer beads. Kareem seemed glassy-eyed, and I hoped that my husband was not reliving his youthful nightmare of being trampled to death on this day. I leaned close and stared, but my husband studiously avoided my eyes. Amani was caught up in her solitary meditations, and I thought that my daughter's face seemed afire.

Satisfied, I smiled, and patted her hand, thinking that I had accomplished much good in bringing my family together for the holy event.

Soon we arrived in the city, which is enclosed by the

Valley of Abraham and surrounded by two mountain ranges to the east, west and south. Makkah is set in a rugged landscape that consists mainly of solid granite, but the ancient city is the most beautiful of sights to all Muslims.

I chanted, 'Here I am, O God! Here I am!' Outside the Holy Mosque of Makkah, our family met a specially appointed official guide who would lead us through the rituals of *Haj* and would perform as our Imam, or minister, during our prayers. Sara and I remained with our daughters, while Kareem and Assad walked away with our sons. All around us other pilgrims called out their prayers to God as we pushed through the expansive marble steps of the Holy Mosque. Taking off our shoes at the entrance of the mosque, we continued to walk and to pray, 'God, You are the peace, and from You peace proceeds. O God of ours, greet us with peace.'

As the Prophet always moved with the right side of his body, I was careful to enter the white marble courtyard of the Holy Mosque by stepping through the Gate of Peace with my right foot first.

There are seven main gates that open into the immense courtyard, and crowds were surging through each of those gates. On the sides of the mosque, white marble columns rise high into the air, while elaborately carved minarets tower above the columns. There are red silk carpets that run the length of the courtyard, and here pilgrims were sitting and reading silently or meditating about God.

The cry of the *muezzin* rang out, and we were called to prayer. There is a section of the courtyard reserved for women only, but Sara and I, with our daughters, lined up in a row behind the men who were in the front, joining other Muslims in prayer, rising and falling in the prostrations so familiar to all Muslims the world over.

I felt myself humbled. I am of the royal family, but before the eyes of God, I was at one with all classes of people. To the side and back of my family were the poorest of God's people, yet they were as rich as I, in the eyes of God.

When the prayers finished, we streamed forward towards the Kaaba, which is a simple stone structure that has a single door six feet up from the marble floor. Fifty feet high and thirty-five feet long, the Kaaba is in the centre of the sacred mosque. This is the spot where three millennia ago, Ibrahim, known as Abraham to Jews and Christians, first dedicated a house of worship to a single God. In the Koran, God says that 'The first house of God that was built for people is the one in Makkah.' It is towards this structure that one billion people turn five times each day to bow down and pray.

A huge black velvet cloth embroidered in gold with verses from the Koran is draped over the Kaaba. I knew that at the end of the annual *Haj*, the cloth would be taken down and replaced by a new cloth that had been woven in a special mill in Makkah. Many pilgrims would pay large amounts of money to take a bit of the beautiful cloth to their country as a memento of their sacred journey to Makkah.

In a corner of the Kaaba is the Black Stone, which is the symbol of Muslim love of God. The Black Stone is framed in silver. The Stone had been honoured by Prophet Mohammed. The *Hadith*, or sayings and traditions of the Prophet, says that our Prophet kissed the Black Stone as he helped to place it in the Kaaba. For this reason, the stone is particularly sacred to all Muslims.

In our next sacred rite of pilgrimage, the *tawwaf*, or the circumambulation, people began to walk around the Kaaba.

Keeping the Kaaba on our left, we circle the Kaaba, while reciting, 'God is most Great. O God, grant us good in this world and good in the hereafter, and protect us from the torment of the fires in hell.'

After we completed this ritual, I saw Kareem. He motioned with his head for us to come. We were fortunate, for Kareem has arranged for us to be taken inside the Kaaba to offer additional prayers.

My family and I climbed a portable staircase that had been rolled up to the structure to enter through the door which is high above the ground. The door had been inscribed in silver with verses from the Koran. Inside the Kaaba is the most sacred spot in the world for Muslims.

The interior of the Kaaba was very dark, and I prayed in each corner of the structure, asking God to keep the devil away from my daughter, Maha, and to bless the other members of my family. In light of the recent Gulf War, I also requested that God assist Muslims in keeping peace. Not forgetting my main focus in life, I prayed that God would guide the men of Arabia in their interpretation of the teachings of the Prophet, and to release their wives, sisters, and daughters from the bondage wrapped so tightly around us in our daily lives.

I heard the sobbing of a child and looking through the darkness witnessed my own daughter, Amani, weeping. Through her cries, I heard her ask God to help her divorce herself from the world of royal luxuries, to be better equipped to stamp out human wickedness. She pleaded with God to swallow up all the sins of mankind and to cure the ills of the world.

Amani was having a religious experience.

Amani's eyes were red, but she ignored my touch of love, tenderly given as we left the Kaaba.

Once we had departed the Kaaba, we walked to the Station of Ibrahim, which is located in the Holy Mosque, and there we performed two more prostrations. Bowing to God, we acknowledged to ourselves that the ritual of circling the Kaaba was not a worship of that structure, but a worship to God, the One and Only One, the Eternal and the Absolute, and none except God deserves to be worshipped.

We then left the courtyard of the Holy Mosque to begin our next rituals, which would take place at the Well of

Zamzam, and the Mas'a, or the Running Place. This spot is in the plains that surround Makkah.

Once again, Sara and I separated from the male members of our family. Though we would perform the exact rituals, we would do so with those of our own sex.

It was in the plains surrounding Makkah that Ibrahim, weary of Sarah's ill persecution of Hagar, allowed Hagar to leave with his son, Ismail. It was then that Ibrahim left with Sarah and Isaac to travel to Palestine. Christians and Jews know that Ibrahim's descendants in Palestine developed the Jewish faith, while his descendants in Makkah went on to establish the Islamic faith.

Thus, by one great man, Ibrahim, two of three great monotheistic religions, Judaism and Islam, are joined.

Hagar and Ismail travelled through the desert with nothing more than a bag of dates. Searching desperately for water for her young son, Hagar ran between the two hills of Safa and Marwa, seeking to find a well of water from which she could nourish her child. A miracle happened. The Angel Gabriel replenished a well that had gone dry, at the feet of Hagar's son, Ismail. Thus God saved Hagar and her son. This well, which was named Zamzam, still runs clear and fresh.

While Hagar ran over rocky terrain in the boiling sun, we pilgrims run between the hills of Safa and Marwa in an air-conditioned gallery. This convenience was built by the men of my family in order to reduce the number of annual casualties suffered each year at the *Haj*. Old, sick, and handicapped pilgrims carried on the shoulders of the faithful used to run seven times between the hills, regardless of the heat. Sunstroke and heart attacks were not uncommon.

There are signs posted in the gallery which tell men when to run and when to walk, while women are instructed to walk. While moving between the hills, pilgrims recite verses from the Koran and chant, 'God is great'. After seven trips, my daughters and I drank the waters of the Zamzam and sprinkled drops of the liquid on our clothing. The mountain spring is no longer visible, as the waters of the well are now delivered to pilgrims through hundreds of water taps that are covered with a beautiful marble vault.

Just as we were about to depart the waters of Zamzam, we heard a loud commotion that swept through the crowd of pilgrims. Curious, I walked towards a group of Muslim women from Indonesia and asked them in the English language if they knew the source of the excitement.

One of them replied, 'Yes!' Three men had fallen and been trampled upon, and they had heard that two of the men had died!

I could not catch my breath! I could think of nothing but my husband! Kareem! Had his nightmare come true, after all?

I ran back to my sister and our daughters, my eyes wild with terror, with my incoherent words making no sense.

Sara grabbed my shoulders and demanded to know what was the trouble.

'Kareem! I have heard some men have been trampled. I fear for Kareem's life!'

Thinking that I had viewed his body, my daughters began to moan, and Sara raised her voice, demanding to know why I thought one of the dead men might be Kareem.

I told Sara, 'A dream! Kareem suffered a dream that he would be crushed at *Haj*! Now, some men have been trampled to death in the area where he was last seen.'

Sara, like me, has learned that there is much in life that is not for our understanding, that unexplained forces move through our lives. She was concerned, though not yet as hysterical as I.

Just as we were about to split into three groups to search for our men, we saw that two stretchers with bodies covered in white sheets were being carried through the crowd. I ran as fast as I could, and screaming, ripped the sheets from the bodies of the dead, first one, and then the other.

The four hospital workers from Makkah stood frozen to the spot, now knowing what to expect next from a woman who was clearly deranged.

Neither of the dead men was Kareem! Both were old, and it was easy to see how they could be pushed to their deaths.

I held the sheet in my hand, and stood over the body of one man, crying out in great relief that I did not know the dead. I was standing in that position just as Kareem, Assad, and our sons followed the sounds of shouting women to see what calamity had occurred.

Kareem could not believe his eyes! His wife was laughing with joy at the sight of a dead man! He pushed through the crowd and caught me by my wrists, pulling me from the scene.

'Sultana! Have you gone quite mad?'

Sara quickly explained what I had feared, and Kareem's angry look softened. Embarrassed, he had to speak in great detail of his fearful nightmare that he had shared with his wife.

The atmosphere was electric with emotion. The crowd began to mumble and menacingly look in my direction, as the wives of the two now dead realized their tragedy and learned that I had laughed like a hyena at the deaths of their husbands.

We hurriedly left the area, while Assad revealed our identity to some guards. With their protection Assad gave a gift of 3,000 *riyals*[2] to each of the families and told them that we were members of the royal family. He quickly explained my fear of Kareem's dream and pacified the angry crowd.

After we escaped the scene, my family began to laugh nervously, and later, as time erased the shame of my conduct, we came to think of the incident as hilarious, and it has amused us ever since.

[2]About £500.

Our rituals were completed for the first day of *Haj*.

We then returned to our palace in Jeddah which is situated beside the Red Sea. During the drive, in an attempt to put the experience of the men trampled out of our minds, each of us shared our profound experiences of the day. Only Amani was strangely quiet and withdrawn.

I thought to myself that there was something perplexing about my youngest child's demeanour.

The feeling of impending doom would not leave me, and once we were back in our home, I followed Kareem around until I could focus my thoughts and articulate what was in my heart and on my mind. I accompanied him from the entrance hall to our bedroom out onto the balcony, and then back into the bedroom and into his library.

An abyss divided our moods.

Looking at me in exasperation, Kareem finally asked, 'Sultana, what can I *do* for you?'

Unsure of what my concerns were, I had difficulty expressing myself. 'Have you noticed your daughter, Amani, today?' I asked. 'Amani is worrying me. I feel that a strange mood is oppressing our daughter. I don't like it.'

In a weary tone, my husband insisted, 'Sultana, stop looking for danger where there is none. She is at *Haj*. Aren't all pilgrims engrossed in special thoughts?' He paused and then added in a malicious tone, 'Except *you*, Sultana.'

Kareem then stood silent, but he gave me a withering look that spoke clearly of his desire for solitude.

Irritated, I left Kareem in his library. I searched for Maha, but she had retired to her bedroom and was sleeping. Abdullah was not around. He had gone with his Auntie Sara to their villa. I felt terribly alone in the world.

I decided that I would go to the source of my worry. I walked to Amani's bedroom, and when I heard her mumbling voice, I held my ear to the door and tried to understand the words that she was saying. My daughter was praying, and her voice pleaded with God with an urgency that awakened my memory of another that I had eavesdropped upon from behind a locked door. Suddenly, the memory of that other voice in another time struck me as to why I was so tormented with anxiety. Lawand! Amani was praying with the same sort of isolated longing that I had often heard from the locked room of her cousin, Lawand!

The atmosphere that had surrounded Amani from the moment of our participation in the first ritual of the day had seemed vaguely familiar. Now, on this day, Lawand's insanity had re-emerged in the chilling intensity of Amani's eyes.

I told myself that Amani was going the way of her cousin, Lawand!

While still a teenager, Lawand, who was a first cousin of Kareem on his father's side of the family, had attended school in Geneva, Switzerland. Her parent's decision to send her abroad for schooling had proved a grievous mistake. While in Geneva, Lawand had disgraced her family by becoming involved with several young men. In addition to her sexual involvements, Lawand had become addicted to cocaine. While moving secretly out of her room one evening, Lawand was captured by the headmistress, who called her father in Saudi Arabia, with a demand that he come and collect his wayward child.

When the family got a whiff of their daughter's activities, Lawand's father and two brothers had flown to Geneva and had taken the girl to a drug rehabilitation centre in that country. Six months later, when her treatment was completed, she was brought back to Saudi Arabia. The family was exhausted with shame and fury, and as punishment a decision was reached to confine Lawand to a small apartment in their home, until they were satisfied that she had realized her reckless offence to Muslim life.

When I heard the verdict, another came to my mind. Through the blur of distance, I could think of little but

Sameera, my sister, Tahani's best friend. Sameera was a brilliant and beautiful young woman, who so long ago had been deprived of her freedom and forced into the dark prison of the 'Woman's Room'. While Lawand would one day secure her freedom, only death would remove Sameera from her incarceration.

Now, within my thin sphere of expectations, I found myself thinking that Lawand was fortunate! Relieved that Lawand's father was not of the unfeeling character that could confine his daughter to life imprisonment, or to death by stoning, I experienced sad relief in lieu of passionate anger.

How fortunate is the human being who has no memories, for memories often remould the victim of suppression into the image of their suppressor! With terrifying seriousness, I listened as the men of my family mouthed the law of obedience, saying that the calm structure of our conservative society rested upon the perfect obedience of children to their parents, and wives to their husbands. Without that obedience, anarchy would rule the day. The men of my family firmly stated that Lawand's punishment was fair.

I visited the family on many occasions, listening with profound sympathy to the grief of Lawand's mother and her sisters. Often, the women of the family talked to Lawand through the locked door. Initially, Lawand begged for forgiveness and pleaded with her mother to set her free.

Sara and I smuggled notes of encouragement to this cousin, advising her to recall the wisdom of silence and to read the books and play the games that female members of the family placed through the small opening that had been constructed for the delivery of food and for emptying the pail containing body wastes, but Lawand had little interest in occupying her time with quiet pursuits.

After several weeks of confinement, Lawand returned to God and began to pray, declaring that she had seen the error of her ways, and swearing to her parents that she would never again commit a single wrong.

Taking great pity on her daughter, Lawand's mother beseeched her husband to set her daughter free, saying that she felt certain Lawand would now return to the pious life.

Lawand's father thought perhaps that Lawand was speaking with deceit, since he had told his daughter that her confinement would end when her mind once again embraced the proper thoughts of a believing Muslim.

Before long, Lawand prayed all of her waking moments, failing to respond to our worried voices. I could easily see that Lawand was hallucinating, for she spoke to God in her prayers on an equal basis, shouting out that she would represent him on earth, teaching his followers a new moral code of which only she, Lawand, had knowledge.

After one particular visit, when Lawand's mother and I overheard her madly rejoicing in the confines of her room, I told Kareem that I was certain that Lawand had lost her mind.

Kareem spoke to his father, who in turn, visited his brother's home. As the eldest brother of Lawand's father, Kareem's father had authority over the family. On my father-in-law's advice, Lawand's father opened the locked door and released his daughter from her prison. Lawand would now be allowed to rejoin her family in a normal life.

Lawand's eleven-week confinement had ended, but the family tragedy ripened rapidly. During the course of her prison sentence, Lawand had disciplined herself to ascetic austerity, and came out of her imprisonment seething with Islamic fervour, claiming that a new day had dawned for Islam.

On the day of her release, Lawand informed her family that all Muslims must denounce luxury and vice, and promptly pounced upon her two sisters for wearing kohl (black powder) on their eyes, rouge on their cheeks, and nail polish. After she made her sisters cower on the sofa, Lawand ripped an expensive necklace from her mother's neck and rushed to throw precious stones down the kitchen drain. The women of the house could barely restrain her, and the family disturbance resulted in various minor injuries. Lawand was given a shot by one of the palace physicians and a prescription for drugs that calm the mind.

Violence hid its face for a while, but nevertheless survived, and from time to time Lawand would lash out with blunt passion, directing abuse at whoever was handy.

After she ripped Sara's gold earrings from my sister's ears, shouting out that to wear such gleaming finery hurt the eyes of God, I thought to protect myself by purchasing a small canister of mace while I was on holiday in the United States. I hid the item in my luggage, even from the eyes of Kareem, and began to carry it in a small bag when I visited Lawand's home.

As is my disastrous misfortune, Lawand selected an afternoon when I was paying a visit to demonstrate her renewed religious fervour.

Lawand, her mother, two sisters, and I were having a pleasant chat while sipping tea, eating pastries and discussing my last trip to America when Lawand suddenly became restless, her eyes flashing about, seeking some affront to God.

In her temporarily disordered mind, she began to criticize her mother's choice of clothing, which Lawand stated was much too immodest for a believing Muslim. In fascination, I watched as Lawand carefully folded her table napkin and very courteously covered her mother's neck with the fabric. Then, without warning, Lawand began to curse. She made a sudden wild leap in the air, twisting her body in mid-air to face me.

I saw that Lawand was eyeing my new pearl necklace, and remembered too late Kareem's warning that I should not wear jewellery in her home.

Lawand's pale ascetic face, twisted in passionate and divine conviction, awed me, and I felt the acute danger that she posed. I quickly dug in my small bag and brought out the mace, warning my cousin that she should quit the room or sit down immediately, or I would be forced to defend myself.

Lawand's mother began to scream and to tug on her mad daughter's sleeve. I braced myself for an attack when Lawand pushed her pawing mother from her side and rushed at me, forcing me into a small corner between a lamp and a chair.

The worst was yet to come.

Sara, who had agreed to meet me at Lawand's home, entered the villa at that exact moment. I saw that Sara held her youngest child in her arms.

Sara's jaw dropped when she saw that Lawand had cornered her youngest sister between a chair and a lamp, and that I was holding a weapon in my hand.

Knowing Lawand's weakness, Sara quickly regained her composure and subtly attempted to persuade Lawand to stop her foolishness. For a short moment, Lawand, with feline deception, pretended to submit to Sara's wisdom. She dropped her aggressive stance and began rubbing her hands together nervously.

Not trusting someone who is known to be a lunatic, I yelled for Sara to take her baby and run from the room! At the sound of my excited voice, Lawand turned back to me and then with all the fury of one who is insane, bounded towards me with outstretched hands, making for my pearl necklace.

I squeezed the mace container with both hands and Lawand dropped to her knees. In the back of my mind, I remembered reading that it takes double power to disable the insane, so in my excitement, I emptied the container and maced not only Lawand, but her mother and one sister, who had come to Lawand's aid.

Lawand recovered from the mace attack rapidly, but had lost her will to fight.

Her father finally realized that his daughter needed long-term professional attention, which she received in France and within a year enjoyed a full recovery.

Lawand's mother and sister required immediate medical attention. The Pakistani physician summoned to treat the women had difficulty in maintaining professional seriousness, when informed that one royal princess had maced three other princesses who were members of her family.

Everyone in Kareem's family thought that I had acted with haste in macing my opponent, but I refused to let myself be crucified for defending myself against a woman who had lost her mind, and I told them so. Indignantly, I added that instead of criticism, I deserved their appreciation for my deed, for the event had led their daughter to recovery.

While there is a tendency of some to dismiss my actions as those of a female of excitable emotion, I am a woman of deadly seriousness when it comes to women's issues.

A wise man was once asked what was the most difficult truth in life to uncover. His reply was: 'to know thyself'. While others might harbour doubt, I know my own character. Undeniably, my personality has been doused with an overabundance of spontaneity, but it is in this exuberance that I gain my power to do battle against those in command of females in my land. I can claim some degree of success in bending the bonds of tradition.

Now, in my memory of Lawand's temporary and unhinged obsession with unhealthy fundamentalist fervour, I attached great significance to my daughter's extreme infatuation with our religion.

While I believe in and honour the God of Mohammed, it is my considered opinion that the masses of humanity who are engaging in loving, struggling, suffering, and enjoying are living life as God intended. I have no desire for my child to turn her back on the rich complexity of life and reaffirm her future through the harsh asceticism of a militant interpretation of our religion.

I ran to my husband. I said, in a rush of words, 'Amani is praying!'

Kareem, who was quietly reading the Koran, looked at

me as though I had finally lost all reason. *'Praying?'* he asked, his voice tinged with disbelief at my reaction over another's communication with God.

'Yes!' I cried. 'She is exhausting herself with prayer.' I insisted, 'Come! See for yourself!'

Regretfully, Kareem laid his Koran on his desk and with an expression of incredulity, humoured his wife by following me from the room.

As we entered the hallway leading to Amani's door, we could easily hear the sound of her voice, rising and falling with the intensity of her words.

Kareem left my side and burst into Amani's room. Our daughter turned, displaying a face lined with pain and haggard with sorrow.

Kareem spoke softly. 'Amani, it's time for you to take a small rest. Go to bed. Now. Your mother will wake you in an hour for the evening meal.'

Amani's expression appeared stricken, and she did not speak. Still bound to Kareem's influence, she lay across the bed, fully dressed, and closed her eyes.

I could see my child's lips as they still moved in silent prayer, uttering words that were not meant for my ears.

Kareem and I quietly left our daughter. Drinking coffee in our sitting-room, Kareem confessed that he had a small degree of concern but was sceptical of my exaggerated fears that Amani was sinking into a medieval passion, darkened with thoughts of sin, suffering and hell. He sat quietly for a short while and then announced that my apprehension was directly linked to Lawand's unhinged denunciations of human wickedness. He told me that Amani's religious revival did not result from insanity, but was essentially linked with the overpowering joy of *Haj*.

'You'll see,' he promised. 'Once we've returned to the normal routine of life, Amani will lapse again into the habit of accumulating wandering beasts, and her religious fanaticism will seem another age.' Kareem smiled and asked a small favour. 'Sultana, please, allow Amani some peace to turn from her daily problems to a oneness with God. It is a duty of all Muslims.'

With a grimace, I nodded my head in agreement. Somewhat relieved, I hoped that Kareem was right.

Still, not leaving such importance to chance, in my prayers that evening I indulged in long hours of pleading with God that Amani would once again be the child she had been prior to our attending *Haj*.

I suffered varying nightmares throughout the night: I dreamt that my daughter, Amani, left our home to join an extremist religious organization in Amman, Jordan, that doused gasoline on the clothing of working Muslim women, setting alight and burning to death those women whom they deemed non-believers.

Chapter Six

HAJ

Arab lands will now go the way of Iran. Egypt will not be the first to fall, nevertheless it shall fall. The women will be the first to suffer loss of human rights. We women were offered our rights as human beings first by Nasser then by Sadat. The courts have already struck down the humane law giving women the right to divorce husbands who take second wives. Egyptian women cringe to think of what is yet to come, often joking that soon we shall share the unfortunate fate of our Saudi sisters.

Comments of an Egyptian feminist pilgrim made to Sara Al Sa'ud, during the *Haj* of 1990

I thought that God must have heard my stirring appeal, for the following morning Amani seemed her usual self. It was as if sleep had erased the apotheosis of human suffering that I had witnessed on my daughter's face the day before. She giggled and joked with her sister, Maha, as they ate their breakfast of fresh yogurt and melon and munched on pieces of kibbeh that had been left from our evening meal.

Our driver delivered us to the Valley of Mina, which is approximately six miles north of Makkah. We would spend the night in Mina, in an air-conditioned and well-equipped tent for which Kareem had made arrangements. The children seemed quite excited at the prospect, since we had never performed that particular ritual in the past.

Along the way, we passed hundreds of buses carrying pilgrims to the valley. On the sides of the highway, thousands of the devout were slowly walking the six-mile journey. Muslims of every colour and nationality were performing their duty by attending *Haj*. I carefully watched their contrasting faces as we slowly passed them by, and there was no doubt that God's name was on every lip.

Thinking that Amani had returned to normal, I once again found myself glad that I was a part of this wonderful gathering of the faithful, and I happily looked forward to the last days of *Haj*.

It was while we were in the Valley of Mina that Kareem met an old friend of his from youthful days spent in England. The man, Yousif, was from Egypt. One moment Kareem was standing by my side, and the next he was heartily embracing a man none of his family had ever seen.

Looking at the man from a distance, I saw that he had a long, slightly curving nose, projecting cheek-bones, and a curly beard. What most caught my attention was the indisputable and concentrated scorn that blazed in his eyes when his gaze fell upon the females in Kareem's family.

Kareem called out the man's name in a loud voice, and I remembered hearing of this person from my husband. Thinking back, I recalled some of what Kareem had told me about this particular acquaintance. During the years of our married life, each time we had visited our villa in Cairo, Kareem's memories had been stirred regarding his Egyptian schoolmate. His plans were to look up his old friend and share the pleasure of exchanging life's joys and pains. On each occasion, the fullness of our family life had prevented Kareem from seeking out his old friend.

Now, after a quick view of the man, I was glad that Kareem's plans had never materialized, for I felt myself in invisible conflict with a malevolent character that, to my eye, had been conspicuous in his dislike for women.

I wondered what had produced such changes in Yousif's life, for I distinctly recalled that Kareem had told me that Yousif had such attractive manners that women had found it hard to resist him and that Yousif had never slept alone.

Kareem and Yousif had known each other during their student days when they had resided in a land not their own. While in London, Yousif had been a carefree, happy individual who was interested in little more than merrymaking with Western women in gambling casinos. Kareem had said that the man had been noticeably brilliant and had little need to study his lessons, and that had been a good thing, for Yousif introduced a different girlfriend each week. In spite of Yousif's insatiable lust for female company, Kareem had predicted a great future for his friend in the legal and political system of Egypt, for Yousif had a quick mind and a pleasing manner.

Yousif had graduated from law school one year ahead of Kareem, and they had not seen each other since that time.

As Yousif and Kareem began to share their news, my daughters and I stayed in the background, which is our way when the man is not of our family, but we could overhear all that Kareem and Yousif were saying.

Apparently Yousif had changed radically from his years as a student, for after a short conversation, it was evident that he and my husband no longer enjoyed much in common.

Yousif was strangely reticent regarding his career, and when Kareem pressed him on his profession, the man would say little more than that he had changed from the youth of Kareem's memory and had become more attached to the traditional ways of Islam.

Yousif proudly told Kareem that since they had last met, he had married and divorced one woman, who had given him two sons, and had married a second woman, fathering five sons in that union. The man delighted in boasting about the joys of having seven sons. Yousif did mention that he had full custody of the first two children, and that the boys had been forcibly taken from the influence of his first wife, who was a modern woman who insisted upon working outside the home. She, Yousif said, with ill-concealed disgust, was a teacher with new ideas about women and their station in life.

Yousif spat on the ground when he mentioned his first wife's name, and said, Praise to God, Egypt was returning to the teachings of the Koran, and Egyptians would soon have the law of Mohammed ruling their lives, rather than the unsettling system of secular law that encouraged women to come out of *purdah*, or complete seclusion.

At this bit of information, I began to come to life and was about to intrude on their conversation and tell the man some of my thoughts, when I was struck dumb by further revelations from Kareem's friend.

Yousif proudly told Kareem that his greatest blessing from God was that neither of his marriages had been cursed with the birth of daughters, and that truly, women were the source of all sin, and if a man had to waste his energies in guarding women, he had little time for performing other, more important duties in life.

Without waiting for Kareem's response to his shocking comments, Yousif launched into a story of a man whom he had met while in Makkah. He said that the man was an Indian Muslim and that this Muslim was thinking of remaining in Saudi Arabia since there was a warrant out for his arrest in India. Two days after his departure to Saudi Arabia, the authorities in India had discovered that he and his wife had murdered their baby daughter by pouring scalding water down her throat.

Yousif asked for Kareem's opinion on the matter, and before my husband could speak, he resumed his loud, rude speech, and said that he, himself, thought that the man should not be punished, since he was the father of four daughters and had desired a son to the point of madness. While Yousif acknowledged that the Prophet had not condoned such a practice, he thought that in such a case the authorities should not intervene on a private matter that had harmed no-one but the baby girl.

Yousif wondered if Kareem could offer assistance on obtaining a work visa for the man, and possibly offer him a job in Saudi Arabia so he would not have to return to his country and face trial.

Yousif had not bothered to discover the sex of Kareem's children, and Kareem had begun to breathe heavily. Knowing Kareem's thoughts on such matters, I thought that my husband might strike his old friend and fling him to the ground.

The back of Kareem's neck turned red, so I knew that my husband blushed in anger. I decided that he could see from the back of his head, for he motioned with his hand for me to stay away. Kareem curtly informed his old friend that he, himself, had been blessed with two beautiful daughters and one son, and that he loved his daughters as he did his son.

A man with thick skin, Yousif gave his condolences to Kareem over the life of our girls, saying that it was too unfortunate that Kareem was the father of daughters. Without taking a moment to breathe, Yousif began to argue the benefits of sons, and wondered why my husband did not take another wife? Kareem could, after all, allow me to keep the daughters, and he could raise our son.

Kareem responded in the calm demeanour of a man who is very angry by reminding Yousif of the teachings of Mohammed. He asked, 'Yousif, you say you are a practising and good Muslim. If so, do you not recall the words of the Blessed Prophet when a man entered the mosque and approached the Prophet?'

I knew the story well, since I have always quoted the fairness of the Prophet with regard to women, in fighting the extremists in my land.

Yousif listened with a blank face, and it was evident to my eyes that here was a man who had no interest in the words of the Prophet if those words did not agree with Yousif's thoughts on life.

Kareem plunged ahead, a man intent on teaching another a good lesson by using intellect, and the teachings of a man anointed by God to spread his word, instead of resorting to brute force. Frankly, I desired to see Yousif be beaten and bloodied by my husband's fists, but I did have a moment of pride when Kareem spoke with the passion of a *muezzin* reminding the faithful to come to prayer, as he told the true story of Prophet Mohammed's reminder to all fathers about the equal value of their children, regardless of the sex.

> A man entered the Mosque and approached the Prophet. He sat down and began to talk. After some time, the man's two children, a boy and a girl, followed their father into the Mosque. The boy came in first, and received much praise and a loving kiss from his father. The boy settled on the man's lap, while the man continued talking to the Prophet.
>
> Some time later, the man's daughter arrived at the Mosque. When she approached her father, he did not kiss her, or put her on his lap, as he had done with his son. Instead, he motioned for the little girl to sit in front of him, and went on talking to the Prophet.
>
> The Prophet was greatly concerned when he saw this. Why, he asked, do you not treat these children equally? Why did you not kiss your daughter as you kissed your son, and let her, also, sit on your lap?
>
> The man felt ashamed when he heard the Prophet say those words. He understood that he had acted in an improper manner towards his two children.
>
> Sons and daughters are both gifts of God, the Prophet reminded him. Both are equally great gifts, and so they should always be treated equally.

Kareem glared at Yousif, his expression seeming to say, now, what do you have to say to that!

This Yousif fellow was a rude man. Ignoring Kareem's obvious discomfort at his attitude towards women and the message of the Prophet's words, he started his tirade against women once again, quoting remarks from the *Green Book*, written by President Qadaffi of Libya, a man who was known to cling to the strictest interpretation of the proper role of women in Islam. Seeing that he had not won over Kareem to his way of thinking, he concluded his efforts by reminding Kareem of the breakdown of the family unit in the Western countries, stating that, 'God has assigned a specific duty for men and for women. Women are created for procreation, nothing else! Kareem, come now, who can deny that by nature all women are exhibitionists? This tendency cannot be changed, but it is a man's duty to keep her away from all men, otherwise, she will squander her beauty and give to any man that asks, her charms . . . '

Furious, Kareem turned his back and walked away from his friend Yousif. His face was an ugly mask as he led his women from the scene.

In a loud voice, he said to me, 'That Yousif has become a dangerous man!'

I glanced back at Yousif. Never have I witnessed such evil in another's face.

Kareem called his brother-in-law Mohammed on his portable telephone, and asked him to make some delicate enquiries about the activities of Yousif, telling Mohammed that the man was extremely radical and possibly an instigator of violence.

Within hours, Mohammed returned Kareem's call and said that Kareem was on the mark, that the man was a skilled lawyer whose clients were members of the Gamaa Al Islamiya, an Egyptian Islamic extremist group formed in the early 1980s that was responsible for militant violence in Egypt.

Kareem was astonished. Yousif represented men that were attempting to overthrow the Egyptian secular government! The Egyptian internal security authorities had told

Mohammed that there had never been charges lodged against the man but, when in Egypt, he was kept under careful surveillance. Mohammed added that he had placed Saudi Security around Yousif to ensure that he did not incite security problems while in Saudi Arabia.

A little less than a year later, Kareem was saddened but not surprised at the news that Yousif had been arrested in Assiut, in southern Egypt, as a principal leader of the Muslim extremist group. While watching a news programme, Kareem spotted Yousif's face – his old friend was looking out on the world from a cage. Kareem followed his case closely and seemed somewhat relieved that Yousif had not been sentenced to death, while I thought that the world was a more dangerous place with such men among the living and would have welcomed his demise.

In spite of the fact that we were at *Haj* and knew we should not concentrate on worldly matters, the man Yousif had made such an impression on our daughters' moods, that Kareem thought it best to talk the matter through and give our daughters the comforting knowledge that men like Yousif were only a passing phase in the long history of Islam.

After the dinner hour, our family sat and discussed the man, Yousif, and what he represented in the Muslim world.

We asked each of the children their thoughts on what they had heard that day.

Abdullah spoke first. Our son was plainly disturbed, saying that Islam was on the move and that it would affect each of our lives, for the extremist groups were calling for the downfall of the Saudi monarchy. He envisaged Saudi Arabia going the way of Iran, with the disposal of the rulers with a man like Khomeini leading our country. Abdullah predicted that his generation of Al Sa'uds would live out their lives on the French Riviera, and such a thought was distressing to our son.

After hearing what the man had to say about females and their value, Maha was spitting mad and wanted her father to have Yousif arrested, and charged as a spy. She would have liked to see him beheaded, even if it was on trumped-up offences!

Amani was reflective and said that Muslim love of all things Western was making men such as Yousif gain power in Muslim countries.

Kareem and I looked at each other, neither of us liking our youngest child's turn of thought.

Maha pinched her sister, accusing her of supporting the man's words.

Amani responded to the charge and said 'no', she did not, but she did consider the possibility that life was simpler when women's roles were more defined and not open for discussion and change. She mentioned that in the bedouin life prior to the building of cities, men and women were not so confused as they were today.

It was as I had feared! My daughter's thoughts were harking to the past. She seemed to be losing pride in her femaleness, and I wondered what I could do to reinforce her worth as a modern woman in an advancing civilization.

Abdullah was unfeeling and began to laugh, asking Amani if she longed for the time that female babies were buried in the sand! It was not too late to take up the practice, he said, the man Yousif could introduce us to such a man who had recently killed his own daughter!

Knowing Amani's mental state was delicate, Kareem gave his son a stern look and said that the matter was no joke, that the evil practice was a terrible problem in India, Pakistan and China. Kareem told us that he had recently read an article in a foreign newspaper that quoted statistics that were startling. Kareem said that tens of millions of females were missing in those lands, and no-one seemed particularly interested in finding out the fate of those victims.

My husband felt so strongly about the matter that he insisted upon discussing further the evils of the practice of infanticide, by telling our children a story that I was not aware my husband knew in such detail.

The children moaned and said that they were too old for stories from their father, but my husband insisted, saying that while statistics made little impact on our emotions, individual tales of horror bring tears to eyes and generate action on social issues in the world community.

With new thoughts about my husband, I listened to Kareem as he told the famous Muslim tale that had been passed down by professional storytellers from the time of Prophet Mohammed.

Kareem said that, 'Prior to the founding of the Islamic faith by Prophet Mohammed, there was a tribe in Arabia that practised the inhuman deed of burying alive their baby daughters, in much the same manner that baby girls are murdered today in other countries.

Qais bin Asim was the chief of this tribe. When Chief Asim embraced Islam, he confessed a dreadful tale to Prophet Mohammed.

' "O Messenger of God! A daughter was born to my wife when I was away from my home on a journey. My wife was fearful that I might bury the child alive, and after nursing her for a few days, sent this child to her sister so that she might be cherished by another. My wife prayed that I might be merciful to the child when the girl became older.

' "When I came back home from the journey I was told that my wife had given birth to a dead child. Thus, the matter was forgotten. During the time, the child remained being loved by her aunt. Once I went out of the house for a whole day, and my wife, thinking I would be out much longer, thought it safe to call her daughter home and enjoy her company for some time in my absence.

' "Unexpectedly, I changed my mind and came home earlier. When I entered my home I saw a very beautiful, neat little girl playing in the house. When I looked at her I suddenly felt a surge of strong and spontaneous love for her within me. My wife sensed my feelings and thought that my blood had called to my own blood and my fatherly love and affection had sprung up naturally for the girl. I asked her, 'Oh, my wife, whose child is this? How charming she is!'

' "Then, my wife told me about the truth of the girl. I could not control my joy and eagerly took the girl in my arms. Her mother told her that I was her father and she began loving me dearly, and calling out to me, 'Oh my father! My father!' At those moments I felt an indescribable pleasure when this girl child put her arms around my neck and showed me affection.

' "Days went by in this way and the child remained being nourished by us and was free from any worry or discomfort. But, there were times when this girl caught my attention and such thoughts came to my mind: I have to give this girl to another man in marriage. I will have to bear the insult that another man will know my daughter as his wife. How will I be able to face other men, knowing that my honour is ruined when this child is bedded by a man. These thoughts took hold of my mind and I was tortured incessantly. At last these thoughts aroused my indignation and made me devoid of patience with the girl. After some time of thinking, I decided that I had to do away with the stigma of shame and humiliation for me and for my ancestors.

' "I decided I had to bury the girl alive.

' "I could not confide this plan to my wife, so I asked her to get the child ready, that I was going to take her to a feast with me. My wife gave the girl a bath, clad her in pretty clothes, and made her ready for the feast. The little girl was excited, bubbling with cheerfulness, believing that she was accompanying her father on a joyful occasion.

' "I left the house with the girl. She was leaping with joy and pleasure, holding my hand every now and then, and running ahead of me, prattling to me with squeals of innocent laughter and gaiety.

' "By this time I had become blind to the girl, and was impatient to get rid of her as soon as possible. The poor child was unaware of my sinister intentions and followed me merrily.

' "At last I stopped at a lonely spot and began to dig into the ground. The innocent girl was surprised to see me doing this and asked repeatedly, 'Father, why are you digging in the earth?'

' "I paid no attention to her questions. She could not know that I was digging a pit to bury my own beautiful daughter with my own hands.

' "While digging in the earth, dust and sand fell upon my feet and clothes. My lovely daughter would clean the dust from my feet and clothes while saying, 'Father, you are spoiling your clothes!'

' "I was like a deaf person and did not look at her, and pretended that I heard nothing she said. I continued my task and finally had dug a pit large enough to serve my purpose.

' "I grabbed my daughter and threw her into the pit, and began to fill the pit with great haste. The poor girl was looking at me with frightened eyes. She began to cry frantically and screamed, 'My dear father, what is this? I have done no wrong! Father, please, do not hide me in the ground!'

' "I kept on doing my work like a deaf, dumb and blind person without paying any attention to her pleadings and entreaties.

' "O Great Prophet of God! I was too heartless to have pity on my own child! On the contrary, after burying her alive, I heaved a huge sigh of relief and came back satisfied that I had saved my honour and pride from humiliation."

'When Prophet Mohammed heard this heart-rending story about an innocent girl, the Holy Prophet could not control himself and tears fell upon his cheeks. He asked the Chief of the Tribe of Asim, "This is too cruel! How can one, who does not pity others, expect to be pitied by the Almighty God?" '

* * *

Kareem looked into the faces of his children. 'Prophet Mohammed, upon hearing this story, became very gloomy, and he related another story that was similar in its horror.'

> A man came to Mohammed and told him that he had once been very ignorant. He said that he had no knowledge and no guidance until the Prophet came and made God's wishes known.
>
> This man said, O Messenger of God! We worshipped idols and killed our children with our own hands. I once had a little and very charming daughter. When I would call her she would run into my arms laughing with joy and pleasure. One day I called this girl to me, and she readily came. I asked her to follow me, and she did. I walked too rapidly, and this girl came running with her small steps. There was a deep well at a short distance from my home. When I reached this well, I stopped and the child came to the well, trotting after me. I caught hold of that child by the hand and threw her into the well. The poor child cried and called out for me to save her. Father, was the last word on the child's lips.

'When the man finished his story, the Prophet wept for a long time, and the tears were so plentiful that they wet his beard. Our ignorance about females was washed away by the shedding of his tears, and today, it is considered a vile and cruel act for a man to bury alive, to throw down into wells, or to harm their female children.'

I hugged each of my daughters. In our hearts, it was as if the Prophet himself were near us, and it seemed as if the tragic tale of the two young girls had occurred in the present and not centuries prior to our existence. Who could doubt that our Prophet had done much to abolish unjust practices and cruel customs? He had been born in an evil time, when pagan Gods were worshipped, when men took hundreds of wives, and the practice of infanticide was common. Prophet Mohammed had great difficulty in abolishing these evil practices, and what he could not abolish, he restricted.

I told my family that, in my opinion, the remaining traditions of that era were what kept us women in bondage, and not the Koran. Few people know the facts, that the Koran does not call for veiling, nor the restrictions women endure in the Muslim world. It is the traditions passed down that so hinder us from moving forward.

A lively discussion ensued as to why the position of women was one of subjection to men, with Maha insulting her brother Abdullah by reminding him that her marks at school were better than his in every subject.

Just as Abdullah opened his mouth to respond, I warned my children not to make the conversation personal.

Then I brought up the obvious, that the physical vulnerabilities of a woman can be traced to that most important function of human accomplishments, the absorption of her strength in carrying, nursing and rearing children. I have always known that this one fact doomed females to a subordinate status in all societies. Instead of attaining honour for being producers of life, we are penalized!

To my mind, this fact is the scandal of civilization!

Abdullah, whose favourite instructor at school was a Lebanese philosophy professor, showed off his knowledge by giving us a history lesson on women's slow climb from the beginning of life until the present moment. That women had been nothing more than beasts of burden in the earlier days, tending to the children, gathering wood for the fire, cooking the meals, making the clothes and boots, and working as pack animals when the tribes were on the march. The men, Abdullah said, risked themselves in the capture of the game, and their reward for providing the tribe with meat was to rest the remainder of the time.

Teasing his sisters, Abdullah flexed his muscles, and said that brute force kept men to the fore, and if his sisters were truly interested in equality, then they should work out with his weights in our exercise studio, rather than read books in their spare time.

Kareem had to restrain our daughters, to keep them from piling on top of their brother. Maha dodged her father's arms and gave a kick to Abdullah's private parts, and Kareem and I both were astonished at her knowledge of his weakest area.

I smiled at my children's antics, but nevertheless my heart was gloomy as I thought of how we women had suffered from the moment of creation. From the beginning of time, we were used as slaves to do the work, and that practice still continued in many countries of the world. In my own country, women were now considered nothing more than things of beauty, sexual toys for man's enjoyment.

I have personal knowledge that women are equal to men in endurance, resourcefulness and courage, but I was ahead of my time in the backward land of Arabia.

Kareem became quiet. Then he broke the silence and said that he was remembering his old friend, Yousif, and the wrongful path that he had chosen.

I was pleased that Kareem had witnessed Yousif's disintegration as a civilized man, for it was if my husband finally became what I wanted him to be, in his recognition of the evil that sprouts and takes hold in society when such men gain power.

Kareem mulled over his thoughts. 'Sultana, you know, it is unsuccessful men, such as Yousif, who mould the myth that women are the root of all evil. I know now that it is a paralysing disillusionment that is so attractive to men, but this disillusionment regarding women does nothing more than create a hateful barrier between the two sexes.'

Kareem looked at his son and said, 'Abdullah, I hope that you will never accept such obstinate resistance to the worth of women. It will be up to your generation to abandon the subjugation of women. I am sad to say that the men of my generation have given new form to women's oppression.'

I could only imagine what my daughters were thinking, since I did not know, but Maha seemed bewildered and angry that she was born into a society so reluctant to adjust to social change, while Amani, recently attached to her consoling faith, appeared burdened by the traditional sanctions that favour the subjugation of women.

Weary of men such as Yousif and of the life they envisage for women – all of whom they consider wicked and therefore strive to control – I could not reconcile myself to the dark years ahead when women would be forced to protect themselves from the growing movement of extremists who called so loudly for their banishment from a normal life.

As I prepared myself for bed, I felt that the sparkle had gone from the occasion of *Haj*. This, in spite of Kareem's new-found philosophy that spoke of enlightened liberation within our family walls.

The following morning, our faces were drawn from our late evening. Silent throughout our morning meal, we prepared ourselves for the most important day of *Haj*.

We were driven five miles north to the hill of Arafat. This was the spot where, according to history, Adam and Eve united after their wanderings. It was also on this site that Ibrahim had been ordered by God to sacrifice his son Isaac. Lastly, this was the place where Prophet Mohammed had delivered his final sermon. Four months later, he was dead.

Disheartened, I barely moved my lips as I uttered the words of the Prophet: 'You have to appear before your God, who shall demand from you an account of all your actions. Know that all Muslims are brothers. You are one brotherhood, no man shall take from his brother unless by his free consent. Keep yourselves from injustice. Let him who is present tell this to him who is absent. It may be that he who is told this afterwards may remember it better than he who has now heard it.'

Walking up the steep side of Mount Arafat, I cried, 'Here I am, O God! Here I am!' This is the day when God erases all our sins and confers his forgiveness.

For six hours, my family and I, with the other pilgrims, stood in the heat of the desert. We prayed and read from the Koran. My daughters, like many other pilgrims, held an umbrella over their heads for shade, but I felt the need to suffer the effects of a baking sun, as a testimony of my faith. Many men and women were fainting all around me, and they were carried off on stretchers to the sunstroke vans, manned by hospital attendants.

At dusk, we moved to the open plain between Mount Arafat and Mina. We rested for a while and then once again began our prayers.

Abdullah and Kareem gathered small stones for the following morning's rituals, and without family communication, for each of us showed signs of physical weariness, we rested fitfully that last night and prepared ourselves for the final day of *Haj*.

The last morning, we chanted, 'In the name of God Almighty I do this, and in hatred of the Devil and his pretence! God is Great!' We each cast seven sets of the small stones gathered by Kareem and Abdullah at the stone pillars that symbolize the Devil. These pillars stand along the road to Mina. This is the very spot where Ibrahim drove Satan away when the Devil tried to tell him not to sacrifice Isaac as God had ordered. Each of the stones represented a bad thought, or temptation to sin, or burden endured by the pilgrims.

We were cleansed of our sins! Now, in the final ritual of the *Haj*, we travelled to the plain of Mina. There, sheep, goats and camels were being butchered to commemorate Ibrahim's willingness to sacrifice his beloved son to God. Butchers roamed throughout the crowd of pilgrims, offering to butcher an animal for a certain sum. Once paid, they held the animal with care, and faced its head toward the Kaaba at the Holy Mosque, while praying, 'In the name of God! God is Great!' After their prayer, the butchers quickly slit the throat of the animal, allowing the blood to drain prior to skinning the beast.

Hearing the cries of the poor beasts and watching the blood run freely, poor Amani screamed as one insane, and dropped to the ground in a faint. Kareem and Abdullah carried our daughter to one of the small trailers which were alongside for the faint of heart and the weak.

They soon returned, saying that Amani was resting comfortably but was still crying, paralysed with grief at what she deemed was the senseless slaughter of many beasts.

Kareem gave me an 'I told you so' look. I felt some small degree of happiness that a recognizable part of Amani's personality had survived intact and hoped that Kareem was right in his assessment that once we departed Makkah that our daughter would be her old self.

As we watched the violent activity, I reminded myself that it was an important ritual, that the animals are sacrificed to remind the pilgrims of the lessons they have learned at *Haj*: sacrifice, obedience to God, mercy to all men, and faith.

Since a child, I had always been fascinated with the skinning process, with the butcher cutting a thin slit in the leg of the animal, then pumping air through the slit to separate the skin from the flesh. The animals grew larger and larger before my eyes, while the butcher struck the body of the animal with a strong stick to distribute the air evenly.

The four days of celebration now began in earnest. I knew that Muslims all over the world were joining us in the celebration, their hearts longing to be at the Holy city of Makkah. Shops were closing, families were receiving new clothes, and vacations were being taken.

As a close to our pilgrimage, we cut off locks of our hair and then exchanged our plain garb for colourful dresses, while the men put on clean cotton *thobes*, the white of the garment shining as bright as newly spun silk.

That afternoon, the actual feast started. Amani was still pale but had recovered sufficiently to join in the festivities, though she refused to partake of any meat.

Our family gathered at our tent, and we exchanged small gifts and congratulated each other. We said our prayers, and then sat together at a long table and ate a wonderful meal of lamb with rice.

What remained of our feast was given to the poor. While many of the pilgrims would pray and repeat their rituals over the next few days, our family decided to return to our home in Jeddah to celebrate further.

We prepared our departure.

My children were now entitled to place the honoured title of *Hajii* before their first name. In spite of the fact that I knew they would not do so, this term of respect reminds all Muslims that a person has fulfilled the fifth pillar of Islam. I knew that we had pleased God by doing *Haj*.

Now, I prayed for God to please me by releasing my daughter, Amani, from the fundamentalist leaning that seemed to grip her soul. I knew that mental instability could lend sanctity to the most extreme doctrine. I did not want my daughter sacrificed to the militant ideals so common to many religions, that I had struggled diligently against from the moment of understanding.

It was not to be. Whether I had pleased God or not, his decision concerning my daughter failed to please me.

The trip to Makkah would later prove to be both fortunate and misfortunate for my family. While Kareem and I grew closer than we had since the first few years of our marriage, and Maha and Abdullah sought to live the lives of responsible citizens of our land, Amani became a gloomy recluse.

My deepest fears became reality.

Chapter Seven

EXTREMIST

Let us imagine a desert country lying in absolute darkness with many living things swarming blindly about in it.

Buddha

Haj was completed and summer was upon us. The hot desert air had nagged us little during our Pilgrimage to Makkah, for our minds were on other, more important matters connected to our spiritual oneness with God.

From Makkah we travelled to our palace in Jeddah, thinking to return to Riyadh the following day. It was not to be. While I was organizing the palace staff for our departure, Kareem entered the room and said that he had cancelled our flight: air traffic control had informed him that a particularly turbulent sand storm was on the way from the Rub Al-Khali desert and moving towards Riyadh. Even without sandstorms, nearly 4,000 tons of sand routinely settles on Riyadh every month. Wanting to avoid this terrible storm of sand that stings the eyes, fills the pores, and covers everything, I was pleased to remain longer in Jeddah, in spite of the fact that Jeddah's humid temperature is more oppressive than the dry desert heat of Riyadh.

Once the children had heard the news, Abdullah and Maha became excited at postponing Riyadh and their normal routine for a few days. Our two eldest children pleaded with us that we take a small holiday while in Jeddah. I looked at my husband and smiled. The smile faded from my face when I noticed that Amani was sitting off by herself in the corner of the room, her nose in the pages of the Koran. Amani was rapidly becoming a gloomy recluse and seemed unconcerned as to where she might be. It appeared to me that my youngest child had raised barriers against a normal desire for harmless fun, for in the past nothing thrilled Amani more than to swim in the lapping, warm waters of the Red Sea.

Determined not to allow Amani's activities to depress me further, I nodded my head, yes, in response to Kareem's questioning eyes. So, in spite of the humidity and the heat waves that were dancing in the air, Kareem and I decided to remain in Jeddah for an additional two weeks, for we could see that our two eldest children were sorely tempted by the blue mirror of the Red Sea waters that we could see from the walls of our palace.

Like many members of the royal family, I preferred the lively port city of Jeddah to staid Riyadh. I was looking forward to taking my daughters shopping in Jeddah's modern shopping malls and entertaining family friends who lived there, and the holiday loomed pleasantly before my mind. Had not Amani chosen this time to expand the growing gap between herself and her family, it would have been a perfect time in an otherwise imperfect life.

I was down on my knees in the long corridor which connected the various wings of the palace, when Maha made the discovery that her mother was attempting to overhear the voice of her sister, Amani, through a small crack in the door onto the Turkish baths and indoor garden area.

'Mummy! What are you doing?' Maha called out in a loud, laughing voice, even as I tried to wave her away with my hand.

From inside the room, Amani stopped speaking, and I heard my daughter's determined footsteps as she made her way towards the door. I made a desperate attempt to spring to my feet so that I could move myself away from the door, but my high heel caught in the hem of my long dress. I was struggling to free myself when Amani flung the door open and stood staring down at her obviously guilty mother.

I was unnerved at my daughter's accusing face, for her piercing eyes and tight lips made it plain that she clearly understood the situation.

Unable to acknowledge my despicable deed, I began to rub my fingers against some red threads that were worked into the hall carpet, and with what I hoped was a lilt to my voice, began to lie with the intensity of one who knows that their listeners see through her lie.

'Amani! I thought you were in your room!' I exclaimed.

I returned my gaze to the carpet at my feet, seriously studying the red of the carpet. 'Darlings, have either of you noticed the red stains on this carpet?'

Neither of my daughters responded.

With a frown, I gave the red threads a few more rubs, and with my heel still caught in my dress, I stood up hunched over and limped down the corridor. Short on explanation, I mumbled, 'The servants have become quite lax. I fear that the stain is permanent.'

Amani, unable to allow me the pleasure of believing that my small lie had been convincing, spoke to my back. 'Mummy. This carpet is *not* stained. Those are red roses woven into the pattern of the carpet!'

Maha could not restrain herself, and I heard her as she began to giggle.

Amani called out, 'Mummy, if you wish to hear my words, you are most welcome. Please, come into the room where I am speaking.' The door leading into the garden room slammed with a thunderous clap.

Tears formed in my eyes, and I rushed to my bedroom. I could not bear to look at my beautiful daughter, for since we had returned from Makkah, she had begun to clothe herself from head to toe in black, even going so far as to wear thick black hosiery and long black gloves. In the privacy of our home, only her face remained uncovered, as my child wrapped her beautiful black hair in a stiff black headcovering that reminded me of something a goat-herding Yemeni woman would wear. When Amani ventured outside our palace walls, she added a veil of thick black fabric that hindered her vision, even though the religious officials of Jeddah were much more relaxed in pursuing women with unveiled faces than were those of Riyadh. Our desert capital is known throughout the Muslim world for its diligent morals committees, which are composed solely of angry-faced men who harass innocent women on the city streets.

Nothing I could say or do could persuade my daughter to dress in greater comfort than the heavy black cloak, veil and headdress, a forced manner of female dressing that strikes most Muslim believers in other Islamic lands as nothing less than ridiculous.

I could not control my sobs. At great risk to my happiness, I had battled most of my life for my daughters to have the right to wear the thinnest of veils, and now, my dear child dismissed my small victory as if it had no value.

And, that was not the worst! Not content with her new-found discovery of our faith, Amani felt a missionary zeal to convert others to her new way of thinking. Today, Amani had invited her closest friends, along with four of her younger cousins to our home, to hear her read from the Koran and to speak to those girls of her interpretation of the Prophet's words, which sounded distressingly like the interpretation I had so often heard from the Government's Committee for Commendation of Virtue and Prevention of Vice.

The intonation of Amani's childlike voice was ringing in my head as I closed the doors to my private quarters and lay crossways on the bed, wondering how I was going to tackle this latest crisis of motherhood.

Whilst eavesdropping, I had overheard Amani as she had read from the holy Koran:

Do ye build a landmark
on every high place
to amuse yourselves?

And, do ye get for yourselves
fine buildings in the hope
of living therein forever?

and when ye exert
your strong hand
do ye do it like men
of absolute power?

Now fear God and obey me
And follow not the bidding
of those who are extravagant,
and make mischief in the land,
and mend not their ways.

My knees shaking, I had listened in horror as Amani stressed the Saudi royal family's similarity to the ostentatious sinners in the verse of the Koran.

'Look around you! Witness the wealth of the home from which I speak! A palace fit for a God could be no finer! Are we not discarding the very words of God in embracing opulence of costly indulgence that no human eyes are fit to see?'

Amani's voice went soft, as if she were speaking in a whisper, but I had closed my eyes and leaned closer, listening with great care. I could barely hear Amani's words. 'Each of us must banish extravagance from our lives. I will set the first example. The jewels that I have received from the wealth of my family name, I will give to the poor. If you believe in the God of Mohammed, you, too, must follow my example.'

I did not hear the audience's response to their leader's outlandish demand, for at that moment, my elder daughter, Maha, had made my unwelcome presence known.

Now, remembering Amani's promise to divest herself of her jewels, I pushed myself from the bed and hurried to my daughter's bedroom. There, I opened the safe that she shared with her sister, and removed a large quantity of expensive necklaces, bracelets, earrings and rings, locking those items into the safe in Kareem's office. I had taken Maha's cache of jewellery along with Amani's, for who knew what offence Amani might commit in her turbulent religious state.

I knew that the total value of Amani's jewellery alone was well into millions of dollars, and it had been given her by people who loved her and wanted to provide economic security for her future. I promised myself that if Amani genuinely desired to provide for the poor, then money would be given to her for this purpose.

Feeling depressed and unappreciated for our generosity, I remembered the millions of riyals that Kareem and I have quietly donated over the years to the poor of the world. In addition to the required *zakah* liability, or percentage of our annual income not needed for our daily living expenses, Kareem and I contribute an extra fifteen per cent of our income for education purposes and medical care to various Muslim countries less fortunate than Saudi Arabia. Never have we forgotten the words of the Prophet, 'If you give alms openly, that is well, but if you give them to the needy in private, it is even better for you, and will atone for some of your bad deeds. Allah is aware of all you do.'

Thinking of the funds provided to build medical clinics, schools and private dwellings in the poorest of Muslim lands, I felt a keen desire to remind Amani of the enormity of the financial contributions made by her parents. Had my child discarded our charitable activities as meaningless? Or was her true desire to turn our family into beggars, like those who benefited from our great wealth?

Returning to my bed, I lay quiet for over two hours, thinking thoughts, discarding wild ideas, not knowing how to do battle with a force that is higher than any man.

Darkness had fallen over my room when Kareem came home from his Jeddah offices.

'Sultana! Are you ill?' Kareem switched on several lamps and walked to my bed, peering down at my face with concern.

'Your face is flushed. Do you have a fever?'

I did not answer my husband's questions. Instead, I took a deep, tortured breath. 'Kareem, one of your flesh and blood is plotting the overthrow of the monarchy.'

Kareem's face turned from pale brown to bright red in a matter of seconds. 'What?'

I feebly waved my hand in the air. 'Amani. Today, our daughter held a meeting of young princesses and good friends. I accidentally overheard her speaking. She's using the Koran to turn her young cousins and acquaintances against the leadership of our family.'

Kareem clicked his tongue in the Arab manner that denotes disbelief. He laughed. 'You're crazy, Sultana. Amani is the least likely of our children to incite violence.'

I shook my head. 'No more. Religion has strengthened our child. She's beginning to resemble a hungry lion rather than a gentle lamb.' I repeated to Kareem what I had overheard.

Kareem made a face. 'Sultana. Believe me when I say this latest passion is nothing more than a passing phase. Ignore her. She'll soon tire of her excesses.'

It was clear that Kareem himself was tired of the topic of Amani's religious conversion. I had talked of little else during the past week. Amani's passionate embrace of all things extreme in our religion tortured her mother, while her father dismissed his daughter's fervour with a joke and a prediction that it would be short-lived.

My hopes were dashed that Kareem and I would share and resolve this latest crisis, unlike our unity in Maha's case. I felt the fight ease from my body. For the first moment since giving birth to Abdullah so many years before, I grew weary of motherhood, and wondered how many more generations of women could be enticed to burden themselves with the solitary and thankless production, nourishing and guidance of the human race.

With a rasping sound in my throat, I cried out to my husband, 'How lonely a woman's life is!'

Fearing that I would react in an unsettled manner to my grief, Kareem patted me tenderly, and asked sweetly if I would like my dinner served to me in private in our quarters. He said that he would take the evening meal alone with our children, if that were the case.

With a sigh of martyrdom, I decided not to stay alone. I had been in solitude for many hours, and I did not want to give Amani the idea that her mother was sulking. I pushed myself off the bed and told my husband that I would freshen up for dinner and see him downstairs.

Kareem and I met in the small family sitting-room, and since we were an hour early for dinner, I asked my husband to go for a stroll with me in the Turkish bath and garden area.

Remembering the evening that we had shared before, Kareem thought that I was feeling romantic, and his eyes brushed my face with tenderness.

I returned his smile but, in reality, I wanted to examine the garden area and see what evidence, if any, my child had left of her religious meeting with her friends and her royal cousins.

We entered our large beautiful courtyard that had been designed by a famous Italian fashion designer, and over the years, many of our royal cousins had attempted unsuccessfully to copy the loveliness of this unique 'Turkish room'. The first thing one sees is a flowing waterfall at the back of the room. Clear water falls from it into a large circular pool full of exotic fish. A stone path encircles the pool and beautiful flowers, tenderly cared for by our staff of gardeners, line the walkway. There are two raised sitting areas to left and right. Lush, green foliage that was imported from Thailand drapes over the rattan furnishings which are scattered with pastel-coloured cushions. Glass-topped tables are set about in the sitting areas, and it is a most pleasant spot for our family to enjoy morning or evening coffee.

The walls are made of special tinted glass, but the greenery is so abundant and dense that we are shaded from the hot rays of the sun. A pathway leads around the waterfall, and Kareem and I walked on these stones, which are carved with the faces of wild animals. I felt sad as I walked on the face of a giraffe, for I remembered that Kareem had the stones especially carved for Amani, as a surprise for our animal-worshipping child.

The walkway took us to the Turkish bath area. Our home in Cairo has such a room too, and I had requested the Italian designer to study that design and duplicate it at our palace in Jeddah.

The Turkish bath house contains four baths, each one set in a different style and size. There are steps that lead to each bath, and over one of the larger baths is an arched bridge made of stone. Steam was rising from the water and dissipating in the cool air.

My family have enjoyed many wonderful times in the Turkish baths, and Kareem and I, just the evening before, prior to our evening of romance, had soothed ourselves by enjoying a lengthy steam bath.

There was nothing visible to the eye to indicate that Amani had held a religious meeting in our home. Yet my head still thundered with the words that I had overheard. I desperately wanted Kareem to acknowledge the seriousness of Amani's new passion, for our daughter was now talking of becoming a female Imam, a woman who would minister to other women's religious needs. While I wanted my daughter to live the life of a good Muslim, I had no desire for her to further the bondage of women under the strictest interpretation of the traditions that so hobbled females in our land.

Sensing correctly that Kareem was not burdened by Amani's passionate attraction to everything that I had fought against since an early age, I thought to remind him of where such religious passion could lead, for I knew that my husband was sensitive on the subject of the Al Sa'uds' legitimate claim to the throne and the wealth and privilege that accompanied our envied position.

Knowing my husband's life was firmly centred in a fashionable life of luxury that could hardly be afforded without the vast wealth of our country's oil fields, I gestured at the lovely décor of the Turkish bath. 'This', I said to Kareem, 'is what our daughter believes is a great sin, to enjoy what God has seen fit to provide our family.'

My husband made no response.

I needled him further. 'Kareem, we must take action. Or, do you want your own flesh and blood to lead the revolt that will bring down the house of Al Sa'ud?'

Kareem, still not believing his daughter capable of serious mischief, refused to analyse Amani's disenchantment with our royal status any further, saying only that our daughter should be left to her consoling faith, even if it was against her mother's obstinate resistance.

Holding me tightly by my shoulders, Kareem forbade me to mention the subject again, making a ridiculous statement.

'Sultana,' he said, 'I decided long ago that each of us must respect the other's delusions, or there will be no peace in our home. Now! Drop this disagreeable subject!'

After days of soul-searching, I finally reached the understanding that I was not to blame for my daughter's new direction in life. I reached the conclusion that Amani's zeal for a cause was a direct result of Saudi Arabia's horrendous poverty that had been relieved by sudden and enormous wealth. To get to the heart of the matter, I had to go back in time.

Many people, Muslims and Christians alike, despise Saudis for their unearned wealth. Yet, few bother to understand the wretched poverty endured by all Saudi Arabians until the mid-1970s. I highly resent this hasty analysis of our current situation.

Many years passed after the actual discovery of oil under the sand of the desert before our people benefited from the riches guaranteed by oil production that had been organized by American companies. In the beginning, King Abdul Aziz, my grandfather and the founder of Saudi Arabia, trusted the smooth-talking men who made false promises, not understanding that the deals struck put millions into the pockets of the Americans and paltry sums into the coffers of Saudi Arabia. Only when the American oil companies were forced to be fair did they behave in a principled manner.

Thus, due to the disproportionate method of dividing the proceeds from the oil wealth, it took many years for the bedouin desert tents to be replaced by luxurious villas and palaces to house our people. Meanwhile people of Saudi Arabia suffered greatly. Infant mortality in Saudi Arabia was among the highest in the world, for there was no money, doctors, or hospitals to treat the sick. Saudi diets consisted of dates, camel milk, and goat and camel meat.

I can remember seeing the desperate look in the eyes of one of the wealthiest men in the kingdom, as he shared the horrifying tale of his early years. A brilliant and highly respected man of business, he spent the first fifteen years of his life going from door to door in the mud-hut village of Riyadh, in an attempt to sell small bags of goat's milk. He was the man of the family when he was only seven years old, for his father had died from a slight infection he had contracted from his sword when slaughtering a camel for the *Haj* feast. The infection had turned to gangrene, and his father had ended his life screaming in great pain.

As was the custom of the day, the young boy's mother was wed to a surviving brother of his father, a man who had many children of his own. The young boy felt responsible for his five younger siblings. Four of them were buried by his own hand, their death a result of poor nutrition and medical facilities. His brutish climb to prosperity was a tale of Dickensian horror.

After a youth spent amid dire poverty, it was quite natural for the first Saudi generation to use the power of wealth to pamper their offspring, showering them with everything money could buy. While Kareem and I grew to adulthood without need in our lives, we understood the vital force of poverty, since the vestiges of poverty in our parents' generation made a lasting impact on our youth. However, the children born from our generation never knew deprivation, even secondhand, and so did not realize what it really meant to be poor.

Civilization followed a natural course, for concentrated wealth balanced insecurely upon a lost heritage may at any moment be dismissed as of no value. It was only a matter of time before shaky foundations would begin to tumble.

The conventions and traditions accepted by past generations were questioned by my generation. The generation that followed mine often followed their animal instincts wholly without restraint. This primitive rejection of social order, brought forth a natural backlash of religious fanaticism and disdain for extravagant wealth.

Now, those who are fanatical are the offspring of my generation. Having never known life without great wealth, and spared the knowledge of the consequences of wrenching poverty, our children and the children of our acquaintances are scornful of the economic ease of our lives and are searching for a greater purpose than the accumulation of additional riches.

My child, Amani, became a leader of a group of women who strove and still strive to be even more militant than the men who lead the faithful to overturn the throne claimed by the Al Sa'ud clan.

While Amani sought to save the souls of those she knew as relatives, or claimed as friends, she brought forth a confession from her cousin, Faten, the child of Ali, that none of us could ever have imagined.

No man has been haughtier with women than my brother, Ali. As a child, he treated his ten sisters with contempt. As a young man living in America, he bedded and casually discarded hundreds of Western women. As a husband, he treated his wives as slaves, caring little about their happiness, careful to wed girls at first puberty so that they knew little of man's nature and accepted his perverse behaviour as normal. In addition to four wives, Ali settled one concubine after another in his home. As a father, he virtually ignored his daughters and showered affection on his sons.

It was only natural that his son, Majed, Faten's brother, grew into a sadistic youth who considered women nothing more than sexual objects.

Looking back, I know now that Majed would have been beheaded, or shot to death by a firing-squad, had his crime become common knowledge. Nothing could have saved Majed this fate, not even the fact that he is the son of a high-ranking prince, for his sin was without precedent in the Al Sa'ud family.

We had returned to our home in Riyadh, where each afternoon after school Amani continued her daily Koran sessions with those relatives who were interested in returning to the times of darkness, when women would remain silent on all issues of life that did not occur within the confines of their homes.

It was a Wednesday afternoon, and I watched from my bedroom balcony as one after another of my daughter's friends and relatives left our driveway in the safety of their chauffeur-driven limousines. Faten, my brother Ali's daughter, was last to leave, and I thought it odd that she and Amani talked for so long, and exchanged passionate embraces on more than one occasion. Sadly, I guessed that Faten, in her desperate unhappiness as daughter of my unfeeling brother, had fiercely seized the cause my child had offered her.

Desperate to return to a normal relationship with my child, I cautioned myself not to introduce the topic of religion ever again with Amani, to let God lead her where he wanted her to go. Still, I hoped to interest Amani in a game of backgammon, or cards, to see if I could focus her mind on something other than her faith.

When I timidly knocked on my daughter's door, there was no response. I heard the sound of weeping and entered her room. A sense of irritation swept through me, for there sat Amani, holding the Koran in one hand and wiping tears with the other. I wanted to shout that religion was not meant to bring sadness, but I resisted the urge and knelt at my child's feet. I patted her knee and calmly began to question her on the cause of her grief.

Expecting to hear that she had received some message from God not meant for my ears, I was startled when she replied, 'Mummy, I am truly grieved by what I must do!'

Then my child threw herself in my arms and wept as one who has heard the most devastating news!

'Amani! Daughter! What is this?'

'Mummy!' A spasm went through her small frame as she sobbed. 'A terrible sin has been committed. I have learned a loathsome secret. God has told me to make this sin public.'

'What sin?' I shouted, alarmed that Amani had somehow heard of Maha's unnatural love relationship with her girlfriend, Aisha, knowing that if their affair were made public, that my daughter and our family would suffer greatly.

Amani looked at me with her big eyes. 'Faten has confided a secret that is troubling her soul. This sin is too terrible to reveal, yet I must.'

Mollified that Amani was not speaking of her sister, Maha, I speculated on the latest of Al Sa'ud scandals that might be plaguing my child. In a family the size of the Al Sa'ud clan, there is much gossip regarding the ungovernable conduct of the young princes, and on rarer occasions, the youthful princesses. Male members of the family will often be featured in foreign newspapers after a great gambling loss or being caught in a sexual misadventure with foreign women. After family holidays in the West, more than one princess has returned to the kingdom expecting an illegitimate child. Rarely is the complete truth revealed, as the various relatives rush to cover their children's misdeeds, in order to prevent their personal misfortunes from becoming common knowledge throughout the Al Sa'ud clan.

Amani blurted out, 'Mummy. It's Majed. Majed has committed a sexual sin.'

I had difficulty in maintaining a serious face. 'Majed? Amani, Majed is his father's son.' I pulled my daughter's face to mine, warning her, 'If you speak of this matter, the men of our family will do nothing more than share a laugh at your expense. Ali is proud of his son's success with foreign women.'

Everyone in our family knew that Majed, Ali's second son, participated in foreign activities in our country, attending parties in foreign compounds, dating non-Muslim women from the hospitals and foreign airlines. This activity was generally frowned upon by Muslim families, but Ali thought it a perfect opportunity for his second son to enjoy sexual freedom in a land where such activities are strictly forbidden between people of the Muslim religion.

My heart ached when I saw the seriousness of Amani's expression as she explained further. 'No, Mummy. You don't understand. Majed has performed a sexual act without the consent of the woman.'

I had no idea of what my daughter spoke. 'Amani, what do you mean?'

My daughter began to cry again. Between her convulsive sobs, she asked that I go and find her father, saying that she needed his guidance in her decision on whom to inform of Majed's terrible conduct.

Hurt that Amani desired her father's opinion over my own, I nevertheless went through the house, looking for Kareem. When I finally located him with Abdullah and Maha in the games room, playing a lively game of pool, I felt a twinge of jealousy, thinking to myself that all three of my children preferred their father to their mother. I had to bite my tongue to avoid blurting out Kareem's distressing character flaws in an attempt to redirect my children's devotion.

All three members of my family jumped when I loudly yelled, 'Kareem! Amani needs you.'

'Just a moment. It's my turn.'

'Kareem. Your daughter is weeping. Come, now.'

My husband gave me a filthy look. 'What have you said to her, Sultana?'

Already testy and wrongly accused, I used my hand to knock each of the brightly coloured pool balls into the holes at the side of the table. I walked away, unconcerned with the disappointed moans coming from Kareem and Abdullah.

'Now,' I shouted over my shoulder. 'The game has ended. You've won. Now, perhaps you can tend to your child.'

Kareem was on my heels as we entered Amani's room. The tears had gone from my daughter's eyes, and she had the fixed look of one who has made a decision.

Kareem spoke first. 'Amani? Your mother said you needed to tell me something?'

'Father, Majed has to be punished for what he's done. I've carefully read everything that is written on such matters, and there's no other way. My cousin *must* be punished.'

Kareem sat on a chair and crossed his legs. He had a squeezed, funny look on his face, as though for the first moment he realized that Amani had gone too far in her religious quest.

His voice quiet, he asked, 'What has Majed done that's so terrible?'

Still an innocent girl, Amani's face turned a bright red. 'I'm ashamed of what I have to say.'

'Just say it,' Kareem prodded.

Embarrassed at speaking thus in the presence of a man, even her own father, whom she had purposely requested to share the confidence, Amani stared into her lap. Her face was clear and innocent as she told us a tale of evil blackness.

'One evening Majed attended a party at one of the Western compounds. I believe that it was the compound for Lockheed employees. While there, he met an American woman who took an interest in the fact that he was of the royal family. As the evening went on, Majed became drunk, and the woman thought better of her promise to go with Majed to a friend's apartment. When Majed understood that he had wasted his evening and that there would be no sex that night, he left the compound in an angry mood. On the way home, he went to visit a friend who happened to be in a hospital with minor injuries from a car accident. While at this hospital, Majed became angrier, and in his drunken condition, he slipped from room to room searching for a blonde or foreign woman whom he could coax or pay to have sex.

'It was after midnight, and there were few employees who were not sleeping.'

Amani's bottom lip began to tremble, and Kareem had to persuade her to continue. 'And . . . what happened then, Amani?'

The accusation tumbled from my daughter's mouth. 'Majed had sex with a woman in the hospital who was a patient, a woman who had been seriously injured, and was not conscious.'

I could not move. As one who had been turned to stone, I listened as my daughter and my husband continued to speak.

Kareem shook his head in disbelief. 'Amani. Faten told you that?'

'Yes, Father. And, more.'

'Amani. No. Faten is imagining this. It can't be true. It's too sick to be real.'

'I knew you would resist the truth,' Amani accused. 'There's proof.'

'Proof? What proof? I would like to know.'

'Well, there was a man from Pakistan working in that area of the hospital. He discovered Majed leaving the room, and when he examined the patient, he saw that the sheets on her bed had been disturbed. He followed Majed and threatened to call the authorities. When he was told that Majed was a prince, he demanded money. To shut him up, Majed gave him what he had in his pocket.

'Amani!' Kareem, highly dubious, cautioned his daughter. 'Watch the words that come from your tongue. Rape! Blackmail! This is too much to believe!'

'It's true! It's true! You'll see! Now there's going to be trouble.' Amani's words rushed, one atop the other, as she tried to convince her father. 'Now, it's been discovered that the woman who was in a coma, a Christian woman from another land, is with child! Even though she's been in the hospital, unconscious, for six months! She's three months with child! There's a big investigation in that hospital, and Majed is afraid that his name will be made public in the scandal.'

Thinking for the first time that there might be some truth to the story, for the details were many, I began to breathe heavily, wondering how we could avoid this scandal.

Amani tearfully completed her tale of horror, 'Faten caught him trying to break open the safe in their father's office, in order to steal cash. When cornered, Majed confided in his sister that the Pakistani has demanded a lot of money. This man wants 1,000,000 *riyals*[1] to remain silent about Majed's royal identity. Majed can't ask his father for that amount of money without an explanation, and the man's going to name him. Majed's been given one week to come up with the money.'

Kareem and I stared at each other, wondering if what we were hearing was the truth.

I recalled terrible words that Majed had once used to Abdullah, ridiculing my son for his refusal to have sex

[1]Roughly £172,000.

with what Abdullah had claimed was a particularly ugly American, a woman who was twice my son's age but had been willing to have sex with a young prince for money. Majed had accused Abdullah of being a man who did not like women, saying, 'A true man can become excited over a she-camel!' I vaguely recalled that Majed had then told Abdullah something about the woman looking better than the last woman he had 'ridden' – a woman who had been unconscious and had not known what fun she was missing.

When discussing the incident, we had assumed that the woman must have been drunk. Now, in the light of what Amani was saying, had that woman been unconscious from an injury? Had Ali's son raped a woman who had no ability to speak for herself? The timing of Abdullah's confidence now fitted in with Amani's story.

I wanted to ask Kareem about that conversation, for Abdullah had told him about it, and he had shared the story with me. I remembered that from that time onwards Kareem had forbidden Abdullah to accompany his cousin Majed to foreign parties.

Kareem came to when Amani said, 'Majed has to be punished. I will have to tell Wijdan to inform her father of Majed's misdeed.'

I heard Kareem's teeth as they ground against each other. He, as I, knew that Wijdan's father was a religious man who worked out of the royal mosque. While he bore no special animosity towards members of the royal family, he was a man of religion who followed his conscience. He would be a difficult man to buy off, and if nothing else, would insist on discussing the matter with the religious council and the King. The last thing our family needed was for that particular man to be told of the situation.

Besides, I still hoped in my heart that a mistake had been made and Majed was innocent of such unspeakable and indecent behaviour.

Kareem instructed his daughter, 'Amani, this is not a topic for young girls to be discussing. I'll investigate these charges, and if they're true, I give you my word that Majed will be punished. Now, I must have your promise that you will tell no-one of what you've said.'

Expecting Amani to disagree, I was pleasantly surprised when my child seemed relieved to discharge the problem to her father. She promised him all that he had asked.

Within three days, Kareem had discovered the ugly truth. Indeed, there was a Christian woman in a local hospital who had suffered a serious head injury in a car accident within the kingdom seven months prior to Kareem's investigation. She had been unconscious for that length of time. Now, the hospital staff and the family of the woman were in a crisis, for the medical staff at the hospital had discovered that the woman was four months' pregnant! There was an ongoing inquiry at that institution to find the guilty party.

Amani's horrifying story was true!

Kareem said that Ali must be told, and my husband requested that I accompany him to my brother's home. For once in my life, I experienced no glee regarding my brother's misfortunes.

My stomach churned as we entered the side gate into the enormous compound that housed Ali's four wives and seven concubines. As our car entered the gateway, I caught sight of many women and numerous children gathered on the portion of the lawn partly hidden by green foliage. The children were playing, while the women were gossiping, playing card games, or knitting.

How strange, I thought, that over the years the women that my brother had wed, along with the concubines he kept, had developed close and loving relationships. It was rare that so many women attached to one man could maintain such a successful and friendly rapport.

I could not imagine sharing Kareem with one woman, let alone ten. I thought perhaps that the lack of love in my brother's manner caused the women to seek friendship and companionship with those of their own kind. Or perhaps my brother inspired no love at all from his women, and each one welcomed the intrusion of another to seduce Ali away from the marriage bed.

That thought brought a smile to my face.

But when I remembered the tragic reason for our visit to my brother's home, my smile vanished.

Ali was in a jolly mood, and he extended a friendly welcome to our unexpected and unexplained visit.

After an exchange of pleasantries, and our third cup of tea, Kareem broke the bad news. It was not an easy exchange, and, as Kareem informed Ali of what he had learned, Ali's expression changed from that of a contented man to one lost in sorrow. For the first time in my life, I felt sympathy for my brother, recalling words I had often heard spoken by those wiser than me. 'Those whose hands are in the water should not expect happiness from those whose hands are in the fire.'

Ali was a man with his hand in the fire.

Majed was summoned, and the boy's arrogant countenance cracked when he saw the furious look on his father's face. I wanted to hate the boy, but I remembered an incident that had occurred when I was but a child. After being corrected for some minor infraction, Ali once called our mother an 'ignorant bedouin' and had moved to kick at his own mother. When my sisters and I had begged our mother to beat Ali with a big stick, our mother had sadly responded, 'Why blame a young boy for resembling his father?'

Now, just as Ali had resembled our father in character and behaviour, Majed was the image of Ali.

Kareem and I left my brother and his son when Ali began to strike Majed with his bare hands.

A week later Ali confided to Kareem that the problem had been 'handled'. He reported that he had located the Pakistani orderly and had made the man very rich. With the cash he was given, the Pakistani invested his money in Canada, and with Ali's assistance would soon receive a passport to that country. Our family would hear no more from that troublemaker, Ali had declared.

Shaking his head in bafflement, Ali had told Kareem, 'All this disruption, for a woman.'

Neither the hospital nor the family of the woman raped by Majed was ever aware of the truth of the matter, that the guilty party was a royal prince.

Majed was sent away to school in the West.

Amani, convinced that no punishment could be worse than banishment from the land of the Prophet, was pacified.

Once again, wealth had abolished family responsibility for a crime committed.

I suppose I should not have been angry or surprised, for as my brother said, it was only a woman.

It seemed that nothing disturbed the male domination of my country, even when one of their own was guilty of the most heinous crime.

Chapter Eight

LOVE AFFAIR

When love beckons you, follow him, though his ways are hard and steep.

Kahlil Gibran

Amani and her sister, Maha, awoke me from a pleasant afternoon nap. Through the thick doors leading into my private quarters, I could hear my daughters screaming at each other.

What had Amani done now? I thought to myself, as I quickly dressed. Since Amani's religious conversion, she liked to tell people what she thought of them, never hesitating to enumerate her brother's and sister's immoral acts, searching endlessly for a pretext to censure her siblings.

My son, Abdullah, was loath to fight. Dreading Amani's incalculable, and apparently unappeasable wrath, Abdullah, more often than not, simply ignored his sister. On the rare occasions that Amani's demands were simple to fulfil, he capitulated.

Amani did not find such agreement possible with Maha. With her older sister, Amani was dealing with a female character who was at least as strong as her own, for Maha's violent temper had characterized her from her first breath.

I followed the sound of my daughters' shouts. Several of the servants were standing in the doorway of the kitchen, but they were disinclined to interrupt what to their eyes was lively entertainment.

I had to push my way into the room.

I had arrived at an opportune moment. Maha, who is twice Amani's size and much fiercer than her younger sister, had reacted violently to Amani's latest regulation. As I rushed towards my daughters I saw that Maha had her younger sister pinned to the floor, rubbing her face into the pages of the morning newspaper!

It was as I had thought!

Just the week before, Amani and her religious group had come to the conclusion that the kingdom's daily newspapers were made holy since the pages contained the word God, the sayings of the Holy Prophet, and verses of the Koran. The committee had decreed that newspapers were not to be walked upon, eaten upon, or thrown into the trash. At the time, Amani had given notice to her family of the religious decision, and now she had violently apprehended Maha committing an irreverent act – heedless of her noble instruction.

The result had been predictable.

I shouted, 'Maha! Let your sister go!' Spurred on by her anger, Maha seemed not to hear my excited command. I made a futile attempt to pull Maha away from her sister, but my daughter was determined to teach Amani a lesson. Since Maha was stronger than Amani and me together, she was the victor in our three-way struggle.

Red-faced and breathing with great effort, I looked to the servants for assistance, and one of the Egyptian drivers moved quickly to intervene. The man had strong arms and was successful in separating my daughters.

One battle always invites another. Verbal insults replaced physical force. Maha began to curse her baby sister who was weeping bitter tears while accusing her elder sister of being a non-believer.

I proposed to mediate but could not be heard above the mayhem. I pinched the skin on my daughters' arms until they were silenced. Maha stood in smouldering sullenness. Amani, still on her hands and knees, reached to straighten the pages of the ripped newspaper. My daughter kept her devotions to the end!

The causes for religious fervour are many, and the results are endless. I had a thought that some people appear at their worst in their religion. Certainly, that was the case with Amani. In the past, I had felt both doubtful and hopeful that religion could, in time, soothe rather than incite Amani. But now I felt with dull certainty that would not be the case.

My patience did not equal my anger, and I led my daughters by their ears into the sitting-room. With a firm voice, I called for the servants to leave us to ourselves. I glared at my children, thinking ungallantly that I had made a grievous mistake in inflicting such troublesome characters upon the world.

'The wailing of the newborn infant is nothing more than a siren of warning sung for a mother,' I said to my daughters.

My face and glance must have shown me as a madwoman, for my daughters' expressions were stricken. They held a curious respect for their mother's moments of insanity.

Thinking to avoid a second larger quarrel with three participants rather than two, I closed my eyes and took a deep breath. Once calmed, I told my daughters that each of them would have an opportunity to speak but that there would be no more violence.

Maha burst out, 'Too much! Too much! Amani is driving me insane! She will leave me alone, or . . . ' I could see that Maha was searching through her mind for the worst possible insult, 'I'll slip into her room and rip up her Koran!'

Amani gasped in horror at the thought.

Knowing how spirited and daring Maha could be when she was determined to do a thing, I forbade my daughter the irreverent act.

Her fury unleashed, Maha continued. 'This stupid idea

of not discarding old papers! We'll have to build a large storeroom to house them.' She looked at her sister, 'You've lost all good sense, Amani!' Maha looked back at me and charged her sister with dictatorship, 'Mother, from the moment we departed *Haj*, Amani no longer feels my equal but my master!'

I agreed completely with Maha. With impressive speed, I had seen my daughter's religious beliefs pass from confusion to a flourishing vision. Her sense of divine righteousness was producing ridiculous household sanctions that excluded no-one.

Just a few days before, she had discovered one of the Filipino gardeners proudly displaying a pair of rubber sandals that had been imprinted with the name of God on the sole of the shoe.

Instead of receiving anticipated praise for his purchase, Amani had shrieked in rage, grabbing the poor fellow's shoes and accusing him of blasphemy, threatening him with severe punishment.

In tears, the young man had confessed that he had purchased the shoes in Bahtha, a popular shopping souq located in the downtown district of Riyadh. He had thought that his Muslim employers would be pleased to see that the name of God was printed on his shoes.

Calling the shoes the work of the devil, Amani had called a special meeting of her religious group and had stunned them all by revealing the sacrilegious shoes.

Word had spread to other religious groups, and pamphlets had been distributed in the city, advising people not to buy or wear such shoes.

The shoes were rather shocking, since Muslims are taught not to walk on any item bearing God's name, even going so far as to forbid our shoes from lying sole up, in case that might be some insult to our maker. Yet, Amani's reaction had been somewhat drastic since the young Filipino was not of our faith and not acquainted with our truths. My daughter had been cruel in her angry denunciations.

Since an early age, I have been drawn to the idea of a kindly God, a being that does not find sin in every human delight. I knew with certainty that my child was not acquainted with the God of Mohammed, as taught to me by my loving mother. I sent a questionable prayer to my maker, asking that Amani's gloomy devoutness take a holiday.

My thoughts returned to the present crisis, and I looked upon my daughters.

With Maha's threat of defacing her Koran looming as a real possibility, Amani promised to refrain from inspecting her siblings' habits.

Maha declared that if Amani would only leave her to her own inclinations, however distracting they might be to her sister, she would commit no further violence.

I hoped that the truce would stick, but I had my doubts, for Amani was readily moved to judge all before her, never really happy except when making religious war. And Maha was not one to bear the taunts of her sister timidly.

My two daughters, trapped in a family unit, were too volatile a mixture for everlasting peace.

I abandoned desolation and yielded to motherly affection. With the deepest love, I embraced each of my daughters.

Maha, always quick to anger and prompt to forgive, gave me a genuine smile of peace. Amani, slow to pardon those she deemed in the wrong, was stiff and did not yield to my affection.

Exhausted by the responsibilities of motherhood, I wistfully observed my girls as they went their separate ways.

All at once, the room was empty of their mad energy, but the consoling quiet was not comforting. I felt edgy, and told myself that I was in need of a stimulant.

I rang the bell for Cora and asked that she bring me a cup of Turkish coffee. Then, without knowing my reason, I abruptly changed my mind and asked instead, that she mix me a strong drink of bourbon and Cola.

Cora stood open-mouthed with surprise. It was the first occasion that her mistress had requested a drink of alcohol during the daylight hours.

'Go on,' I demanded.

I sat, reading the newspaper without absorbing the news. I admitted to myself that I was looking forward to my drink with discomfiting anticipation, when Abdullah arrived at home.

Abdullah moved with speed through the door into the hallway. I caught a glimpse of my son's face and did not like what I saw. Accustomed to his gentle character, I saw by his dark expression that he was torn by agony.

I called out, 'Abdullah!'

Abdullah strode into the room. Unasked, he let his anguish be unconfined.

'Mother! Jafer has fled the kingdom!'

'What?'

'He's run away! With Fouad's daughter, Fayza.'

Staggered by confusion and scepticism, I could not speak. With my mouth hanging open, I sat and stared at my son.

Still in his early twenties, Jafer Dalal was a young man admired by all who knew him. He was both handsome and strong, with a serious but kindly countenance bespeaking quiet wisdom and calm strength. He was a charming conversationalist, a gentleman of refinement and courtesy. Jafer was one of a but few young men that Kareem trusted completely with the women of his family.

Jafer was Abdullah's dearest and most cherished friend.

Often I told Kareem that I would like to have known Jafer's parents, for never has a man been better raised. But that could never be, for Jafer's mother died when he was only twelve and his father was killed in the Lebanese civil war when Jafer was seventeen. Jafer's one brother, four years his senior, had been critically wounded in the Lebanese war and was a permanent resident of a nursing facility located in the south of Lebanon. Orphaned while still a teenager and without any siblings to offer him shelter, Jafer moved from the only home he had ever known and travelled to live with an uncle in Kuwait, who managed some businesses for a wealthy Kuwaiti.

As a Palestinian Sunni Muslim born and raised in the refugee camps of Southern Lebanon, Jafer did not have an easy life.

After the Iraqi invasion of Kuwait, the PLO stood behind Saddam Hussein. It was not surprising that after the war ended there was much resentment by Kuwaiti citizens towards the large Palestinian population. While Jafer's uncle and his family had remained loyal to their Kuwaiti sponsor and could have remained in Kuwait, there was such a backlash of dislike towards anyone with a Palestinian identification that the Kuwaiti sponsor recommended that the family move to another land. The kindly man did not want such a fine family to risk danger by remaining in Kuwait. 'Let a few years pass,' he promised, 'and the crisis will pass.'

This Kuwaiti sponsor co-owned a business with Kareem, and he suggested to my husband that Jafer's uncle would make an excellent employee for a particular job opening in that company's offices in Riyadh.

As there was some bitterness at the time between our king and Yasser Arafat with regard to the Gulf War, there was a political move in Saudi Arabia to avoid employment of people with Palestinian nationality. As a high-ranking prince, Kareem could do as he pleased. On the recommendation of his Kuwaiti partner, he employed Jafer's uncle.

After the man arrived in Riyadh, he became one of Kareem's most entrusted employees, assigned with difficult tasks and responsible posts. Jafer accompanied his uncle and so impressed my husband that he was given a management position in Kareem's law offices.

From the moment Abdullah was introduced to Jafer, the two young men became fast friends, Abdullah claiming Jafer as the brother that he never had.

Jafer came into our lives only two short years ago, yet he quickly became a beloved member of our family.

Conspicuously attractive, Jafer drew much female attention wherever he went in the city. Abdullah claimed that women passed his friend notes of invitation while in hotel restaurants. Once when Jafer accompanied Abdullah to the King Faisal Specialist Hospital and Research Centre to visit a royal cousin hospitalized there, three foreign nurses volunteered their telephone numbers to Abdullah's friend after the briefest of conversations.

I thought Jafer wise beyond his years, for it appeared that he lived a life of celibacy, in a land that frowned upon illicit relationships between men and women.

Sensing that the young man was lonely and was of an age to settle down, Kareem reproached Jafer for persistent bachelorhood. Making serious offers to introduce Jafer to Lebanese or Palestinian contacts, men who might introduce him to marriageable Muslim women from those countries, Kareem declared that it would be a tragedy if Jafer avoided love, adding that even good men could be ruined by too much virtue!

With a wink in my direction, Kareem mischievously added that all men should experience the pleasures and tribulations of female companionship.

In jest, I made a threatening move towards my husband, for I knew the truth – that Kareem, a happy father, could not have borne a life without children.

Kareem failed in his attempt to provide female company to a young man whom he had grown to respect and love. Jafer never accepted Kareem's generous invitation to meet women.

Abdullah added to the mystery by saying that his friend was polite but firm in refusing all offers of female companionship.

I was puzzled but so consumed by the problems presented by my daughters, that I thought little more of Jafer's private life.

Looking back, how could we have thought that a full-blooded, sensual man like Jafer scorned all that love had to offer?

The truth as to why Jafer had deferred marriage was made known in a most devastating manner that threatened to end tragically.

My thoughts returned to my son.

Abdullah, who had loved Jafer with perfect sincerity, let his grief overflow. There was something disarmingly childlike about my son as he complained, 'Jafer never told me about Fayza.'

It was the darkest time of Abdullah's young life. My son's dishevelled innocence pierced my heart.

At that moment, Kareem arrived, as angry as Abdullah was sad.

'Abdullah!' he shouted. 'You've risked your life and the lives of innocents!'

Kareem told me that when Abdullah had been informed of Jafer's disappearance, he had become distraught and had left Kareem's offices in a dangerous mood. Fearful for his only son's safety, Kareem had followed in hot pursuit. My husband claimed that Abdullah had driven his car through the streets of the city at high speed. Kareem said that at one point Abdullah's car crossed the centre lane and forced a line of drivers from the road.

'You could have been killed!' So agitated at the possibility, Kareem reached across and slapped our son's face.

The sharp slap shocked and silenced my husband.

Over the years of my children's turbulent growth, I have pinched and slapped all three of our offspring with irresistible pleasure.

Never had Kareem struck one of our children!

Kareem was as stunned by his action as I was, staring down at his offensive hand as though it were not his own.

He embraced his shivering son and apologized, saying that in the course of following Abdullah's reckless path, he had gone out of his mind with worry.

The room was filled with emotion, and it took many

moments for the mystery of Jafer and Fayza's hidden romance to be completely revealed.

Fayza was the daughter of Fouad, Kareem's partner in three foreign businesses. Fouad was not of the Al Sa'ud family but weakly related by marriage to a daughter of a royal.

Many years before, Fouad had been allowed to wed into the royal family, even though he was not from a clan of the Najd, nor was his tribe particularly close to the Al Sa'uds. Generally, Al Sa'ud women were wed out of the family for political or economic reasons. While Fouad was from a prosperous Jeddah trading family, his family had bitterly fought the Al Sa'uds during the early days of the formation of the kingdom.

Anxious to unite his family with the rulers of the land, Fouad had offered an immense dowry for Samia, a princess who, we often said in kindness, had been spared the distracting handicap of being a great beauty.

No-one in the royal family could believe Samia's good fortune, for she was long resigned to remaining a spinster, cruel gossip about her bad skin, small eyes, and bent back having stripped away all possibilities of marriage.

Fouad, determined to attach himself to the respected Al Sa'ud clan, had heard of Samia's lack of attraction through women who knew her family, but his only desire was to marry a woman of many virtues. He had been forewarned by the lurid stories that were bandied about by his female relatives telling of alluring women who made the most miserable wives, for carefully coiffured and richly garbed women could think of little besides expensive homes, many servants and endless jewels.

Fouad knew sound advice when he heard it. Denouncing the lure of beauty, he said that he desired a woman of humour and warmth. The particular princess he sought, while uncongenial to a poet's dream, was one of the more popular royals, well loved for her charm and grace.

Thinking that Fouad was a fool, Samia's family had accepted his offer, and a wedding was held.

Fouad was well pleased with his wife, for she had a sense of humour that Fouad knew would see them through the tribulations of marriage. His new bride facilitated matters by falling deeply in love with her husband. Theirs was the happiest of unions.

Fouad was a Saudi man who adored his one and only wife and was the proud father of three sons and one daughter. In one of the stranger quirks of nature, Fouad, a plain-faced man, and Samia, a woman who was pitied for her appearance, produced the most dazzling offspring. Their three sons were strikingly handsome, while their only daughter was a ravishing beauty.

Fayza was the only girl I have ever seen who rivalled Sara's youthful splendour. Stories about her fair complexion, wistful dark eyes, and long coal-black hair stirred the blood of Saudi Arabian men who could only imagine the girl's physical attractiveness from hearsay.

Fayza had other irresistible qualities. She had inherited something of her mother and was a girl of rare, dry wit and often livened our female gatherings.

I was sorry that Fayza was older than my son, for I thought Abdullah would have loved her intensely, had he the opportunity.

Beautiful, witty and smart, Fayza was a university student at a women's school in Riyadh. She was in the first courses of pre-dentistry and had aspirations to open a children's dental facility.

Fouad confided that while he wanted his daughter to obtain a degree, that in reality she would have little need for working skills. He proudly confided in Kareem that at the completion of his daughter's education, Fayza would be married into a wealthy family. Meetings had already been conducted, and Fouad had his pick of three influential families. When his daughter graduated, he would allow her to have supervised meetings with each of the three young men in question, allowing his child to have a say in her future.

When Kareem told me Fouad's plans for his child, I

felt great joy, thinking how far we have travelled since the days of my youth! None of my sisters had a voice in the choice of their husbands. And, Sara! Who among us could forget the nightmare that Sara endured in her first marriage to an evil man. It had been a cruel union that had scarred my sister, almost claiming Sara's life.

In my family I was the only daughter privileged to meet my husband before he became my intimate partner in life, and that decision had resulted from nothing more than the actions of a spirited girl, combined with the determination of a curious suitor.

Now! A man raised in the strictest of times was casually speaking of allowing his child the opportunity to take part in the selection of her husband.

How happy I was at the news!

Yet I did not let myself rejoice for too long, for I knew that most women in my land were still used as nothing more than political or economic prizes. Nevertheless, I assured myself, each individual battle won would eventually lead to widespread and enormous victory!

And, now! Fouad's dreams for his daughter's future had come to nothing. His only daughter, a beautiful woman sought by the wealthiest of men in my land, had eloped with a penniless Palestinian refugee!

'How did this happen?' I asked my husband.

With their lawyer's minds and information gathered by Samia, Kareem and Fouad had pieced together the drama of the two lovers.

Weeks after Jafer had begun his work at the firm, Fouad's family had come into the office to sign some papers. Fouad had acquired some rather large business interests abroad, and he had put some of those businesses in the names of his children.

Jafer was responsible for the clerical aspects of the documents. When Fouad's family arrived, they were ushered into Jafer's office, where the young man was told to obtain the necessary signatures. As our religious customs demand, Samia and her daughter, Fayza, were veiled. Feeling protected in a locked office, in the presence of a trusted employee, both women had thrown their veils off their faces, onto the top of their heads, for the purposes of reading and signing documents.

Now, in the midst of the controversy, Samia had the dimmest recollection that her daughter and Jafer had stared at each other for too long a time. Samia, innocent in her inherent goodness, had not connected her daughter's nervous behaviour and crooked signature with the medley of incredible fancies that were playing upon her child.

At the time, Samia had listened without hearing and looked without seeing.

The handsome young man, Jafer, had offered them tea, and Samia had watched her daughter as she gratefully received the attentions of the man, their hands lightly brushing in the innocent exchange of pens and cups of tea. She told her husband that, at the time, she had thought that the touches were accidental.

Kareem reported that Fouad had screamed insults, blaming his wife, telling her that all men are by nature villains, and that she, the mother of an innocent girl, should have been more astute to Jafer's evil nature! Fouad had moaned, claiming that Jafer was nothing more than a man with a poem on his lips and a dagger in his pocket!

Samia could recall nothing more, other than that her child had seemed flushed and feverish while in the company of Jafer.

Fayza's personal Filipino maid, Connie, knew many details. She was carefully questioned by Kareem and Fouad. The two men discovered that there was no end to the intrigue of the two lovers, and according to Connie, it was Fouad's daughter, rather than Jafer, who had pursued the affair.

Connie reported that, from that first day, Fayza had been stricken by a great love. A weakening love that made the girl forget to eat and sleep. Torn between loyalty to her family and drawn by sexual desire for Jafer, Fayza had confessed to her maid that love was the victor, that she would have the man, Jafer, or no man at all.

Connie said that she had never seen a girl so taken by a man.

Knowing the plans of Fayza's parents for their lovely daughter, Connie found herself in an unenviable position. She could not report the truth about her young mistress, yet she knew that she should. Connie swore to Fouad that she reminded Fayza that the daughter of a wealthy Saudi family, with close connections to the Al Sa'uds, could not end up with a Palestinian clerk.

Such a situation could only lead to misfortune.

Having a tendency to lapse into criticism of our male-dominated society, I thought of where the blame might be placed. Thinking of Saudi Arabia's restrictive social customs, I interrupted Kareem and told him I had come to a conclusion, that Fayza's over-reaction to a charming, handsome man made a mockery of our system. My voice thick with frustration, I declared that if men and women could only meet each other under normal circumstances, that delusions of instant love would be more infrequent.

While I do believe that great attractions lead to genuine love, such as it had with my sister, Sara, and her husband, Assad, such a happy outcome is rare. When life is filled with harsh social restrictions, when young men and women rarely have the opportunity to enjoy the other's company in ordinary social occasions, spontaneous emotions are quick to rise to the surface, often ending in terrible personal tragedies.

With an irritated look on his face, Kareem said he would quit the room if I insisted on burdening the conversation with my well-known theories of the subjugation of females in the Saudi culture!

Abdullah looked at me with longing, his eyes begging me not to make a scene. For the sake of my son, I agreed to be quiet.

Kareem, subtly pleased, continued to tell of the drama.

Fayza, telling Connie that her heart had been a willing

recipient of love, knew that Jafer had loved her, too, but that he was vulnerable in his low position to her elevated status. She feared that he would never take the initiative.

Fayza boldly called Jafer at his office, asking him to meet her, promising that her family would never know.

Jafer, while acknowledging to Fayza that no woman had ever affected him as she had, refused the tempting offer, asking the girl what benefit there would be would be only temporary bliss, for when the relationship ended, unbearable mental torture would ensue.

Fayza gleefully confided to Connie that Jafer was snared, that she was certain she would soon see him, for their telephone conversations had become hot with passion, with Jafer warning her that if he ever had her, that he would never give her up. His words were delightful to hear!

Fayza persisted. After two weeks of increasingly intimate telephone conversations that only served to further their desire, Jafer's resolve had weakened. They agreed to meet at the Al-Akariya, a large shopping mall in the city of Riyadh.

At last, a veiled Fayza, masquerading as a relative of Jafer, walked beside the man whom she had sought. The two walked from shop to shop, getting to know the other. They aroused little suspicion, for they appeared to be nothing more than an Arab man with a veiled woman, a common sight in our city.

Their walking relationship was unnatural, but they were too fearful to seat themselves at a restaurant to share a meal, for they knew that restaurants in our country are the principal target of the active and increasingly familiar morals committees that harass people of every nationality who live in Saudi Arabia.

Such committees are composed of menacing men who unexpectedly surround and enter eating establishments, demanding identification of the restaurant patrons. If proof is not forthcoming that the men and women sharing a table are not husband and wife, brother or sister, or father and daughter, these frightened people will be arrested and escorted to a city gaol, with punishment freely given. The legal penalties vary according to the nationality of the 'criminal'. Muslim offenders can be flogged for their social misconduct, while non-Muslims are gaoled or deported.

In the beginning, Jafer and Fayza adjusted their morals to the situation.

Over time, Jafer located an apartment where they could meet in privacy. A sympathic Lebanese friend offered his place. Since Fayza, as a woman, was not allowed to drive, she was forced to trust a family driver. Knowing that his participation could result in deportation or worse, Fayza lessened his hesitation by offering the man a large sum of money.

Out of this tempting attraction a great love blossomed. The lovers accepted they could never love another. Jafer asked Fayza to marry him. Just as they were building up their courage to make their love known to their families, a crisis occurred. One of Saudi Arabia's wealthiest men approached Fouad for the privilege of the beautiful Fayza to wed his eldest son. Pressure mounted for Fayza to agree. Fouad declared that the prospective bridegroom was matchless.

'How long I have toiled to build a perfect relationship that my father would so readily destroy!' Fayza had cried out to Connie.

The desperate lovers made their decision to flee the country.

Fouad had been tricked, his honour tarnished, and now he would stop at nothing to find his only daughter!

Knowing how difficult it was for females in Saudi Arabia to travel freely, I asked, 'How did Fayza manage to leave the kingdom alone?'

'She didn't,' Kareem replied, 'leave alone.'

I was pleased to hear that Fayza had not committed the sin of travelling alone. Saudi women are forbidden by our religion to travel without a male member of her family as an escort. This particular restriction is taken directly from the words of the Prophet who said: 'She who believes in Allah and the Last Day (meaning the Day of Judgment) must not travel any distance which is normally covered by one day's and one night's travelling unless accompanied by a *mahram*.'

A woman's *mahram* is any of her relatives to whom she cannot be married, such as her father, brother, uncle, nephew, stepfather, father-in-law or son-in-law. She is allowed to travel with her husband as a matter of course.

I discovered that Fayza had talents in the art of treachery. She told her parents she needed some time away from the mounting pressures on her. She hinted to her mother that a positive response would be forthcoming to the marriage proposal if she could only enjoy a small holiday. She thought she would like to visit her cousin, a girl who had married a man from Dubai. Could she be rewarded with a weekend before she pledged herself to marriage?

Samia was bedridden with a sprained back, so Fayza's younger brother was taken along as his sister's required male escort.

Why should a connection be made that Jafer had taken his annual holiday during this same period? In their wildest imagination, no-one in the family linked the young man with Fayza.

Once in the safety of Dubai, removed from the dangers of Saudi Arabia, Fayza had out-manoeuvred her younger brother, slipping her passport from his travel bag while he was in the shower, and making an ordinary pretence to shop with other females. Her brother volunteered to drive, dropping them at the Al Ghurair Centre on his way to meet a Saudi friend who was staying at the Chicago Beach Hotel, located on one of the most beautiful beaches in the Emirates.

From the Al Ghurair Centre, a popular shopping area, Fayza had whispered to her cousin that she had to seek a toilet but that she would soon return. Her cousin, intent upon selecting perfume, had thought little of the deception, promising Fayza that she would wait for her in the shop.

Fayza was not seen again. To her cousin's horror, she had disappeared.

A frantic search had ensued, with Fouad and his wife fearing the worst for their daughter's safety. Had their child been kidnapped, raped or murdered? While such crimes were rare in the Emirates, occasionally violent acts were committed.

When Connie learnt of her well-loved mistress's strange disappearance, she collapsed into a weeping fit and confessed Jafer and Fayza's activities.

A father's love knows no reason. Not believing that his innocent daughter could be so devious, all blame fell upon Jafer's head.

Neither Kareem nor I had ever heard of Fouad resorting to abuse or force. Fouad was known to all as a soft-spoken, kindly man. This was not the case in the emotional upheaval he suffered after his daughter's flight with a man. He fired the unfortunate Connie, putting her on the next flight to Manila. In his wild rage Fouad burst into Kareem's offices, and physically assaulted Jafer's uncle. There was a terrible scene, with Fouad threatening the life of the man if his daughter were not returned unharmed, still a marriageable virgin.

The police were summoned by a frightened Indian secretary in a neighbouring office.

In Saudi Arabia, liability for public disorder falls upon the foreigner, never upon a Saudi. Fouad was questioned by the police and apologies were made for their interference in a private matter. Had Kareem not been higher in rank and influence than Fouad, Jafer's uncle would have been imprisoned.

Everyone in my family felt saddened by the insoluble problems of human life, and no-one knew the appropriate action to take.

Sara and I visited Samia in her home. Muttering that 'life without love would be a mistake', I said everything wrong, causing poor Samia's ugly face to grow uglier still, while Sara knew how to express intense feeling in her own quiet way.

Bewildered by her child's rash flight, Samia had difficulty speaking and began to stutter anxious responses to Sara's kind sympathy. She appeared prematurely senile in her inconsolable grief.

When we left Samia's home, I asked my sister, 'How can the outworn traditions of our society be changed, without painful destruction of the older generation's expectations?'

In my opinion, I believe that marriage brought about by love is most natural and rewarding, while most inhabitants of my land scorn love and look only for respect and companionship after marriage.

How would we Saudi Arabians ever reconcile our differences?

Unable to determine his daughter's whereabouts without professional assistance, Fouad contacted private investigative agencies in France and America. One week after his child disappeared, Fouad discovered that she was in Nevada, registered in a hotel as Jafer's wife!

The moment the information came to Fouad, he travelled with his three sons to America, vowing to bring Fayza home. He promised his wife that their daughter would not remain with a Palestinian. Caught up in his tyrannical affection, he said that Fayza's death would be preferable to his shame.

This bit of news created a furore in our household.

I bit my nails until they bled.

Abdullah fell into a melancholy that threatened his health, sensing that nothing would ever be the same again.

Praying for the souls of the lovers, Amani glumly predicted that her prayers would not be answered, that the lovers had foolishly taken their paradise on earth, and that fires of molten hot metal would welcome them as they exited this earth.

Abdullah glared at his sister and cuttingly remarked

that perhaps Jafer felt Fayza's feminine perfection was worth quitting heaven for.

Caring deeply for both Jafer and Fayza, Maha became hostile to anyone who criticized the lovers, declaring that no man or government should have authority over true love.

Hearing the news that Fouad and his sons were *en route* to the United States, Abdullah and I pleaded with Kareem to make contact with Jafer, to warn him to flee. I told Kareem that Fayza's male relatives needed additional days to accept the crucial fact that Fayza now belonged with another. Their extreme anger could not prevail, time would ease their rage.

It was not to be. My husband infuriated me, remaining true to the Saudi male policy of accepting any injustice, if that injustice involved a man's obsession with his women or the family honour. Thinking to incite him to action, I insulted Kareem, telling him that I was disappointed to learn that I had wed a man who failed to probe into the deeper complexities of life, but who, instead, was a dull, unfeeling type who tended to remain on the surface of things.

As I left my husband standing open-mouthed in amazement at my attack, I could not resist one final incivility. 'Kareem, how can you have no conflict between logic and feeling? Aren't you human?'

Silently I retreated, but secretly I had Abdullah take action. At my urging, he searched Kareem's office and brought forth information that had been provided by the investigative services.

Triumphant, we were careful to hide ourselves from Kareem or Amani, making our telephone call during the long evening prayer, knowing that Kareem was in the mosque and Amani was locked in her room, facing Makkah, saying her prayers.

With shaking fingers, Abdullah punched the number of the Mirage Hotel in Las Vegas, Nevada, where Jafer and Fayza were known to be registered.

As I watched the brooding face of my beautiful son patiently waiting for the hotel operator to ring the room, I was possessed by the fever a mother has for her children, desiring for Abdullah's pain to leave his body and enter mine.

Jafer answered the telephone!

Abdullah tortured himself trying to find the right words to make Jafer understand that he was in great danger.

His friend was dismayed at their rapid discovery but felt secure in his married state. 'What can they do, now?' he asked Abdullah.

When Abdullah shared his words, I grabbed the telephone from my son's hand. 'They can do plenty, Jafer,' I yelled. 'Fouad's honour has been attacked, his only daughter vanished with a man not thought suitable! Don't be a fool! You're an Arab, you're aware what reactions such anguish will bring an Arab father!'

Jafer tried to soothe my fears, claiming that their love would see them through any persecution.

Fayza came to the telephone, speaking softly into the receiver that Jafer still held in his hand. Fayza's sultry voice told of the wonderful love that had prevailed, in spite of the substantial hindrance of the laws of our land.

'Fayza, you're still only twenty and have broken free from our inflated traditions. Your father can't do this. Fouad is a man of desert mentality, and he can only flow down the main stream. In his mind, you've committed a shocking offence. Leave that place! Have a meeting with the men of your family at a later date.'

My pleas for the lovers to vanish made no impact. How weak my words were to their brave spirits. Courageous, Jafer said that he would face the fury of Fayza's family.

I returned the telephone to my son, thinking that I had done all that I could do.

I thought, is it a glory or a disaster that they have no suspicion yet of the extent of their tragedy? I realized the narrow limits of their lovers' vision. Jafer and Fayza were blinded, believing that the strength of their great love could conquer the challenge of her furious and disapproving family.

Fretting in hopeful silence, I could only hope that Jafer and Fayza could delay destiny for a while.

It was four days before Fouad returned to the kingdom.

His voice low and uneasy, Kareem called me from his offices and reported that Fouad and his sons had returned from America.

My throat closed around the words that I could not ask.

After a dry pause, Kareem added that Fouad had returned with his daughter but without her husband.

My voice returned; 'Is Jafer dead?' I asked, wondering already how we would break the cruel news to Abdullah.

'No. Jafer isn't dead.' Kareem answered, his voice causing me to doubt his words even as he spoke them.

I was quiet, waiting for news that I was not sure I wanted to hear.

'Sultana, I'm coming home. We'll tell Abdullah what has happened together.'

'What happened?' I screamed, thinking that I could not bear to wait for Kareem to make the twenty-five-minute drive from his office to our home.

I heard a click and then a dead line. I told myself that my husband's news must be dreadful, for Kareem, like most Arabs, had a habit of putting aside unpleasant truths until the last possible moment.

Fouad had told my husband little, only that there had been a minor physical scuffle in the hotel room, and that Jafer had been left unconscious but without serious injury.

Fayza? Naturally, his daughter had been traumatized by the incident and was now at their palace under sedation. Without the influence of Jafer, Fouad believed that his daughter would hasten to submit to her true self.

I looked at Kareem and announced with certainty, 'Jafer is dead!'

'Nonsense. They were in America.'

Two weeks later we received a telephone call from Jafer. He had returned to Lebanon. We finally learned the truth of the matter.

Jafer's words to me were, 'All is lost.' He paused. 'Except for my skin, which is safe.'

'Abdullah!' I called out. 'It's Jafer! Come quickly!'

Kareem, Maha and I stood round Abdullah as he spent long moments quietly listening to his dearest friend, comforting the caller with reassurances. 'What could you do? You had no choice.'

With a start, I heard my son say, 'I'm coming!', that he would soon be on his way to Lebanon, that nothing could keep him from his friend's side.

I grabbed Abdullah's arms and began to shake my head, 'No', vigorously.

My feet left the floor as Kareem yanked me from my son's face.

Abdullah hung up the telephone. With tears running down his face, my son buried his head in his hands and began to weep bitter tears. His words were muted, difficult to understand. 'Jafer's ruined! He's ruined!'

'What is this about Lebanon?' I enquired, too agitated at the thought of Abdullah travelling to that country to consider Jafer's condition.

'Hush, Sultana,' Kareem ordered.

Abdullah finally calmed himself and explained how Fouad and his sons had taken Fayza from Jafer.

A telephone call had awakened them in the night. Fayza's father and brothers were in the lobby. 'Could they come up, please?' Fouad's tone was civil, Jafer was encouraged and felt no fear of physical assault.

When Jafer opened the door, he felt pleased and smiled.

Fouad and his sons took no time to talk. Provoked by Jafer's smiling face, which he now feared they had mistaken for a smirk, Fayza's brothers set upon him. Caught by surprise, Jafer was no match for four men.

Jafer said that he was hit on the head with a heavy object, and blackness overcame him.

Hours later, when he revived, his new bride and her male relatives were gone.

Jafer said that he knew all was lost once they had stolen Fayza away from him. He was well aware that it is illegal in Saudi Arabia for a Saudi girl to marry a man not a Saudi national. He could receive no legal assistance in claiming Fayza as his own, despite their married state, for their union was not recognized in Saudi Arabia. Had Jafer been a Saudi and Fayza a Palestinian, there would have been no difficulties, for Saudi men can marry whom they wish.

In spite of that knowledge, Jafer had flown to London, making a desperate attempt to re-enter the kingdom, but had been told that his resident's visa for Saudi Arabia was no longer valid.

Jafer, having feared Kareem's scorn, now overcame his fear and asked to speak to my husband. He wondered if Kareem, with his princely status, could help?

Kareem said that he could but would not. Now that he knew Jafer was alive, he had no intention of placing him in a position that ensured his murder. Kareem warned Jafer that for certain Fouad and his sons would kill him if he returned to the kingdom.

Kareem had never said so, but I knew that my husband would never forgive Jafer his deception. Kareem had suffered acute embarrassment that an employee he had trusted had conquered and stolen the beloved only daughter of an old friend and business associate. His intense love for Abdullah had kept him silent.

Never one to promise more than he could give, Kareem recommended that Jafer try to find a life for himself in Lebanon, that it seemed the country was finally returning to peace.

'How sad,' I said. 'It is the end of a magnificent love story. And, now Jafer stands alone against an overwhelming power.'

Standing quietly to the side of the room, my son was an unforgettable figure clad in his white thobe. He was straight and tall and suddenly looked a man. His face was sad, and with dramatic intensity, Abdullah said no, that was not the case. Jafer would never be alone, for he would not forsake his friend. He was going to visit him in Lebanon.

Kareem and I refused our son permission to travel to that country, but Abdullah seemed to care not for our consent and said that he would go nevertheless.

Such a trip would invite a thousand calamities! I was miserable as I prepared myself for bed, plotting to stop my son from his sentimental journey.

I should have known I would fail, for it is impossible to rule a son in blossoming manhood, for such youthful vitality does not easily accept defeat.

Chapter Nine

ABDULLAH

We will give it unto our children, and they unto their children, and it shall not perish.

Kahlil Gibran

After the distressing incident with Jafer and Fayza, I underwent a persistent and depressing change, retreating into myself, for my son, Abdullah, plotted his trip to Lebanon with such inspired devotion that I came to believe him when he said that nothing would hinder the potentially perilous journey.

Kareem cautioned me to restraint, for he said that our son's ardour would cool as the difficulties of travel to Lebanon became apparent.

I grew cross with my husband, and with a voice raised in disbelief asked how he could remain calm, while those to whom we had given life tortured my mind with grief.

With a mysterious half-smile, Kareem reminded me that Abdullah's passport was locked in the safe. It would be impossible for our son to leave the kingdom.

For these reasons, my resistance to Abdullah's plan was sporadic, unorganized and ineffectual. In a matter of days, my once close relationship with my son became one of strained silences.

Everyone who lived in our palace fumed and despaired. While Abdullah packed his suitcases, his sister Amani mourned to see how little she could do to improve the morals of her brother and older sister. Spurred on by her faith, Amani began to spy on our employees. Horrified by what she called the looseness of our staff of sixty servants, for there are many secret romantic encounters among those who serve us, Amani set herself out with blunt directness to reform our Christian and Hindu servants into the superior Muslim faith.

After a hundred quarrels with my daughter's inconsiderate and indiscriminate vigour against those who practise a different religion from our own, I finally acknowledged that I had met my match in Amani, who continued to distance her mother in sheer perseverance.

I spent many hours in the solitude of my room, mulling over the lives of my children.

When my three offspring were infants, they gave my life great joy and meaning. In the days of their early childhood, only Maha generated chaos, and I had no reason to anticipate peril at every turn. In those pleasurable times, moments of parental happiness vastly overshadowed the dark intervals of fear and worry over the fate of these small beings to whom I had given life.

Now that my children were nearing adulthood, I came to the frightful conclusion that the only prerequisites to motherhood seemed to be a precarious dependence upon chance, for nothing I said or did altered my children's unpredictable behaviour.

As one who has enormous difficulty in adjusting to failure, I took to my bed, complaining to Kareem that nothing in my life was progressing as I had hoped. My psychological decline came at a time of Kareem's busiest period of business expansions, and as his free moments were limited, he was ill-equipped to console and liberate my soul from melancholy, that mental interloper which had intruded and dismantled my joyful pursuit of happiness.

I felt increasingly alone. Suppressing every display of emotion other than self-sympathy, I began to sleep poorly and overeat, gaining unwanted pounds. Continually ignored by family members whom I was attempting to manipulate, I became progressively bad-tempered with my family and the servants. I even acquired a disgusting habit of twisting, pulling and biting on my hair. The length of my hair became shorter, and the thickness became thinner until Kareem, after noticing my habit, sarcastically commented that he had thought I had employed a new, and more enthusiastic hairdresser, when in reality I was behaving like a child by pulling it out.

I was quick to snap an ugly retort, unfairly accusing Kareem of loving none but himself, that I, alone, had to keep watch over our children.

Gently impatient, Kareem's eyes took on a distant look, and I felt that he left me without leaving the room. When his spirit returned, he said that he had laboured to remember a comforting verse that he had once read about the rearing of spirited children. Kareem recited, 'You may give your children love, but not your thoughts, for they have their own thoughts.'

'Kahlil Gibran,' I said.

'What?'

'That verse, it is from *The Prophet*. And, it was *I* that read that particular verse to you while we were awaiting the birth of our firstborn.'

Kareem's stern face softened as a smile parted his lips, and I wondered if he was remembering the happy moments so long ago that we had spent with our infant son.

That was not the case, for he complimented me by saying, 'Sultana, you're an amazing creature. How can you remember such a thing?'

Kareem had always marvelled at my memory, for once I'd read or heard something, my recall never failed in accuracy.

I was pleased with his recognition, but the cause of my discontent was too deep and varied to be so easily dissolved. In a collision with my children, my mad passion had blinded me to my husband's clear and logical mind. With no-one else to battle, I continued to snarl at my husband. In contempt I compared Kareem with Nero, the mad fiddler of Rome, blind to disaster even when his kingdom was aflame.

Angered by repeated insults, Kareem thought better of his solicitous sympathy and left me alone to consider his parting observation, which was not comforting. His spiteful words were, 'Sultana, you have it all. Yet, you fear everything, and understand nothing. I predict that you will, one day, be committed to an institution for the insane.'

I hissed like a snake and Kareem left, not to return for two days.

Shortly after our heated exchange, I was unconsciously twisting my hair with one hand, while idly thumbing through one of my many foreign publications, when I read an article featured in an American magazine that told of a rare disease that strikes only females, causing women to pull their hair out until they become completely bald. Once bald, those unfortunate women then progressed to eating their eyebrows, eyelashes and body hair.

I let go of my hair. Did I have that disease? I ran to view my image in the mirror, and to search through my scalp for bald spots. My hair did seem thin. Now I was truly worried, for I had never cured myself of vanity, and had no inclination to be bald! Besides, in the Muslim religion, it is forbidden for a woman to be bald.

Time proved that I did not have the disease, for unlike the women in the article, my attachment to beauty quickly helped to cure myself of that habit.

In spite of my success in retaining my hair, I feared that my passion for life was cracking, and I told myself that if my debilitating depression were not conquered, I would be overcome by premature old age. Feeling sorry for myself, I imagined that I would have a slow death through the gradual diminution of my senses.

I was saved from my self-destructive behaviour by my dearest sister.

Sara, a contemplative genius, was sensitive to my

blunted lust for life, and she began to spend many hours by my side, humouring me with her undivided attention. Sara understood my feelings perfectly, and knew that worry over Abdullah and Amani now ruled my life.

My sister looked upon me with great pity when I tearfully told her that, 'Sara, if I have to live my life over again, I do not believe that I could survive it.'

Sara's mouth broke into a half-smile, as she wryly observed, 'Sultana, few of our family will survive if *you* are to live your life again.'

Our laughter filled the room.

My sister was so dear. Sara was not without problems of her own. Her life was disturbed by the actions of an unruly child, yet she found time to come to my aid in my moment of great need. While four of my sister's five children strived for perfection, Nashwa, Sara's teenage daughter born on the same day as Amani, relished controversy.

In strictest confidence, Sara told me to be thankful that Amani had attached herself to religion, for Sara had the opposite problem with Nashwa. Her daughter was wildly attracted to members of the opposite sex, and twice Assad had discovered Nashwa meeting Saudi teenage boys in a music shop at a shopping centre in the city.

Tears streamed down Sara's face as she confided in me that her daughter flirted outrageously with every male that entered their palace grounds. In a voice filled with disbelief, she said that the week before, Nashwa had begun an explicit sexual conversation with two of the younger Filipino drivers. One of Nashwa's brothers had overheard the conversation and, when confronted, Nashwa boldly acknowledged her action, stating that she had to do *something* to interrupt the monotony of life in Saudi Arabia.

Assad had been forced to fire those young drivers, and employ older Muslim men from Egypt who would respect the Muslim way: to ignore the wilful women of the house.

Just that morning, Sara had overheard her daughter

speaking with a female friend on the telephone, the two girls were discussing in great detail the girl's eldest brother's good figure. It seemed to Sara that Nashwa had a crush on this boy, and now my sister had to reconsider or regulate her daughter's visits to that home.

Sara's face was drawn with worry over the outcome of Nashwa's loose morals and unbecoming conduct, saying that she had often heard that one of the oversights of nature was that beauty and virtue often arrive in separate packages. Nashwa, my sister said, was an innocent-faced beauty who was sadly lacking in virtue.

I had to agree that my difficulties with Amani paled in comparison with my sister's problems with Nashwa. There was some consolation in the knowledge that Amani's piety had the approval of the religious authorities, while Nashwa's activities could embroil Sara and Assad in that never-ending web of the Saudi religious and legal system.

Once again the thought came to me that Nashwa was my true child, while Amani must be attached by blood to Sara. I thought to ask Sara about the matter, but had a moment of speculation that an exchange of daughters might result from my baseless confidence to my sister. I reminded myself that in my country, it is better to wrestle with a persistent religious fanatic rather than the problem of a young girl habituated to sexual stimulus.

In an effort to raise my sister's spirits, I told her that too often when dealing with our children, a parent sees little but the defects. I thought to mention some of Nashwa's good traits, but could find nothing to say.

Sara and I were still for a time, looking at each other. We knew instinctively that we understood each other perfectly.

With her daughter in mind, my sister began to ponder the progress of civilization, and questioned the theory of how it had been possible for animals to turn into humans, for our children had been sheltered from all worldly concerns, lavished with creature comforts, provided with intelligent pursuits and moral guidance, yet the careful organization of their lives had made little impact on their development.

Sara said that she had come to the conclusion that human outcome was linked to nothing more than genetics, and her children might as well have grown like weeds, instead of meticulously tended plants. 'Besides,' she said with a laugh, 'the radicals of one age become the reactionaries of the next, so who's to know what will eventually happen to our offspring?'

Since it always lightens one's burdens to be reminded of the details of another's troubles, even if that person is one greatly loved, I felt more cheerful than I had in days.

I laughed and agreed with my sister, saying that the seeds we had planted had not all flowered. Thinking that all of life is in God's hands anyway, I promised myself that I would worry no longer.

Sara went to enquire of her youngest children, who were playing in our palace playground located next to Amani's zoo, while I promised to bathe and dress myself for a visit to Fayza. Neither Sara nor I had seen the poor girl since she had been forced to return to the kingdom, though we had heard, with some surprise, that she had recovered and was now seeing close friends and relatives.

Enjoying uncommon peace for the first time in days, I was unprepared for a shocking telephone call from my husband.

His voice was alarmingly intense. 'Sultana, go to the safe and locate Abdullah's passport.'

'Why?' I asked.

Kareem told me to shut up and do as he said.

Thinking the worst, I dropped the telephone receiver to the floor and ran rapidly into my husband's home office on the first floor of our home. My hands refused to cooperate with my memory and it required three attempts to open the combination safe.

My husband kept his passport in the office safe, while those of his wife and children were locked inside another safe in his home office.

My fingers riffled through the various documents and papers. Abdullah's passport was missing!

I was then struck with the horrible realization that I could only account for two out of four passports. Looking closely, I saw that Maha's passport had disappeared along with her brother's.

What was going on? How had this happened? No-one, other than Kareem and I, knew the combination of this particular safe.

'No!' I said to myself when I could not find the special papers of permission that Kareem kept signed for the women of his family to travel outside the kingdom without the company of a male member of our family.

I was confused. Had Maha travelled alone? Or, had she and her brother fled the kingdom together?

Kareem's private telephone began to ring in his office.

My husband had tired of waiting for my return to our personal line that I had answered in our bedroom. He shouted, 'Sultana! What is going on?'

I told Kareem of my unsettling discovery.

'And the dollars?'

I had not thought to look for the large amount of dollars that we kept in our safe for the purpose of fleeing the kingdom should a religious revolution ever grip our land. It was money that we hoped we would never be forced to use to bribe safe exit from our country.

I opened the large drawer at the top of the safe. It was as Kareem had expected. The money was no longer there! As our fears of unrest in Arab lands had grown, the money had increased. Abdullah had taken over a million dollars in cash from his parents' safe. Had my son lost all his good sense?

'The dollars have disappeared,' I glumly reported.

'Go, see if Maha is at school. I'm on my way to the airport.'

I cried out, 'Hurry!' I knew that my son was on his way to Lebanon. But, how was Maha mixed up in this? Surely, Abdullah was not taking his sister with him to that dangerous land. I was giddy with fear and confusion.

'I'll try to call you from the car. Now. Do as I say. Find Maha!'

I fetched a simple dress and hastily pulled it over my head. Reaching for my *abaaya*, veil, and *shayla*, I threw on my outer garments as I ran through my home, calling out for my sister, Sara, to accompany me to Maha's school. I yelled at Cora to find Mousa, the youngest of our Egyptian drivers, a man who, I knew from past experience, could be urged to break the city speed limit.

Maha's school was fifteen minutes by car from our palace, but we arrived in ten minutes. Along the route, I told Sara what little I knew of the situation.

The seventeen girls in Maha's history class were taking notes while listening to a male instructor who was featured in the centre of the room on a large television screen. The lesson was being given via video, since it is forbidden in Saudi Arabia for a male professor to come into personal contact with female students.

Maha's face turned crimson red as I burst into her classroom, calling her name. Seeking the face of my child, I hovered over her desk, and said, 'Maha! You're here!'

Maha pushed my arms from her neck, exclaiming, 'Where did you think I was?'

I told the headmistress that I needed my daughter to return home. Without a hint of curiosity over my excited behaviour, the supervisor calmly instructed Maha to gather her books. She asked if Maha would be away for longer than a week. Since I did not know, I said that she would. The supervisor said that she would have Maha's instructors save my daughter's lessons for her return.

'Mother! What is going on?' Maha wanted to know as we settled ourselves in the car.

'I feared that you were with Abdullah.'

'Abdullah?'

My son was supposed to be at his school, at a different location, which was an institution that girls did not attend.

Maha looked at me in astonishment. 'Mother, you're behaving like a mad woman.' She looked at Sara for confirmation. 'Auntie, what's wrong?'

Sara explained the mystery of the passports, saying that we could not fathom why Abdullah had taken his sister's passport.

My sister's eyes met mine across the head of my daughter. Sara's thoughts matched mine perfectly.

'Fayza!' We uttered her name in unison.

I told the driver to take us to Fouad and Samia's home. 'Quickly!'

Abdullah's plans ran clear through my mind. My son had taken Maha's passport for Jafer's wife, Fayza! Abdullah had plotted her rescue. It was Fayza who was travelling on Maha's passport. Fayza was going to Lebanon with my son, not Maha! With veiled faces, it is quite possible for Saudi women to travel abroad using someone else's passport.

When Maha understood the significance of her brother's deed, she pleaded with me for us to return to our home.

'Mother! Let them go!'

It was a difficult moment. If I made no move to notify Fayza's parents, then I was an accomplice in my son's unwelcome intrusion into another man's private affairs by restoring his daughter to the arms of her husband. If I was the cause of Fayza's continued separation from a man whom she had loved enough to wed, then I could never again claim to battle for the rights of women in my land.

Sara and I stared at each other for many moments. Sara's eyes were clear and penetrating, and I knew that my sister was reliving the horrible sexual abuse that she had endured in her first marriage. Had our mother not revolted against our father, risking a divorce and possible permanent separation from her own precious children, Sara would have remained in sexual bondage to a man whom she hated, never knowing the wonderful love that she shared with Assad.

My decision was the result of the intolerance and

severe restraints upon women in my country. I thought to myself, women in my country had endured man's harsh abuse through too many centuries.

Wanting to live up to the best, and not the worst in my ancestry, I instructed Mousa, 'Take us home.'

Maha burst into laughter, and kissed me time and again, crushing me against the seat of the car.

Sara's eyes grew luminous. My sister smiled, and squeezed my hand, saying, 'Sultana, don't worry, you've made the correct decision.'

With muscular exaggeration, Mousa's eyes grew wide, and his mouth opened and closed, reminding me of a bird which was suffering from the desert sun. His face grew darker in colour, and I could see that he violently disagreed with the turn of events.

I spoke in French, a language he did not understand. 'Look at the driver's face,' I told my sister and my child. 'He doesn't approve.'

'What man in this country would approve a woman's right to choose her husband?' Maha wanted to know. 'Tell me one! And . . . and . . . I'll wed him!'

I looked back upon the day and felt a rush of recognition. My heavy spirit at last achieved tranquillity, for I understood that my daughter shared the blood of one who was enlightened, yet had no knowledge of his liberation.

'Abdullah.' I answered quietly. 'Your brother. My son. Abdullah is such a man.'

In happy silence, I stared at my daughter's face, but was imprisoned in my past. I saw the form of my firstborn as he had lain in his mother's arms. The emotions that I had lived on the day of his birth came to me in a flash, such a rush of joy that by its nature must be brief. I had wondered then if my newborn son would uphold and thereby harden the harsh system towards females in my land. I had prayed that it would not be the case, but that he would influence our country's history to my liking and help to bring change to the rigid social customs of Saudi Arabia.

It was difficult to judge Abdullah's actions calmly, but

in an honest appraisal of his activity, I knew that my deepest desire had been realized. A male child born of my womb *would* remodel the land of my birth.

How brave my bold son was!

No longer caring about Mousa's reaction, I spoke in Arabic, reminding Sara and Maha that the men of Kareem's generation had once displayed a voice of reason when it came to their women, but that voice had been stilled and silenced by the clash of militant men of religion. Grieving over the timid men of our age, I no longer looked to them for relief.

But hope was not lost, so long as we women of Arabia gave birth to men such as Abdullah.

I told Maha and Sara what I knew to be the truth, that my beloved son was a prince who would one day use all of his power and influence to enhance the status of Saudi women.

Renewed by my son's brave act, I talked of nothing else the remainder of the trip home, scandalizing Mousa with my frank discussion of complete freedom for all women, even for his own wife, a woman whom he forced to live with his parents in a small village in Egypt, while he worked in Saudi Arabia.

Kareem was impatiently awaiting my return. He did not seem surprised that I expressed great happiness, and I imagined that my husband judged incorrectly that my improved mood was linked to the safe recovery of our daughter. Never did he know that my happiness was attached to our son and the fact that Abdullah had turned his back upon injustice, and his face towards a free life for all people.

Maha was a bit frightened by the intensity of her father's blazing eyes, and she mentioned some small task that required her time.

Sara gathered her children and went home to Assad, whispering in my ear that I should call her as soon as possible.

I could hear Amani's voice in the background, rising

and falling with the sounds of her deeply felt communication with God.

Finally, I was alone with my husband.

I thought that Kareem's face was hardened by the oppressive weight of his discovery, and I was unprepared for his ruthless accusations.

He declared his feelings without questioning his wife. 'Sultana, there's a whiff of you in Fayza's flight.'

For a short moment, I was silenced by his insinuation. As one who runs to extremes in anger, I appeared at my worst when I struck out at Kareem's arm with my fist.

Well acquainted with my passions, Kareem was prepared. He sidestepped, avoiding the blow.

Over the years, Kareem had disciplined his reactions so that he appeared moderate, always making me appear the worse in our conflicts. Today was no exception. 'Sultana. This is no time to fight. Our son and Fayza have fled the kingdom.' My husband grabbed me. 'You *must* tell me their travel plans.'

All my denials were futile in convincing Kareem that while our son might have inherited my talent for conducting brilliant deception, I had no hand in his action to reunite Jafer with his wife.

Like the town thief who is not believed when a loaf of bread is stolen, my past reached into the present and a frightening avalanche of opinions flamed out against an innocent woman.

I was paying a dear price for my militant past.

I thought that Kareem's conduct as a husband might have been more loyal, and I told him so.

Kareem asked how he could believe me. He said that he had married a woman who was half angel and half devil, and the devil in me often ruled the angel, and when it came to issues that concerned women's lives, that I could not speak without lying and could not act without treachery!

Angrier than I have ever been, for what human endures false censure with grace, I spat at Kareem's feet and left the room, promising never again to enter a conversation with the man whom I had wed.

Kareem thought it best to bury his doubts, for he was concerned that, without my assistance, he might not succeed in finding his son, or in returning Fouad's daughter. Kareem said that he apologized if he were in the wrong and that I must save our son from committing an offence that would further entangle Abdullah in another man's personal affairs.

Suspecting his true motives, I refused to answer his request for forgiveness, squeezing my eyes shut so I did not have to view his face and motioning with my hand for him to go away.

As soon as the door slammed, my pleasure at revenge faded at once.

Where was my son? Was he safe?

For five days there was no peace in our home, for Kareem and I had no peaceful communication. Amani prayed and wept, while Maha sang love songs and celebrated Fayza's escape.

Is anything in life sweeter than success?

With a singleness of purpose, Fayza avoided all the traps that had been set to ensnare her and was reunited with the man she loved.

I could have never anticipated Fouad's and Samia's reaction to Fayza's desperate flight to her husband. Prepared for Kareem to be forced to use his position of prince for protection of our only son, I was pleasantly surprised by Fouad's meek acceptance of his daughter's elopement.

On the fifth day after their disappearance, Abdullah called us from Cyprus. Abdullah had no fear of our reaction and declared firmly to our protests that he had administered justice, not vengeance, in bringing Jafer and Fayza together.

My breath left my body when Abdullah confided that Fayza had telephoned her parents an hour before, and that Fouad and Samia had left their anger behind them and wanted nothing more than a second opportunity to welcome Jafer as their son. Fouad told his child that if she and Jafer would not turn their backs on her family, he promised he would not 'step in the same raging river twice'.

How true it is that humanity refuses compromise during prosperity, and reaches out for arbitration when weak. Swayed by great fear of never seeing their beautiful daughter again, Fouad and Samia had come to the conclusion that they would accept her marriage to someone beneath them in wealth and status.

Being of a suspicious nature, I thought perhaps it was a trick to ensnare Jafer in a land where he had no rights. Once in Saudi Arabia, he could be imprisoned on the slightest pretence, if that were Fouad's wishes.

Fayza's parents did not confirm my pessimism.

That day, Fouad and his family flew to Greece and met Jafer and Fayza in a golden land where men had been civilized from an early age. Thoughts more bitter than death were put to rest, and Jafer and Fayza at last found happiness in the family unit that had once challenged the legitimacy of their marriage.

Special permission was obtained for Fayza to wed a Muslim from another land, and a second, more festive wedding was held in a hotel in Cairo, Egypt.

Kareem and I travelled there with our two daughters to join our son for the occasion.

Jafer and Fayza insisted that male and female guests come together for a reception at the Mena House Hotel. Their great love even made a dour Kareem smile, even though he was a prince ashamed that his son had interfered in his friend's life at home. Kareem's tension was released when Fouad confessed that there could have been no other ending, for long before Abdullah had rescued Fayza, his daughter's extreme misery had led Fouad and his wife to the knowledge that Fayza must be reunited with Jafer. Their daughter's grief could not be ignored. Fouad assured my embarrassed husband that they, themselves, had been on the brink of parental surrender the day that Fayza had fled.

Kareem and I watched as Fouad grasped Jafer and Fayza as if they were one. From the look on Jafer's shining face as he watched his wife, it was clear to see that he loved Fayza more madly than before.

How pleased I was! A Saudi woman was happily wed to one forbidden.

I whispered in Kareem's ear, 'See, every straight line can be forced into a curve!'

A family tragedy was transformed into a scene of great harmony.

Later that evening from the courtyard at our Cairo villa, Kareem and I watched the loveliness of the Egyptian sky.

My husband surprised me with a heartfelt apology. Hovering nebulously between shame and love, Kareem promised that he would not prejudge me again, that he had been told by Abdullah that I was not privy to his plot to free Fayza.

As though it were an afterthought, Kareem reached into his pocket and brought out the largest diamond that I had ever seen. The stone was set in a gold chain. My husband tenderly fastened the necklace around my neck, and I felt his lips as they brushed my shoulder.

A few years ago, I had hated the bitter emptiness of my married life. Just the month before I had hungrily sought the meaning of life. The moment was a breeding ground for all sorts of emotions – affection, regret, and most of all, confusion. Was Kareem that rare phenomenon, a Saudi husband who was gentle, virile, practical and intelligent? Had I been wrong in my assessment of his character?

How could a Saudi man be the answer to my happiness, for I had fought against Saudi men for all my life long?

I had once heard that a miser is never satisfied with his money, nor a wise man with his knowledge. Was I a woman who would never know fulfilment? That possibility was frightening.

Another thought came to my mind, an Arab proverb, 'If your husband is made of honey, do not consume him.'

I looked at Kareem in a new light. Remembering the numerous insults that I had inflicted upon my husband, I prayed that God would shorten my tongue and increase my powers of reason.

I smiled at my husband. Suddenly, I felt many wounds heal – injuries suffered from my husband's earlier conduct in our marriage.

For some reason, my scars could scarcely be detected.

Chapter Ten

FATMA

Something was dead in each of us
And what was dead was Hope.

Oscar Wilde

The following afternoon, Kareem and I were sitting together with our children on the veranda at our villa in Cairo. An immaculate flower garden encircled the large covered porch, and the sweet scent of roses and honeysuckle permeated the air, reminding one of the wealthy British presence that had once infiltrated an unenthusiastic Cairo. My husband and I were savouring the coolness of the spacious shady area, for there was not a hint of an afternoon breeze, and the concrete structures of the overcrowded city had retained the oppressive heat of the day, dulling the senses of Cairo's eight million occupants.

Our three children whispered among themselves, claiming that we had once again been forgotten by 'Forgetful Fatma', as they often called our Egyptian housekeeper when she was out of earshot.

I warned my children not to make fun, that Fatma was no longer young and her feet had difficulty moving her abundant body. Still, I stifled a smile, thinking that the children were probably right in their assessment of the circumstances, that Fatma had more than likely begun some new chore, entirely forgetting her employers as they waited impatiently for a cool drink. Fatma *was* absent-minded and did have a consistent inability to remember why she left one room to go into another. Many times Kareem had complained, saying that Fatma should be let go and a younger, more energetic woman hired in her stead, but I resisted his urgings since the woman was dependable and had always displayed a genuine love for my three children.

Kareem accused me of being unable to part with Fatma since the woman delighted me with lively tales of Cairo scandals. But that was not the case.

Fatma had been employed as our permanent, live-in housekeeper since we had purchased the villa many years before. Abdullah had been only two years old at the time Fatma came into our lives, and our girls were not yet born, so Fatma was a constant in their young lives.

Just as I pushed myself from my chair to go and remind Fatma of our earlier request, I heard the familiar scraping of her loose sandals as they struck the marble floor of the interior hallway leading to the veranda.

I looked at Kareem, and he gave an irritated shake of his head. My husband had no understanding of why he should be inconvenienced by the aging of a servant.

Feeling mischievous, I said, 'My husband, do not forget that God is watching you.'

Kareem tartly replied, 'Sultana, do not concern yourself regarding my relationship with God.'

The children thought that we might slip into an argument and ruin the afternoon, so Amani wrapped her arms around her father's neck, while Maha began to rub my shoulders and begged me not to lose my temper.

I felt too good to fight and said so. About that time, my attention was drawn to Fatma. Recalling the graceful and slim Fatma of years past, my eyes affectionately followed the woman's heavy figure as she painstakingly opened the double glass doors that led from the villa onto the veranda. Fatma was enormous and had great difficulty balancing the tray stacked with crystal glasses and a matching crystal decanter filled with freshly squeezed lemonade.

Like many Egyptian women, Fatma had struggled with a weight problem from the moment she bore her first child. With each new addition to her family, she had grown larger and larger, until a childish Abdullah had fearfully questioned me, asking me how Fatma's skin could continue to hold her figure together.

Slowed by her weight, Fatma took many moments to walk the few steps from the doorway to the table of white painted rattan.

Abdullah jumped to his feet and took the tray from a reluctant Fatma, insisting that he would serve the family.

Kareem and I exchanged glances, and I saw that my husband bit the inside of his lip to keep from protesting. Ever since he was young, Abdullah was easily affected by the suffering that comes so often undeserved to mankind. I felt proud of Abdullah's sensitivity, but I knew that his father had no desire for his son to do the work of servants.

To distract Kareem, I asked our son to tell us more of his experiences in Lebanon, for since we had met Abdullah in Cairo, we had enjoyed little private time to hear of his adventure. I remembered that in Kareem's youth, he had spent many happy moments in the beautiful city of Beirut, for large numbers of the Saudi royal family had travelled to Lebanon for rest and relaxation before the days of the mad and senseless war that had destroyed that once lovely land.

Abdullah saw hope where Kareem said there was none. Abdullah said that he had been impressed by the Lebanese spirit, marvelling that the Lebanese people had not only survived, but had endured a most vicious civil war with their optimism intact, refusing to acknowledge that they could not surpass their brilliant past. Abdullah thought that given half the chance, the Lebanese would once again rise to claim an exalted place in the Arab world.

Abdullah paused and looked at his father. He wondered

if Kareem might be interested in investing money in that country.

Kareem rewarded Abdullah with an approving smile. My husband is a man who seeks economic opportunity at every chance, and our son's previous lack of interest in such matters had always been a weight on his mind. Kareem's smile quickly vanished when Abdullah added that the infrastructure of Lebanon was almost completely in ruins and that there were many good causes to which Kareem could donate funds.

I almost dissolved into laughter when I saw Kareem's pallid face. Kareem sat up straight and tried to show some interest, but my husband had difficulty in concealing his desperation; he looked at his son as if he were seeing him for the first time.

I knew that my husband had not yet recovered from Abdullah's proud announcement that he had donated the bulk of the one million dollars that he had taken from our safe to the hospital that housed Jafer's older brother. My husband had no heart to reprimand his son for a good deed and had gazed at Abdullah with sad affection, in spite of his agony at losing one million dollars.

Kareem had confessed to me later that in his mind, money donated to Lebanon was equivalent to tossing good money after bad, for who knew when the guns of destruction would once again flame across the Lebanese sky. Let the Lebanese show that they are serious about peace, and Kareem would look into the possibility of assisting those fellow Arabs.

Abdullah had been stricken by the lack of facilities at the institution where Jafer's brother had been, and now he spoke again of that place. He said that he could not forget the wretched condition of the war wounded who lived in the hospital. Abdullah's eyes welled with tears as he told of men and women without limbs, confined to small rooms, for there were no prosthetics or wheelchairs. Abdullah discovered men tied to wooden tables, men who had no movement in their bodies, men stoically accepting the idea of a life devoid of a single pleasure.

Abdullah said that he had learned a tragic truth, that a large number of the Lebanese wounded had no surviving family members to provide funds for their care.

In anguish, Abdullah asked, 'Does the world neither know nor care of the damage done to that country?'

I reminded Abdullah of a happy thought. That Jafer's brother had been luckier than most, since Jafer had routinely sent money for his medical expenses, but even his situation was bleak when compared to the most advanced health care facilities that our oil wealth guaranteed the inhabitants of our land. Jafer's brother would now enjoy the latest treatment available, for Fouad had insisted upon taking his son-in-law's brother from Lebanon to Saudi Arabia to live as one of his family.

Now our son wanted his father to distribute more of his personal wealth for the needy of Lebanon. Abdullah thought that a new hospital supplied with the latest equipment would be an auspicious beginning.

I leaned forward with keen interest to hear my husband's reply, for I knew that it was painful for Kareem to refuse any wish of his beloved son.

Kareem closed his eyes in concentration and began to rub his forehead with his hand, when without warning our family gathering was intruded upon by the most pathetic howling.

Baffled, we looked at each other and then realized that the strange noise was coming from the inside of our villa and the sound was made by Fatma!

A look of relief flashed across Kareem's face, for his son's interest was diverted. Abdullah was the first to move inside the villa, and my daughters and I followed Abdullah inside, leaving Kareem on the veranda.

My first thought was that Fatma had burned some part of her body, for she was standing over the kitchen stove, frying beef and onions for our dinner. I quickly saw that her weeping had not interrupted her cooking task, for she continued to stir the ingredients in the pan and seemed not to realize that her wails had penetrated the stone wall of the villa.

'Fatma! What is the problem?' Abdullah asked.

Like the voice of doom, Fatma replied, 'Oh, Abdullah! The female most blessed is she that has never been born! Next to her in happiness is the female who dies in infancy!'

Bereaved to madness, Fatma began to thump her chest.

Maha grabbed the wooden stirring spoon from Fatma's hand, while Amani began to console the poor woman with soothing sounds and comforting words.

Abdullah gave me a questioning look with his brown eyes.

I shrugged, as confused as he. I had no thought other than Fatma's husband might have divorced her and taken a younger wife, though they had seemed a well-satisfied couple in the past.

Fatma's husband, Abdul, doubled as our gardener and family chauffeur, and the couple had often said that they considered themselves fortunate to work for wealthy people who paid a good wage and who were rarely in the country. They were guaranteed plenty of free time to spend with their children, who lived in an apartment in Cairo with Abdul's mother. Yet, I knew that by law Egyptian men, like Saudi men, have full power over their women, and it was not unusual for an old man to take a second wife, or even to divorce his first wife and take a younger, more attractive woman into his home.

My own experiences have taught me that men are generally the root cause of female grief. Thinking of Fatma's bitter words of female misfortune, I imagined a man as their cause, for nothing is more demoralizing to a woman of Fatma's age than to be abandoned by a husband of many years.

Abdullah, Amani and I led Fatma to a large chair in the sitting-room, while Maha tended to Fatma's unfinished tasks.

Fatma moaned as she walked, holding her hand on the

top of her head, like someone trying to stop the pain.

Wanting to get to the cause of her grief, I waved my children from the room, and asked her point blank, 'Fatma, has Abdul divorced you?'

Fatma raised her head and looked at me, her languid eyes blinking at my question. She repeated my words, 'Abdul? Divorce *me*?' She then smiled, but only with her lips. 'That old man? Let him try! I'll crack his bald head open like an egg and fry his brains on the pavement.'

I had to struggle to keep from laughing aloud, for in the past, Kareem had often commented that, in his opinion, Abdul lived in fear of his wife, and there was at least one married woman in the Arab world who had no need of feminine advice from me.

Abdul was half Fatma's size, and once Kareem had come upon the couple and had seen with his own eyes Fatma strike her husband on the back with a large board.

I asked, 'Then, if it's not Abdul, what's the problem?'

Fatma's heavily wrinkled face fell, and she became lost in her own morose thoughts. She sighed so heavily that I knew her sadness had a heartfelt source, and I asked myself with dismay what could be behind her mental anguish.

'Fatma?' I reminded her of my presence.

Suddenly, her face turned ominous, and Fatma's despair burst forth.

'It's my granddaughter, Alhaan! Her father is an evil being, a donkey of a man, that Nasser! I would kill him with my bare hands if my daughter would allow it! But no! She says, she and her family must live their lives as they see fit!'

Fatma's eyes flashed with anger, and her huge bosom heaved with indignation. 'My own daughter demands that I stay out of her family matters!' She looked at me aghast and asked, 'Can you imagine that? To have no say in my own granddaughter's life?'

Feeling utterly bewildered, I asked, 'What has Nasser done to his child? To your granddaughter?'

Surely, I thought to myself, if the mother of the child had no objections, the harm to the child must not exist.

'That Nasser! He's from a small village. What does he know?'

I drew back in surprise as Fatma spat upon our newly carpeted floor.

Fatma was talking in every direction, cursing Nasser, crying out for her daughter, and begging God to help her grandchild.

I lost my patience, and raising my voice, I demanded to know. 'Fatma! Tell me, now! What's happened to your granddaughter?'

Disconsolate and at a loss, Fatma tightly squeezed my hand and said, 'Tonight. Tonight they'll make Alhaan into a woman. They have an appointment with the barber at nine o'clock. This ritual I do not believe is necessary. None of my daughters were so treated. It's that Nasser! Can you help me, Mistress, please . . . '

The past surged up in my mind. How well I remembered the horrible story told to me by my oldest sister, Nura, when she too had been made into a woman.

Kareem and I had not yet wed, and I was young, only sixteen years old. My mother had recently died, and Nura, as the eldest daughter, was instructed to answer my questions regarding female circumcision. I had not known until that time that Nura and our two sisters closest to her in age had endured the horrific rite, and as a result had been subjected to life-long pain and suffering.

In Saudi Arabia's not so distant past, circumcision of women had not been infrequent, with each tribe following a different custom. Just this past year, I had read a book that my son had purchased while in London. The book was titled *The Empty Quarter* by St John Philby, a respected British desert explorer. With assistance from my grandfather, Abdul Aziz Al Sa'ud, the founder and first king of Saudi Arabia, John Philby had carried out extensive exploration in Arabia in the 1930s.

I had taken the book from my son's room and had

derived great pleasure reading the man's history of Arab tribes that make up the population of Saudi Arabia, until I came across a section of the book that told of the Englishman's findings on female circumcision. Knowing what I know, I had imagined the brutalization of my own sisters and had cringed and cried out when reading a conversation John Philby had documented with the Arab men of the desert:

> But his strong subject was sex, and he loved to poke fun at Salih by dilating on Manasir practice in the matter of female circumcision. Take it from me, he said, they let their women come to puberty with clitoris intact and, when a girl is to be married, they make a feast for her circumcision a month or two before the wedding. It is only then that they circumcise them and not at birth as do the other tribes – Qahtan and Murra, Bani Hajir, ay, and 'Ajman. Thus their women grow up more lustful than others, and fine women they are too and that hot! But then they remove everything, making them as smooth as smooth, to cool their ardour without reducing their desire . . . the girls are dealt with in their tents by women who know their business, and get a dollar or so for the job. They are expert with the scissors, the razor, and the needle, which are all used for the operation.

The idea that such brutalization would make a woman lustful! I wondered at the information provided to the Englishman and came to the conclusion it was nothing more than brash male talk, for I had been told that the procedure made a woman chaste, rather than passionate.

My grandfather, Abdul Aziz Al Sa'ud, was a man who was ahead of his time, and he looked for better ways in all matters. Coming from the Najd, he did not believe in the circumcision of women, or in the flaying circumcision of men, which was as terrifying as female circumcision.

In the flaying circumcision of men, the skin is removed from the navel down to the inside of a man's legs. On witnessing such brutality, our first king forbade the practice. In spite of my grandfather's decree, the old ways died slowly, and people were willing to risk punishment to carry on with what they had been taught by those who came before them.

My own mother paid no heed to the new ruling, and three of her daughters were subjected to the cruel practice of female circumcision.

While some tribes forbade circumcision of their women altogether, others excised the hood of the clitoris only. The cutting of the hood of the clitoris is the least common method, and is the only procedure that is analogous to male circumcision.

Then, there were those poor women who belonged to tribes in Arabia who removed the whole clitoris, along with the labia minora. This is the most common method of female circumcision and is comparable to removing the head of a man's penis. Three of my sisters had suffered this cruel procedure. The remainder of the women in our family had been spared the rite of circumcision, due to the intervention of a Western physician and my father's insistence to my mother that circumcision of females was nothing more than a pagan practice that must be halted.

There is another, more atrocious and dangerous method of female circumcision, named the pharaonic circumcision. I could scarce imagine the pain experienced by the women who received the pharaonic circumcision. This process is the most extreme, and after the rite is completed, a girl is left without a clitoris, labia minora, or labia majora. If such a procedure were done on a male, it would involve amputation of the penis, and the scrotum around the testicles.

How barbarous were these old customs that still lingered in our present day! In Saudi Arabia, much had been accomplished to eradicate the tradition, and most women in my country no longer experience the terrible custom.

The men of my own family had forbidden the pagan tradition, but still some families of African descent who lived in Arabia were prepared to risk punishment rather than forgo the rite, swearing that nothing other than the reduction of female pleasure would preserve female chastity.

I had known that the practice of female circumcision was thought to have begun along the Nile valley, and I had speculated in my mind that the barbaric ritual might end where it had begun. Yet, many women in Egypt and throughout the continent of Africa were still subjected to this most inhumane ritual.

Over the years, when my own family no longer practised this rite, I had been successful in pushing the thought of female mutilation from my mind.

Fatma tugged on my arm. Her imploring gesture brought me back into the present. With great sadness, I recalled the face of the young girl Alhaan, for she had visited her grandmother in our villa on many occasions. She was a pretty child and had seemed bright and happy. I imagined an indelible image of the girl being led to the barber, undressed by her mother, with small legs spread before the man with a sharp razor.

I recoiled in horror. In disbelief, I wondered how the mother of that girl could condone such evil inflicted on her beautiful daughter? Yet, I knew that many mothers were allowing such intolerable practices, for it is estimated by world health organizations that female genital mutilation affects between 80 and 100 million women worldwide. So much pain inflicted on little girls!

With hope in her voice, Fatma examined my face carefully and asked, 'Mistress, can you save my granddaughter?'

I moved my head slowly and heavily. 'What can I do, Fatma, that you cannot. I'm not of your family. My interference would be resented.'

'You're a princess. My daughter would respect someone who's a princess.'

I had learned long ago that those who have no wealth

believe that money has provided wisdom along with economic freedom, but this was a matter of deeply ingrained culture. Instinctively, I knew that Fatma's daughter would not welcome my intrusion.

I waved my arms helplessly. 'What can I do, Fatma? Since I reached the age of understanding, I've wanted female freedom from such practices.' My voice fell low, along with my spirits. 'Now, it seems that the world is becoming darker and darker for those of our sex.'

Fatma remained silent, and a sorrowful look came into her black eyes.

I assured her. 'If I could, I would help your granddaughter. I've no authority to voice my opinion.'

Fatma looked disappointed but spoke words devoid of reproach. 'I understand, Mistress.' She stared at me from half-closed lids. 'But, I beg you to come with me. To try?'

Surprised at Fatma's stubbornness, I felt my resolve soften. I felt a shiver run through my body and asked in a weak voice, 'Where does your daughter live?'

Fatma's thick lips exploded with her excited reply, 'Very close, not more than a short ride in a car. If we leave now, we can get there before Nasser comes home from work.'

I summoned all my courage and stood to my feet. I told myself that, in spite of anticipated failure, I must make an effort. I knew that I would be forced to lie to my husband, or he would forbid me to go. 'Fatma, go and get your things. And say not a word to anyone of this matter.'

'Yes, Mistress! I knew that it was God's will that you would help me!'

I watched her as she hurried away, moving faster than I could ever remember. Despite our vastly different worlds, the two of us had become comrades fighting for the same cause.

By the time I combed out my hair, applied lipstick, and located my handbag, I had decided to tell Kareem that Fatma had just that morning learned that her daughter was ill with a rare female disorder, but she refused treatment, saying that if it was God's will that she die, then she would not reverse his decision by accepting treatment from any man. Fatma had pleaded with me to go and convince her daughter that she must fight to live for the sake of her own children. To be more convincing, I would complain that I did not want to go, but how could I forgive myself if the woman died and I had made no effort. It was a weak scenario, but Kareem shied away from female problems and would more than likely grumble but make no move to stop me from going.

As it turned out, I was not forced to tell such a wild tale, for Abdullah said that his father had received a telephone call while I was talking to Fatma. Kareem left a message for me with Abdullah that he was going to join one of his royal cousins in a Cairo casino and that he would not be home until later that evening. I knew that my husband wanted to put time and distance between himself and his son's earlier request to donate millions of dollars to a failing Lebanese economy, and I had a sense that his excuse to leave our home was as dishonest as the lie I had been prepared to tell. Kareem shares a common trait with most Arabs. My husband cannot say no, but would rather tell a small lie and disappear from the sight of the person who requires an answer.

'Good!' I muttered under my breath. Kareem's discomfort at being in his son's company had come at an opportune time.

After advising me of his father's message, Abdullah turned his attention back to the television set, and I saw that he was mesmerized, watching an Egyptian soap opera that was greatly favoured by Arabs from many lands. I noticed that Amani's lips had formed a disapproving pout. My daughter was not pleased at her brother's selection: that particular show was not allowed in Saudi Arabia, since there were many scenes that hinted at sexual impropriety.

'Abdullah, I need you to drive me to Fatma's daughter's home. Can you come?'

My son looked for any opportunity to drive the new white Mercedes that Kareem had purchased and shipped into the country for our Cairo home. I knew from past experience that Kareem would have taken the older Mercedes into the busy district of downtown Cairo, since he greatly feared the driving practices of the taxi drivers in that teeming city.

Abdullah flicked the remote control button, turning off the set. He gallantly leapt to his feet. 'I'll get the car.'

The Cairo streets were crowded with vehicles of every description, and the traffic was almost at a standstill. Pedestrians threaded in and out of the traffic. People hung onto the sides of buses already packed with humanity; they clung precariously to the doorways or windows as if it were the most natural method in the world to travel.

As our car inched through the city streets, I gazed in amazement at the mass of people who had descended on the city of the Pharaohs, and shuddered as if I had seen some terrifying sight, for it was easy to see that Cairo could not continue to exist as it was.

Abdullah interrupted my thoughts, asking me the point of our errand.

I swore him to secrecy. When I told him of Fatma's source of sorrow, a flash of anger swept over his face.

Abdullah said that he had heard of such things but had thought such tales were exaggerated. 'Is it really true?' he asked. 'Are such things done to young girls?'

I thought to tell him about his Auntie Nura but reconsidered, for it was such a private matter, and I knew that my sister would be keenly ashamed if my son knew of her mutilation. Instead, I told him the history of female circumcision.

While my son was pleased that the custom was ending in our own land, he felt sickened that so many women worldwide suffered unnecessary pain.

We were silent for the rest of the trip, each of us swamped by our own thoughts of the evening's business.

Fatma's daughter lived in a small alley branching off

from a main shopping road in the city. Abdullah paid a shop owner for the privilege of parking our car on the pavement in front of his clothes shop and promised the happy man a generous bonus if he would ensure that no damage occurred while we were away.

Abdullah guided us, hands on our backs as we weaved through the pedestrian traffic and entered the alleyway that led to our destination. The alley was too small for cars, so we walked down the middle of the stone-paved street. Strong cooking odours drifted into the street, as we passed a number of cafés specializing in Arab dishes.

Abdullah and I exchanged many glances, for we had never visited the poorer sections of Cairo, and the close living quarters and poverty of the inhabitants was a shock to us both.

Fatma's daughter lived in a three-storey building at the centre of the alleyway. The building faced the local mosque, which looked worn and was in urgent need of repair. The bottom floor of the building was a bakery, while the two top floors were rented out as apartments. Fatma pointed up and said that her daughter, Elham, lived on the top floor. Incredibly, Elham must have been looking down at the crowd from the flat-roofed building, for she recognized her mother, and began to yell Fatma's name, which we could barely hear over the loud noise of city life.

Abdullah, not knowing this particular family's custom that women may meet men not of their family, for in Egypt the custom varies from family to family, told me that he would wait for me in a small café we had passed that served shawarma sandwiches, which are thin slices of lamb that has been turned and cooked on a spit and placed into a piece of Arab bread, with tomato, mint and onion as added taste. Shawarma sandwiches were a big favourite of all my children. Abdullah said he was becoming hungry.

I agreed with my son and watched his tall slim figure as he walked jauntily through the crowd.

Elham and three of her four daughters met us on the stairwell, all four speaking at once, demanding to know if there had been some illness or tragedy in the family.

My first thought was that Elham looked identical to Fatma when she was young.

Elham gazed at me in fascination when Fatma introduced me as a princess from Saudi Arabia, her employer, for I had never met this particular child of Fatma's, even though I had met most of Fatma's children and grandchildren. I grew very conscious of my showy jewellery, for in my haste, I had not remembered to remove my large diamond earrings or my opulent wedding ring, which I realized was more than conspicuous in such poor surroundings. Elham's youngest daughter, a girl of only six, was slapped by her mother as she rubbed her small fingers across the stone in my ring.

At Elham's insistence, we were led into her small sitting-room, and she left us for a short time to go and boil water for tea. Fatma had two granddaughters in her lap and a third at her feet. Alhaan was nowhere to be seen.

I examined my surroundings and could see that Elham lived a simple life. I tried not to stare at the threadbare floor coverings and the torn loose covers, for I did not want my attention to be misunderstood. There was an open brazier in the middle of the room, and a square table pushed against the wall was piled with religious books. A small gas lamp hung down from the ceiling, and I wondered if the apartment was not supplied with electricity. I noticed that Elham's home was spotless, and it was evident that she was a proud woman who went to great measures to keep the dust and bugs out of her simple home.

Elham soon returned, serving sweet tea and small almond cookies that she said she had baked herself for the family celebration that they were having that evening. She mentioned to her mother that Alhaan was excited over the event and was on the rooftop, reading the Koran and quietly preparing herself for the most important day in her life.

The atmosphere remained cheerful until that moment, as Fatma brought up the topic on our minds, pleading with her daughter to cancel the planned evening ritual, to spare her child great pain and suffering.

Fatma talked in a rush and seeing that she was making no dent in her daughter's determination, pointed to me and said that if Elham would not listen to her own mother, then she should pay heed to a woman who had been educated by bright minds, a woman who had learned from respected physicians that the mutilation of girls was not encouraged by our religion and was nothing more than a custom that had no basis or meaning in modern life.

The tension built, and though Elham was polite and listened to my thoughts on the matter, I could see the lines of her face were set and her eyes were glassed over with stubborn determination. Knowing from Fatma's confidences that the family was notably religious, I shared my knowledge of religious thought, saying that nothing in the Koran spoke of such matters, and if God considered it a necessity for women to be circumcised, then surely he would have given that message to Prophet Mohammed when he revealed his wisdom to his messenger.

Elham admitted that while excision or infibulation of girls is not mentioned in the Koran, the practice was founded upon the customs of the Prophet so that it became *Sunna*, or tradition for all Muslims. She reminded me of a well-known *hadith*, or tradition addressed but not recorded in the Koran. This *hadith* says that Prophet Mohammed one day told Um Attiya, a matron who was excising a girl, 'Reduce but do not destroy.'

It was this tradition that Elham and her husband were going to follow regarding female circumcision, and nothing I could say would alter their decision.

We discussed the issue until I could see the light begin to leave the room. Sundown was approaching. I knew that Nasser would return to his home soon, and I had no desire to confront the man of the house over such a delicate matter. I made some small mention that it was time for me to return to my children.

Fatma, sensing failure, began to wail and slap at her cheeks until her face was completely reddened.

A look of distress flickered in Elham's eyes at her mother's grief, but she said that the decision had been reached by her husband and that she agreed with his thinking. All four of her daughters would undergo the rite of circumcision at the proper age.

I could see that Elham wished me to leave. Understanding that I could do nothing to halt the frightening shadow cast over the lives of the female children of this home, I stood and said my farewells.

With quiet self-assurance, Elham's eyes met mine, and she politely bade me goodbye. 'You have honoured my home with your presence, Princess Sultana. Please, come again another day for a longer visit.'

Against her daughter's wishes, Fatma insisted upon staying for the ceremony, saying that if the evil deed was going to be done, that she wanted to supervise the barber's work to make sure he cut nothing more than the tip of her granddaughter's clitoris.

I submitted to the inevitable, leaving Elham's home without accomplishing my goal. My feet felt leaden as I walked down the long staircase. In an effort to give myself time to calm my nerves, I stood motionless on the steps and recited aloud a verse from the Koran, 'You cannot lead aright whomever you wish, it is God who leads whomever he wishes.'

My son was waiting, sitting at a small table in the front of the café. His questioning gaze followed me as I made my way to his side.

He peered at me with expectation. 'So?' he asked.

I shook my head, 'No. There is nothing to be done.'

Abdullah's face clouded as I admitted my failure.

'Come,' I said. 'Let's go home.'

I glanced over my shoulder as we left the small alley,

gazing into the night. Elham's home had melted into the darkness as though it had never existed.

When my son began to talk, I urged silence pressing my hand against his lips.

I was unable to control my weeping.

Without speaking, my son drove his sobbing mother home.

As soon as I arrived back at our villa, I called out for my astonished daughters to abandon their current activities and pack their belongings: our family would leave Cairo as soon as their father returned from the casino.

I whispered to Abdullah that the city that I had loved since a child was in danger of losing my affection, though I hoped that our evening's experience would not result in my vigorous dislike of everything Egyptian.

Abdullah's eyes flashed with understanding, and I was gratified to see that my son appreciated the reasoning behind my words.

Kareem soon arrived with the odour of alcohol spread about him, which brought on a sudden and prolonged prayer from Amani for God to look past her father's sinful acts and restore Kareem to the status of heaven's most favoured. In the context of her plea, Amani began to describe the burning agony of hell that awaited members of her family.

Already in a foul mood, I quickly wearied of Amani's enthusiastic fanaticism. I was incensed that she would take it to the point where she spoke critically of her family. Face to face, I told her in no uncertain terms that I had not yet received notification that God had appointed my daughter to the sacred role of frightening mankind into decency.

I reached across to pinch the skin on her face, but Kareem grabbed my hand and held it tight to his chest, ordering Amani to leave our presence, suggesting that she complete her prayers in the privacy of her room.

Kareem then became noisy in the irritating manner of a drunkard, saying that he had often observed my inability to control my destructive temper, and he thought that the time had come to teach me a useful lesson.

We looked at each other for a time. Kareem stood still, waiting for my response. His lips were curled in contempt, and it was easy to see that Kareem was in a rare mood to fight.

I quickly scanned the room for a weapon with which to bang my husband's head, for I am a woman who meets threats with violence, but Kareem knows me well and placed himself in a position between me and the brass pot which I had decided to use against my husband.

The will to fight left my body in a rush, for there are times when I can think reasonably, and Kareem is twice my size. Without a weapon, I am at a notable disadvantage and once disarmed can be quickly overcome. Besides, it was best that I decided not to escalate our disagreement into a brawl, for my past had taught me the impossibility of winning an argument with Kareem when he was drunk. But I was filled with scorn, and had difficulty remembering why I had ever loved Kareem in the first place.

Wishing to avoid a confrontation that could provide me with no benefit, I knew that I must recapture the favoured position.

I laughed, and said to Kareem, 'Look at you! You look like an elephant threatening an ant!' I then smiled at my husband and said that I was more than pleased that he had returned early, that I yearned for his companionship at a time of great sorrow.

Kareem was not at his prime mentally, and was easily bested. Bewildered for a short moment at my change in tactic, he fell easily into my trap and became very remorseful for his unthinking words, patting my shoulder, offering apologies, and wondering why his dear wife was distressed.

I looked at my watch and saw that it was nearly nine o'clock. Half insane with the consciousness that the innocent child, Alhaan, would soon undergo female mutilation, I instantly forgot my thoughts of self, and with tremendous sadness I told my husband that there is no loveliness in life for women and that in my mind it would be advantageous for all females to die.

Kareem could not fathom the reasoning behind my dark ideas. He asked, was my life not perfect? Was there anything that I desired that my husband did not provide?

Knowing that my main source of inner conflict rested with the social injustices directed towards women, he reminded me that together we had ensured that in our home, our daughters felt little of the prejudice that exists against females in our land. What more could one man do, he wondered, than to protect those whom he loved.

Kareem smiled sweetly and tenderly brushed my lips with his fingers.

I had a quick thought that Kareem *was* endowed with a winsome charm that atoned for his less admirable traits.

Unsure how to address the ambiguous issue of my general dissatisfaction with female status, Kareem announced that it was my inescapable destiny to be born in Saudi Arabia, and in the end women must accept the limits imposed by our culture. My husband reminded me that God knew all things, and his purpose in planting my feet in Saudi soil had not been made known to those bound on earth.

My emotions in a whirl, I once again felt dislike for Kareem, regretting that all men could not be turned into women and live in our limited and often cruel world for sufficient time to attain understanding. I wanted to rage at my husband's distance from my knowledge of the pain that women endure.

How can woman bind man to the grief that walks the earth and settles at the feet of each woman by turn? Sensing the futility of longing for men to suffer women's position in society, while women enjoy the status of male rank, I told myself that I was too keyed up to be capable of a normal conversation and suggested to my husband that we go to sleep early, and then rise refreshed to a day of new thoughts.

Because he follows a set pattern of fighting, and then sleep after drinking alcohol, Kareem agreed and willingly prepared himself for bed, while I located the children and gave instructions for them to eat their evening meal without us and be available with packed bags to leave Cairo in the morning.

By the time I returned to our quarters, my husband had begun to breathe deep and peacefully as one already at rest.

With my mind in conflict between my own rebellious thoughts and Elham's traditional beliefs, I considered what Kareem had said, that I was a woman at odds with my fate. Yet, in spite of my second-class status, I knew that I could never yield to meek acceptance of female circumcision.

Before falling into a troubled and unsatisfying sleep, I vowed to myself that my fury over the fate of girls such as Alhaan would outlive the barbaric custom that had aroused it.

Chapter Eleven

MONTE CARLO

To call women the weaker sex is a libel; it is man's injustice to women. You will guard your wife's honour and be not her master, but her true friend. Let not either of you regard another as the object of his or her lust.

Mahatma Gandhi

Fatma's face was contorted in an effort to appear cheery as she bid us good morning. She had been hard at work in the kitchen when the family awakened and seemed distraught at our abrupt announcement that we were leaving Cairo and travelling to Monte Carlo that very morning. There, on the French Riviera, we would join three of my sisters and their families who were holidaying in the small principality of Monaco.

I had already imagined in my mind the scene of her granddaughter's circumcision and knew that the tragic evening did not lend itself to words. Still, I manoeuvred a quiet moment away from my family to enquire about Alhaan's safety.

With clasped hands and a steely glint in her eyes that reflected her lingering anger, Fatma said that the child had not fared well. On her son-in-law's instruction, the barber had removed all of the girl's clitoris, along with her labia minora. Fatma said that special compresses had to be made to stop the flow of blood.

Feeling undeserved guilt that I had had no ability to halt Alhaan's brutalization, I asked in alarm, 'Do you fear further complications?'

Fatma tried to relax her expression when she saw that my eyes were filling with tears and realized that I was becoming distraught.

'Mistress,' she hugged my neck as she spoke. 'The deed is done. Now we must live with it. You did all that you could. I bless you for your love of another who is not of your own blood. Take comfort from my belief that Alhaan will recover.'

I could find no words to speak. Fatma turned me loose and her eyes met mine. Our gazes stayed fixed on one another for a long time. Neither of us looked away or moved, and I felt a great love surging from Fatma to me.

Fatma moistened her lips before she continued. 'Princess Sultana, you entered my dreams last evening, and now I feel that I must convey the message of the dream.'

I held my breath, afraid of what I might be told, thinking that I had never fared well in supernatural predictions.

Fatma gazed at me with sad affection. 'Mistress, you are surrounded with life's possessions, yet you appear empty. This discontent comes from having the heart of a child in the body of a woman. Such a combination will bring great difficulties to one's soul. Neither you, nor any other child of God, can resolve all of mankind's problems. I was told to tell you that it is not shameful to bow to reality and that you should allow the lust for conflict to cool in your veins.'

My mother's face appeared to me as a dark dream of disconnected memories. There was no doubt in my mind that my mother was using the form of the earthbound Fatma to communicate with her youngest child. Fatma's words were just the sort of advice that my mother had often made to me in the days of my childhood. When I was young, her words of wisdom were unclear and seemed to have no connection to me. Now that I was an adult, that was no longer the case.

I had known then, even as a child, that when my mother understood that she was dying that her only regret in passing from earth was that she was leaving my untempered character without a firm guide. Her fears had been that I would react to adult controversy in the same hasty manner with which I had confronted problems when I was a child, when I had no goal but success, embroiling myself in one conflict after another.

My beloved mother was communicating with me!

I felt a warm glow throughout my body and felt calmer than I had in days. My memories were no longer obscure, and I keenly felt my mother's divine presence.

I had no explanation to give for the sudden whimpering that I heard arise from my throat, or for the sobbing and incoherent woman who threw herself into Fatma's strong arms, a woman who still felt as a child, longing with all her heart to have but one short moment with the woman who had given her life.

I cried out to a sympathetic Fatma, 'How blessed are those who still have their mothers!'

When leaving the city of Cairo, I could not help but think of the gloomy fate awaiting many young girls in the country of Egypt. I whispered to my son that such tragic events make Egyptian life less bright and cheerful than is fitting in such a country.

Late that afternoon, our private plane landed at the Nice-Côte International Airport. My three sisters' husbands had rented a large villa in the hills above Monaco, which they had assured Kareem was a short drive from the airport. On short notice, Assad had arranged for three limousines to meet our arrival and transport our family and baggage from the airport to the villa.

Actually, at one time the villa had been a palace belonging to a French aristocrat and had over sixty rooms, so there was more than enough space for our combined families. None of my sisters was married to a man who had taken more than one wife, so our group of eight adults and sixteen children was considerably small for an Arab gathering of four families.

There are three highways which go from Nice to Monaco, but none of us had a desire to travel the coastal road, or the Inférieure Corniche, which is generally traffic-packed. The Moyenne Corniche is the middle road, and the Grande Corniche is the high road.

I expressed a desire to take the Moyenne, since I knew it was the best road of the three and had wonderful views of the coastline.

Kareem disagreed, saying that our daughters should choose the road we would travel.

I pinched the flesh on his leg, indicating that his idea was not sound, but he continued to ask their opinions.

As I knew they would, Maha and Amani began an immediate squabble, with each of them insisting upon a different route.

I whispered to Kareem, 'I told you so.'

Our daughters had never reached agreement on any issue, regardless of the subject, since the time they had learned to speak. I admitted to myself that nothing in our lives had been simple since I had given birth to three children.

The driver settled their argument by saying that a truck loaded with eggs had suffered a mishap, and that the Moyenne was temporarily blocked. Since two of the three roads were congested with traffic, he suggested that we take the Grande.

Like the baby she is, Amani pouted, but Maha and Abdullah were joyful, pointing out various interesting sights that they had not remembered from our last trip to Monaco over three years before. The drive took us along the precipices of the Maritime Alps' southern slopes and the scenery was spectacular.

I couldn't help commenting that, after viewing the uninspired brown and beige shades of desert countries, the lush greenery of Europe was restful to my eyes.

Amani took my comment as a slur upon the home of

the Prophet, whereupon Kareem lost his patience and asked his daughter *please* to omit religious interpretations of the simplest social remark.

I thought to myself that my own precious daughter was becoming thoroughly unlikable. My love flowed as strongly as ever, but there were moments when I suffered extreme distaste for Amani's overbearing and 'holier than thou' attitude.

Pleased that my family's confined journey was coming to an end, I was happy to see my sisters Sara, Tahani and Nura, when our car pulled up the circular driveway to the front of the villa. How welcome I felt that the three of them had evidently been eagerly waiting by the door for our arrival.

My pleasure was short-lived.

'Reema has been hospitalized!' Nura announced as soon as we had completed our greetings and my three children had left the area to go and seek out their cousins.

'What?' I responded, while trying to imagine what illness had struck the fifth sister in age in our family.

'She's been injured,' Sara volunteered, while exchanging a meaningful look with Nura.

'Yes?' My voice was so low that the sound barely left my throat. I had a sudden fear of a car accident, for traffic accidents are the main source of death in Saudi Arabia, where many young boys recklessly race their vehicles through the streets.

My sisters and I stood without speaking, awkwardly facing one another. I moved my weight from foot to foot, waiting for someone to enlighten me about my sister's condition.

Kareem and Assad stood to the side of our small gathering, watching but not speaking.

When no-one spoke, my stomach churned. Was my sister dead, and was there no-one in my family with the nerve to tell me?

Finally, I asked weakly, 'Is her injury serious?'

'It seems that it isn't life-threatening,' Nura stated.

The Arab manner of avoiding bad news is maddening! I felt the urge to scream, for someone to tell me all that there was to know, to release me from the agony of attempting to force small bits of information from my reluctant sisters.

'What's happened?' I demanded. 'Anything is easier to accept than this torturing doubt!'

My sisters looked at each other strangely. Surely, Reema was dead!

'Let's go into the villa,' Assad suggested, as he placed a tender hand on Sara's arm. 'I'll have tea prepared.'

I followed Sara into the villa, taking no notice of the rooms as we passed them by. I was thinking of poor Reema. The fifth daughter in our family had always inspired family sympathy. From the date of her birth, Reema had not been blessed with obvious skills or beauty. While my sister was not born with a face scarred or misaligned, there had been nothing in her appearance that brought forth envy from other young mothers.

Nura had once confided that Reema was the only daughter whom our mother had felt no need to protect with the blue stone that was believed to ward off evil spirits, for who would wish the evil eye upon an infant so displeasing in appearance?

In addition, the young girl Reema had been cursed with a heavy figure that brought her cruel taunts from unfeeling children.

Of my nine sisters, Sara is the most beautiful. Of the remainder of our female family members, four sisters are notably pretty, three sisters are appealing, another sister is elegant and graceful, while Reema lacks a single mark of beauty. In a family of ten daughters, Reema was the unattractive sister who failed to excel in school or in games. Her one outstanding accomplishment was her ability to duplicate our mother's cooking skills, improvising delectable Arab and French dishes that did nothing to help her expanding figure.

Living in a country where nothing is more admired than female beauty, Reema was not esteemed.

Once we had settled ourselves in the sitting-room, Kareem and Assad left us to go and arrange tea. As the door was closing, I heard Assad speaking in a low voice to my husband, and knew that Kareem had discovered Reema's fate before her own sister had.

'I must know the truth. Tell me. Is Reema dead?'

'No.' Nura responded. Yet, my sister's gloomy face reflected the seriousness of the situation.

'She was attacked by Saleem,' Tahani finally said.

I felt cold all over. 'Truly?' I asked.

With tremendous emotion, Nura added, 'Our dear sister was viciously attacked by her own husband.'

'Why would Saleem want to hurt Reema?' I wondered. 'Surely, she gave him no motive!'

Like many unattractive people, Reema had always been pleasing in character, striving to make all around her feel delightful and gay, as if her joyful countenance could outwit nature, eliciting admiration from those in her company.

Saleem? My memory of Reema's husband flashed through my mind. Saleem, like Reema, was not blessed with physical beauty. But he was known to be a most quiet and gentle man. As we often say in the Arab world, 'every pot has its cover'. Saleem was considered a perfect partner for Reema, and their union seemed to suit them. His violent action was completely unexpected and out of character.

I put to Nura the most logical possibility, 'Did Saleem lose his mind? Is that why he assaulted Reema?'

I was not prepared for what I heard.

Approximately a year before Saleem's attack on his wife, Reema had expressed great anxiety to her oldest sister, Nura, that a dark secret was consuming the light in her life. Reema said that her dear husband was undergoing a bizarre personality change that had begun with a strange restlessness and dissatisfaction. Suddenly the formerly contented Saleem had been overcome by the blackest melancholy. Where Saleem had once been well pleased with his home, he was now irritable, finding endless fault with his wife and four children. He no longer expressed an interest in his work, and for many days he would remain in bed until mid-afternoon. Saleem was caught in the tyranny of his own emotions, which prevented the entire family from living a normal life.

While Reema's attachment to Saleem had increased during the years of their married life, Saleem coldly told Reema that he had never loved her, that as a matter of fact he had never known love at all, and had married Reema for no reason other than to gain prestige from her family name.

Reema confronted Saleem's unreasonable hostility with faithful love and genuine concern. Reema told Nura that she feared that Saleem must have a brain tumour, or at least be suffering from a chemical imbalance. Why else would a man so radically change, when nothing in his life had undergone trauma?

Reema pleaded with her husband to seek medical attention. Instead of looking for professional help for his misery, Saleem dwelled on his unhappiness. Saleem, a man who rarely drank alcohol, began to drink with increasing frequency. When drinking, he would become violent towards Reema and the eldest of their daughters.

Reema told Nura that she feared she would soon be divorced, separated from her two youngest sons, for Saleem had threatened to liberate himself from Reema, insisting that was the only way to free himself from his unhappiness.

Nura was helpless at giving advice, for Saleem was from a family that none of our family could approach without tension, for their family had recently requested that one of Nura's daughters be wed to their youngest son. The engagement did not materialize, since Ahmed and Nura had already arranged a different husband for their child. Saleem's family had held themselves at a distance since that time, taking offence where none was intended.

Nura said that while Saleem slowly pulled himself together so that he began to function at work, his contempt of Reema only grew more intense. Saleem began to take frequent trips to the Far East, and Reema knew from some of the brochures that she found in her husband's belongings that the trips were not of a business nature. Saleem was participating in sexual junkets to Bangkok and Manila.

Just the month before, Reema had come to Nura's home with a bruised face and a horrifying story. Our sister had discovered her husband in bed with one of the Sri Lankan maids. When she protested, Saleem had come at her with his fists and threatened Reema with the loss of her children if she dared open her mouth to anyone in his family. Saleem's family was known to be devout and religious, and they would have expressed great shame at his conduct, though they would have been helpless to change his mood.

While it is true that many Saudi men turn to secret pleasures with women to whom they are not wed, none of the females in our family had married a man so insensitive as to flaunt sexual relations with a servant in his own home.

Reema, perplexed and not sure where to turn, went to an Egyptian female Imam, asking that the woman put in writing the answer to the question: Does Islam permit a man to have sexual intercourse with his maidservant without marrying her? Surely, her husband would heed a religious ruling, if she brought it to him in writing. To go against the teachings of the Koran would be unthinkable in the mind of our pious sister!

Nura said that Reema had confessed that she was going to confront Saleem with the ruling. Nura had cautioned our sister, concerned that Saleem no longer enjoyed total sanity.

I asked if Nura recalled the words of the ruling.

She replied that she had taken a copy for herself and

filed it with her other religious material. Who knew what other woman might have a need for the information at a later date?

Nura said that to the best of her memory, 'the Imam's ruling clearly states that Islam does not allow a sexual relationship between a master and a servant'. The idea was outrageous, and only through marriage could a sexual relationship exist in Islam.

The Imam acknowledged that what happens in actual life is not always sanctioned by Islam and that there were many cases in the kingdom which had been brought to her attention involving a master forcing his servant to yield to his wishes, exploiting her weakness in their relationship to get cheap fulfilment of carnal desire.

The Imam had ruled that such a relationship was illicit and led to the three evils expressly forbidden by Islam. The evils of which she spoke were: 'Any relationship which adversely affects the moral fabric of society, or leads to promiscuity, or affects the rights of any individual. In Islam, the only lawful way to have sexual intercourse is through marriage.'

Reema's courage in seeking an outside opinion caused me some surprise, for she was meek in nature.

'Was the ruling the cause of Saleem's attack?' I asked my sisters.

Nura answered in the negative, causing me some surprise.

'Then?'

Sara began to weep and left the room, saying that she could not bear to hear the details again. Tahani rose to follow her, but Assad was standing near the door. I caught a glimpse of him wrapping his arms around his wife as he led her to a private corner.

Tahani returned and sat by my side, and began to pat my hand nervously.

I thought to myself that I was being prepared for some distressing details.

'The physician would not tell us the full details, but

Father and Ali went to his office and were told the truth of the matter, for Saleem finally confessed to the physician what exactly had happened to Reema.

'It seems that Saleem had just returned from a short trip to Bangkok and had smuggled in pornographic video tapes. After a night of drinking and viewing the tapes, Saleem thought to have sex with his wife, although he had not displayed affectionate interest in Reema for some time.

'When Saleem awakened Reema in the middle of the night for sex, he was told that she was having her monthly period.'

With half-shut eyes, Nura leaned back on the sofa.

Like all Muslims, I know that the Koran forbids sexual relations during a woman's menstrual cycle. The Koran clearly states: 'They ask, concerning women's courses, respond: they are a hurt and a pollution, keep away from women in their courses, and do not approach them until they are clean, but when they have purified themselves, you may approach them in any manner, time, or place, ordained for you, by God.'

Had Reema fought her husband, only to be raped and beaten during a time she was forbidden to him?

I could tell that Nura was thinking of what she was going to say and how she was going to say it. I watched Nura's face as it became white with anger. 'Saleem, in a drunken state, became angry at his wife's condition and refusal.' My sister took a deep, ragged breath. 'Sultana, Reema was badly beaten, and then Saleem raped his wife in a region of her body not allowed to her husband. The physician at the private clinic informed Father that Saleem's attack was so violent and brutal that emergency surgery was performed. For the remainder of her life, Reema will be forced to wear a colostomy bag.'

My mouth opened in a soundless howl. Reema? Disabled and encumbered for life? I found myself seething with hostility. Now I understood why Sara had fled the room, for she herself had been subjected to that same type of sexual abuse when wed against her will to her first husband, a man who was sick in his head.

I got to my feet and stamped my foot so hard that a vase tottered and threatened to fall from a tall stand. 'If Saleem were in this room, I would attack him with my hands,' I shouted. In an uncontrolled rage, I asked, 'And Saleem? Has he been gaoled?'

Tahani made a clicking sound with her tongue. 'Gaoled? He's Reema's husband. He's free to do as he likes.'

Nura's face was becoming even paler in her grief and bitterness over the fate of our innocent sister.

I protested, 'But his conduct was forbidden! Surely, we can make a case for a religious investigation!'

Nura looked at me with great love mingled with sadness. 'Sultana, you speak as a child. Who, in our land, will take the side of a woman against her husband? Our own father and brother have directed that this is a personal matter between Reema and Saleem and that no-one of our family is to interfere.'

Tahani confided, 'Father prohibited us from telling you, but we decided that we must, for when you see Reema next, her condition will be obvious.'

I insisted, 'Reema must divorce him! That, at least!'

Nura reminded me of the reality of Reema's situation. 'And lose her children? Both girls have reached puberty, and the boys are now eight and nine. Saleem has the right to take them from their mother. And that he would do. He has already threatened her with their loss. Sultana, Reema would die without the presence of her children.'

When Nura saw that I was still fiercely angry, she asked, 'Tell me, Sultana, could you live if your children were taken from you?'

In my land, in the event of a divorce, the mother has the right to retain her children if they are still suckling. But in most cases, a mother maintains custody of daughters until a girl child reaches puberty. In the case of male children, the boy should be allowed to remain with his mother until he is seven. When he reaches his seventh birthday, he is supposed to have the option to choose between his mother or father. Generally it is accepted that the father have his sons at age seven. A son *must* go with his father at the age of puberty, regardless of the child's wishes.

Often, in the case of male children, many fathers will not allow the mother to retain custody of a son, no matter what the age of the child. I have personally known women who have lost custody of their children at young ages, never seeing those that they gave birth to again. Unfortunately, if a father seizes the initiative and takes his children, there is no authority to enforce the return of the children to their mother.

I knew that if Saleem refused Reema visits to her children, then my sister would be banned from their presence for ever. There was no court of law that would reverse the husband's final decision about the destiny of his children.

I moaned, thinking of the possibilities we would know if we had male support. If only the men of her family, our father and Ali, would stand behind Reema, then her position in negotiating for her children would strengthen. Since our father and brother thought that a man should be unencumbered to do as he would with the females in his family, they would be of no assistance to Reema.

It was a serious moment.

'Perhaps Saleem will come to his right mind,' Nura hopefully suggested.

'Never try to straighten a dog's tail. In vain you do,' Tahani muttered to no-one in particular.

After further discussion, my sisters and I decided that we were needed in Riyadh. We would leave our husbands in Monte Carlo with our children, and travel back to Saudi Arabia the following day.

Later that evening, Kareem tried to lift my downcast spirits by reminding me that my sister had not died from her injuries and where there was life, change might come. He said that a better day would soon be known, that in his opinion, Saleem was suffering from nothing more than a male crisis that would pass.

Kareem had become concerned when I promised him that Saleem would suffer for his attack on the gentle Reema.

Trying to ease my murderous rage, he had joked, 'Sultana, I don't wish to see you ready for the executioner's sword! You must spare Saleem's life.'

My husband continued to speak, but I listened to his words without hearing, thinking that it was most lamentable that so much ignorance should prevail in a land that is home to a great religion.

Chapter Twelve

HOME

A girl possesses nothing but a veil and a tomb.

Saudi Arabian proverb

Our brother, Ali, met us at the King Khalid International Airport twenty-two miles from Riyadh. He seemed preoccupied and curtly informed us that we would be taken directly to the private clinic to visit our sister, Reema, for she was suffering a particularly bad day and had continually asked for Nura since early morning.

The traffic was heavy, and the drive took more than an hour. Each of us was lost in our thoughts of Reema. At the beginning of the journey, the conversation was strained and sparse, with nothing of any consequence being said.

Ali, tiring of the silence, confided that he, himself, was involved in a family crisis. With a touch of annoyance in his voice, my faithless brother said that Reema's unfortunate injury could not have occurred at a worse time, and that he had been greatly inconvenienced by the necessity of becoming involved in Saleem's private family affair. In all earnestness, Ali wondered aloud what Reema had done to arouse Saleem's hostility.

Ali was blaming Reema for Saleem's unprovoked attack!

Sara and Tahani looked quickly at Ali, and I detected in their evasive glances faint reprimands at his unfeeling comment.

I could not restrain my tongue and said, 'Ali, with

each day, your ignorance grows while your intelligence shrinks!'

I felt a keen urge to slap my brother, but not wanting to appear less than admirable in front of Nura and Tahani, consoled myself with silent criticism of Ali. Ali was only a year older than me, but he looked no less than ten years my senior, with lines in his face and pouches under his eyes. In his youth, Ali had been handsome – vain about his looks. In middle age he had grown a bit stout, and his chin had doubled. Ali's affluent, over-indulgent lifestyle was clearly evident in his face and form. I was cheered to see his physical appeal decaying.

My eldest sister's face clouded, and in a voice filled with tenderness and concern, asked Ali what crisis there was in his life.

Out of ten sisters, only Nura truly loves Ali. The emotions of the remaining nine sisters for their only brother range from pity, contempt and envy, to open dislike. Nura, understandably, is protected from acute disapproval of her only brother by the division of many years, for Nura is the oldest child among us, and Ali is one year from the youngest. Nura was married with children when Ali was born, and was mercifully spared his overbearing spoiled conduct. In addition, Nura inherited the kindly character of our mother and belonged to that minority who instinctively make apologies for those around them, while accepting the most feeble explanations for inexcusable deeds. Thus, Nura's reaction to Ali's insensitive statement differed from that of his other three sisters.

Ali frowned slightly. He looked out of the car window and then said distantly, 'I have divorced Nada.'

Nura gasped. 'Again?'

Ali looked at Nura and nodded.

'Ali! How could you? You promised Nada that never again would you divorce her!'

Nada was Ali's most beautiful and favoured wife. He had married her seven years before, and together they had had three lovely daughters.

Under Muslim law, a man's freedom to divorce his wife is justified in the Koran. This system of the threat of divorce looming over a woman's security is most unsettling to women in my land. It is intolerable that many men stretch this ruling to the utmost of its flexibility, demanding divorce for the most trivial causes, ending with the continuous social degradation of their women.

Women do not have the same options, since a divorce in a woman's favour is given only after a thorough investigation into her life. More often than not, women will not be allowed to divorce, even when there is just cause. This female lack of a freedom so enjoyed by males creates one-sided, often cruel methods of male control and power over their women. The words of divorce slip most easily off the tongue of a man who wishes to punish his wife, 'I divorce thee', or 'I dismiss thee', sending the woman into exile from her married home, often without her children.

Ali, a man rarely in control of his tongue or his temper, often used divorce as a weapon against his wives.

I knew that my brother had divorced each of his wives at least once, and Nada had been divorced twice. More times than not, Ali's anger receded, he would repent the divorce and retain the wife he had divorced the day or night before. Ali had this benefit, for men are not only given the option of divorcing their wives with the greatest of ease but are allowed to take back the divorce and resume their marriage as if nothing out of the ordinary had occurred. Under Muslim law, a man is given this option twice. If a man divorces his wife for a third time, then the procedure becomes more complicated.

In a fit of anger, Ali had divorced Nada for the third time and, according to our law, he could not resume marriage with Nada until she had married another man and had then been divorced by that man. Through his childlike conduct, Ali had finally and truly divorced himself from the only one of his wives for whom he felt true affection.

I tried not to smile as I quoted words from the Koran, doing my best to remember every word.

'You may divorce your wives twice; after that you must either retain them with kindness, or put them away with benefits. If then the husband divorce her a third time, it is not lawful for him to take her again, until she shall have married another husband.'

I stuck my face in my brother's and asked, 'Ali, who is Nada now going to wed?'

Ali glared at me with bulging eyes, and answered coldly. 'La! La! (no, no) Nada has no desire to wed another!'

'Ha! Nada is famous within the female community for her beauty. Once it is known that she is free, many mothers and sisters will send their sons and brothers to ask for Nada. Wait and see!'

Sara intervened, not wanting our lifelong, unending feud to lead to a fierce argument in a confined area. 'Ali. What led to this divorce?'

Ali was clearly embarrassed to say. He said that the matter of the divorce was private, but he did ask Sara and Nura if they would visit Nada, to convince her that the words were spoken in haste, and as such, Ali should be given another opportunity to prove that he had no real desire to divorce Nada. If Nada chose to ignore the situation and did not notify the authorities, then Ali might be able to avoid an order to allow Nada to leave his home, thereby becoming eligible for another man to pursue.

Nura and Sara agreed to talk to Nada.

The car began to slow down, and Ali peered through the dark blue curtains of the limousine and then pointed at the black assortment of veils, *abaayas*, and *shaylas* that were spread over the car seat. 'Hurry. Prepare yourselves. We're there,' he commanded.

It was a struggle for the four of us to cover ourselves in the black garb of decency within the small space of the car. Ali had met our private aeroplane on the tarmac, so we had not bothered with our required outer coverings until the last moment.

We had arrived at the private clinic that Ali said was owned jointly by a Lebanese and a Saudi Arabian. The clinic was one often frequented by royal family members when confidentiality was desired. I was acquainted with three princesses who routinely entered the clinic for treatment of drug and alcohol abuse.

Our family was escorted inside the building through a little-used door; we were met there by one of Reema's physicians. The man informed us that he was an internist, a specialist from Beirut, and had recently been hired by the owners of the clinic to care for members of the royal family. It was easy to see why the man had been selected to treat influential Saudis, for he was a tall, attractive man, deferential, yet with an air of confidence that provided us with a sense of well-being for our sister's safety.

The physician walked between Nura and Ali, and though I made an attempt to lean forward and involve myself in their quiet conversation, I failed to hear the words that he spoke. We passed a group of Asian nurses who were clustered around an elongated nurses' station. Once close, I could tell by their accents that they were Filipinos.

The windows in Reema's room were still closed, but the blinds were slightly open, allowing a small amount of the sun's glow to penetrate and wash the room in a soft light. The room was completely white, and above Reema's head hung a large pearl-white chandelier that looked strangely out of place in a clinical setting.

Reema was resting, but when she heard us she opened her eyes. I could see that my sister suffered a moment of confusion before reality rushed back to her. Her face was of the palest hue, and her eyes were those of a frightened child. My sister was receiving fluids from bottles hanging from metal stands, and I could not count the tubes that had been placed in her arms and nose.

Nura rushed to her side, placing her arms around the form that was Reema. Sara and Tahani held hands, fighting back tears, and I could scarcely see as I flung myself in a white armchair. I bit my lips until I tasted blood, and

I pressed my hands into the arm of the chair with such force that I broke three fingernails.

Ali, uncomfortable with our display of grief, whispered to Sara that he would return within the hour to escort us to our homes. Before leaving, he reminded Sara that it was imperative that she see Nada on that very evening.

I was seething with rage at the sight of my wounded sister and thought to myself that I would like to send the hottest fire raging throughout the whole country. Let the evil of my land die with the flesh of those Saudi men who dared to use the holy Koran as a basis to molest those of my sex!

I attempted to calm my thoughts, for there was no purpose in creating chaos and adding to Reema's pain. I remembered the Prophet's promises of punishment to those who so sin, but my religion could not soothe me, even in the knowledge that Saleem would suffer everlasting agonies in hell for what he had done to my sister. I had no patience to wait for divine intervention. Nothing would cool my boiling blood but the sight of Saleem's mutilated remains!

Once comforted by Nura, Reema talked to each of her sisters in turn, pleading with us to treat Saleem with the same courtesy as before, reminding us that one of the duties of good Muslims is to forgive those who do wrong. Seeing the anger in my face, Reema quoted a verse from the Koran. 'Sultana, don't forget the words of the Prophet: forgive, even when angry.'

I could not hold back my words. Remembering the text of the Koran that followed, I replied, 'Let evil be rewarded with evil.'

Sara pinched me on my buttocks, reminding me not to cause further anguish to our sister. I left Reema's side and stared out of the small openings of the window, seeing nothing of what I was looking at.

Reema began to speak once again. I could not believe what I was hearing and was chilled by Reema's words, which were delivered with the impassioned eloquence of a woman whose reason for living was at stake.

I returned to my sister's bedside and stared at her face.

As the intensity of Reema's feelings increased, her brow became furrowed, and her lips grew tight with determination. My sister said that Saleem had repented and had promised that there would be no other violence. She was not going to be divorced, nor would she seek a divorce.

Suddenly I realized what was in Reema's heart. My sister's only fear was to be deprived of her children, and those four children were the inspiration for Reema's ability to forgive Saleem for his heinous attack. She would accept any indignity so long as her relationship with her precious children was not severed.

Reema asked, would we assure her that no-one in our family would seek retribution on her behalf?

It was the most difficult promise ever to pass my lips, and my tongue would scarce obey my mind. But my word was given, and I knew that I had no choice but to abide by my sister's sincere wish.

Once recovered, Reema would return to the home of the man who had an infinite capacity for cruelty, well hidden for many married years. I knew that, once unleashed, Saleem's ugly temperament would not soften. There was nothing that we could do.

Our frustration only increased when an Egyptian nurse employed at the clinic confided in Nura that Saleem had visited his wife earlier that day. In the presence of that nurse, Saleem had lifted his wife's hospital gown, viewing the hole that had been made in her side for her bodily waste to be expelled, and had expressed shocking disgust at the sight.

The nurse said that Saleem had then made a most callous remark, telling his wife that while he would not divorce her, that he would never again come to her bed, for he could not bear the sight or smell of one so repugnant.

I marvelled at my ability to control my rage.

My sisters and I had entered the clinic as a united force, swelled with determination to snatch our sister from the grasp of her evil husband. Defeated by Reema's legitimate apprehension of the possible loss of her children, we retreated from the clinic as nothing more than a group of black shrouded and nameless wives, without the ability to force justice upon a single man.

The sting of defeat was unbearable.

Who could deny that the main bulwark of Saudi social order remained male dictatorship?

Since our husbands and children were still in Monte Carlo, my sisters and I decided that we would remain together in Nura's house. From the clinic, we had Ali transport us to her home. Nura and Sara pledged to Ali that they would have one of Nura's drivers take them to visit Nada that evening and said that it was best for him to stay in the home of another wife that night.

Once we had telephoned our husbands in Monte Carlo, advising them of news of Reema, Tahani pleaded exhaustion and retired early to bed. I insisted on accompanying Sara and Nura to Nada's palace. I was forced to make a second promise, guaranteeing that I would make no suggestions to Nada for her to quit Ali while she had the opportunity.

My sisters know me well. Admittedly, I had already made a plan in my mind to try and convince Nada that she must quickly move to marry another. My brother had treated women with contempt all of his life and in my opinion it was time for him to learn not to use divorce as a weapon. Perhaps if he lost the only wife for whom he felt affection, then he would temper his bullying tactics.

Now, I had a second difficult promise to keep.

It was nearly nine o'clock in the evening when we arrived. Ali's compound seemed more peaceful than we had ever seen. We saw none of his wives, concubines or children as our car drove through the wide circular drive that wound around the four palaces belonging to our brother. Nada's palace was the third building within the compound walls.

Nada's Egyptian housekeeper informed us that her mistress was having a bath but was expecting us and had instructed the housekeeper to bring us to her living quarters.

We followed the woman to the interior of Ali's home.

Nothing about my brother is modest. The influence of Saudi oil wealth was evident at every turn. Conspicuous consumption met my eye as I entered the front hallway laid with white marble that was the width of an airport terminal. The towering staircase gleamed with the glow of silver, and I remembered Ali's proud announcement that the columns bracing the structure were coated with real silver. Fifteen foot high doors with solid silver doorknobs led into Nada's private living quarters.

I tried not to gloat, recalling that my brother had taken a serious financial loss with the worldwide run on the silver market in the 1980s. In his greed, Ali must have purchased more of that precious metal than we had realized, only to see his fortunes tumble. Now, Ali's financial loss was the gain of a silver enhanced palace!

I had never visited Nada's bedroom, though I had once received an invitation to view the bedstead. I had been told by a shocked and saddened Sara that the bed was carved in solid ivory, and now I saw that that description was true. Ali had once bragged about the number of elephants that had died to support his bulky frame, but now I could not recall the figure that he had quoted.

Looking around my brother's opulent home, I had a vision of justified Al Sa'ud exile from the Kingdom of Saudi Arabia, for such inherent corruption of wealth deserved no other fate. Would we one day share royal displacement with the likes of King Farouk of Egypt, the Shah of Shahs of Iran, or King Idris of Libya. There was one certainty in my mind, that if the working class of Saudi Arabia ever viewed the private living quarters of Prince Ali Al Sa'ud, revolution was inescapable.

This terrifying idea numbed my body.

At that moment, Nada swept into the room, her hair fashionably coiffured; she had a haughty expression, and her opulent bosom was crammed into a blinding gold lamé dress. It required little imagination to understand how our brother was ensnared by his infatuation for his most beautiful wife. Nada had achieved fame in our family through her daring fashions and her will to do battle with a man who had met little resistance from women throughout his life. In spite of Nada's ability to torture Ali, I had always thought the expression in her eyes looked subtly malicious and had never veered from my opinion that Nada's itch for gain had been her only purpose in marrying Ali. I did remember Sara's words that it was Nada's insecurity in her marriage that made her appear what she was not, for she had no idea when Ali might dispense with her, as he had other women. Such a position creates the need to accumulate future economic security. But I still had my lingering doubts about her true nature. I did admit to myself that Nada had paid dearly for the softer luxuries, for married life with Ali surely must be grim.

Nada said, 'Ali sent you, didn't he?'

I watched Nada's face, thinking that she was pouting and mourning, as if our visit were all a mistake. I alternated between like and dislike, and as Nura and Sara gathered round our sister-in-law, I excused myself, saying that I was going to the bar to fetch myself a drink.

The house was completely quiet and there was no-one about. After preparing myself a gin and tonic, I felt no desire to rejoin my sisters, and I wandered through my brother's palace, finding myself in his private study located on the lowest level of his home.

I was overcome by childlike curiosity, and displayed the traits of a voyeur, sifting through my brother's personal belongings and making a discovery that first puzzled me and then brought great amusement.

I opened a small packet on the top of his writing desk,

and read with vague curiosity about a set of undergarments that my brother had obviously purchased during a recent trip to Hong Kong.

A flimsy sheet of instructions accompanied the underpants, and I read the sheet with interest.

> Wonder Garment: Congratulations on the purchase of your new Wonder Garment! The garment that you have purchased should be worn daily. This garment is guaranteed to improve the wearer's sexual performance.
>
> The secret of these miracle underpants lies in the 'strategic' pouch which maintains the sexual organs at the correct temperature and under optimum conditions.
>
> The Wonder Garment is recommended for all men, but most especially for those who maintain an active sexual life and for those who sit down at their work.

I began to giggle, and an evil spirit came over me. I stuffed the slim plastic bag containing the undergarment and instruction sheet under my long dress. I had no thought of what I was going to do with the item but felt an urge to share the secret with Kareem. Feeling as I had in the days of my childhood rivalry with Ali, I gleefully imagined how my brother would frantically search through his home for the magical pants.

I met my sisters on the staircase and could see from their eyes that they had had no success with Ali's wife.

Nada was leaving Ali.

Unlike poor Reema, Nada was not worried that her children would be taken, for Ali had little love for his female offspring and had made no secret to his wife that their three daughters were of no value to him, and that they would be allowed to live with their mother.

I left without saying goodbye. I cradled my gin and tonic in the car. My theft of Ali's personal possessions had brought forth childish emotions, and I felt quite daring as a princess in the House of Al Sa'ud riding through the streets of Riyadh, enjoying an alcoholic drink.

I asked Sara why Nada was leaving the tempting life of an Al Sa'ud, for in spite of my brother's distasteful character, Nada had a dubious family background, and it would be difficult for her to duplicate the wealth enjoyed as a wife of Ali. It had been Nada's great beauty, and not her family connections, that had won her a husband of immense riches.

Nura said that from what she could gather it seemed that Nada and Ali's divorce had come about over an evening of love.

Nada had tearfully confessed to my sisters that she had been divorced on three occasions over the issue of sex, saying that Ali insisted she accommodate him at odd hours in the night, often waking her from a heavy sleep. The week before, Nada had refused her husband sex, and Ali had insisted, saying that when a man calls his wife to intercourse, that she must not resist him even though she might be on a camel! When Nada still refused, Ali had divorced her.

Sara then told me that Nada had made a surprising second declaration, saying that while she had some affection for Ali's other wives, she had grown increasingly weary of the bastards that sprang from Ali's infidelities, for our brother was the father of seventeen legitimate children and twenty-three illegitimate offspring. The compound that Nada called home was overrun with her husband's concubines and their children.

At the mention of all that sexual activity which produced endless offspring, I could not avoid thoughts of Ali's Wonder Garment and laughed until tears streamed down my face, refusing to divulge the source of my uncontrolled merriment to my two sisters, who feared that the day's events now threatened their youngest sister's sanity.

Epilogue

O God, make the end of my life the best of my life,
And the best of my deeds, their conclusion, And the
best of my days, the day on which I shall meet Thee.
O God, make death the best of those things we choose
not, But which we await; And the grave the best
dwelling in which we shall dwell, And, then death,
make best which follows death.

A Pilgrim's Prayer

It had been a week since we left our families in Monaco. In two days our husbands and children would return to Saudi Arabia.

On this night, each of the ten female children of my mother had gathered in Nura's home. We were blessed that Reema was among us, for that morning Reema had been dismissed from the clinic and had come to stay in the home of her oldest sister until her health was further improved.

The occasion was bittersweet, for we had come together on the twentieth anniversary of our dear mother's death. This was an annual ritual that we had never failed to commemorate, for our mother was sorely missed, even after twenty years. On past occasions we had celebrated our mother's memory by calling to mind our favourite childhood stories of her – telling of the wonderful influence she had had on our lives. Tonight, due to our sadness over Reema's recent tragedy, our mood was subdued, and our woeful spirits led us to themes more sorrowful than in the past.

'Twenty years?' Sara mused. 'It cannot be so long since I looked upon my mother's face.'

Each of us agreed that the years had moved more rapidly than we liked.

I had a sudden realization that of ten daughters, eight were now older than our mother had been at her death. Sara and I were the two exceptions. When I gave voice to this thought, there were many moans and frowns.

Nura demanded, 'Sultana! Say no more! Please!'

Nura now had grandchildren, and our eldest sister's age had become a topic forbidden in the past few years.

Reema asked us to hush, saying that she had a small story about our mother that she had never shared, for she had thought that I might take offence.

My eyes flashed with interest and surprise, and I agreed that nothing Reema might say would create controversy.

'You must promise, Sultana! And, keep your word, no matter what your emotions!'

I laughed and agreed, my curiosity aroused.

When I was only eight years of age, Reema had been called into our mother's bedroom, and Mother had asked Reema to give her a solemn promise. Shy Reema had been awed at the thought of a special secret that she, alone, would share with our mother. In great anticipation, she had given her word that no-one would know of their conversation.

Mother told her that she had made a disturbing discovery about Sultana. Mother told Reema that 'Sultana is a thief!'

My eyes popped in surprise, while my sisters burst into loud laughter.

Reema held her hand in the air, asking for silence so that she could complete her story.

Mother had caught her youngest child stealing from personal belongings of others in our home. Mother said that I had been discovered stealing toys, books, candy, cookies, and even items for which I had no use, such as Ali's record collection. Mother told Reema that she had tried every tactic and punishment and nothing succeeded, that I was a child who could not be shamed into obeying her mother. Now, Mother needed Reema's assistance in saving my soul.

Mother made Reema swear that each time she prayed, for the rest of her days on earth, Reema would never cease to ask God to protect Sultana, guide Sultana, and forgive Sultana.

With teary eyes glistening, Reema looked at me and said, 'Sultana. I have wearied of worrying about your sinful conduct. That promise has been a great burden, for I am a Muslim who not only prays the five obligatory daily prayers, but who prays on many other occasions. A promise made to my dear mother can never be broken, so I know that I must pray for you until I pass from this earth. But, now, I pray that you are no longer a thief and my prayers have been answered!'

The room burst with the sound of eight other voices, for each of my sisters was whooping with laughter, screaming over the sounds of the others. Once calm had returned, we made the discovery that my mother had requested and received the identical promise from each and every sister! Each had been convinced that she was the only sibling privy to the secret that her baby sister was a little thief! For twenty years, none had broken her promise by telling. When the truth of the situation came over us, our wild and hysterical laughter could be heard throughout Nura's palace.

I felt a keen sense of relief. Surely I was protected by many of God's angels, for each of my sisters was devout and said many daily prayers.

In a joking manner, Tahani asked me point blank, 'Sultana, we would like to know if God has answered our prayers. Have you taken anything not belonging to you since the time of your youth?'

I could see that my sisters expected me to reply in the negative, for they could not imagine that I was still a petty thief. I could not keep my face free from a trembling smile and began to fidget, remembering Ali's Wonder Garment that was packed away with my belongings in the room that I was occupying.

Surprised at my hesitant reaction, Nura said, 'Sultana?'

'Wait a moment,' I said, and ran to get the garment that I had stolen from Ali's home.

No-one could believe their eyes or ears when I returned to the room wearing Ali's underpants, and when I read the instruction sheet and placed two bananas into the special 'strategic' pouch, Nura tried to be firm in her disapproval, but hysterical laughter overwhelmed my sisters, and three had to leave the room, while another claimed that she had wet her pants.

We could not control our glee, even after three of Nura's servants came running into the palace, fearful of the tremendous noise that they had heard from distant gardens.

After calm had returned, the telephone rang, and our thoughts switched to more serious matters. The caller was Nashwa asking for her mother, Sara. It seemed that Nashwa was telephoning from Monaco to complain to her mother about her cousin, Amani. My daughter had been following her cousin in Monaco and had appointed herself a one-woman 'vice and social corruption committee'.

Nashwa's indignation was running high, for Amani had gone so far as to take her cousin's make-up, nail polish, and sunglasses, saying that for Nashwa to wear such things made her a violator of Islamic mores!

Nashwa told her mother that if someone did not control Amani, she was going to have three French friends follow Amani that evening and strip off her clothes, leaving her clad only in her underwear in an area filled with tourists. That should get the prude's mind on other topics rather than Nashwa's morality.

The evening's conversation shifted away from Ali's underpants, and none of my sisters could shake the ironic thought of Sultana's daughter caught in religious fervour, while Sara's child was happily lounging in discos.

I left the room for a moment to call Kareem, advising him of the tension between our child and her cousin. My husband said that he had already decided to keep Amani by his side until she was safely returned to Riyadh, for our daughter had on that day confronted a manager of a hotel in Monte Carlo, demanding that he provide separate elevators in his establishment for men and women, advising him that members of the same sex that were unrelated had no business confined together in a close area.

I rolled my eyes in disbelief, agreeing when Kareem declared that Amani would be put into counselling when they returned to the kingdom. Maha's successful recovery from her earlier mental inbalance had turned Kareem into a staunch believer of psychiatric counselling.

I lived a short moment of relief, thinking of how Maha had rejoined our family as a responsible girl. My eldest child's thoughts now centred on her education and plans for a normal life.

When I re-entered the room, there was a heated discussion of the threat of militant fundamentalism that was now challenging our family's leadership of Saudi Arabia and my thoughts returned to Amani and her extreme interest in her faith. Each of my sisters stated that her husband had expressed great fear of the growing gap between the monarchy and the pristine ideological movement now gathering power. The Islamic fundamentalist leaders are known to be young, educated and urbanized. This group preaches an uncompromising return to the Koran and is on a collision course with our regime, which is linked with modernization and westernization of the kingdom.

I said little even though I had done much investigation of the movement, for my own child was part of an extremist group that had indicated opposition to the monarchy. I felt too close to the subject at hand and made myself busy preparing pillows to place behind Reema's head.

I asked myself, what disturbances would I live to see in the land that I called home? Would my own child be a part of the opposition that brought down the legitimate government of Saudi Arabia?

When talk of the Muslim extremists ran dry, Reema said that she had another bit of news that she wished to share.

I hoped that no further sin of mine was going to be made public knowledge, and I tried to make my expression unconcerned.

Reema spoke without emotion, saying that Saleem had made plans to take another wife.

While our mother had been greatly humiliated by our father's taking of four wives Reema was the first of my sisters to undergo such an ordeal.

My chest tightened and my eyes flooded with tears, but Reema asked that none of us cry, that she would happily live her life as an ignored wife. Nothing could shake her resolve to live a life of peace, so long as she was not separated from her children. She declared in a loud voice that she was happy, but Reema's eyes spoke a different truth.

I knew that my sister had loved Saleem with a true and honest love. Reema's reward for being a faithful wife and loving mother had not come to her on earth.

For her sake, Reema's sisters made a pretence of belief and congratulated our sister on her small victory.

Nura announced that Nada had once more become Ali's wife. Our brother had signed a document giving Nada wealth in her own right, along with a trip to Paris to purchase diamonds and rubies fit for the Queen of England.

When Tahani asked how he had overcome the religious edict that forbade him to remarry Nada, I was not surprised to hear that Ali had hired a Saudi cousin to wed Nada without consummating the union. After the marriage, a divorce had taken place. Then Ali and Nada had wed again.

I quoted from memory my Islamic knowledge of such a deed and told my sisters that such was not allowed. The Prophet himself said that God curses men who are parties to such an arrangement, for it is nothing more than a trick against God and is considered a grave matter.

'Who is going to intervene?' Sara asked.

Nura admitted the truth – no-one. 'But, God knows,' she added, and each of us felt great sympathy for Ali, for he had piled yet another sin upon his soul.

The evening was coming to an end when the telephone rang once again. One of Nura's servants came and said that Tahani was wanted on the telephone.

Those of us who had left our loved ones in Monaco thought perhaps another crisis had come about and told Tahani to spare us details of our children's follies.

We heard Tahani cry out, and we rushed to her side. Once she replaced the telephone on the hook, it took us many moments to calm our sister, and our fears were high that a member of our family had met with misfortune.

A grief-stricken Tahani finally spoke. 'Sameera has died.'

No-one could speak, no-one could move.

Could it be true?

I counted on my fingers, trying to calculate the number of years that dear girl had spent locked in the 'Woman's Room', a padded cell in the home of her savage uncle.

'How long?' Sara asked, seeing me struggle with my memories.

'Almost fifteen years,' I told her.

'I have committed a grave sin,' Tahani confessed. 'For many years, I asked God to take her uncle from this earth!'

We had heard that Sameera's uncle was wrinkled and frail, and that knowledge had given us hope that after his death, Sameera would return to us.

I sarcastically commented, 'We should have known that such a one could not be depended upon to die soon enough.'

Sameera was born fortunate, to a mother and father who doted on their only child. When her parents had been killed in a car accident, her father's brother had assumed control over her life. Sameera had fled from him with a young man whom she had loved. Tricked into returning to the kingdom, Sameera had been wed to a man not of her choice. When the discovery had been made that she was no longer a virgin, her uncle's fury had led him to confine his niece to the 'Woman's Room'.

Over the years, many had tried to win Sameera's release, saying that her sin did not merit eternal earthly punishment, but her uncle felt that he alone knew the wishes of God, and his harsh verdict had not been lifted.

Sameera had been brilliant, beautiful and sweet in temperament. What nature had given her, cruel fortune had taken away. This woman whom we had loved had been slowly consumed by the horrors of solitary confinement.

Tahani began to sob, her cries chopping through her words. It took her many moments to reveal that Sameera had been buried on this day. Sameera's auntie had confided that despite her emaciation, Sameera was still beautiful when wrapped in the white linen shroud in which she would appear before God.

How could we bear the pain of her cruel death?

Choking back sobs, I tried to remember a verse from Kahlil Gibran on the question of death. I first whispered it, and as my memory of it returned, I slowly raised my voice, until all could hear me. 'Only when you drink from the river of silence, shall you indeed sing. And, when you have reached the mountain top, then you shall begin to climb. And, when the earth shall claim your limbs, then shall you truly dance.'

My sisters and I joined hands, remembering that we were like a chain – as strong as the strongest link, weak as the weakest link.

As never before, we belonged to a sisterhood more powerful than that of our own blood. Never again would we sit back and wonder at the cruelty of men and the obscene arbitrariness of innocent female death, brought about by men's evil.

I said, 'Let the world know that the women of Saudi Arabia are gaining strength in the knowledge that they are right.'

My sisters looked at me one by one, and for the first time, I knew that each of them understood why I do the things that I do.

At that moment, I promised myself that somehow the moral order of our world would be changed, and right would triumph some day.

The great movement of human rights for women in Saudi Arabia had just begun and it will not be defeated by men of indoctrinated ignorance.

The men of my land will grow to mourn my existence, for I will never cease to challenge the evil precedents that they have allowed to flourish against the women of Saudi Arabia.

A Few Facts about Saudi Arabia

With an area of 864,866 square miles, Saudi Arabia is one-third the size of the United States and the same size as Western Europe. It extends from the Red Sea in the west to the Persian Gulf in the east, and borders Jordan, Iraq and Kuwait in the north, and Yemen and Oman to the south. The United Arab Emirates, Qatar and Bahrain lie to the east. A harsh desert land with no rivers and few permanent streams, Saudi Arabia is home to the Rub Al-Khali (Empty Quarter) which is the largest sand desert in the world. The mountain ranges of Asir Province rise to over 9,000 feet in the south-west.

The nation is composed of tribes who can trace their roots back to the earliest civilizations of the Arabian peninsula. The ancestors of modern-day Saudis lived on ancient and important trade routes and much of their income was realized by raiding parties. Divided into regions and ruled by independent tribal chiefs, the various warring tribes were unified under one religion, Islam, led by the Prophet Mohammed, in the seventh century. Before the Prophet died at the age of sixty-three, most of Arabia had become Muslim.

The ancestors of the present rulers of Saudi Arabia reigned over much of Arabia during the nineteenth century. After losing most of Saudi territory to the Turks, they were driven from Riyadh and sought refuge in Kuwait. King Abdul Aziz Al Sa'ud, father of the present-day king, returned to Riyadh and fought to regain the country. He succeeded and founded modern Saudi Arabia in 1932.

More than one-quarter of the world's known oil reserves lie beneath the sands of Saudi Arabia.

In 1933, Standard Oil Company of California won the rights to prospect for oil in Saudi Arabia. In 1938, oil was discovered at Dammam Oil Well no. 7, which is still producing oil today. The Arabian American Oil Company (ARAMCO) was founded in 1944 and held the rights to continue to search for oil in the kingdom. In 1980, however, the Saudi government assumed ownership of ARAMCO.

The kingdom's oil wealth has ensured that Saudi citizens live an opulent lifestyle enjoyed by few. With free education and interest-free loans most Saudis prosper. All Saudi citizens, as well as Muslim pilgrims, receive free health care. Government programmes provide support for Saudi Arabians in the case of disability, death or retirement. The entire country is an impressive socialist state. Economically, Saudi Arabia has developed into a modern, technologically advanced nation.

Saudi Arabia is an Islamic state and the law is based on the *Shari'a*, the Islamic code of law taken from the pages of the Koran and the *Sunna*, which are the traditions addressed by Prophet Mohammed. The Koran is the constitution of the country and provides guidance for legal judgments. Executive and legislative authority is exercised by the King and the Council of Ministers. Their decisions are based on *Shari'a* law. All ministries and government agencies are responsible to King Fahd Ibn Abdul Aziz Al Sa'ud (officially known as 'The Custodian of the Two Mosques').

Today Saudi Arabia has a population of approximately 14 million, of which 95 per cent belong to the Sunni branch of the Muslim faith while five per cent belong to the Shiite branch. The Shiite population suffers much discrimination and injustice from the Sunni government, since there is great distrust and dislike between the Sunni and Shiite sects.

As the heartland of Islam, Saudi Arabia occupies a special place in the Muslim world. Each year, millions of Muslim pilgrims journey there to Makkah to pay homage to God. For this reason, Saudi Arabia is one of the most traditional Muslim countries and its citizens adhere to a strict interpretation of the Koran.

A Muslim has five obligations, called the Five Pillars of Islam. These obligations are: (1) Profession of faith: 'There is no god but God; Mohammed is the messenger of God.' (2) A Muslim should pray five times a day, facing the city of Makkah. (3) A Muslim must pay a fixed proportion of his income, called *zakat* to the poor. (4) During the ninth month of the Islamic calendar, a Muslim must fast. During this time, called Ramadan, Muslims must abstain from food and drink from dawn to sunset. (5) A Muslim must perform the *Haj*, or pilgrimage, at least once during his lifetime (if he has the economic means).

Saudi Arabia uses the Islamic (hegira) calendar based on a lunar year rather than the Gregorian calendar which is based on a solar year. A lunar month is the time between two successive new moons. The lunar year contains 12 months, but is 11 days shorter than the solar year. For this reason, holy days gradually shift from one season to another. Lunar year dates are derived from AD 622, the year of the Prophet's emigration, or *Higra*, from Makkah to Madinah. The Islamic holy day is Friday. The work week in Saudi Arabia begins on Saturday and ends on Thursday.

The Saudi *riyal* is the basic monetary unit in Saudi Arabia. The *riyal* consists of 100 *halalahs* and is issued in notes and coins of various denominations. There are 3.75 *riyals* to the American dollar.

The recent history for the women of Saudi Arabia starts in 1963, when, despite religious protests, the first school for girls opened in the Kingdom of Saudi Arabia. Saudi Arabia's third king, Faisal, and his wife Iffat, were the driving force behind women's rights in the Kingdom. At the assassination of King Faisal on 25 March 1975, the movement to further women's position in Saudi Arabia came to a halt. In 1977, King Khalid, the fourth King of Saudi Arabia, issued two decrees: one that forbade a woman to travel outside her home unless escorted by a male member of her immediate family, and another that decreed a Saudi woman would no longer be allowed to travel abroad to study unless she was accompanied by a male member of her immediate family. Women have never been granted the right to drive or to study or work in the presence of men.

During the 1991 Gulf War, a new atmosphere of freedom reigned briefly for women in Saudi Arabia, because of the presence of Allied troops and Western journalists. With the withdrawal of the troops and news reporters came further harsh restrictions on the female population by the religious authorities. In addition, a law was passed in the Kingdom forbidding women to drive. Prior to the driving demonstration of Saudi women during the Gulf War, the ban on female driving had been one of social restriction rather than legal law.

Human rights groups have recently sprung up to protest violations of all human rights, including that of women, but the Government has been actively disbanding these groups, even arresting and imprisoning some of their members.

While large numbers of Saudi women are becoming educated and their power is growing within their homes, their personal freedoms have lessened outside their walled villas.

Glossary

Abaaya	A black, full-length outer garment worn by Saudi women
Abu	Father
Al Ras	School for girls in Saudi Arabia
Al Sa'ud	Ruling family of Saudi Arabia
Assiut	Village in Southern Egypt
Bedouin	A nomadic desert people, the original Arabs
bin (or ibn)	Follows a man's given name and precedes a father's, grandfather's or great grandfather's name which means 'son of'
Dhu al-Hijah	The twelfth month of the *hejira* calendar
Dhu al-Qida	The eleventh month of the *hejira* calendar
Gamaa Al Islamiya	Islamic extremist group formed in Egypt in the early 1980s
Green Book	Qaddafi's Green Book: Philosophy of Colonel Qaddafi of Libya
Hadiths	Sayings and traditions of Prophet Mohammed which help to formulate Islamic law
Haj	Annual pilgrimage to Makkah made by those of the Islamic faith
Hajii	Pilgrim who makes the pilgrimage to Makkah (A title that denotes honour)
Hijira	Islamic calendar which started on the date that Prophet Mohammed

fled Makkah and escaped to Madinah (622)

Ihram Special time during *Haj* that all Muslims refrain from normal life and dwell on nothing but religious matters

Imam Person who leads communal prayers and/or delivers the sermon on Fridays

Jeddah Saudi Arabian city located on the Red Sea

Kaaba Islam's holiest shrine, a sacred sanctuary for all Muslims. The Kaaba is a small building in the Holy Mosque of Makkah, nearly cubic in shape, built to enclose the Black Stone, which is the most venerated Muslim object

Kohl A black powder used by Saudi Arabian women that goes on the eyelid to enhance the beauty of a woman

Koran The Holy Book of all Muslims that contains the words of God as they were given to Prophet Mohammed

La Arabic word meaning 'no'

Madinah Second holiest city of Islam. The burial place of Prophet Mohammed

Mahram Male to whom a woman cannot be married, such as her father, brother or uncle, who is allowed to be a woman's escort when travelling. Must be a close relative

Makkah Holiest city of Islam (also known as Mecca). Each year, millions of Muslims travel to Makkah to perform the annual pilgrimage

Morals Police Religious authorities in Saudi Arabia who have the power to arrest those they believe commit moral wrongs or crimes against Islam or go against the teachings of Islam

Mut'a Temporary marriage allowed to those of the Islamic faith

Mutawwa The religious police, also known as the morals police. Men who seek out, arrest, and punish those who do not abide by Saudi religious law

Muezzin The crier who calls the faithful to pray five times a day

Najd The traditional name for central Arabia. The inhabitants of this area are known for their conservative behaviour. The ruling family of Saudi Arabia are Najdis

Purdah A practice of confining women to their homes. This total seclusion of females can occur in some Muslim countries

Purification The ritual of cleansing prior to offering prayers to God practised by Muslims

Riyadh The capital city of Saudi Arabia which is located in the desert

Riyal Saudi Arabian currency

Rub Al Khali An enormous desert wilderness which occupies the south-east portion of Arabia. It is often referred to as the 'Empty Quarter'

Sana'a The capital city of Yemen

Shawarma Popular sandwich sold in Saudi Arabia and other Arab countries made of lamb, beef or chicken wrapped in pita bread, mixed with sauces and tomatoes and peppers

Shayla Black gauzy scarf worn by women of the Muslim faith in Saudi Arabia

Shiite The branch of Islam that split from the Sunni majority over the issue of Prophet Mohammed's successor. One of two main sects

Sunna Traditions of the Islamic faith as addressed by Prophet Mohammed

Sunni The majority orthodox branch of Islam. Saudi Arabia is 95 per cent populated by those of the Sunni sect. The word means 'traditionalists'. One of two main sects

Taif Mountain resort city in Saudi Arabia which is located close to Makkah

Thobe A long shirtlike dress which is worn by Saudi men. It is usually made of white cotton, but can be made of heavier, darker-coloured fabric for the winter months

Umrah A short pilgrimage (to Makkah) undertaken by those of the Muslim faith which can be made any time of the year

Umm al Qurrah 'Mother of Cities' or 'The Blessed City' which is Makkah

Veil Black fabric which is used to cover Saudi Arabian Muslim woman's face. The material can be sheer or thick

Woman's Room Room in a man's house used to confine Saudi Arabian women who go against the wishes of their husbands, fathers or brothers. The punishment can be for a short period or a life sentence

Zakah — Obligatory alms giving required of all Muslims which is the third pillar of Islam